The Marginal Seabed: United Kingdom Legal Practice

THE
MARGINAL
SEABED

UNITED KINGDOM
LEGAL PRACTICE

GEOFFREY MARSTON

CLARENDON PRESS · OXFORD
1981

Oxford University Press, Walton Street, Oxford OX2 6DP

OXFORD LONDON GLASGOW
NEW YORK TORONTO MELBOURNE WELLINGTON
KUALA LUMPUR SINGAPORE HONG KONG TOKYO
NAIROBI DAR ES SALAAM CAPE TOWN

Published in the United States by
Oxford University Press, New York

British Library Cataloguing in Publication Data

Marston, Geoffrey
 The marginal seabed: United Kingdom legal
 practice.
 1. *Submerged lands - Great Britain*
 I. *Title*
 344.1064'69164   *KD4456.S*   *80–41305*

ISBN 0–19–825369–9

Typeset by Oxprint Ltd, Oxford
Printed in Great Britain
at the University Press, Oxford
by Eric Buckley
Printer to the University

To my Parents

Arthur and Mabel Marston

Preface

This work is a revised version of a doctoral thesis submitted in 1973 to the University of London. Its primary purpose is to set out, in a relatively condensed form, the practice of the legislature, executive, and judiciary concerning the bed and subsoil of the sea (together referred to as the solum) adjacent to the dry land of the United Kingdom and to its inland waters. Its secondary purpose is to provide a brief analysis of the legal status of such solum in the light of the material above.

The study has been compiled in large measure from official papers available to public scrutiny under the 'Thirty-Year Rule' in the Public Records Act 1967. There is the probability that some relevant papers have not been released to the public archives for one reason or another. There is the certainty that there are more papers of relevance in the public archives which the author has failed to discover.

Two areas of practice are omitted from the scope of this study. First, the work does not cover practice pursuant to the Continental Shelf Act 1964. Secondly, it does not cover practice in former or present British territories outside the United Kingdom. The author is well aware of the legal problems which have arisen in the United States, Canada, and Australia over the marginal sea and solum. It is hoped that the contents of this work will not be irrelevant to persons interested in those problems.

Finally, although the study purports to cover the whole United Kingdom, the author is conscious of his English origin, and apologizes in advance to those in Scotland and Northern Ireland who may find the material on their jurisdictions deficient.

GEOFFREY MARSTON

18 November 1980

Acknowledgements

Chronologically, I ought first to acknowledge my indebtedness to certain persons in the Attorney-General's Department, Canberra, ten years ago, including the late Sir Kenneth Bailey, without whose initiative I might never have become interested in this subject.

I wish to thank the staff, at all levels, of the Public Record Office, London, for their help over the years; the Secretary and Keeper of the Records of the Duchy of Cornwall for permitting me to examine documents in his custody; Dr J. H. Baker, Fellow of St. Catharine's College, Cambridge, for making me an annotated transcription of Hardres' report of the Sutton Marsh case; the Maitland Fund of the University of Cambridge for material help in preparing the final text for publication; and Mrs U. M. Tollman for secretarial assistance.

Transcripts of Crown-copyright records in the Public Record Office appear by permission of the Controller of H.M. Stationery Office.

Finally, I recall the memory of my late friend, Professor D. P. O'Connell, QC, whose writings on this and associated subjects have been a constant source of intellectual challenge to me during the last decade. He read the typescript of an earlier version of this work shortly before his last illness and advised me to seek its publication. It was in Oxford on 11 June 1979, on learning of his untimely passing, that I followed his advice.

Contents

Preface   vii

Acknowledgements   viii

Abbreviations and Notes   xii

Part One   Description

  I   HISTORICAL DEVELOPMENT UP TO THE
CROWN LANDS ACT 1829   1
     A. The pre-Stuart Period   1
     B. The Stuart Period   5
     C. The post-Stuart Period   15

 II EXECUTIVE AND LEGISLATIVE
PRACTICE 1829–1876   22
     A. Introduction   22
     B. The Seabed   24
     C. The Subsoil   50

III JUDICIAL PRACTICE 1829–1876   56
     A. English Judicial Decisions   56
     B. Scottish Judicial Decisions   68
     C. Irish Judicial Decisions   73

IV THE CORNWALL SUBMARINE MINES   75
     A. Practice up to 1856   75
     B. Arbitration before Sir John Patteson
1856–1858   83
     C. The Patteson Award   90
     D. The Cornwall Submarine Mines Act 1858   91
     E. Arbitration before Sir John Coleridge 1866–1869   94
     F. The Coleridge Award   110
     G. The Reaction to the Coleridge Award   110

V   *THE QUEEN* v. *FERDINAND KEYN*:
     THE *FRANCONIA* CASE   114
     A. Introduction   114
     B. Court for Crown Cases Reserved—First Hearing   115
     C. Court for Crown Cases Reserved–Second
        Hearing   120
     D. Summary of the Arguments   129
     E. The Judgments   130

VI   THE REACTION TO *R.* v. *KEYN*   138
     A. The Events of 1877   138
     B. The Events of 1878   144
     C. The Events of 1880–1881   149
     D. Conclusion   151

VII   THE CHANNEL TUNNEL SCHEME 1874–1883   152
     A. The Negotiations   152
     B. The Excavations   156
     C. The Litigation   159

VIII   EXECUTIVE AND LEGISLATIVE
     DOMESTIC PRACTICE AFTER 1876   165
     A. The Seabed   165
     B. The Subsoil   173
     C. Conclusion   191

IX   JUDICIAL PRACTICE AFTER 1876   192
     A. English Judicial Decisions   192
     B. Scottish Judicial Decisions   204
     C. Opinions of the Judicial Committee of the Privy
     Council   213

X   EXECUTIVE EXTERNAL PRACTICE AFTER
     1876   220
     A. The Fisheries Arbitrations   220
     B. Law Officers' Opinions to the Colonial Office   221
     C. The Views of Sir Cecil Hurst   223
     D. The Gulf of Paria   231
     E. Practice within International Organizations   239

Part Two Analysis

XI THE DELIMITATION OF THE MARGINAL
SOLUM 249
A. The Shoreward Limit 249
B. The Seaward Limit 260
C. The Downward Limit 269

XII THE HISTORICAL AND JURIDICAL BASES
OF THE CROWN'S CLAIM TO THE
MARGINAL SOLUM 270
A. The Historical Basis 270
B. The Juridical Basis 272

XIII THE LEGAL STATUS OF THE MARGINAL
SOLUM 286
A. On the Basis of the Traditional Claim 286
B. On the Basis of the Territorial Sea Doctrine 293
C. The Application of Statutes 296
D. Conclusion 298

Select Bibliography 299

Table of Statutes, Statutory Instruments, etc. 303

Table of Cases 306

Index 310

Abbreviations and Notes

Abbreviations of Archival Classes in the Public Record Office, London

ADM	Admiralty
C	Chancery
CO	Colonial Office
COAL	Coal Board (incorporates records of the Coal Commission)
CREST	Crown Estate Office (incorporates records of the Office of Woods, Forests, and Land Revenues)
DPP	Director of Public Prosecutions (incorporates some records of the Treasury Solicitor)
FO	Foreign Office
HO	Home Office
MT	Ministry of Transport (incorporates some records of the Board of Trade)
PRO	Public Record Office (private collections)
SP	State Papers
T	Treasury
TS	Treasury Solicitor

Other Abbreviations

BL	British Library
BYBIL	British Year Book of International Law
C., Cd., Cmd., Cmnd.	Command Papers, successive series
HC Debs.	House of Commons Debates, Parliamentary Debates, 5th series
HL Debs.	House of Lords Debates, Parliamentary Debates, 5th series
HCP	House of Commons Papers

HLP	House of Lords Papers
LQR	Law Quarterly Review
P.Debs.	Parliamentary Debates (prior to 5th series)
UNTS	United Nations Treaty Series

Notes

1. Throughout this work, emphasis is given as in the original document.
2. Some abbreviations in the original documents have been expanded for ease of reading.
3. In references to Parliamentary Papers, both the pagination of the individual paper and the manuscript pagination of the volume containing it are given.

PART ONE

DESCRIPTION

Chapter I

Historical Development up to the Crown Lands Act 1829

A. The pre-Stuart Period

There is ample documentary evidence for the proposition that at least from the early fourteenth century the Kings of England claimed to exercise certain legal rights in the surrounding sea.[1] There exists little specific evidence, however, that in the early years this claim extended to property rights in the sea itself or in its bed and subsoil. Stuart A. Moore, in his work on the history and law of the foreshore, cited a case decided in 1286 in which the Crown claimed *petram in fundo maris juxta Portland*, but it is not clear from the extract cited whether the bed in question was under the open sea as opposed to a harbour or estuary, or whether the Crown was claiming as original owner of the stone.[2]

In the view of one authority, 'We do not, however, find in these old records any hint that the kings of England looked on the sea itself as part of their patrimony, or that they considered themselves entitled to exclude foreigners from passing through it, or from appropriating its produce.'[3] On the other hand, some thought that the claim had always been one of ample scope. Thus, in his dedicatory epistle dated 19 November 1652 to the Parliament of the Commonwealth of England in respect of his translation of John Selden's *Mare Clausum*, Marchamont Nedham wrote:

Moreover, our own Municipal Constitutions every where declare the same, as may bee seen by the several Presidents and Proceedings thereunto relating; which manifestly shew, that by the Common Law of the Land, our Kings were Proprietarie Lords of our Seas. That the Seas were ever under the Ligeance of our Kings, and they sovereign Conservators of the Peace as well upon the Sea as Land.[4]

According to Fulton,[5] the notion that the Crown had the

[1] See, e.g., Fulton, ch. 1; Wade, (1921–2), 2 *BYBIL* 99.
[2] Moore, 95.
[3] Wade, 107.
[4] John Selden, Nedham translation, at page c.
[5] Fulton, 362.

exclusive right of property in the sea itself, and in the soil beneath it, originated in a treatise written in 1569 by Thomas Digges.[6] Digges set out to show that the foreshore (i.e., the area between high and low-water marks) belonged to the Crown in right of its prerogative and had not, in general, been granted out to private persons. He summarized his principal argument in a paper which he wrote later in order to answer objections made against views expressed in his treatise. In this paper[7] Digges wrote that

. . . in this estate regall of Englande wee see that the Kings of most auncient times have in the right of theire crowne helde the seas abowte this Ilande so proper and entire unto them as not onlie whatsoever treasure, precious stones or other comodities of any value, the seas shoulde yelde or caste up upon the shores, were and are of dewtie reputed the Princes, but also all wracks whatsoever (that almost no prince hathe) are here in respecte of the king's most absolute prerogative and right in the seas entirelie adiudged his.[8]

He then turned to the status of the soil:

And also to make it manifest yt the soile of the seas is also intirelie the King's, no man can let fall any anchore in any roade aboute this Realme but he paiethe for breakinge the King's grownde to the officers of the Kinge. Hereof it cometh to passe yt the L:Admirall hathe in his pattente *Anchorage*, *Buyage* &c. So that wee maie necessarielie conclude, that suche manner of purchasinge propertie by occupacion was of auncient time where contries laie wast not inhabited by anie nor within the limitts of any kings *Territorie*.[9]

Digges's conclusion, as set out in the treatise, ran as follows:

. . . reson techeth that as the sea of all waters is the cheefe, and as Salamon sayth the fountayne whence all Rivers take theyr *Originall*, so the propertye thereof ought unto the cheefe the Kinge himself to bee attributed. For that no subject cann have propriety therein the Civill lawes plainly affyrme, makinge a most manifest distinction betweene the sea, and fressh Rivers . . .[10]

After discussing the arising of islands in the sea, the property in

---

[6] *Arguments prooving the Queenes Maties.propertye in the Sea Landes, and salt shores thereof, and that no subiect cann lawfully hould eny parte thereof but by the Kinges especiall graunte*: BL, Lansdowne MS 100, article 6; Moore, 185–202. J. W. Pycroft, who reproduced these texts in 1855, attributed authorship to Sir Richard Onslow (Pycroft, *Arguments relating to Sea Landes*, dedication to Serjeant Merewether).

[7] *Arguments against the Queenes Prerogative and interest in Land left or gained from the Seaes, and armes thereof with answeres to everye obiection*: BL, Lansdowne MS 170, article 7; Moore, 202–11.

[8] Moore, 203.

[9] Ibid.

[10] Ibid., 185–6.

the soil of ports and harbours, and the right to wreck, Digges continued:

So in the greate salt river I meane the sea envirroninge the whole Ilande, and in the salt shores thereof, the greate and cheefe lorde of the whole soyle the Kinge himself only muste have interest and propertye, and no man ells nether by prescription nor eny other waye, save only by the Kinges especiall graunte maye claime propertye in them.[11]

He was soon to be in a position to put his theories into practical application. In 1571, a Commission was granted out of the Exchequer to five commissioners, one of whom was Digges, to enquire whether any lands recovered from the sea around the coasts of Kent were in the valid possession of their occupiers.[12] The Queen granted the lands in question to Digges by Royal Patent and he promptly took action to recover them from their occupiers by means of informations filed in the Exchequer. In these he was not successful.[13] The argument on behalf of Digges can best be seen in the following extract from an information filed by the Attorney-General on 21 June 1575 against William Hammond in respect of marsh and foreshore at Richborough, Kent:

Quod cum Domina Regina nunc ratione praerogativae suae proprie-tatem habeat tam in littoribus maris infra et per totum regnum Angliae et in ipsa terra fundo arena et solo sub eodem mari quam in omnibus terra solo fundo et arena et per totum praedictum regnum quae aliquo naturali maris fluxu salsis undis fuere infra tempus memoriae hominum absque innaturali et extraordinari cursu seu impetu ventorum sive tempestatum inundatis et ratione ejusdem prerogativae suae intitulata sit gaudere et habere et ad usum suum proprium gaudere habere et retinere debeat omnes ejusmodi terras quae infra totum praedictum regnum aliquo naturali maris fluxu seu cursu salsis aquis fuere inun-datas et postea fuerunt vel erunt relictas sive recuperatas a mare ejusve littoribus aut ab aliquo membro vel brachio maris ubicumque fuerit infra regnum suum Angliae . . .[14]

In 1580, the Court of Exchequer gave judgment for the defen-dant, Hammond, stating that the land had been in his possession for sixty years and 'is but only averred to belong to the Queenes Highnes'.[15]

---

[11] Ibid., 191.
[12] For the texts of the Commission and Royal Patent, see Moore, 212–15.
[13] e.g., 3 Dyer 326b.
[14] Moore, 221–2, from Exch. Q.R. Memda., E., 17 Eliz., roll 87.
[15] Moore, 221–3, from Eccl. D.B., T., 22 Eliz., vol. 6, fo. 390.

In 1575, the theories of Digges were again canvassed, this time in the case of *Attorney-General* v. *Sir John Constable*. This was a suit by information charging that Sir John Constable took wreck of the sea *magis ex opposito manerii et dominii de Holderness*. Constable pleaded that the wreck had been found between low-water mark and the firm land. His counsel, Plowden, argued:[16]

. . . we ought to consider to what place the bounds of England extend, and then to whom the property of the sea and of the land under the sea belongs, and to whom belongs the property of the land between the greensward and the low-water mark, and within what county and parish the said soil is . . . Firstly, the bounds of England extend to the middle of the sea adjoining which surrounds the realm; but the Queen has all the jurisdiction of the sea between France and this realm by reason of her title to France, and so it is of Ireland; but in other places, as towards Spain, she has only the moiety; for there is the same reason concerning the sea as concerning great and public rivers in a kingdom, and these belong to those who have the land adjoining, so that every one who has the land bounding on the rivers shall have, by reason of his soil adjoining, interest in the said rivers. . . . The same reason is of the sea and of the salt water, for in this our Queen has the jurisdiction and governance of all things within the said bounds of England to the midst and between France or Ireland and this kingdom, and has all the jurisdiction of the sea in respect of her title to the land on either side. This can be understood by 40 Assizes 25, where in appeal against sixteen (persons) it was said by Chard that a Norman was master of a ship accompanied with Englishmen, and they robbed certain Englishmen, and in the Norman it was adjudged only felony, but in the Englishmen it was adjudged treason, because they did it on their lands on the wastes of England; so, if the servant kill his master, it is treason, and thus it is by Glanvill, if the homager kill his lord, on account of the trust reposed in them.

Plowden then drew a distinction between jurisdiction and property:

But although the Queen has jurisdiction in the sea adjoining her realm, still she has not property in it, nor in the land under the sea, for it is common to all men , and she cannot prohibit any one from fishing there, and the water and the land under it are things of no value, and the fish are always removable from one place to another. And also Bracton says, lib. 2, cap. 2: If an island is born in the sea, which rarely happens, it belongs to the occupant; and with this Britton agrees; which proves that the Queen has not property in the sea nor in the land under it. And that which Digges in his book and also Robert Carey urged to the contrary is

---

[16] Moore, 227–9, from BL, Hargrave MS 15, fo. 95d.

not to be regarded, for they rely on the saying of Bracton in another place, that the Queen shall have the island born *propter superintendentiam*, and this seems to be understood of a common river or of an arm of the sea within her realm; but I marvel much that the Admiral uses in his Court to hold pleas of robberies and other things done upon the coast of Spain, which is altogether out of his jurisdiction and the authority of this kingdom.

Judgment was given for Constable,[17] though neither in this case nor in the latter case of *Attorney-General* v. *Sir Henry Constable*[18] is there any record of the Court pronouncing upon the legal status of the seabed below low-water mark.

In 1591, articles were promoted against one Dulinge for erecting a weir at Braunston in Devon, without a licence from the Admiral. The articles ran in part:

Firstly, that you know or believe that, as well our most serene lady, Elizabeth, queen of England that now is, as all and singular her illustrious and invincible progenitors and predecessors, kings of England, from and for time whereof the memory of man runneth not to the contrary, have in right of their royal prerogative [and] in right of their kingdom ever been lords and owners, as also she, our lady Elizabeth, queen that now is, is now owner and proprietor of the sea adjacent to and encircling and washing [the shores of] the realm of England, at least for 300, 200, 100, 50, 40, 30, 20, or 10 miles from land or shore, towards the deep sea, and of all and singular the rights, privileges, fruits, emoluments, hereditaments, profits, royalties, and lordships, whatsoever they may be, arising coming and issuing from the said sea and shores, and of all lands lying beneath and under the sea, and overflowed by it . . .[19]

B. The Stuart Period

The advent of the Stuart kings gave impetus to the claim of the Crown to be owner of all water areas in and adjacent to the territory as well as the foreshore. In 1610, during its argument in the case of the *Royal Piscarie de le Banne* the Crown maintained that

[l]a mer est del ligeance del Roy, come de son Corone d'Engleterre; mes est auxy son proper inheritance; and pur ceo le Roy avera le terre que est gained hors del mer . . .[20]

---

[17] (1575) 1 And. 86.
[18] (1601) 5 Co. Rep. 106a.
[19] Marsden, *Select Pleas in the Court of Admiralty*, vol. II, 174.
[20] (1610) Davis 55, 56.

Writers, too, espoused the claim of the Crown to be the owner of the bed of the sea, although it should be noted that Selden, who presented the first version of his work *Mare Clausum* to James I about 1618, did not base his theory of dominion over the 'British seas' on a theory of property in the seabed. In 1622 Serjeant Robert Callis gave a series of lectures at Gray's Inn on the subject of the Statute of Sewers, 23 Hen. 8, c. 5, in which he began a chapter entitled 'The Sea within the Realm of England' as follows:

First, touching our *Mare Anglicum*, in whom the interest therein is, and by what law the government thereof is, is a fit question, and worth the handling. And in my argument therein, I hope to make it manifest by many proofs and precedents of great worth and esteem, that the King hath therein these powers and properties, *videlicet*—
1. *Imperium Regale.*
2. *Potestatem legalem.*
3. *Proprietatem tam soli quam aquae.*
4. *Possessionem et profitum tam reale quam personale.*
And all these he hath by the common laws of England.[21]

Callis then referred to various proclamations and statutes, to the work *De Acquirendo Rerum Domino* of Bracton, and to the cases of Sir Henry Constable and the Banne Fishery. His conclusions read:

So I take it I have proved the King full lord and owner of the seas, and that the seas be within the realm of England; and that I have also proved it by ancient books and authorities of the laws, and by charters, statutes, customs, and prescriptions, that the government therein is by the common laws of this realm.[22]

After discussing *Lacey's Case*,[23] Callis continued:

But the King hath neither the property of the sea, nor the real and personal profits there arising, but by the common laws of England, and in proof thereof the book 15 and 16 Eliz. in Dyer, where the grounds gained from the sea pertained to the Queen . . . which must needs be by the common law of England; for no law gives the King any soil, but only the common laws of England. . . .

And there is a statute made in 13 R. 2. c. 5. which restrains the Admiral that he do not meddle with any thing done within the realm, but on the seas; by which it may be collected, that the seas be not within the realm of England: But in my opinion the intent of that statute did rather limit the Admiral how far he should extend his jurisdiction, than any way to set forth the bounds of this realm: wherein my conclusion herein

21 Callis, 39.
22 Ibid., 41.
23 (1582) 1 Leon. 270; 2 Co. Rep. 93.

is, That my statute hath his extent within all the realm of England; and that English seas being within the realm, be within the bounds of my said Statute of Sewers; and that statute-law is in full power on the seas, as by the cases and statutes mentioned formerly doth appear.[24]

Callis next considered the legal status of an island which might suddenly appear out of the sea adjacent to the coast of England. He wrote:

But whether the Laws of this Realm be of force in the said new-sprung up Sea Islands, or not, is a question: It appears in *Calvin's Case*, and in the case of the Tanistry in the Irish Reports, That if the King conquer an Island or Nation, the same is no part of England, nor the laws of England there in force, till the King shall so declare the same, but the own proper Laws seem to be in force there; . . .
I am of opinion, that in this new-sprung up Island the Laws of England are there in force, because when it was Sea, the same was under the Government of these Laws; and although the nature and quality thereof be changed, *viz.* dry Land for full sea, yet the same Laws and Government remain in force; so that I hold this new Island within the Statute, and that the property thereof is the King's.[25]

Later, in discussing whether a subject could be seised of land, he stated, that 'no prescription, or custome can fetch lands farther than the low-water mark'.[26]

In 1633, Sir John Boroughs, in his treatise *The Soveraignty of the British Seas*, claimed that

. . . it is manifest that by the common law of the land the king is proprietary Lord of our seas; that the seas of England are under the legeance of the king, that the king is the sovereigne conservator of the peace as well upon the sea as land, that not only things floating on the superficies of the water but such as lye upon the soil or ground thereof, belong properly unto the king, whereupon I conclude, That *Rex Maris imperio Dominio et fundo possidet*.[27]

About this time, the question of the legal status of the seabed adjacent to the coasts of England arose incidentally in the course of litigation in the Court of Exchequer. In 1635, the Crown filed an information of intrusion against Sir Cornelius Vermuyden, William Wyld, Lord Gorge, and Michael Oldsworth, in order to recover 7,000 acres of marsh, called Sutton Marsh, which were parcel of the seashore of Lincolnshire and which had been left

[24] Callis, 41–2.
[25] Ibid., 46–7.
[26] Ibid., 49.
[27] Boroughs, 36 (1651 ed.).

derelict by the sea. The defendants claimed that by the custom of the country the owners of lands had alluvion and increment. Judgment, however, was given for the Crown on a demurrer.[28]

In 1637, further argument was heard in what appears to have been the same case.[29] The argument of the Attorney-General, Sir John Bankes, began:

First, he conceived that the King is seised of the British seas and the soil thereof in right of the Crown (*jure Coronae*). And this he endeavoured to prove by authority and reason, and by answering the objections against it.

Bankes then discussed the rules relating to wreck and to land gained from the sea. He continued:

Secondly, this realm is an island surrounded by the sea, and it is bounded by the sea like a forest is.

The second reason is because no subject can take title to the soil, for all the soil of this realm belongs to the king unless it passes from the king by grant . . .

Third reason. All the profits of the sea belong to the king; ergo the soil itself does. For what is the land but the profits? And anchorage is due to the king, which shows that the soil belongs to the king . . .

Fourth reason is because such lands have been in the Crown and anciently granted by it . . . And in several kings' reigns such grants have been made of such lands and of salt-marshes; as in Abergavenny, Portsmouth, Yorkshire, Gloucestershire, Essex, Lincolnshire, Norfolk and Kent. And copperas stone cast by the sea upon the land belongs to the king and has been demised by him.

Fifth reason. If a common person's meadow is overflowed by water and then becomes dry again, without question the subject shall have it back. Now the shore is the king's great mead, and therefore the same privilege should be to the king as to the subject. And if one grants *aquam suam* the soil passes, for *cujus est solum est ejus usque ad coelum* . . .

Sixth reason. The king has the soil of navigable rivers and of the ports, which are called gateways of the realm (*janua regni*); therefore, by the same reason that the arms of the sea belong to the king, the body itself does. For the body can privilege the branches . . .

Seventh reason. If the king regains Calais, a subject who had lands

---

[28] Hale, *De Jure Maris*, ch. 6; Moore, 398.

[29] Transcriptions of the Crown's argument and the judgments of Weston and Trevor BB. were printed by Moore from BL, Lansdowne MS 1081, fo. 178 *et seq.* (Moore, 295–303). The judgments of Davenport C.B. and Denham B. were not transcribed by Moore. The present transcription has been made for the author by Dr J. H. Baker, primarily from Cambridge University MS Gg. 2. 20, fos. 1044–54, 1107v–1116v, a manuscript report by Thomas Hardres.

there at first shall not have them back, even though he has evidences to show for them. So it is of lands gained by the enemy, as 7 Edw. 4.

Eighth reason. Subjects and lords of manors have taken sea shores by grants. The cases of 5 Edw. 3 and 39 Edw. 3, 5, have been objected, where waif and stray and royal fish can be claimed by prescription. And Coke, 5 Rep. 107, makes an inference out of these books that the soil belongs to the subject. Answer: (1) it is only Lord Coke's inference, (2) these things can be cast above the high water mark, (3) they were granted first, and so good. Objection that all the lords would lose their privileges. Answer: it is not so in all cases; also they might have it by grant, and then all is well.

The Court of Exchequer, Davenport C.B., Denman, Trevor, and Weston BB., unanimously gave judgement for the Crown. In the course of his judgment, Trevor B. stated:

The King has these lands *jure Coronae*; for, just as the king is supreme lord upon the land, so also upon the sea. And in 11 Hen. 7, 7, just as he has common law to rule the land, so he has martial law and maritime law to rule the sea, and forest law for the government of that. And all the land at first was derived out of the Crown; and so it has been, as our case is, in all commonwealths in foreign nations. Also, the king by his prerogative has all things of excellency, such as royal mines, and likewise the sea, being the chiefest and most excellent of waters. For, as it is said, all inferior rivers flow and reflow to and from the sea. By the same reason the king shall have it . . .

The third question is whether custom prevails against the king.

Negative. For, as it was in the king so long as it was parcel of the sea, now that it is made parcel of the dry land it shall not be taken from him.

Denman B. stated:

And if the sea belongs to the king, the soil, which is less worthy (*minus dignum*), also belongs to him. If a man grants his fishing-water or pond (*aquam piscarium sive stagnum suum*), the soil passes as an accessory and less worthy thing. So it is of a grant of all the wood (*de toto bosco*). And, if the soil did not belong to the king, there would be fractions and divisions of the inheritance, which the law will in no way allow; for at some times of the day it would be the king's, and at other times of the day it would be the subject's. In 6 Ric. 2, Proteccion 46, the sea is called the inheritance of the Crown. And in 22 Ass. *brachium maris*, which is the flow and reflow, is called parcel of the sea.

The judgment of the Chief Baron of the Exchequer, Sir Humfrey Davenport, discussed in some detail the question of property rights in the sea. He remarked:

Now, to discuss in whom the inheritance thereof, especially of the sea, belongs; and also touching the property thereof. I hold that by the common law of the land, without the help of any statute, during the time that these things remain in their natural and proper courses they belong to the Crown as parcel of the flowers and royal branches thereof.

After discussing the civil law position as irrelevant to England, he continued:

And *mare, littora maris*, and so on, are settled in the king *jure Coronae* as well before as after the reliction, for three reasons:

First, because the sea and sea-shores are visible and real inheritances and within the realm, and parcel of the Crown, and within the allegiance of England, and within the king's protection . . . And that the sea is parcel of the Crown and within the realm, and the king's inheritance, appears in 6 Ric. 2, Proteccion 46; with which agrees Sir Henry Constable's Case . . .

Second reason. The sea is ruled by the laws and customs of this realm ~. . .

The third reason: if the common law should be according to the Imperial law, the common law would commit suicide (*felo de se*). For this realm is an island, and the sea is the wall thereof. Now, if the walls thereof were not part of the realm and were *nullius in bonis*, what would become of the realm? It would expose our land to invasions and incursions . . . Now for authority in this point. The Mirror of Justices—which can be cited as authority, as it was in time of Henry VI—says that the rights of the Crown include amongst others the sovereignty and dominion of the sea. And the chief ports of the land belong to the king as parcel of the Crown; and the rest of the realm was conferred on others for the defence of the realm. Judicial records, statutes and customs make the law. Now, it appears by many judicial records that the possession of the sea and the government thereof belong to the Crown *jure Coronae*: see Selden in his *Mare Clausum*, which is a record in this court by the king's command.

Further judicial consideration of the status of the sea, though not its bed in particular, took place in the 'ship-money' case, *R*. v. *John Hampden*,[30] which was argued before all the judges in the Exchequer Chamber shortly after the Sutton Marsh case above. On behalf of the King, the Attorney-General, Sir John Bankes, declared of the King's alleged dominion:

This dominion is not only upon the land, but it is upon the sea. And so the king he hath not only a dominion at sea but he is 'dominus maris Anglicani'; he is both owner of the sea, and of the soil under the sea. And so it was resolved lately, by my Lord Chief Baron, and the rest of the

---

[30] 3 Cobbett's State Trials 825, 1023.

Barons in the Exchequer, in the case of Sutton Marsh, Mich. 13 Car. . . .
That not only the dominion of the sea, but the very soil belongeth unto
the king.[31]

Sir Humfrey Davenport, Lord Chief Baron, in giving his
opinion in the case, stated:

. . . for the king is lord of the sea; as it was argued at bar, in a cause
brought before us the barons of the Exchequer, where we did
unanimously agree, and adjudge that the king was, and is in my
conscience, rightly true lord of the very propriety and ownership of the
seas.[32]

Sir John Finch, Lord Chief Justice of the Court of Common
Pleas, remarked in the course of his opinion that 'Sea and land
make but one kingdom, and the king is *sponsus regni* . . . The soil of
the sea belongs to the king, who is lord and sole proprietor of them
. . .'[33] Sir John Brampston, Lord Chief Justice of the Court of
King's Bench, in the course of his opinion declared that 'the sea is
within the kingdom . . . It is the ancient custom of England, that
the king is lord of the narrow seas.'[34]

Still more judicial consideration of the seabed occurred in
Johnson v. *Barrett* in 1646, in which Hale appeared as counsel for the
Crown in respect of an action of trespass concerning a quay at
Yarmouth. The report stated:

But it was clearly agreed, that if it were erected beneath the low-water
mark, then it belonged to the King. It was likewise agreed, that an
intruder upon the King's possession might have an action of trespass
against a stranger; but he could not make a lease, whereupon the lessee
might maintain an *ejectione firmae*.[35]

The nature of the Crown's claim at this time can be gathered
from the information in the 1662 case of *Attorney-General* v. *Ceeley*,
which read:

Whereas our Sovereign Lord King Charles that now is during all the
time of His Majesty's reign over England hitherto hath been and still is
seised in his demesne as of fee *in right of His Crown of England* of and in the
ground and soil of the coasts and shores of the seas of and belonging to his
Kingdom of England, and of and in the ground and soil of all and every
the ports, havens, arms of the sea, creeks, pools, and navigable rivers

[31] Ibid., 1023.
[32] Ibid., 1210.
[33] Ibid., 1225–6.
[34] Ibid., 1246.
[35] (1646) Aleyn 10, 11.

thereof into which the sea doth ebb and flow *or hath used to ebb and flow*
. . .[36]

It was about this time that Sir Matthew Hale was writing his
three treatises *De Jure Maris et Brachiorum ejusdem, De Portibus Maris*,
and *Concerning the Customs of Goods Imported and Exported*. These
three works appear to have originated from an earlier draft by him,
A Narrative Legall and Historicall Touchinge the Customes, which is
printed in full by Moore.[37] In these works there are several specific
references to the status of the seabed. In the *Narrative*, Hale wrote,
'. . . the soyl not only below the low water marke, but between the
high water and low water marke, doth belonge to the Kinge, and
are part of the wast demesnes of his Crown'.[38]

Attached to the *Narrative* was another paper by Hale, *Concerninge
the Right of the Kinge to the Shore etc.*, which Moore concluded was a
draft of an argument for use in the Sutton Marsh case. In this
paper, Hale argued that *recessus maris* belonged to the King
because

. . . the sea, at lest so much thereof as adjoines nearer to our cost then to
any other foren cost: as it is within the Kinges jurisdiction, which
amongest other evidences thereof appears by the booke 6 R. 2, *protection*
46, wher Belknap affirmes the sea to bee of the ligeance of the Kinge as of
his Crown of England, so likewise it is the Kinges in propriety as his
roiall waste, and therfor hee hath those *bona caduca* or *vacantia*, as *floatsam*
etc., partly in respect of the right of property which hee hath in the soyle
underneath the water; and therfor questionlee the Ilands neare adjoining
to our cost are parcell of the Kinges inheritance, as being part of that
greate royal wast covered with the British Ocean: and no more evident
right can there bee of ownership or propriety then to bee master of comon
right of such profits as any way the sea adjoining yeelds . . .[39]
as the Kinge hath right of jurisdiction or dominion of so much at lest of
the sea as adjoines to the Brittish coast nearer then to any forren coast:
which appears by Belknap, 6 R. 2, *protection* 46; so as soone as any matter
of profitt happens upon or by reason of the said sea capable of propriety,
it doth presently belonge to the Kinge unles some other better title doth
interpose: such are wrecks, floatsam, etc. *Insulae natae in mari*, etc.; therfor
though the Kinge cannot have propriety in the water, yet when any
thinge therein emergeth that is capable of propriety it is the Kinges as
aforesaid: The sea is the Kinges royal wast *de communi jure*. But to leave

[36] Moore, 314, from Exch. B. & A. Chas. 2, Cornwall, 49.
[37] Moore, 319–69, from BL, Hargrave MS 98. Fulton, 543, put its date at about 1636.
[38] Moore, 347.
[39] Ibid., 358.

that doubtful question whither the soil of the sea be the Kinges *aqua marina adhuc coopertum*.[40]

Hale then went on to declare:

The narrow seas, or at lest so much therof as adjoines to the English shore, is within the Kinges jurisdiction or roialty, 6 R. 2, *protect*. 46, etc.: and likewise in right of propriety; for although the use of the sea be comon, yet the propriety thereof belonges to the Kinge as a royal wast: which is the reason that as well all the *bona vacantia* upon the seas belonge to the Kinge as the right of his admirall jurisdiction, so likewise ilands in the sea, which although by civil law *fiunt occupantis*, yet in our law they are annexed in point of interest to the crowne, who is therof presently in possession, and so prevents any right to bee acquired *per occupationem*.[41]

Hale expanded these views in his treatise *De Jure Maris et Brachiorum ejusdem* which is also printed in Moore's work.[42] In chapter 4 of this treatise, Hale expressed the following opinion:

The narrow sea, adjoining to the coast of England, is part of the wast and demesnes and dominions of the king of England, whether it lie within the body of any county or not. This is abundantly proved by that learned treatise of Master Selden called *Mare Clausum*; and therefore I shall say nothing therein, but refer the reader thither.

In this sea the king of England hath a double right, viz. a right of jurisdiction which he ordinarily exerciseth by his admiral, and a right of propriety or ownership. The latter is that which I shall meddle with.[43]

Hale supported his thesis by reference to the Crown's right of fishing in the sea, its right of property in the foreshore and its right to *maritima incrementa*. The last topic he divided into three aspects: increase *per projectionem vel alluvionem*, increase *per relictionem vel desertionem*, and, finally, increase *per insulae productionem*. In respect of the first he argued that: 'The reason why this belongs to the crown is, because in truth the soil, where there is now dry land, was formerly part of the very *fundus maris*, and consequently belonged to the king.'[44] He used a similar argument to support the second aspect: 'This doth *de jure communi* belong to the king; for as the sea is parcel of the wast or demesne, so of necessity the land that lies under it, and therefore it belongs to the king when left by the sea.' Similarly, Hale considered in respect of the third aspect

[40] Ibid., 362.
[41] Ibid., 367.
[42] Ibid., 370–413.
[43] Ibid., 376.
[44] Ibid., 380.

that islands 'are part of that soil of the sea, that belonged before in point of propriety to the king . . .'[45]

In chapter 6 of *De Jure Maris*, after discussing the first Sutton Marsh case, Hale continued:

The King of England hath the propriety as well as the jurisdiction of the narrow seas; for he is in a capacity of acquiring the narrow and adjacent sea to his dominion by a kind of possession which is not compatible to a subject; and accordingly regularly the king hath that propriety in the sea: but a subject hath not nor indeed cannot have that propriety in the sea, through a whole tract of it, that the king hath; because without a regular power he cannot possibly possess it. But though a subject cannot acquire the interest of the narrow seas, yet he may by usage and prescription acquire an interest in so much of the sea as he may reasonably possess, viz. of a *districtus maris*, a place in the sea between such points, or a particular part contiguous to the shore, or of a port or creek or arm of the sea. These may be prescribed by a subject because they may be possessed by a subject, and prescribed in point of interest both of the water, and the soil itself covered with the water within such a precinct; for these are mainorable [sic], and may be entirely possessed by a subject.

The civilians tell us truly, *nihil praescribitur nisi quod possidetur*. The king may prescribe the propriety of the narrow seas, because he may possess them by his navies and power. A subject cannot. But a subject may posses a navigable river, or creek or arm of the sea; because these may lie within the extent of his possession and acquest.[46]

About this time, there were a few examples of grants by the Crown of areas of seabed, apparently still under the open sea. Thus, by letters patent in the name of James I, the property of St. Michael's Mount in Cornwall was granted in fee to Robert, Earl of Salisbury, in 1611. The letters patent included the following provisions:

And further, of our more abundant special grace and of our certain knowledge and mere motion we have given and granted, and by these presents for us, our heirs and successors, do give and grant to the aforesaid Robert Earl of Salisbury, his heir and assigns, all and singular the lands heretofore overflowed by the water of the sea which are now gained from the sea and reduced to dry land, [and] the lands now overflowed by the water of the sea which hereafter shall be gained and reduced to dry land, abutting, adjoining, or adjacent to the aforesaid

---

[45] Ibid., 383.
[46] Ibid., 399–400.

lordship, manor, farm, lands, tenements, and other the premises before granted in the said county of Cornwall.[47]

In 1676, the year of Hale's death, a similar grant was the subject of litigation. By letters patent, James I had granted to an individual certain lands which comprised the manor of Holbeach in Lincolnshire. A clause was added to the letters patent granting

. . . nec non totum illud fundum et solum et terras suas contigue adjacentes quae sunt aqua cooperta vel quae in posterum de aqua possunt recuperari.

After the grant was made, one hundred acres of land, formerly under the sea, became derelict. It was argued for the King that the lands which he had by his prerogative could not pass by general words and that therefore the grant of lands yet to be recovered was void as it transferred only a bare possibility and was too indefinite. The defendant, who was claiming under the grant in the letters patent, argued that the soil was in the King, that he could grant it, and that subjects were capable of holding property in the sea. According to the report in Levinz, Montague C.B., with the advice of the Chief Justices of the King's Bench and Common Pleas, held that nothing passed by the general words in the original letters patent and that the patent was void in respect of the one hundred acres of reclaimed land. According to the reports in Modern Reports and Sir T. Raymond, however, no judgment was given.[48]

C. The post-Stuart Period

For more than a century, executive, legislative, and judicial practice regarding the seabed and subsoil of the marginal sea was scanty. The absence of practice shows in the following remarks in the 7th Report of Commissioners of His Majesty's Woods, Forests, and Land Revenues, presented to Parliament in 1830:

From the time of the passing of the Civil List Act of Queen Anne [1 Anne, st. 1, c. 7], by which the Estates of the Crown were rendered inalienable, except for the limited terms therein mentioned, till the year 1786 [26 Geo. 3, c. 87] the management of that Property does not appear to have,

---

[47] Patent Roll, 9 James I, p. 10 (See pp. 107–8 below).

[48] *Attorney-General* v. *Farmen* (1676) 2 Lev. 171; *sub nom. Attorney-General* v. *Sir Edward Turner* (1676) 2 Mod. Rep. 106; *sub nom. Attorney-General* v. *Sir Edward Farmer* (1676) Sir T. Raymond 241. The area in dispute was on the shores of the Wash, a feature which might not have been regarded as open sea.

on any occasion, engaged the attention of Parliament or of the executive Government.[49]

Throughout this period, Acts of Parliament, at first public then private, were passed to sanction the construction of piers and other works abutting on the foreshore and in many cases clearly running out into the sea. These Acts did not expressly recite the claim of the Crown to be seised of the sea and soil thereof; they did sometimes contain an assertion that the piers, or part of them, were 'out of the body of any county of this realm'.[50]

The decline in the intensity of the Crown's activity did not mean that it had expressly abandoned its claims. In one of the few instances of executive practice found during this period, the Lord Mayor, Sheriffs, Commons, and Citizens of Dublin claimed, in August 1752, under a charter of Queen Elizabeth made in or about 1585, to be entitled to exercise the Office of Admiralty at that port and to receive in consequence the droits and perquisites thereof including that of anchorage.[51] They claimed that this charter rendered void a grant of Admiralty functions and perquisites in Ireland, including anchorage, made by the Crown on 17 May 1751 to one Richard Read. The Admiralty submitted the following questions to the Admiralty advocates and civilians sitting at Doctors' Commons:

Whether Anchorage, and the Duties and Profits thereof, Did (at the time of Queen Elizabeth Granting said Charter to the City of Dublin) of Right belong to, and were Grantable by the Crown, or the Lord High Admiral or Commissioners of the Admiralty for the time being; And whether any Right to the Profits of Anchorage of Ships in the Port of Dublin, was by the general Words above Quoted from the said Charter, Granted to the said City of Dublin; and, if any such Right was granted whether it extended any farther from the City of Dublin, towards the Sea, than to Low Water Mark.

On 28 February 1753, Dr G. Paul replied:

The Dominion of the British Seas, must be held to be an indispensable appendant to the Crown of Great Britain and his Majesty has not only a General Empire over the water, But also a more peculiar and stringent Title to the Land and Water joyned in Ports and Navigable Havens, below the first Bridge, and also to those places on the Sea Coast which the saylors call the King's Chambers which are described by the writers

---

[49] *HCP*, 1830 (508, p. 1) xvi, 1.
[50] e.g., 33 Geo. 2, c. 35 (New Shoreham Pier).
[51] The papers for this incident are in ADM 7/298.

on maritime affairs to be The Land and Water between a Peninsula or Promontory of Land where the Sea and Land joyn together, and from which places farthest extended into the sea, a direct line may be drawn to the next projecting Point, on the same Coast. Therefore I humbly apprehend that the Dutys arising from anchorage belong to, and are only grantable by his Majesty.

The other civilians who were consulted, Jervis, Ryder, and Pinfold, made no mention in their replies of the soil under the sea.

Towards the end of the eighteenth century, a dispute arose in connection with the ownership of the Ham oyster grounds which was to be the forerunner of much litigation concerning this area of the coast. The Ham grounds were described as 'bounded on the North by a certain place called the Spaniard; on the South by a part of the Kentish Coast; on the West by the Island of Shepey [sic], and on the East by a certain place called the Flats; at low water some parts of the Ham grounds are dry, and others are covered; but the depth varies from one to two and a half fathom water'.[52] According to the Crown, fishermen from Whitstable and Faversham had for many years occasionally dredged for oysters but they were frequently interrupted by the Water Bailiff of the Court of Admiralty, 'it being generally understood that the King is Lord of the Soil'.

The Crown wished to grant a 31-year lease of the soil of the fishery to certain persons who, before they proceeded to stock the fishery, wanted to know whether they could do so free from the interference of others. Accordingly, in 1789, the Land Revenue Office prepared a Case Stated for Stewart Kyd, of Counsel, which, after stating the above facts, asked, 'Whether a Lease from the Crown to A.B. & C. for the Term of 31 Years of the Arm of the Sea called the Ham, will give them an exclusive right to the Fishery during that period?' Kyd delivered his opinion on 27 December 1798. he began:

By the Civil Law, the Sea, Arms of the Sea, and navigable Rivers, where the Tide ebbs and flows as far as high water-mark were the property of the Public; no one had or could have there an exclusive privilege of navigation or Fishery; but every Individual might navigate or fish, and do such Things on the shore as were necessary to the exercise of those Rights. . . .

By the feudal Law the King or Prince was considered as the Representative of the Public, and in that Character the property of the Sea, Arms of the Sea, and navigable Rivers where the Tide ebbs and flows

[52] The papers for this dispute are in CREST 40/43.

became vested in him. Craig: *de jur. feud*: lib. 1, D. 15 s. 13. From which it might naturally have been concluded that the King was the ostensible proprietor *in trust* for his Subjects against foreign Nations without infringing on the right of the Individual to navigate and fish. It was so as to navigation; but the King under the fictitious Character of *Proprietor* assumed the Prerogative of granting to particular Individuals the right of Fishery on the Coast of the Sea, Arms of the Sea, and navigable Rivers where the Tide ebbs and flows, in exclusion of his other Subjects. Vid: Craig: ibid: s. 13. 15.

I think it will appear from a careful Investigation of what is to be found in our Books on this Subject that the English Law corresponds pretty nearly in this respect with the feudal.

Kyd was 'inclined to think' that the King might grant an exclusive right of fishery in the arm of the sea in question.

This was not the end of the dispute, however, since three years later the grantees, under a document executed on 18 March 1799, brought an action in the King's Bench claiming that various defendants had broken into their fishery and taken oysters therefrom. The defendants replied that, as subjects of the realm, they had the liberty and privilege of fishing in the Ham Grounds and dredging up oysters. The grounds were described in the pleadings as an arm of the sea lying and being below the low-water mark. In a transcript headed 'Plaintiff's Case' it was stated:

If every Grant by the Crown of any part of the soil of the Sea were to be invalid in case any subject had previously been accustomed to fish upon the place granted, the prerogative of the Crown in this respect would be reduced to nothing. There is no part of the Coast without a fishery of some kind or other and in particular Oysters and Brood are dredged for on most parts of the Coasts of Kent Essex Norfolk Suffolk Hants and other Counties and it would be strange to say that the King cannot legally grant any part of the soil of the Sea on any of those Coasts.[53]

The action, *Kelsey* v. *Baker*, was heard before Heath J. in late 1803. He immediately non-suited the plaintiffs on the basis set out in a note endorsed on one of the documents in the case:

If the King possessed it exclusively, he could grant it exclusively.
If he has it as a Trustee, he could not grant it.
The King is prima facie seized in trust for his subjects.[54]

The action appears then to have been settled, the plaintiffs surrendering their grant.

[53] CREST 40/44.
[54] Ibid.

In 1795, the Attorney-General filed an information against one Richards, praying that the defendant might be restrained from making any further erections in the harbour at Gosport and that a wharf which he had constructed there be removed. The information stated 'by the royal prerogative, the sea and sea-coasts, as far as the sea flows and reflows, between the high and low-water marks, and all the ports and havens of the kingdom, belong to His Majesty'. In the course of argument for the defendant it was stated:

It is clear, that as far as the jus privatum of the Crown is concerned, a grant of the soil of the sea-coast, or of a harbour, is good. But, if the argument be true, that no possession could ever be taken of the soil while overflown, no grant or feoffment of land covered with water could ever be good.

But on the contrary, Lord Hale says (*De Portibus Maris* p. 85) that there are a thousand instances of licence from the King to build new wharfs or keys, in which licence the right to the soil, within high and low water mark, or beyond, is necessarily included.[55]

In fact, the Court held that the grant by which Richards claimed the foreshore as against the Crown had not included the *locus in quo*.

Fifteen years later, a further information was filed by the Attorney-General in respect of another wharf at Gosport claimed by the defendant under the same grant. This time the House of Lords held that the *locus in quo* was not within the area granted. In the course of argument, the defendant stated, 'It is admitted that the sea and sea coasts round the Kingdom, so far as the sea flows and reflows between the high and low water marks, are the property of the Crown, and may be granted and transferred, subject to the jus publicum.'[56]

Statements by both writers and judges to the effect that the Crown owned the soil of the marginal sea became frequent as the nineteenth century advanced. Joseph Chitty, junior, in his treatise on the prerogative published in 1820, wrote with references to Hale (*De Portibus Maris*), Selden and Craig:

The King has an undoubted sovereignty and jurisdiction, which he has immemorially exercised through the medium of the Admiralty Courts, over the British seas, that is, the seas which encompass the four sides of the British islands; and other seas, arms of seas, and navigable (but not

---

[55] *Attorney-General* v. *Richards* (1795) 2 Anst. 603, 611.
[56] *Parmeter* v. *Gibbs: Re Portsmouth Harbour* (1813) 10 Price 412, 424.

unnavigable) rivers, within and immediately connected with the territories subject to his sway.

The law of nations and the constitution of the country have clothed the
Sovereign with this power, that he may defend his people and protect
their commercial interests.

By implication of law the property in the soil under these public waters
is also in the King . . .

As to the soil or *fundum maris*, there can be no doubt it may be claimed
either by charter or prescription, for every prescription respecting a
franchise generally supposes a grant, which in this instance could be
made by the King, yet it is to be observed that the soil can only be
appropriated *sub modo*; for, according to Lord Hale, though the dominion
either of franchise or propriety be lodged by prescription or charter in a
subject, yet it is charged or effected with that *jus publicum* that belongs to
all men.[57]

In the context of accretion, Chitty wrote:

The King is also by his prerogative, on principles of expediency or as lord
paramount of the soil, the owner of such lands as are covered by the
narrow seas adjoining the English coasts, or by arms of the seas or
navigable rivers, within his dominions; and is therefore entitled to
maritima incrementa, or lands which increase by the casting up of sand and
earth from the sea.[58]

Finally Chitty considered the classic hypothesis of an island
appearing in the 'King's seas'. He observed that, '. . . these *prima
facie* and of common right also belong to the King, for they are part
of that soil of the sea that belonged before in point of propriety to
the King . . . '[59]

The following year, in *Blundell* v. *Catterall*, Holroyd J. remarked:

Neither in Lord Hale's treatise [i.e., *De Portibus Maris*] nor elsewhere,
does it appear that there is a common law right in the King's subjects in
general, or any of them, to appropriate the seashore, or the soil even
below the low water-mark, for general purposes, though temporary only,
to their own use, without the King's grant or licence, even where that can
be done without nuisance to his subjects. Such an appropriation by any
of the King's subjects, without his grant or licence, though it were not in
law a nuisance, would be . . . where the soil remains the King's, a
purpresture, an encroachment, and intrusion upon the King's soil. . .[60]

[57] Chitty, 142–3.
[58] Ibid., 206.
[59] Ibid., 207.
[60] (1821) 5 B. & Ald. 268, 298.

In the lengthy case of *R.* v. *Lord Yarborough*, Best C.J., in 1828, addressed the House of Lords as follows:

All the writers on the law of England agree in this, that as the king is lord of the sea, that flows around our coasts, and also owner of all the land to which no individual has acquired a right by occupation and improvement, the soil that was once covered by the sea belongs to him.[61]

An alternative report of the same address read:

As the king is lord of the sea, so he is owner of the soil covered by the sea, but that right may be confined in particular places by local custom, and then the custom must be pleaded and proved.[62]

---

[61] (1828) 2 Bligh N.S. 147, 157.
[62] (1828) 1 D. & C. 178, 186.

Chapter II

Executive and Legislative Practice 1829—1876

A. Introduction

On 19 June 1829, the Crown Lands Act received the Royal Assent.[1] The long title proclaimed it to be an Act 'to consolidate and amend the Laws relating to the Management and Improvement of Her Majesty's Woods, Forests, Parks, and Chases; of the Land Revenue of the Crown within the Survey of the Exchequer in England . . .' The Act placed the possessions and land revenues of the Crown under the management of the Commissioners of Woods.

Although it made no specific mention of the Crown's claim to the ownership of maritime territory, the Act marked the beginning of a sustained effort by the Crown to assert the rights which it claimed over the foreshore and bed of the sea. By 1859, an anonymous commentator in the *Law Magazine and Law Review* could write:

. . . the subject of the crown's rights to the soil of the seashores, to the bed of the sea, and to the bed and soil of navigable rivers, after having scarcely been stirred—there are not half a dozen exceptions—since the date of the treatise *De Jure Maris* (which is commonly attributed to Lord Hale), has of late years sprung into life again, has been much canvassed, and made wear a somewhat more compact and finished appearance than heretofore.[2]

Within a year of the 1829 Act coming into force, a treatise was published by Robert Gream Hall which supported the Crown's maritime claims in vigorous terms.[3] Hall began by asserting the Crown's 'dominion and ownership' over the 'British seas' and continued:

This dominion and ownership over the British seas, vested by our law in the King, is not confined to the mere usufruct of the water, and the

---

[1] 10 Geo. 3, c. 50. The Scottish land revenues were transferred to the United Kingdom Treasury by the Act 3 Will. 4, c. 13, s. 1, of 1833.

[2] (1859) 6 *Law Magazine & Law Review* 99–100.

[3] Hall, *Rights of the Crown and the Privileges of the Subject in the Sea-shores of the Realm*, 1830.

maritime jurisdiction, but it includes the very *fundum* or soil at the bottom of the sea. 'The sea is the King's proper inheritance', and he is 'Lord of the great Waste', both land and water; *'tam aquae quam soli'*. Selden, in his celebrated treatise on the Dominion of the Seas, would seem to contemplate this ownership of the King, as combining both jurisdiction and ownership; the one, indeed, would seem to involve the other, if Selden's doctrine to its full extent be admitted.

There are eminent writers upon natural and upon national law, who have controverted Selden's doctrines, and have denied the King of England's exclusive dominion, and consequently his ownership over the British seas; but however this may be, and probably will ever continue, *vexata quaestio* between such writers, we know that the writers on the common and municipal law of England, as well as the decisions of our judicial courts, all speak the same language, and appropriate the dominion of the British seas *tam aquae quam soli*, to the King.[4]

Hall continued:

The title of the King of England to the land or soil *aqua maris cooperta*, is similar to his ancient title to all the *terra firma* in his dominions, as the first and original proprietor and lord paramount . . . That part of the land which the King and his ancestors *have never granted out to the subject*, remains to the King, as his *demesnes*, in absolute ownership. The *terra firma* of England has become, almost entirely, the property (by grant and tenure) of the subject; but the *terra aqua maris cooperta* still remains to the King in wide and barren ownership.

Some rare and antique instances may indeed be found of actual grants, by Kings of England, of certain portions of land *under the sea*, *i.e.* of both sea and land, to a certain extent. These grants have been made in such places where some creek or bay has afforded the means of exclusive possession. Thus, the tract ascribed to Lord Hale [*De Jure Maris*] . . . recites a grant of King Canute 'de terra insulae Thanet, tam in terra quam *in mari* et *littore*'; and another of William the First, 'Abbati Sancti Augustini de tota terra Estanore, *et totum littus usque medietatem aquae*'; and the author of the tract adds, 'If the King will grant lands adjacent to the sea, together with a thousand acres of land covered by the sea adjoining, such grant will pass the soil itself; and if there should be a recess of the sea, leaving such a quantity of dry land, it will belong to the grantee.'[5]

Hall summed up his argument on this aspect as follows:

. . . the king is absolute owner of the ground or soil under the surface of those seas which are within, or parcel of the British dominions.[6]

[4] Hall, 2–3, as reprinted in Moore, 668–9.
[5] Ibid., 6–7; Moore, 671–3.
[6] Ibid., 7; Moore, 673.

It is proposed to distinguish between the practice relating to the bed of the marginal sea on the one hand, and that relating to its subsoil on the other.

B. The Seabed

The period under survey was punctuated by the Crown Lands Act 1866,[7] which, unlike its predecessor of 1829 and the Crown Lands Act of 1845,[8] made specific mention of the bed of the sea in drawing a distinction, for the purpose of assigning responsibility to government departments, between the bed of the sea on the one hand and minerals and mines under the bed of the sea on the other.

The background to the legislation appears from a report to Parliament made by the Commissioners of Woods, Forests, and Land Revenues dated 1 February 1866.[9] This contained the following passage:

By the common law the shores and bed of the sea and of all tidal navigable rivers below ordinary high-water mark are vested in the Crown, subject to all public rights of navigation . . .

The right of the Crown is of a two-fold character.

First:—A right of property in the soil which may be granted to a subject, and may be enjoyed by the grantee so that he does not obstruct the public right of navigation.

Secondly:—A right of jurisdiction for the protection of public rights; this right is inalienable except by Act of Parliament, and continues to exist in the Crown, although the right of property may have been granted away.

The first-mentioned right, that of property, is, like other territorial rights of the Crown, under the charge of the Commissioners of Woods. The latter right, that of jurisdiction, was, until lately, under the charge of the Board of Admiralty, but by the Act 25th and 26th Victoria, cap. 69, the exercise of it was (except as regards some particular localities) transferred to the Board of Trade, to whom the management of the Crown's right to 'Wreck' had been previously entrusted by the Merchant Shipping Act, 1854.

The same opinion was expressed in respect of Scotland.

The Act received the Royal assent on 6 August 1866. According to s. 25:

---

[7] 29 & 30 Vict., c. 62.
[8] 8 & 9 Vict., c. 99.
[9] *HCP*, 1866 (172, pp. 3–6) lx, 469–72. The original is on T1/6618 B.

4. To enable the Board of Trade to deal more liberally with the title of the Crown in the case of works of public utility.[14].

In 1872, the Board of Trade presented to Parliament the first of a series of papers which were to be issued at intervals until 1919. The paper was entitled 'Statement of the particulars of all cases in which the rights and interests of the Crown in the shores and bed of the sea and tidal rivers have been sold, leased or otherwise dealt with by the Board of Trade under The Crown Lands Act, 1866'. In this first paper, which dealt with the period 1867–71, the Board of Trade set out the texts of the form in which grants and leases of the foreshore and bed of the sea were usually made by it. The 'common form of grant' read in part:

This Indenture, made [date] between the Queen's Most Excellent Majesty of the first part, the Board of Trade acting in exercise of such of the powers conferred by the Acts 10 Geo. 4, c. 50, and 15 & 16 of Her Majesty, c. 62, or any other Act, as were transferred to the Board of Trade by 'The Crown Lands Act, 1866', of the second part, and [name] hereinafter called the grantee, of the third part, witnesseth, that in consideration of the sum [amount] by the grantee, paid to the Accountant of the Board of Trade . . . on behalf of Her Majesty, and with the consent of the Commissioners of Her Majesty's Treasury, signified by their warrant, dated [date], do by these presents grant unto the grantee and his heirs all that piece of land being part of the foreshore and bed of the [a blank was left in the form] below high-water mark situate opposite to [a blank was left in the form] in the parish of [name] in the county of [name] and extending [a blank was left in the form] which said premises hereby granted are intended to be delineated in the plan annexed to these presents . . .
    Except, nevertheless, and always reserving to the Queen's Majesty, Her heirs and successors, out of this present grant, full and free right, for Her and them, and for all persons by Her or their permission (which permission shall be assumed to have been granted unless the contrary be shown), to ride, drive, walk or otherwise pass to and fro over, and to fish and bathe upon, and to gather seaweed or ware from the premises hereby granted, and to land thereon goods and passengers in vessels and boats, but so that erections or works constructed or placed on the said premises, with the consent and approval of the Board of Trade, as hereby provided, shall not be prejudiced or interfered with by reason of the aforesaid exception and reservation.
    . . . To have and to hold the premises hereby granted unto and to the use of the grantee, his assigns for ever.
    Yielding and paying unto the Queen's Majesty, Her heirs and succes-

[14] Moore, 611.

sors, the yearly rent of one shilling on the first day of January in every year, if demanded . . .[15]

The 'common form of lease' was drafted in similar terms, with the necessary changes being made.

British executive practice in respect of the seabed during the period 1829–76, both before and after the above Act, may be classified by subject matter into five categories: (a) reclamations of the bed of the sea, (b) piers, harbours and breakwaters, (c) submarine cables, (d) sedentary fisheries, (e) conservancy.

(a) RECLAMATIONS OF THE BED OF THE SEA

Various local Acts of Parliament passed during this period in order to regulate the reclamation of the seabed have been put forward from time to time as evidence of the Crown's title to the seabed.[16] Usually, these Acts contained a preamble reciting the position of the Crown in respect of the land to be reclaimed. Thus the preamble to the Norfolk Estuary Act 1846[17] stated:

. . . and whereas the Queen's most Excellent Majesty, in right of Her Royal Prerogative, claims to be entitled to the said Tracts of Land . . .

The preamble to the Lincolnshire Estuary Act 1851[18] ran:

. . . and whereas Her Majesty, in right of Her Crown, claims certain exclusive Rights and Jurisdiction in and over the lands to be reclaimed . . .

A third formula was used in the preamble to the South Essex Estuary and Reclamation Act 1852:[19]

. . . and whereas Her Majesty, in right of Her Crown, is or claims to be seised of the Soil and Freehold of the said Marches, Mud Banks, and Waste lands so proposed to be reclaimed . . .

The reclamation Acts usually stipulated[20] that the land reclaimed should be deemed to be within the county adjacent, a provision which could thereby raise the inference that the seabed before reclamation was outside any county, and was not therefore *intra fauces terrae* since all land under waters *intra fauces terrae* was already within some county. However, the areas in which the

---

[15] *HCP*, 1872 (61, pp. 1–18) xxxvi, 209–26.
[16] e.g., by Sir Cecil Hurst, (1923–4) 4 *BYBIL* at 37 note 2.
[17] 9 & 10 Vict., c. ccclxxxviii.
[18] 14 & 15 Vict., c. cxxxvi.
[19] 15 & 16 Vict., c. lxvi.
[20] e.g., the Norfolk Estuary Act 1846, s. 26.

reclamations were carried out, e.g., the Wash, the estuary of the Thames, Pegwell Bay, Castlemaine Estuary, were areas which were not clearly outside inland waters. During the period under review, there does not seem to have been any single reclamation Act which concerned an area of seabed beyond doubt under the open sea.

(b) PIERS, HARBOURS, AND BREAKWATERS

The management of harbours, docks, and piers was an important matter in mid-Victorian Britain and to this end the Government introduced a Harbour Conservancy Bill in August 1846.[21] The preamble of this Bill read in part:

Whereas the power, property and jurisdiction of the Crown of these Realms extended in ancient times over all the seas and shores surrounding the Dominions of Great Britain and Ireland; and the Crown had also the property of the soil in all navigable rivers which have the flux and reflux of the sea, up to high-water mark of ordinary spring tides; and Her Majesty's predecessors have, from time immemorial, exercised that power, enjoyed that property, and enforced that jurisdiction.

The Bill was not proceeded with. Shortly afterwards, on 11 May 1847, the Harbours, Docks, and Piers Clauses Act 1847 was passed without such a fulsome preamble.[22] This Act, the aim of which was to consolidate in one Act certain provisions usually contained in Acts authorizing the making and improving of harbours, docks, and piers, provided in s. 12 that

The Undertakers shall not construct the Harbour, Dock, or Pier, or any Part thereof, or any Works connected therewith, on any Part of the Shore of the Sea, or of any Creek, Bay, Arm of the Sea, or navigable River communicating therewith, where and so far up the same as the Tide flows and reflows, without the previous Consent of Her Majesty, Her Heirs and Successors, to be signified in Writing under the Hands of Two of the Commissioners of Her Majesty's Woods, Forests, Land Revenues, Works and Buildings, and of the Lords of the Admiralty . . .

After referring to Acts authorizing the construction or improvement of harbours, docks or piers, known as 'special Acts'. the statute provided in s. 99:

Nothing in this or the special Act, or any Act incorporated therewith, contained shall extend to alienate, defeat, vary, lessen, abrogate, or

[21] *HCP*, 1846 (626) iii, 153. This formulation was clearly taken from the report of the Tidal Harbours Commissioners: *HCP*, 1845 (665, p. xi) xvi, 279.
[22] 10 & 11 Vict., c. 27.

prejudice any Estate, Right, Title, Interest, Prerogative, Royalty, Jurisdiction, or Authority, of or appertaining to the Queen's most Excellent Majesty, Her Heirs or Successors . . .

Various 'special Acts', taking the form of local Acts, were passed subsequent to this legislation. The first legal difficulty in respect of these seems to have arisen in 1854, following the Great Yarmouth Wellington Pier Act 1853,[23] an Act for constructing and maintaining a pier of that name, which ran in part:

And whereas Her Majesty is or claims to be seised in right of Her Crown of the land to the seaward of High-water Mark at ordinary Spring Tides on which it is proposed to make the said Pier and Works: Be it therefore enacted, That nothing whatsoever contained in this Act shall extend to authorize the Company to purchase, take, use or otherwise interfere with any Land, Soil, Tenements, or Hereditaments, or any Rights in respect thereof, belonging to Her Majesty in right of her Crown, without the Consent in Writing of the Commissioners or Commissioner for the Time being of Her Majesty's Woods, Forests, and Land Revenues . . .

In the 'Book of Reference' mentioned in s. 16 of the Act, the Crown and the Corporation of Yarmouth were scheduled as owners of the beach, and the Crown as owner of the bed of the sea. Shortly after the passing of the Act, the Pier Company entered into negotiations with the Crown, i.e., the Office of Woods, for a lease of the site of the pier below low-water mark. The Crown proposed a lease of 80 years to which the Company countered with requests first for a lease of 999 years and, later, for the fee. The Crown replied that the maximum lease which it would be prepared to grant would be for 99 years though it proposed a sale of the fee. The directors of the Company then stated that all that could be purchased thereby would be the 'base right of driving a few piles into the sand which is covered with water'. They claimed that the case of *Johnson* v. *Barrett*[24] in 1646 concerned a quay in a tidal river not in the open sea, and that the Crown could not prevent them from proceeding with the construction of the pier. The Crown took the advice of the Law Officers, the Case Stated beginning:

Her Majesty is entitled in right of the Crown to the bed and shores of the Sea and of all Navigable Rivers so far as the Tide flows and reflows subject only to such Grants as have been at any time heretofore made by Her Majesty or any of her Predecessors.

[23] 16 & 17 Vict., c. xv.
[24] (1646) Aleyn 10.

The Law Officers, Cockburn A.G. and Bethell S.G., replied on 6 February 1854:

We are of Opinion that an application should be made to the Court of Chancery for an Injunction to restrain the Company from all further proceedings in constructing or opening the pier.[25]

The dispute must have been settled in a manner agreeable to both sides since the earliest sale of land below low-water mark recorded in the schedules of Crown seabed transactions prepared prior to a consultation with the Law Officers in 1878 was in fact that of 1 acre, 3 roods, 9 perches sold to the Great Yarmouth Wellington Pier Company on 3 May 1854 for a purchase price of £80.[26]

On 1 August 1861, the General Pier and Harbour Act 1861[27] became law. The aim of this Act was to avoid the necessity for undertakers of piers, harbours, quays, wharves, jetties, etc. to obtain the passing of a special local Act before they could proceed. S. 3 of the Act provided that the Board of Trade might grant Provisional Orders in respect of such proposed works, provided that the estimated expenditure did not exceed £100,000. By s. 15, such an Order might empower the undertakers to take land on lease or otherwise, to an extent limited by the Order, by agreement. In general, each Provisional Order required the additional approval of the Office of Woods and was to be confirmed by a public general Act of Parliament initiated by the Board of Trade. The Act also provided that the rights of the Crown were to be preserved. The 1861 Act was amended in respect of certain details by the General Pier and Harbour Act 1861, Amendment Act 1862[28] which entered into force on 16 May 1862.

In practice, separate Provisional Orders were often confirmed by a single Act, which recited the text of each Order and laid down the conditions under which the work was to be carried out. Thus the Pier and Harbour Orders Confirmation Act 1862[29] referred to Provisional Orders in respect of works at Carrickfergus, Deal, Oban, St. Ives, Tobermory, and Hastings. In respect of the proposed works at Deal, the Deal and Walmer Pier Order of 19 May 1862, the text of which was set out in the Act, read in part:

[25] The papers for this incident are in CREST 40/54.
[26] CREST 37/336. This consultation, to which frequent reference will be made, is described in detail in Chapter VI below.
[27] 24 & 25 Vict., c. 45.
[28] 25 & 26 Vict., c. 19.
[29] 25 & 26 Vict., c. 51.

. . . The works by this Order authorized comprise the following:—

A pier on iron piles carried out from the South Esplanade, Deal, into the sea to a distance of 920 feet, with a general width of 20 feet, and a width at the head of 40 feet.

. . . The Company [i.e., the Deal and Walmer Pier Company, Limited] shall not construct any work on any part of the shore or bed of the sea below high-water mark without the previous consent of Her Majesty, Her heirs and successors, signified in writing under the hand of one of the Commissioners of Her Majesty's Woods, Forests, and Land Revenues, and then only according to such plan and under such restrictions and regulations as the said Commissioners, or one of them, approve of, such approval being signified as last aforesaid. After any such work is constructed with such consent as aforesaid, the Company shall not alter or extend the same without first obtaining the like consent and approval. If any work be commenced, constructed, altered, or extended contrary to this provision, the said Commissioners may, at the expense of the Company, abate and remove it, or any part of it, and restore the site thereof to its former condition. The amount of such expense shall be a debt due to the Crown from the Company, and shall be recoverable as such, with costs, or the same may be recovered with costs as a penalty is recoverable from the Company.

The Order had earlier stipulated that, 'For the purposes of the works by this Order authorized, the Company may from time to time, by agreement, enter on, take, or use all or any part of the lands shown on the deposited plans as intended to be taken for the purposes of the proposed works.'

The St. Ives Harbour Order of the same date, also confirmed by the Act, provided for the construction of 'A pier 600 feet in length, running 540 feet below high-water mark, in a south-easterly direction, into a depth of water of 30 feet at time of high water, and of 6 feet at time of low water.'

The Hastings Pier and Harbour Order dated 23 May 1862, also confirmed by the above Act, provided for the construction of

(1) A pier, commencing from the site of the Old Fort on the west, and extending about 1,650 feet in a southerly direction, then taking a curve to the eastward, and running in an easterly direction for 1,230 feet:

(2) A pier or breakwater, commencing about 1,200 feet eastward of the other, from the 'Rock-a-Nore', and being carried to the extent of 1,650 feet in a line nearly parallel to the western pier.

For both the St. Ives and Hastings Orders, similar consent and land entry provisions were included to those set out above in respect of Deal.

The corresponding Act for 1863[30] confirmed Provisional Orders made in respect of piers at Blackpool, Deal, and Walmer (amendment of the 1862 Order), Exmouth, Chatham, and Bray. The Order for Blackpool was for a pier 'commencing at or near Bellevue Square and carried out seawards a distance of one thousand five hundred and fifty feet or thereabouts'.

The 1864 Act[31] confirmed Provisional Orders relating to pier construction at e.g., Eastbourne, Sandown, Walton-on-the-Naze, Clevedon, Rhyl, Bray (additional works), Walton (Suffolk), Holywood, Exe Bight, and Lytham.

Three separate Confirmation Acts were passed in 1865[32], dealing with projected works at e.g., Eastbourne, Clevedon, Herne Bay, Hastings, Maldon, Northam, and Shanklin. The Pier and Harbour Orders Confirmation Act 1866[33] confirmed Orders relating to pier construction at e.g., Blackpool (South), Cowes (West), Dawlish, Hornsea, Llandudno, Penzance, Plymouth (Hoe), Redcar, and Scarborough. The Provisional Order for Blackpool (South) provided that the works authorized comprised:

A promenade pier, jetty and landing place commencing at a point on the shore near the Wellington Hotel, and opposite Chapel Street, in Blackpool, in the township of Layton-with-Warbrick, and parish of Bispham, in the County Palatine of Lancaster, and extending thence into the sea in a westerly direction at a distance of one thousand six hundred feet or thereabouts . . .

Although there was a provision empowering the South Blackpool Jetty Company (Limited) to enter on the lands described in the plans deposited, there was no provision whereby the consent of the Commissioners of Woods was needed for any work below high-water mark. The reason was, presumably, that the Crown Lands Act 1866 had transferred full authority over the seabed as such to the Board of Trade.

The Hornsea Provisional Order provided for a pier 'extending seaward in an easterly direction a distance of 1,200 feet or thereabouts', the Redcar Provisional Order the same distance, the Scarborough and Penzance Provisional Orders 'one thousand feet or thereabouts' while the Llandudno Provisional Order provided for a pier of more than 1,670 feet in length.

By the Pier and Harbour Orders Confirmation Act 1866 (No.

[30] Pier and Harbour Confirmation Act 1863, 26 & 27 Vict., c. 104.
[31] 27 & 28 Vict., c. 93.
[32] 28 & 29 Vict., cc. 58, 76, 114.
[33] 29 & 30 Vict., c. 58.

2),[34] which confirmed proposed pier construction at Clynder, Hastings, and Newlyn, authority was given for, *inter alia* 'A promenade pier (to be called the Alexandra Pier) commencing from the Esplanade or beach opposite to the centre of Warrior Square, in the Parish of Saint Mary Magdalen, in the borough of Hastings and county of Sussex, and extending seawards in a southerly direction for a distance of twelve hundred feet or thereabouts.'[35]

The Confirmation Acts, which were placed amongst the local and personal Acts in the annual volumes of statutes, became a regular feature of legislation.

Even before the 1861 Act, the Crown, in the person of the Commissioners of Woods, was selling portions of the seabed. Some of these sales were recorded in the schedules[36] prepared prior to a consultation with the Law Officers in March 1878, although the annual Reports of the Commissioners of Woods and the returns of foreshore transactions presented to Parliament by the Board of Trade made reference to other seabed sales which might also have concerned the bed of the open sea.

The first recorded sale of seabed was that already mentioned, namely of 1 acre, 3 roods and 9 perches sold to the Great Yarmouth Wellington Pier Company on 3 May 1854. This sale, which was listed in the schedule for England, was followed on 21 November 1857 by the sale to the Great Yarmouth Britannia Pier Company for £75 of 'a piece of land, extending seaward from high-water mark, in a direct line, to a distance of 200 yards, and of the breadth of 8 yards, or thereabouts, situate at Great Yarmouth'. This latter sale was recorded not in the schedule but in the 36th Report of the Commissioners.[37] The schedule for England made reference to the sale for £5 to the South Eastern Railway Company of 15 perches of seabed at Dover Harbour in 1859, which might have been the sale of 'a small piece of land, below low-water mark in front of the Lord Warden Hotel at Dover' on 31 December 1859 recorded in the 39th Report of the Commissioners.[38] The 38th Report of the Commissioners,[39] but not the schedule, mentioned the sale on 7 February 1860 to the Bournemouth Improvement Commissioners for £21 of 'a piece of

[34] 29 & 30 Vict., c. 56.
[35] For litigation on this, see *Corporation of Hastings* v. *Ivall* (1875) L.R. 19 Eq. 558.
[36] CREST 37/336 (England), 37/356 (Scotland, Wales, Isle of Man, and Ireland).
[37] *HCP*, 1857/58 (380, p. 48) xxxi, 52.
[38] Ibid., 1861 (391, p. 50) xxxiii, 256.
[39] Ibid., 1860 (421, p. 42) xxx, 678.

land, below low-water mark, containing about 10,209 sq. yards, situate at Bournemouth, as a site for the erection of a pier'. The schedule recorded the sale on 12 April 1860 of 4 roods of seabed at Blackpool to the South Blackpool Company for £10, and of the sale on 29 November 1861 of 31 perches at Folkestone to the South Eastern Railway Company for £105. Sales recorded in the Board of Trade Return[40] but not in the schedule were of part of the foreshore and bed of the sea at Worthing required for a pier, sold to the Worthing Pier Company Limited on 9 October 1861, and of 23 perches below low-water mark at Blackpool sold to the Blackpool Pier Company Limited on 23 July 1862 for £5, though the schedule mentioned a sale of 4 roods to the same company on the same day for the same price.

The schedule listed the following sales of land below low-water mark made between 1863 and 1871: 2 acres, 1 rood, 14 perches at Brighton sold to the Brighton West Pier Company Ltd. on 10 November 1863 (the Board of Trade return described the land sold as extending about 1,000 feet below high-water mark);[41] 32 perches to the Bognor Pier Company on 16 August 1864; 12 acres to the Ventnor Harbour Company on 22 July 1865; 3 acres to the Swanage Pier Company on 29 March 1866; 1 acre to the Scarborough Promenade Pier Company Ltd. on 31 December 1866; 1 rood to the Clevedon Pier Company on 18 November 1867; 2 roods, 22 perches at Southport to the Southpool [sic] Pier Company on 9 May 1869; 1 rood, 20 perches to the Walton-on-the-Naze Pier Company on 31 May 1869; 4 acres, 1 rood, 17 perches to the Hastings Pier Company on 17 January 1870; 2 roods to the Hartlepool Port and Harbour Commissioners on 26 April 1870; 4 acres and 34 perches at Northam Burrows (Devon) to the Northam Pier Company Ltd. on 28 January 1871. There was also a sale of 1 acre, 2 roods, 19 perches to the Eastbourne Pier Company Limited, the year of which was omitted from the schedule.

The schedule for Scotland[42] recorded the sale on 11 June 1855 of 1 acre, 24 perches of land below low-water mark at Nether Buckie, Banff, and of 26½ perches of foreshore and bed of the sea at Girvan Pier on 17 August 1870.

The Board of Trade return mentioned the payment on 9 February 1860 of £1 by the Trustees of Whitby Harbour as acknow-

[40] Ibid., 1863 (42, p. 12) xlviii, 202.
[41] Ibid., 1864 (3, p. 8) xlviii, 368.
[42] CREST 37/356.

ledgement of the title of the Crown to part of the bed of the sea at Whitby upon which a groyne was proposed to be built,[43] and of a similar sum paid by the Commissioner of Bognor on 8 March 1862 as acknowledgement for trespasses committed by removing rocks situated below low-water mark at Bognor.[44]

(c) SUBMARINE CABLES

New technology resulted in several companies seeking to lay telegraph cables on the bed of the sea. Some of these companies were incorporated by local and personal Acts of Parliament. The first of these, the Magnetic Telegraph Company's Act 1851,[45] provided in s. 33 that no works were to be constructed below high-water mark without the consent of the Lord High Admiral or his Office. The second, the Atlantic Telegraph Act 1857,[46] went further. It provided in s. 42 that 'It shall not be lawful for the Company to execute any Works whatsoever on the Bed or Shore of the Sea, or of any navigable River, so far as the Tide flows and reflows, without the Consent in Writing of the Commissioners of Her Majesty's Woods, Forests and Land Revenues, or One of them.'

The third Act, the British and Canadian Telegraph (Northern Line) Act 1859,[47] stipulated in s. 19 for an additional consent for works in the above areas, namely that of the Lord High Admiral or his Office.

The cables laid were later mentioned in the schedules prepared by the Office of Woods for the consultation with the Law Officers in 1878. The schedule in respect of England[48] was headed, 'Schedule of Licences to lay down and maintain telegraphic Cables affecting land below low water mark exclusive of the beds of tidal navigable rivers and upon payment of rent.' This schedule set out the details of four licences granted during the period to persons desirous of laying telegraphic cables on the seabed.[49] The first, dated 2 March 1861 and granted to the Submarine Telegraph Company, was described in the following terms:

This licence is to lay down 8 lines of Cables on portions of the foreshore

[43] *HCP*, 1860 (464, p. 36) lvii, 90.
[44] Ibid., 1863 (42, p. 18) xlviii, 208.
[45] 14 & 15 Vict., c. cxviii.
[46] 20 & 21 Vict., c. cii.
[47] 22 & 23 Vict., c. cvi.
[48] CREST 37/336.
[49] The 1872 Board of Trade Paper listed others, at Newbiggin and Lowestoft: *HCP*, 1872 (61, pp. 5–6) xxxvi, 213–14.

and bed of the sea belonging to Her Majesty so far as British Territory extends in the following directions respectively indicated by red lines on the plan attached to the licence vizt.—

1. From Abbotts Cliff near Folkestone Co. Kent in the direction of Boulogne in France.
2. From the South Foreland Co. Kent in the direction of Calais in France.
3. From Weybourn Co. Norfolk in the direction of Emden in Hanover.
4. From Weybourn Co. Norfolk in the direction of Heligoland and of Ionning in Denmark.
5. From the South Foreland Co. Kent in the direction of Middlekirk in Belgium.
6. From Berling Gap near Beachy Head Co. Sussex in the direction of Dieppe in France.
7. From St. Albans Head Co. Dorset in the direction of Havre de Grace or Cap de la Hague in France.
8. From Abbotts Cliff Co. Kent in the direction of the coast of Belgium.

The term of the licence was stated to be '30 years from 5th January 1861 determinable in certain events mentioned in the Licence including the event of the revocation of certain Charters granted to the Company dated 19th July 1852 and 9th January 1861'. The annual rent was stated to be '£25 for the first 5 cables, and £5 for each of the remaining cables, which were not like the first 5 cables laid down at the date of the licence such rent of £5 to be payable from the quarter day previously to the laying of the cable'. The observations column of the schedule noted that the rent of £25 had been regularly paid as had the rent for cable 6; the two remaining cables had not yet been laid.

The second licence was granted on 4 November 1864, also to the Submarine Telegraph Company. This licence, which was for a term of 25½ years at an annual rent of £5, was described in the schedule as follows:

Licence to lay down and maintain a Cable on the foreshore and bed of the Sea from Dumpton Gap and so far as British Territory extends in the direction shewn by the red line in the plan in the margin of the Licence to be united at a distance of 25 miles or thereabouts from the English Coast with the line of Cable laid down by the Company between Dover and Ostend in Belgium.

The third licence was granted on 8 September 1865 to the Earl of Dudley and R. H. S. Hughes for a term from 5 July 1865 until revoked. In fact, it was revoked by the licensees on 31 December 1866. The description of the licence ran:

Licence to lay down a Cable on the Shore and bed of the Sea, belonging
to Her Majesty at and from the South Foreland so far as British Territory
extends in the direction of Cape Grisnez as shewn by a black line on the
plan in the margin of the Licence.

The fourth licence in respect of England set out in the schedule
was granted on 27 August 1866 to Reuter's Telegram Company
Limited for a period of 30 years from 1 September 1866 at an
annual rent of £5. The description ran:

Licence to lay down a Cable on the Shore and bed of the Sea at and
from Lowestoftness so far as British Territory extends in the direction of
Nordeney [?] as shewn by a red line on the plan drawn in the margin of
the Licence.

The schedule listing licences in respect of seabed outside
England[50] mentioned three instruments. The first was granted on
27 March 1863 to the Electric Telegraph Company 'to lay down
and maintain a line or lines of wire for the purpose of telegraphic
communication between Ireland and England from Greenore
Point in Ireland across the bed of the sea to a point on the shore at
or near Abermawr Bay, Co. Pembroke'. The second, made on 14
October 1864, was granted to the Glasgow, Cantyre and General
Telegraph Company Limited for a line between Cantyre Light,
Co. Argyll and Torr Head in Ireland. The third was granted on 15
November 1866 to the Electric and International Telegraph
Company, for a line between Whitehear near Carrickfergus in Co.
Antrim and Port Nova in Wigtownshire.

There was a major controversy recorded during the period.[51] In
1858, the Submarine Telegraph Company was engaged in
negotiations with the French Government for a renewal of an
exclusive privilege to maintain telegraph cables between France
and England. The British Government regarded such a monopoly
as prejudicial to the general interests of Britain and made repre-
sentations to the French Government accordingly. Meanwhile,
the Foreign Office requested an opinion from the Admiralty on the
powers, if any, which the Admiralty might exercise to prohibit any
further cable being landed on British coasts. On 21 December
1858, the Admiralty replied that it did not have any right in the
foreshore, this being in the Crown and under the management of

---

[50] CREST 37/356.
[51] The papers covering this are in *HCP*, 1859 sess. 2 (212, pp. 1–96) xv, 763–852. The
originals of many of the papers are in T1/6217A.

the Commissioners of Woods and Forests. The Foreign Office then addressed a request for a similar opinion to that Office. On 22 December 1858 the Commissioner, Charles Gore, replied in part as follows:

With respect to the bed of the sea from low-water mark, as far as the territory of England extends, I apprehend the Crown title is indisputable, and that it cannot lawfully be permanently occupied by a subject without license from the Crown.[52]

Gore then referred to the Cornwall Submarine Mines Act 1858, and the Atlantic Telegraph Act 1857, s. 42. He continued, '. . . I think it perfectly competent for this Department to refuse to permit an electric cable to be laid permanently on the bed of the sea from low-water mark to the seaward limit of the territory of England . . . '.

Despite the British attitude, the French Government concluded, early in 1859, an agreement with the Submarine Telegraph Company for a renewal of the exclusive privilege for a period of 30 years. The Treasury thereupon referred the above legal question to the Law Officers, Fitzroy Kelly A.G. and Cairns S.G. Their opinion, dated 16 March 1859, read in part:

We are of opinion that the Crown has power to prevent the laying of any submarine cable on any part of the soil or bed of the sea below low-water mark, and within British territory, and that the Crown has also a similar power with regard to the English foreshore between high and low-water mark, except in those parts where the foreshore, by grant or prescription, has passed out of the Crown into the hands of individuals.
We think the Crown has power below low-water mark, and on such parts of the foreshore as belong to the Crown, to direct the removal of a telegraph cable, or the Crown might direct legal proceedings, in the name of the Attorney General, to enforce such removal.[53]

On 19 March 1859, Gore wrote to the Company, stating that 'by the common law of this realm, the shores and bed of the sea within British territory are vested in Her Majesty in right of Her Crown'.[54] In its reply, dated 26 April 1859, the Company stated that with regard to any part of the bed of the sea beyond the limits of high and low water marks 'whatever may be the rights of sovereignty or dominion appertaining to Her Majesty . . . neither

[52] Paper 212, 37.
[53] Ibid., 55.
[54] Ibid., 56.

the Commissioners of Woods and Forests nor the Commissioners of Her Majesty's Treasury have any concern'.[55]

Gore returned to the charge. In a letter to the Company dated 2 May 1859 he asserted in strong terms the Crown's seabed claim:

The right of the Crown to the property in the soil of the bed of the sea from low-water mark, as far seaward as British territory extends, is indefeasible; and I am unable to enter into any negotiation with the Company which does not distinctly admit the existence of such right.

As instances of the recognition of the Crown's title to the property in the bed of the sea, I may briefly refer to the Cornwall Submarine Mines Act, 1858, section 2; to the Atlantic Telegraph Act, 1859, section 42; and to the judgment of the Lord Cranworth . . . in the last case of the *Lord Advocate* v. *Gammell.*[56]

At an Extraordinary General Meeting of the Company, held on 13 May 1859, its Chairman, Sir Ian Carmichael, stated that the Company 'had no wish to fight the point, although we have been told by legal authority that the question of the title to the bed of the sea is an open question'. He himself did not believe the question to be settled but the Company did not want to contest the matter with its own Government.

Some embarrassment was then caused to the British authorities by a further opinion of the Law Officers, now Bethell A.G. and Keating S.G., of 25 June 1859 to the effect that under its Charter the Company was entitled to construct new telegraphic lines. Following a Treasury Minute, dated 27 June 1859, in which the legal right of the Crown to the foreshore and bed of the sea, within the 'dominions of Great Britain' was described as indisputable, Gore capitulated to the Company. As a parting shot, however, he concluded his letter to it of 7 July 1859 as follows:

The Company have full knowledge of the rights of the Crown, and that the telegraphic cables already or hereafter to be deposited on Crown land will be removed in the event of the revocation of the Company's present charter.[57]

It is significant that in the internal correspondence of the British executive during this incident it was the Crown Lands Act 1829 which was relied upon for the powers claimed by the Office of Woods.

Finally, it was in the context of submarine cables that the

[55] Ibid., 61.
[56] Ibid., 61–2.
[57] Ibid., 89.

Commissioner of Woods, Charles Gore, later made one of the infrequent references to a specific limit to British territory below low-water mark when, in a letter dated 25 November 1869, he remarked to the Treasury that 'the Shore seaward below low-water mark, so far as British territory extends (which limit as your Lordships are aware is 3 miles from low-water mark) is under the charge of the Board of Trade'.[58]

(d) SEDENTARY FISHERIES

The Acts[59] passed to implement the Anglo-French Fishery Convention of 1839 applied to fisheries in general; it was not until a local Act, the Herne Bay Fishery Act 1864,[60] was passed that the legislature concerned itself specifically with sedentary fisheries. This Act empowered the Commissioners of Woods and Forests to grant, and the Herne Bay, Hampton and Reculver Fishery Company to accept, a lease of Crown lands consisting of 'all those Parts of the Foreshore and Bed of the Estuary of the River Thames situated within the several parishes of Swalecliff, Herne, Reculver, Chislett, and Saint Nicholas atWade, all in the County of Kent, or some of them, and Places adjacent thereto . . . containing an Area of Nine Square Miles, or thereabouts'. The Act went on to provide that 'the Oyster Grounds, and all places within the Limits thereof shall for all the Purposes of this Act, and for all other Purposes, civil and criminal and otherwise, be within the Body of the County of Kent'.

This enactment was followed a year later by the Ham Oyster Fishery Act 1865[61] which provided that the Commissioners of Woods and Forests might grant and the Ham Oyster Fishing Company might accept a lease of Crown lands consisting of 'That Part of the Estuary of the River Thames off the North-eastern Coast of the Isle of Sheppey in the County of Kent . . . containing an Area of Two and a Half square Miles or thereabouts . . . '. The Act also provided that 'the Oyster Fishery, and all Places within the Limits thereof, shall for the purposes of this Act, and for all Civil and Criminal Proceedings in any Court whatsoever, be within the Body of the County of Kent . . . '.

The schedule of leases[62] prepared for the 1878 consultation with

[58] T 10/28, fos. 301–2.
[59] e.g., 2 & 3 Vict., c. 96; 6 & 7 Vict., c. 79.
[60] 27 & 28 Vict., c. cclxxx.
[61] 28 & 29 Vict., c. cxlviii.
[62] CREST 37/336.

the Law Officers noted that in the case of the Herne Bay fishery a lease was made on 10 October 1865 for a term not specified in the schedule at a rent of £25 for each of the first 5 years, £50 for each of the next 5 years and thereafter £500 a year for the rest of the term; in the case of the Ham fishery a lease was made on 17 February 1866 at a rent of £10 for each of the first 5 years, £50 for each of the next five years, and £125 a year for the rest of the term. The Herne Bay lease was of 'six square miles below low water mark opposite the Parishes of Swalecliffe, Herne, Beltinge, Reculver, Chislett and Saint Nicholas'; the Ham lease was of '2½ square miles opposite Whitstable off the north east coast of the Isle of Sheppey'.

On 6 August 1866, the Oyster and Mussel Fisheries Act 1866[63] become law. S. 3 provided that:

An Order for the Establishment or Improvement, and for the Maintenance and Regulation, of an Oyster or Mussel Fishery on the Shore and Bed of the Sea, or of an Estuary or Tidal River, above or below, or partly above and partly below, Low-water Mark, (which Shore and Bed are in this Act referred to as the Sea Shore), may be made under this Act, on an Application by a Memorial in that Behalf presented to the Board of Trade by any Person, Persons, Company or Body desirous of obtaining such an Order (which Person, Persons, Company, or Body are in this Act referred to as the Promotors).

The Act went on to provide that the Provisional orders made by the Board of Trade were to be confirmed by an Act of Parliament.

About this time, the Board of Trade requested an opinion from the Law Officers of England and Scotland with regard to the legal status of the foreshore in Scotland and the oyster and mussel fisheries connected therewith. The matter was topical following the decision of the Court of Session in *Duchess of Sutherland* v. *Watson*, discussed in Chapter III below, given on 10 January 1868. The relevant passages from the opinion dated 13 June 1868 and signed by Karslake A.G., Gordon L.A., Brett S.G., Millar S.G. for Scotland, W. M. James QC, and Ivory, were as follows:

13. The bed of navigable rivers, of estuaries, and of the sea, within the realm, belongs to the Crown, and is capable of alienation, but subject always to the rights of the public as above mentioned, in such navigable river, estuaries, and sea. . . .

17. Under the Crown Lands Act, 1866, the rights and interests of the Crown in the foreshore and bed of the sea, previously under the management of the Commissioners of Woods, are transferred to the

[63] 29 & 30 Vict., c. 85.

management of the Board of Trade; and we think that the power of
alienation, by the Board of Trade, of the Crown's patrimonial right
in the foreshore and bed of the sea, is not affected by the Oyster and
Mussel Fisheries Act, 1866.
18. The same powers which may be exercised by the Crown with respect
to mussels on the foreshore, may be exercised by the Crown with
respect to mussels in the bed of the sea below low water-mark.[64]

The Oyster and Mussel Fisheries Act 1866 was repealed and its
provisions incorporated in Part III of the Sea Fisheries Act 1868,[65]
which received the Royal Assent on 13 July 1868. S. 43 of this Act
read:

The Portion of the Sea Shore to which an Order of the Board of Trade
under this Part of this Act relates (as far as it is not by law within the
Body of any County) shall for all purposes of Jurisdiction be deemed to
be within the Body of the adjoining County. . .

The Provisional Orders made under the Oyster and Mussel
Fisheries Act 1866 and, after its repeal, the Sea Fisheries Act 1868,
referred to areas such as Boston and Lynn Deeps, the Firth of
Forth, Blackwater in Essex, Hamble, and Bosham. In other
words, areas which were not beyond doubt outside inland waters.
It is significant that in the schedule of leases[66] affecting land below
low-water mark, exclusive of the beds of tidal navigable rivers,
which was drawn up for the 1878 consultation with the Law
Officers, only two entries were made, the Herne Bay and Ham
leases. It is equally significant that both entries were endorsed
'Estuary' by the Office of Woods. This fact is of relevance to the
litigation over the Whitstable oyster beds which will be described
later.[67]

More significant in the present context was s. 67 of the 1868 Act.
This ran:

The Irish Fishery Commissioners may from time to time lay before Her
Majesty in Council Byelaws for the Purpose of restricting or regulating
the dredging for Oysters on any Oyster Beds or Banks situate within the
Distance of Twenty Miles measured from a straight Line drawn from
the Eastern Point of Lambay Island to Carnsore Point on the coast of
Ireland, outside of the exclusive Fishery Limits of the British Islands,

[64] *Case submitted by the Board of Trade in reference to the Foreshores of Scotland with Opinion of
Counsel thereon*, printed for H.M. Woods in Scotland, pp. 61–2.
[65] 31 & 32 Vict., c. 45.
[66] CREST 37/336.
[67] See Chapter III A below. See also *Loose* v. *Castleton*, Court of Appeal No. 356 of 1978;
The Times, 21 June 1978.

and all such Byelaws shall apply equally to all Boats and Persons on whom they may be binding.

The section went on to provide that observance of the Byelaws was to be enforced through an Order in Council which 'shall be binding on all British Sea-Fishing Boats, and on any other Sea-Fishing Boats in that Behalf specified in the Order, and on the Crews of such Boats'. The above section was introduced into the Bill despite an opinion given to the Board of Trade in May 1868 by the Law Officers, Karslake A.G. and Brett S.G., together with the Attorney-General for Ireland, Sullivan. The opinion stated:

1st. We are of opinion that the Irish Fishery Commissioners have not power to enforce close time or other restrictions on Oyster fishing on the Banks in question outside the three mile limit as against foreigners, and we think it extremely doubtful whether they have any such power against British subjects.
2. We think that such power might be conferred by Act of Parliament as against British subjects, but not, in the absence of treaty, as against foreigners; but we are of opinion that it would not be advisable to insert clauses in order to give such power as against British Subjects in the Bill . . .[68]

Nevertheless, the clause was introduced and, on 23 April 1869, the Commissioners made a Bye-law under the powers conferred by it, proclaiming a close season for oyster dredging.[69] There was no mention that the Bye-law extended to foreign boats or crews. It was confirmed by an Order in Council dated 29 April 1869, again without mention of foreign boats or crews.[70] In the preparation of the British argument for the Behring Sea Arbitration in 1892, the Foreign Office asked the authorities in Dublin for information on whether the Act had ever been enforced against foreign boats at a greater distance than three marine miles from the shore. The reply, dated 22 October 1892,[71] was negative. Accordingly, the following passage was included in the British case at the arbitration:

The law is therefore expressly limited to British boats within the 20 miles. It cannot by the terms of the Act itself apply to any foreign boats.[72]

---

[68] MT 10/57.
[69] For the text, see CO 885/14 (Law Officers' Opinions to the Colonial Office, vol. v, opinion 19A).
[70] Ibid.
[71] Ibid.
[72] FO Confidential Print 6311*, p. 50; FO 881/6311*.

Finally, a further item of Scottish practice should be recorded. In giving evidence to the Parliamentary Select Committee on Scottish Salmon Fisheries in 1860, the Lord Advocate, James Moncrieff, stated:

It was decided by the House of Lords ultimately that the Crown had a property in all the salmon fishing round the coast of Scotland, to the extent to which the territory reaches; and, as the territory reaches three miles from the coast, it must now be held to be the law that the Crown has an absolute patrimonial right to all the fisheries round the coast.[73]

(e) CONSERVANCY

The preamble to the Thames Conservancy Act 1857[74] read in part:

And whereas the Queen's most Excellent Majesty in right of Her Crown is or claims to be seised of the Ground or Soil of the Seas around the United Kingdom of Great Britain and Ireland . . .

The legal problems of conservancy below low-water mark arose in several opinions given by William Atherton, when Admiralty Advocate. He was asked, presumably by the Admiralty, 'as to what proceedings should be taken against the following parties viz. those dredging for stone below low water mark—those taking stones above low water mark and those digging or taking stones at the foot of or from other parts of the Cliff [probably Hengistbury Head].[75]

Atherton's opinion, dated 25 February 1856, began:

1st. As to dredging for stone below low water mark—I am of opinion that the stone thus removed is the property of the Crown lying as it does so near to and forming in part the support of the adjacent coast— After due notice therefore persons persisting in such removal may be proceeded against before Magistrates under 7 & 8 Geo. 4, c. 30, s. 24, particularly as there seems to be no probability of any title, as against the Crown to commit those Acts being set up—Should such summary proceedings be found from any cause ineffectual more formal proceedings at the instance of the Crown as Conservator of the harbours of the Realm should be resorted to.[76]

Atherton was then asked 'to state what further steps and proceedings should be taken to prevent the removal of stones from

---

[73] *HCP*, 1860 (456, p. 19) xix, p. 39. He was referring to *Gammell's* Case (see Chapter III below).
[74] 20 & 21 Vict., c. cxlvii.
[75] TS 25/26, fo. 243.
[76] Ibid.

the Cliff and from above and below high and low water marks'. He replied on 23 May 1856:

I am of opinion that it will be useless to take any further steps for the purpose of obtaining a summary statutable remedy for the removal of stones from above or below low water mark . . .

With reference to the removal of stones below low water mark it may be that an information will lie at the suit of the Attorney General and his opinion should be obtained on the point. I doubt whether the original removal of the rock can be made a general ground of complaint in any of the Queen's Courts: such removal taking place within the Admiralty Jurisdiction. But the severed stone it appears to me continues to be Crown property and in respect of dealing with that when brought above low water mark I think the Law Courts might intervene.

It is laid down by Lord Hale (*De portibus maris*, c. 7) that nuisances 'not within the body of the County but upon the high sea are rectified and redressed by the Court of Admiralty *ex officio*.' The removal of Rock below low water mark would I think upon the evidence be held to be a nuisance as tending to the common detriment with reference to the neighbouring Harbours. But assuming this, I am not sufficiently informed of the course of procedure in the Court of Admiralty to be able to say whether any or what steps towards redress or prevention can be taken in that Court.[77]

The opinion concluded, 'This case is a pregnant instance of the necessity of new statutable powers being vested in the Lords of the Admiralty for the protection of Navigation.'

In the course of a later opinion, dated 24 May 1856, Atherton remarked:

The 'Admiral' now represented by the Lords of the Admiralty was an Officer judicial and executive; but still only an Officer, not a proprietor. As an Officer, also, he had proper jurisdiction only *super altum mare* below low water mark and *extra corpus comitatus*.

In modern practice the understanding appears to prevail that the Admiralty shall effectually represent the Crown as Conservator of the *jus publicum* on the shores of the sea and in all tidal waters. This, of course, can be carried out either by arrangement between Departments, or by new enactment on the subject. Whatever plans shall be adopted it would seem to be just that payments to be made by companies or individuals should go to the Commissioners of H.M. Woods so far as they relate to the value of soil used or taken; and to the Lords of the Admiralty so far as they relate to expenses connected with navigation.[78]

---

[77] Ibid., fos 245–6.
[78] Ibid., fos. 241–2.

Some months later, Atherton was asked for his opinion on certain incidents of the offence of throwing ballast or rubbish into the waters of any port, road, roadstead, harbour or haven, an offence laid down in the statute 54 Geo. 3, c. 159. He concluded his opinion, dated 5 January 1857, as follows:

The point really to be determined is whether the statutable offence has been committed. And if I rightly apprehend the fact (for whether a particular spot be a Roadstead etc. is mainly a question of fact) no such offence can, under the circumstances, be established. I presume the spot selected for the unloading of the mud is below low water mark and near to the Isle of Wight; and it does not appear to me to answer to the description of Port Roads Roadstead Harbour or Haven. It seems to be no part of the 'Port' or 'Harbour' of Portsmouth nautically and the arbitrary limits of the Port for merely Revenue purposes are immaterial. Neither is it a 'Road' or 'Roadstead' which is 'an open passage of the sea being at the same time a safe place for the common riding or anchoring of ships' (Hale, *De Port. Mar.* c. 2) Haven being a place also of 'receipt and safe riding of ships' and which is 'protected by the adjacent land from dangerous or violent winds' (Id.) seems to be a description equally inapplicable.

The Law requires Amendment.[79]

The 'pregnant instance' of Atherton nearly came to birth three years later when Henry Thring was entrusted with the task of codifying the law of civil jurisdiction, including that of the Admiral. Accordingly, he drafted a Bill, entitled the Civil Jurisdiction Bill. In his observations, dated 28 October 1859, communicated with the draft Bill, Thring remarked:

The Limit of the Jurisdiction possessed by the Lord High Admiral has never been defined with great Precision. In earlier Times it encountered popular Opposition, as forming One of the Prerogatives of the Crown; while the Tendency of modern Legislation has been directed to the Restoration in some Measure to the Lord High Admiral of his original Powers and Privileges.

In many Instances, however, it may be doubted whether the Legislature, in setting foot on the Territory of the Lord High Admiral, has not contracted, rather than enlarged its Boundaries; in other Words, whether the Effect of many Statutes that appear to confer Powers is not in reality to take them away, by giving a defined statutory Power of less Extent than the undefined Common Law Jurisdiction would have given by its own inherent Vigour.[80]

[79] Ibid., fos. 270–1.
[80] MT 10/75.

During his discussion of those provisions of his draft Bill which dealt with conservancy, Thring wrote:

The Conservancy Powers of the Lord High Admiral at Common Law consist in the Franchise of erecting Beacons, Lighthouses, and Sea-marks, and of reforming Nuisances on the High Seas and navigable Rivers beneath the first Bridges and Havens.

These Powers must be carefully distinguished from the Right of Property in the Soil of the Sea Shore and of the Sea, possessed by the Crown, to which Attention will hereafter be directed, but which has never vested in or been placed under the Control of the Lord High Admiral.

The above-mentioned Common Law Franchise of erecting Beacons, Lighthouses, and Sea Marks has long since been abandoned by the Admiralty, and become vested by Statute in the Trinity House, the Commissioners of Northern Lighthouses, and the Port of Dublin Corporation; and these Bodies have by recent Legislation been placed under the Control of the Board of Trade. The remaining Franchise of reforming Nuisances on the High Seas and navigable Rivers practically has been reduced to a Nullity and the Conservancy Powers of the Admiralty may be regarded as depending solely on Statute.

Thring then turned his attention to the defects in the conservancy power. In respect of this, he stated:

The Insufficiency of the Common Law as well as of the Statutory Powers of Conservancy have already been adverted to, but it remains to be seen whether the Right of Property in the Sea Shore possessed by Her Majesty as One of the Prerogatives of Her Crown may not be called in aid to supply the Want of Conservancy Power belonging to the Crown in its Office of Admiral.

The legal Expression of this Right of Property is as follows: 'That the Queen is of Common Right seised of the Soil of the Bottom of the Sea, and of the Shore landwards up to the Line of the medium High Tides between the Springs and the Neaps.'

. . . Such being the State of the Law, it is obvious that as the Queen has the Right of Property in the Soil She must possess the Right to protect Her Property from Injury.

For example, the taking away Pebbles, Rocks, or Sand from the Shore will be taking away the Property of Her Majesty; the throwing any Sand, Ballast, or Rock into the Sea will be a Trespass on Her Majesty's Property.

Turning to the procedural problems, Thring commented:

A Difficulty, however, arises from the Nature of the special Remedies reserved to the Crown.

In the Case of a Subject Ejectment is the usual Remedy for the Purpose of determining the Title to Land.

The Sovereign, however, cannot bring an Action of Ejectment, because that Action supposes Dispossession of the Plaintiff, and the Sovereign cannot be dispossessed by reason of the legal Fiction that makes legal Ubiquity One of the Prerogatives of the Crown.

Again, an Action of Trespass is the ordinary Mode of redressing Injuries done to Real Property. In Strictness such an Action appears to be maintainable by the Crown, but in Practice it has fallen into Disuse.

The Result is, that the only Remedy actually adopted is an Information on behalf of the Crown, called 'An information of Intrusion', filed in the Court of Exchequer by the Attorney General.

This Remedy, as may be readily supposed, is too cumbrous and expensive for the effectual Redress of the Encroachments and Trespasses which are constantly being made on the Sea Shore.

Finally, Thring considered the practical difficulties:

A still greater Difficulty arises from the Circumstance that the Right of Property vested in the Crown is exercised by a different Department of the State from that which exercises the Right of Conservancy.

The Right of Conservancy is, as has already been observed, possessed by the Lord High Admiral, while the Right of Property, or Control over the Soil of the Sea Shore, as being a Portion of the Possessions and Land Revenues of the Crown, is placed under the Control of the Commissioners of Her Majesty's Woods, Forests, and Land Revenues, who are permanent Officers, and are not capable of sitting in the House of Commons.

This separation of the Rights of Conservancy and the Right of Property in the Sea Shore by vesting them in different Departments would of Necessity appear to be destructive of the Interests of Navigation; the Bill, therefore, proposes to give the Admiralty the Control over the Soil of the Sea Shore, and to forbid the granting of any Lease or the selling of any tidal Lands without the Consent of the Admiralty.

The Difficulties arising from the special Remedies reserved to the Crown, for any Injuries to the Sea Shore will be cured by giving the Admiralty Power to bring Actions of Ejectment and Actions of Trespass in the usual Way.

Clause 30 of the proposed Civil Jurisdiction Bill, drafted by Thring but never introduced,[81] ran as follows:

Subject to the Reservation of private Rights herein-after mentioned, the Lords of the Admiralty shall, for the Purposes of any Actions, Suits, or

---

[81] The Harbours Transfer Act 1862 (25 & 26 Vict., c. 69) transferred the Admiral's conservancy power to the Board of Trade but no specific mention was made of submarine soil.

other legal Proceedings instituted or defended by them in pursuance of this Act, be deemed to be the Owners of the Soil of the Sea Coast, adjacent Seas, Ports, Harbours, and navigable Rivers of the United Kingdom.

C. The Subsoil

The Cornwall submarine mines, the history of which will be set out separately in Chapter IV, provided the Crown with its first contest over title to submarine strata. In view of the award of Sir John Patteson and the successful passage of the Cornwall Submarine Mines Act 1858, it is not surprising that the Crown then turned its attention to the seabed and subsoil elsewhere in the United Kingdom.

While the Cornwall Submarine Mines Bill was passing rapidly through its Parliamentary stages, there was another Bill before Parliament which touched on the bed of the sea elsewhere. This was the Durham County Palatine Jurisdiction Bill, introduced on 24 April 1858. Its preamble read in part as follows:

... and whereas amongst the Jura Regalia claimed by the Bishop of Durham previously to and at the Time of the passing of the said Act [6 & 7 Will. 4, c. 19] was the Right to the Bed of the Sea adjacent to the said County of Durham, and to the Shore of the Sea between High-water mark and Low-water Mark, and to the Beds and Shores of navigable Rivers . . .

And whereas doubts are entertained with respect to the said Claim, and with respect to the Construction of the said Act how far such Right is or has thereby become vested in Her Majesty . . .[82]

The Bill contained in its clauses several references to the bed of the sea in the context of the claim. The next event is best described in the words of Horace Watson, Solicitor to the Office of Woods, in a letter dated 5 July 1858 to the Commissioner, Charles Gore. Watson wrote:

According to the principle of Sir John Patteson's decision in the case as to the Under Sea Mines round Cornwall, although the Bishop of Durham might have been entitled to the foreshores he could have had no right to the Sea adjacent to and not within the County and from the enclosed letter . . . you will see that on behalf of the Ecclesiastical Commissioners they make no claim to the Bed of the Sea.

The Bill has therefore been amended in the House of Lords by striking out all mention of the Bed of the Sea and by limiting its operation to the

[82] *HCP*, 1857–8 (Bill 61) ii, 39.

Shore of the Sea, and the beds and shores of navigable rivers so far as the tide flows.[83]

The Bill as amended was passed on 23 July 1858.[84]

The Patteson award in respect of Cornwall similarly had its effect in Cumberland. The Crown Minerals Agent, W. M. Smyth, reported to Gore that the Earl of Lonsdale was raising coal from mines running below low-water mark. Following a report by Watson,[85] Gore addressed a letter to the Earl, dated 18 March 1859, in which he pointed out that if the workings did extend so far the Earl should take a Crown lease and pay a royalty on coal raised from that area. The letter ended, 'I may add that in regard to any Coals gotten from under the Sea below low water mark the legal right of the Crown is to recover the value of such Coals at the bottom of the pit.'[86]

The story and its outcome were later recalled by Gore in a letter to the Lords Commissioners of the Treasury dated 30 March 1880.[87] During the reign of Charles II the Crown had granted to Sir J. Lowther (later the Earl of Lonsdale) the foreshore between high- and low-water marks along a stretch of the coast north and south of St. Bees in the county of Cumberland. The Earls of Lonsdale had worked the coal under a portion of this foreshore for upwards of a century and had extended the workings below low-water mark. Gore then recalled:

In the autumn of 1858, my attention was called to the subject of those workings, in consequence of some arrangements that had been made for the grant of a lease of some under-sea minerals adjacent to the county of Cornwall. I was advised that, although the Earl of Lonsdale might have a good title under the Nullum Tempus Act, [9 Geo, 3. c. 16] to such part of the workings beyond low-water mark, as had existed for more than 60 years, he was not entitled to extend those workings to an indefinite distance under the sea.

He recorded that an arrangement, in the nature of a compromise, was then entered into:

By that arrangement, and in consideration of the Crown not making any claim to the mineral substances that had theretofore been raised from beneath the deep sea beyond low-water mark, the Earl of Lonsdale

[83] CREST 22/46, fos. 227–8; See also Watson's letter of 23 June 1858 to the solicitors to the Ecclesiastical Commissioners: ibid., fos. 125–6.
[84] 21 & 22 Vict., c. 45. See also *Journals of the House of Lords*, vol. 90, p. 352.
[85] CREST 22/47, fo. 22.
[86] CREST 9/81, fos. 417–18.
[87] *HCP*, 1881, (307, pp. 69–72) xxx, 805–8. The original papers are in CREST 37/94.

agreed to accept a lease of the mineral substances lying beyond low-water mark in front of the foreshore of which he was owner.

The details of the lease were incorporated into one of the schedules prepared prior to the reference to the Law Officers in March 1878.[88] The lease was made on 27 August 1860 for a term of 31 years from 5 July 1859 and was in respect of the coal, culm, ironstone, and fireclay found within three miles from low-water mark opposite the parishes of Moresby, St. Bees, and St. Bridget Beckermet. A fixed rent of £1 was reserved, with royalties of 2d. per ton on large coal, 12d. on small coal, and 1½d. on ironstone and fireclay. Over the next twenty years the Crown received over £34,000 in royalties under this lease.

The Crown's activities continued to spread geographically. The story was narrated by J. Redgrave, of the Office of Woods, in a memorandum dated 5 March 1878,[89] prepared previous to the reference to the Law Officers in that month. He wrote that, 'A tract of Coal extends at a workable depth along the northern parts of the East and West Coasts of England and also extends further northward on the East Coast of Scotland. That tract is believed to extend far out to seaward below low water mark.'

After referring to the lease to the Earl of Lonsdale, Redgrave continued:

After the grant of that lease applications were received from various Coal Owners, and others, who were desirous to work the Coal below the Sea upon the west as well as upon the East coast. Up to the present time 8 leases including the lease of Coal at Whitehaven, above referred to, have been granted of Coal extending below low-water mark of the open sea. The area of coal demised by those leases is as follows.

Upon the Coast of Cumberland, the area demised extends for an aggregate length of about 16 miles from north to south, and for a breadth in one case of 3 miles from low water mark and in another case of 3 miles from high water mark.

Upon the coasts of Durham and Northumberland the area demised extends for an aggregate length of 24 miles from north to south and for a breadth varying in different cases, from 2 miles below high water mark, to 3 miles below low water mark.

In two cases besides that at Whitehaven the workings have already extended below low water mark.

The schedule of leases of minerals in England, below low-water

---

[88] CREST 37/336.
[89] CREST 37/356.

mark, prepared in the Office of Woods in 1877,[90] showed that, in addition to the lease of 27 August 1860 to the Earl of Lonsdale, a second lease of submarine strata off the coast of Cumberland was being prepared. This was a lease of the coal '3 miles seaward from ordinary high water mark in front of the township of Harrington' to J. V. Longbourne and others for a term of 42 years from 1 January 1877. A rent of £100 was reserved without any indication whether tonnage royalties were also to be paid.

The first recorded lease of submarine mines adjacent to the coast of Durham was one of 31 years from 1 February 1866 to Hugh Taylor and others in respect of the coal, culm, and ironstone extending to two miles from high-water mark in front of the township of Ryhope. A fixed rent of £500 a year for the first three and half years was reserved, increasing to £2,000 a year for the remainder of the term. In addition, tonnage royalties on the minerals excavated were provided for.

On 19 February 1867, a lease of 31 years from 1 January 1866 was made to Earl Vane, later the Marquis of Londonderry, in respect of the coal, culm, ironstone, and fireclay extending to two miles from low-water mark opposite the township of Seaham and Dawdon. This lease was later surrendered in exchange for a lease of 63 years from 1 January 1874 in respect of the minerals extending to three miles from low-water mark. Another lease made to Earl Vane was one of 31 years from 5 January 1868, in respect of the same minerals extending to two miles from high-water mark in front of the townships of Hesildon, Hawthorn, and Easington.[91]

Two other leases of submarine strata adjacent to the coasts of Durham were made during this period; first, a lease made on 10 February 1868 to W. F. Blackett and others for a term of 31 years from 30 August 1867 in respect of the coal, culm, ironstone, and fireclay extending 'about two miles from high-water mark' from the River Tyne on the north, and the southern boundary of the parish of Whitburn on the south; secondly, a lease concerning the Wearmouth Colliery made on 17 February 1868 to Wm. Stobart and others for a term of 31 years from 30 August 1868 in respect of the same minerals extending 'about two miles from high water mark at parts and from low water mark at other parts from the southern boundary of Whitburn Parish to the north boundary of

[90] CREST 37/336.
[91] These leases were the immediate subject of the reference to the Law Officers on 16 March 1878. See Chapter VI below.

Ryhope'. Fixed rent and tonnage royalties were provided for in both the leases.

The schedule contained in its 'observations' column a remark:

The workings in the Ryhope and Seaham Coll. leases have been carried below low water. In the other 3 cases [i.e., Hesildon, Hawthorn, Easington Collieries, Whitburn Colliery and Wearmouth Colliery] the working of the demised coal has not yet been commenced.

Only one lease was recorded for Northumberland in the period. It was made on 31 December 1873 to John Straker and others for a term of 31 years from 1 January 1872 in respect of the coal, culm, ironstone, and fireclay extending '2 miles from high water mark at the north end and 3 miles from high water mark at the south end. The whole sett and veins opposite the Township of North Seaton and Newbiggin.' A fixed rent and a tonnage royalty were provided for.

Two other leases of submarine strata, other than on the Cornish coasts, were recorded in the schedule for England. On 17 September 1864, a lease of one year from 10 October 1864 was made to Caroline Mary Sargent in respect of the Combe Martin Colliery in Devon. The lease, which covered 'all mines and minerals except gold and silver', extended 'from high water mark to a distance seaward in the British Channel of 200 fathoms, within the limits defined by red lines on the plan attached to the lease'. A fixed rent of £5 was provided for. On 21 February 1866, another lease, apparently in identical terms, was granted for one year from 10 October 1865.

The schedule for Wales[92] recorded leases in two submarine areas not endorsed as lying within estuaries or under the beds of tidal navigable rivers. On 10 January 1876, a lease for a term of 31 years from 10 October 1873 was made to Chas. Ranken Vickerman in respect of 'all mines within and under the shore and bed of the sea in front of land adjacent to the parish of Amroth, Co. Pembroke extending seawards a distance of one to one and a half miles'. Two other leases in similar terms were also made.

The second area was 'all that parcel of land being part of the bed of the sea adjoining to the Co. of Flint situate below low water mark as defined on attached plan outside the estuary of the Dee'. This area was leased on 10 July 1876 to John, Lord Hanmer, for a term of 38 years.

It is significant that the Scottish schedule did not record any

[92] CREST 37/356.

lease of submarine strata adjacent to the coasts of Scotland which had not been endorsed 'estuary' by the Office of Woods. In his memorandum of 5 March 1878, Redgrave, after summarizing Crown practice, wrote:

Similar acts of ownership have been exercised over and leases of Coal etc. have been granted in Estuaries such as the Firth of Forth, the Solent, the mouth of the Thames, etc. but no reference is made to them in the preceding statements, which are limited to acts of ownership over parts of the bed of the open Sea.[93]

[93] Ibid.

Chapter III

Judicial Practice 1829–1876

A. English Judicial Decisions

The Crown Lands Act 1829 received the Royal assent on 19 June of that year. Three weeks later, on 9 July 1829, the Privy Council gave its advice in the case of *Benest* v. *Pipon*. Although this appeal came from Jersey, not part of the United Kingdom, it will be discussed under the above heading since the law involved was stated to be the same as English law. Pipon claimed damages from Benest in respect of the cutting of seaweed by the latter on certain rocks where the former claimed an exclusive right since time immemorial. The rocks were described as lying 'within a bay entirely formed by the land belonging to the manor' of Noirmont.[1] In delivering the advice of the Privy Council, Lord Wynford stated:

The rocks where the sea-weed grows, which was the subject of the action in the Court of Jersey, are covered with the ordinary tides. The sea is the property of the King, and so is the land beneath it, except such part of that land as is capable of being usefully occupied without prejudice to navigation, and of which a subject has either had a grant from the King, or has exclusively used for so long a time as to confer on him a title by prescription: in the latter case a presumption is raised that the King had either granted him an exclusive right to it, or has permitted him to have possession of it, and to employ his money and labour upon it, so as to confer upon him a title by occupation, the foundation of most of the rights to property in land. This is the law of England, and the cases referred to prove that it is the law of Jersey.[2]

Lord Wynford continued:

The Islands of Jersey and Guernsey were parts of the duchy of Normandy. The laws of Normandy were introduced into this kingdom by William the First, and superseded the Saxon laws, which before that period were the laws of England. This circumstance accounts for the laws of England and Jersey being precisely the same with regard to land

[1] Records of the Judicial Committee, Plantation Appeals decided in 1829, pt. 2, fo. 383.
[2] (1829) 1 Knapp 60, 67–8.

that is below the ordinary tides, dealing with such land as a part of the bottom of the sea, and vesting the original right to it in the King.[3]

The facts of few, if indeed any, of the actions commenced by the Crown in respect of the 'foreshore', and which were conveniently summarized in a series of Parliamentary Papers,[4] concerned the bed of the open sea below low-water mark. With the exception of the information filed against Lord Falmouth and others in 1855 in respect of submarine mines, described in the next chapter, the great majority of these actions concerned the soil of the foreshore, the bed of the sea *intra fauces terrae*, or the beds of tidal, navigable rivers. In the informations initiating the proceedings, however, the Crown often recited the full description of its submarine claim. Thus, for example, in an information in Chancery filed against Sir Thomas Phillips on 31 December 1857, for erecting a pier on the foreshore of the River Usk in Monmouthshire, the Crown declared:

The sea adjoining the coasts of this kingdom, and all arms, estuaries, creeks, havens, and ports of the sea, and all navigable rivers within these realms, where and so far as the tide flows and re-flows, and the land or ground at or in the bottom or bed thereof respectively, as also the shores, banks and strands thereof respectively, below high-water mark at ordinary tides, and the soil of the same, together with all profits arising therefrom, belong of common right to her Majesty the Queen, and have at all times so belonged to her and her royal predecessors, kings and queens of this realm, in right of their crown, subject nevertheless to such grants by her Majesty or her predecessors as are now in force.[5]

From time to time, the judges delivered dicta which lent support to such wide claims even though the cases in which these pronouncements were made did not directly concern the bed of the open sea. Thus, in 1839, during the argument in *Re Hull and Selby Railway*, a case concerning the shores of the Humber Estuary, the Solicitor-General argued that 'if the sea suddenly recedes, the Crown does not lose its property in the land that was before covered with water'.[6]

In *Duke of Beaufort* v. *Mayor of Swansea* in 1849, which referred to the foreshore at Swansea, Alderson B. said:

[3] Ibid., 68–9.
[4] House of Commons Papers 1857–8 (Paper 314) xlvii, 23; 1860 (Paper 464) lvii, 55; 1861 (Paper 547) li, 45; 1863 (Paper 42) lxviii, 191; 1864 (Paper 3) xlviii, 361.
[5] Cited in Moore, 510.
[6] (1839) 5 M. & W. 327, 329. See also *Marwood* v. *Lord Harewood* (1842, unreported) Cd. 3684, Appendices, 104.

. . . it is quite clear that a subject may hold, not only the lands granted between high and low-water mark, but he might have held below [low-] water mark . . . [7]

In *Attorney-General* v. *Chambers* in 1854, which concerned mines under estuaries and foreshore, Alderson B. and Maule J. declared that, 'The Crown is clearly in such a case, according to all the authorities, entitled to the littus maris as well as to the soil of the sea itself adjoining the coasts of England.'[8]

Similarly, in *Attorney-General* v. *Hanmer* four years later, which concerned the estuary of the Dee, Watson B. quoted without adverse criticism Hale's statement that the main sea was the waste and demesne of the Kings of England, and that the King was the owner of 'that great waste, the sea'.[9]

In the same year, in *R.* v. *Musson*, the question arose whether the occupiers of the Wellington Pier at Great Yarmouth were liable for rates in respect of that part of the pier which projected below high-water mark. The Crown, in fact, did not contend that there was such a liability for the section which projected into the sea beyond low-water mark. In the course of his judgment affirming liability for the section situated between high- and low-water marks, Lord Campbell C.J. declared:

. . . the claim as to the part which is below low water-mark being abandoned, and there is no more ground for saying that it was within the parish than for saying that any part of the land seven miles off at sea is so . . . [10]

In *Ipswich Dock Commissioners* v. *Overseers of St. Peter, Ipswich*, in 1866, which concerned the rating of a dock in a tidal navigable river, Blackburn J. declared:

In *Reg.* v. *Musson* it was rightly decided that what Lord Hale calls the main sea is *prima facie* extra-parochial, and in the absence of evidence that it forms part of a parish it must be taken that it does not; and the same reason, that it is part of the waste and demesnes and dominions of the Crown, would apply to an estuary or arm of the sea; it is a part of the great waste, both land and water, of which the King is Lord.[11]

Meanwhile, there were some cases during this period which,

[7] (1849) 3 Exch.. 413, 426.
[8] (1854) 4 De G. M. & G. 206, 213.
[9] (1858) 6 W.R. 804, 805.
[10] (1858) 22 J.P. 609.
[11] (1866) 7 B. & S. 310, 344.

though not concerned specifically with seabed or subsoil, touched on the status of the open waters adjacent to the coasts of England. The first occasion noted where the Crown unambiguously asserted that any part of the marginal waters was within the realm of England occurred during the argument in *Attorney-General* v. *Tomsett*[12] in 1835. The defendant had been convicted under one of the 'Hovering Acts' of assisting or being otherwise concerned in the unshipping of dutiable goods 'in the United Kingdom'. The goods were transhipped into a boat, hired at Dover by the defendant, at a spot about two miles from the shore but within the limits of the port of Dover as these were defined by Commissioners appointed under the statute 13 & 14 Car. 2, c. 11. The defendant argued that the goods had been unshipped not in the United Kingdom but on the high seas at a place where the Commissioners had no authority to assign the limits of the port. The Solicitor-General, Sir William Follett, appearing for the Crown on a rule for a new trial, argued that since the assistance was rendered at Dover there was no need to consider whether the transhipment had or had not taken place in the United Kingdom. Nevertheless, he went on to argue in the alternative that:

[t]here is nothing to shew that the limits assigned to the port of Dover are not within the kingdom of England; for that is not confined to low water mark; but the narrow seas have always been considered as wholly within the kingdom of England. The statute 1 Eliz. c. 11, to which the statute 13 & 14 Car. 2 refers, and which first authorised commissioners to appoint places for landing goods, directs them to assign places for that purpose in all ports, havens, creeks or roads. Now, roads are on the high seas beyond low water mark; which shews that the legislature considered that the kingdom of England extended beyond low water mark. Besides, this is the case of a British subject, and not of a foreigner, and he is therefore precluded from denying the extent of the king's dominions.[13]

Platt for the defendant replied that the enactment of Car. 2 could not vary the limits of the kingdom of England because 'the commissioners might have had power to vary the limits of the ports, but they had no power to alter the ancient boundaries of the kingdom'.[14]

Despite interjections by Alderson B., who asserted that the Downs and, on the authority of Hale, the narrow seas were within

---

[12] (1835) 2 C. M. & R. 170.
[13] Ibid., 173.
[14] Ibid., 174.

the kingdom of England, counsel argued that the narrow seas were not part of the kingdom. He continued:

No doubt they are part of the dominions of the king of England, and so are the colonies; but it is submitted they are not within the kingdom of England. If they were, they would be within some county, but that is not pretended. The jurisdiction of the admiralty and the common law judges divide between high and low water mark. The warrants of the Chief Justice of the King's Bench, which are tested 'England, to wit', are of no authority in the Downs. . .The statute 6 Geo. 4, c. 108, s. 2, which prohibits certain vessels from navigating within the distance of four leagues from the coast of that part of the United Kingdom which lies within the North Foreland and Beachy Head, shews that the legislature considered the coast, that is, the low water mark, as the verge of the kingdom of England.[15]

The court did not consider it necessary 'to decide upon the present question, whether the unshipping within the limits of the port of Dover assigned by order of the King's commission would have been an unshipping in the United Kingdom, within the meaning of the said statute' since it found that the defendant had been 'concerned in the unshipping' when he hired the boat at Dover.

In *R.* v. *Forty-nine Casks of Brandy*, which conered a Lord of the Manor's claim to casks found floating in the sea, the Admiralty Judge, Sir John Nicholl, made his much-cited remark:

As between nation and nation, the territorial right may, by a sort of tacit understanding, be extended to three miles; but that rests upon different principles, viz. that their own subjects shall not be disturbed in their fishing, and particularly in their coasting trade and communications between place and place during war; they would be exposed to danger if hostilities were allowed to be carried on between belligerents nearer to the shore than three miles: but no person ever heard of a land jurisdiction of the body of a county which extended to three miles from the coast.[16]

In *The Leda*[17] in 1856, Dr Lushington construed the expression 'in the United Kingdom' in the Merchant Shipping Act 1854 as 'the land of the United Kingdom and three miles from the shore'. He followed this ruling in *The Johannes*[18] in 1860 and it was also followed by Page Wood V.C. in *General Iron Screw Collier Company* v. *Schurmanns*.[19] That the decision rested on construction only may be

---

[15] Ibid.
[16] (1836) 3 Hagg. Adm. 257, 289–90.
[17] (1856) Swa. 40.
[18] (1860) Lush. 182.
[19] (1860) 1 J. & H. 180; see also *The Milford* (1858) Swa. 362, 367.

seen in *The Saxonia: The Eclipse*[20] in 1862 where it was held that certain sections of the same Act did not apply to a foreign ship navigating in the Solent within three miles of the coast.

During the period considered in this chapter, the litigation, on which much later attention has been directed and reliance placed for the proposition that the bed of the sea below low-water mark is vested in the Crown, did not directly involve the Crown but was a claim by certain fishermen to levy anchorage tolls on vessels anchoring within a certain area below low-water mark at Whitstable. In 1791, the fee simple of the manor of Whitstable, including an oyster fishery, was conveyed to Edward Foad and James Smith. In 1792, a further deed was executed which declared that the rights of the lord of the manor in 'the said fishery, and the ground and soil thereof' should be the property of Thomas Foad [or Foord]. By an Act of Parliament of 30 April 1793,[21] the Company of Free Fishers and Dredgers of Whitstable was incorporated and empowered to purchase the royalty of fishing or oyster-dredging as well as the ground and soil of the system. Later in that year, the Company accordingly purchased from Foord the fishery, which included, within the area conveyed, the anchorage ground in question. The oyster fishery extended about two miles from the shore, 'far below the ordinary low-water mark'; the anchorage ground was situated within this area 'at the mouth of the east Swale, between the mainland of Kent and the Isle of Sheppey'[22] and abutted on the foreshore.

The vessel of the defendant, Gann, anchored about half a mile from the shore upon part of the land claimed by the Company, but not at that time used as oyster beds. The Company claimed a toll which Gann resisted. The Company accordingly seized a chain belonging to Gann as distress for the sum claimed. This led to an action in conversion by Gann against the individual concerned, one Johnson.

At Maidstone Assizes before Erle C.J. in 1861,[23] Gann argued that the soil of the sea where his vessel had anchored, being below low-water mark, was vested by law in the Crown, and could not be held by a subject. The litigation was referred to the Court of Common Pleas where Hawkins QC and Joyce, on behalf of Gann, argued that a subject could not have a manor out of the kingdom in

---

[20] (1862) Lush. 410.
[21] 33 Geo. 3, c. 42.
[22] See (1863) 13 C.B. (N.S.) 853, 855.
[23] Ibid.

a place which was subject to the Admiralty jurisdiction. Anchorage, they argued, was a franchise incident to a port or harbour but the spot in question was an arm of the sea. 'A right of distress can only exist by the common law; and the common law of England does not extend below low-water mark.'[24]

Counsel for the Company, Lush QC, Denman QC, and Needham, asked the Court whether there could be a right in a subject to the soil of an arm of the sea below low-water mark.[25] The Court, in its judgment of 2 June 1861, replied in the affirmative, giving judgment for the Company. Erle C.J. stated:

There was . . . evidence in this case from which the jury were warranted in inferring that the anchorage in question had been enforced as far back as the time of legal memory: and there is nothing to prevent the plaintiffs [i.e. the Company] from succeeding, unless it be shewn that it is contrary to law to set up such a claim to be exercised below low-water mark. I have listened attentively to the arguments which have been urged on the part of Mr. Gann; but no authority has been brought to our notice which negatives the possibility of the existence of such a right.[26]

Then, in words which have been widely cited in succeeding cases, he declared:

The soil of the seashore to the extent of three miles from the beach is vested in the Crown: and I am not aware of any rule of law which prevents the Crown from granting to a subject that which is vested in itself.

He continued:

Nothing has been cited to shew that such a grant could not be made; and many of the passages cited from Hale go to shew that a district or arm of the sea, or the soil of a navigable river, may be vested in a subject . . .

The other judges, Williams and Byles JJ., each gave judgment in favour of the Company in such a way as to suggest that they considered the spot in question not to be under the open sea. Byles J., for example, stated:

Whether the locus in quo was part of a navigable river, or an arm of the sea, in either case it was originally vested in the sovereign.[27]

In November 1862, an appeal was heard before the Court of

---

[24] *Free Fishers and Dredgers of Whitstable* v. *Gann: Gann* v. *Johnson* (1861) 11 C.B. (N.S.) 387, 401.
[25] Ibid., 405.
[26] Ibid., 413.
[27] Ibid., 419.

Exchequer Chamber under the title of *The Free Fishers of Whitstable* v. *Gann*. On 7 February 1863, Mellor J. delivered the unanimous judgment of the Court (Pollock C.B., Channell B., Wightman, Blackburn, and Mellor JJ.) upholding the decision below. In the course of the judgment, Mellor J. stated:

The only question which was argued at length is a very important one; and with regard to it the authorities to be found in our books are not very direct or clear. [Counsel for Gann] contended that, although the bed of the sea where the claim arose was at one time the property of the Crown, and might possibly have been granted to a subject before Magna Charta, yet that it could only have been lawfully granted subject to the paramount right of navigation, of which anchorage is a necessary incident—unless it could be shewn that the grantee, as a consideration for the grant, had afforded some countervailing advantage to the Crown for the benefit of the public.

That, before Magna Charta, the King could have granted not only the shore of the sea to a subject, but also the bed of the sea itself in what Lord Chief Justice Hale calls 'districtus maris', we think cannot now be doubted: Hale de Jure Maris, cap. 6, pp. 31, 32. The authority of Lord Hale as to this matter has on several occasions been recognized and adopted by judges of the greatest eminence: see the judgment of Holroyd J., in *Blundell* v. *Catterall* 5 B. & Ald. 293.

There may be, and we think that there is, a distinction between the shore, or 'littus maris', and the bed of the sea, with reference to the modes in which a subject may have acquired proprietory rights therein, as well as in the nature and extent of the rights so acquired. It may, we think, be admitted that there is a paramount right of navigation in the sea, in arms of the sea, and in navigable rivers, and that any grant by the Crown of any portion of the bed of the sea, or of the soil of arms of the sea or of navigable rivers, must be subject to this paramount right . . .[28]

Mellor J. concluded as follows:

If the authorities establish, as we think they do, that the soil in the bed of the sea, in a creek or haven, arm of the sea, or 'districtus maris', might have been granted to a subject, it seems to follow that any dropping of an anchor not occasioned by reasonable necessity, but voluntarily, in the bed of the sea so granted, would entitle the owner to compensation for the breaking of his soil.[29]

The case then proceeded to the House of Lords under the title *Gann* v. *The Free Fishers of Whitstable*.[30] Counsel for Gann argued,

[28] *Free Fishers of Whitstable* v. *Gann* (1863) 13 C.B. (N.S.) 853, 857.
[29] Ibid., 859–60.
[30] (1865) 11 H.L.Cas. 192.

on the authority of Callis, that no custom could extend the ownership of a subject further than the low-water mark. Counsel for the
Company, who included Lush and Denman, argued in reply on
the authority of Hale's *De Jure Maris* that a subject could claim by
prescription 'a property in the sea-shore.'

The decision of their Lordships (Lords Westbury, Wensleydale,
and Chelmsford) was given on 3 March 1865. They unanimously
reversed the decisions of the Courts below. In so doing, two of their
Lordships suggested that the *locus in quo* was not under the open
sea but under an 'arm of the sea.' Thus the Lord Chancellor, Lord
Westbury, declared:

The Respondents claim to be entitled by Royal grant to a portion of the
bed and soil (below low-water mark), of the arm of the sea which forms
the estuary of the Thames . . .[31]

Lord Wensleydale, too, made reference to an 'arm of the sea'.
Lord Chelmsford, however, accepted that the case had been
argued on the basis that the *locus in quo* was under the high seas,
and that the case could not be decided on the basis that the *locus*
was a haven or port. On the merits of the case, Lord Wensleydale
stated:

But the principal difficulty I feel is, that the right to the soil of the *fundus
maris* within three miles below low-water mark, and to the fishery in it,
though granted before Magna Charta, is undoubtedly subject to the
rights of all subjects to pass in their vessels in the ordinary and usual
course of navigation, and to take the ground there, or to anchor there at
their pleasure, free from toll, unless the toll is imposed in respect of some
other advantage conferred upon them, or at least on the public.[32]

Lord Chelmsford was even more critical of the status of the
three-mile limit. He declared:

The question is thus simply raised, whether at any period of the history
of this country, the Crown could have imposed upon the subjects a toll
for anchoring their vessels upon the high seas within the limits to which
its right to the soil of the sea-shore extends, without any other consideration moving from the Crown, beyond the permission to use soil for
the purpose.[33]

After citing the passage from Erle C.J. set out above, Lord
Chelmsford continued:

[31] Ibid., 208.
[32] Ibid., 213–4.
[33] Ibid., 217.

With great respect for the learned Chief Justice, I do not think it can be assumed as an unquestionable proposition of law, that, as between the Crown and its subjects, the sea-shore, to the extent mentioned, is the property of the Crown in such an absolute sense as that a toll may be imposed upon a subject for the use of it in the regular course of navigation. In stating the right of the Crown in the seashore, the text writers invariably confine it to the soil between high and low-water mark. The three miles limit depends upon a rule of international law, by which every independent State is considered to have territorial property and jurisdiction in the seas which wash their coasts within the assumed distance of a cannon-shot from the shore. Whatever power this may impart with respect to foreigners, it may well be questioned whether the Crown's ownership in the soil of the sea to this large extent is of such a character as of itself to be the foundation of a right to compel the subjects of this country to pay a toll for the use of it in the ordinary course of navigation.[34]

The next litigation in which the rights in the seabed might have been discussed but were not was that of *Le Strange* v. *Rowe* before Erle C.J. at Norwich Civil Court in 1866.[35] This was an action by a lord of the manor for trespass alleging that the defendant took shell fish and shingle on the foreshore of the manor between high- and low-water marks. Thus, once again, no issue directly arose as to title in the bed of the sea below low-water mark. The plaintiff showed, *inter alia*, that jetties had been run out to sea for a distance of one hundred yards by the plaintiff's orders and for his benefit. Erle C.J. left this to the jury as evidence of the plaintiff's ownership of the foreshore. Nothing appears to have been said about the status of the jetties below low-water mark.

The next litigation concerned with Whitstable oyster ground, *Free Fishers of Whitstable* v. *Foreman*,[36] began in 1867. This was an action by the Company to recover 3s., being three anchorage tolls of 1s. each, claimed as toll for the anchoring of the defendant's vessel on three separate occasions. On two of these occasions, the anchor had been dropped 'somewhat below ordinary low-water mark'; on the third occasion the vessel had anchored between high and low-water marks. In delivering the judgment of the Court of Common Pleas (Bovill C.J., Willes, Keating, and Montague Smith JJ.), Bovill C.J., held that the maintenance of buoys and beacons by the plaintiff company, taken in connection with its ownership of the soil of the anchorage ground, and the benefit to

[34] Ibid., 217–8.
[35] (1866) 4 F. & F. 1048.
[36] (1867) L.R. 2 C.P. 688.

the public therefrom, afforded a sufficient consideration to support its claim to anchorage dues; the present case could be distinguished from the House of Lords decision in *Gann* v. *Free Fishers of Whitstable* since in this earlier case the plaintiff had relied solely on the ownership of the soil of the anchorage ground. Bovill C.J. added that it was possible that the right to anchorage might also be founded on the existence of a 'port' at Whitstable, encompassing the *locus in quo*.

An appeal was taken to the Court of Exchequer Chamber where a difference of opinion occurred. The majority of the Court (Kelly C.B., Channell B., Blackburn and Mellor JJ.), agreed with the reasoning and decision of the Court of Common Pleas. Bramwell B., however, delivered a dissenting opinion concurred in by Martin B. In the course of his dissent, Bramwell B. stated:

It has occurred to me that the anchorage-ground is part of the high seas, open to the navigation of all mankind. Part of it is two miles from land. Now, although within the marine league from shore, and although between two headlands of this kingdom, I take it to be clear that a foreigner might navigate and anchor there. Could any toll be rightfully demanded of him? I think not; and, if not, why of a subject of this realm?[37]

The case then went on appeal to the House of Lords where the Lord Chancellor, now Lord Hatherley, asked the judges to state whether a toll was payable under the circumstances of the case.[38] On the judges answering that a toll was payable as there was evidence of a port existing at the spot,[39] Lord Hatherley and Lords Chelmsford and Colonsay upheld on that basis the claim to anchorage dues. There was no discussion before their Lordships on whether the oyster ground and anchorage ground were *intra fauces terrae* or otherwise although counsel for the shipowner claimed that Whitstable was not a port but an 'open roadstead'. In holding, however, that the *locus* had been 'treated as a creek of the Cinque Ports' and was at one time probably part of a port, their Lordships appear to have excluded the possibility that it was land under the open sea or high seas.

While the Whitstable anchorage cases were passing through the courts a case was heard which could well have raised the whole subject of the status of the seabed adjacent to the coasts of England, but, unfortunately, did not do so. This was *Submarine*

---

[37] (1868) L.R. 3 C.P. 578, 590.
[38] (1869) L.R. 4 H.L. 266, 275, *sub nom. Foreman* v. *Free Fishers and Dredgers of Whitstable.*
[39] Ibid., 275.

Telegraph Company v. *Dixon* decided by the Court of Common Pleas
on 20 January 1864.[40] The plaintiff company claimed damages for
the injury caused to its submarine cable, by reason of its being
dragged and broken by an anchor of the defendant's ship. The first
count of the plaintiff's declaration claimed that the cable was laid
down within three miles of the shore; the second count varied the
distance to eight miles. The defendant pleaded in reply to these
two counts that the cable was lying more than three miles from the
seashore of England and was therefore out of the realm, that the
vessel was a Swedish vessel and therefore not subject to the laws of
England, and, finally, that he had not been negligent. The plaintiff
company replied to the effect that 'one end of the cable was
fastened to the soil of the county of Kent, and carried thence across
the seashore of the county unto and into the sea abutting thereon,
and the part injured was within three marine miles of the seashore
and coast of the county of Kent'. On a demurrer, the plaintiff
company claimed:

And as to so much of the . . . plea as puts in issue the realm, dominion,
sovereignty and jurisdiction of our Lady the Queen in and over the said
high seas, and alleges that the defts. were aliens domiciled in and subject
to the laws of Sweden and not to the laws of England, and that the ship
was a foreign ship on a foreign voyage, and puts in issue the defts.'
liability to answer in this court in respect of the grievances in the first
count mentioned, the plts. say that the said . . . plea is bad in substance.

The Court (Erle C.J., Williams and Willes JJ.) held that the
plaintiff company had a good cause of action, although it did not
seem to hear argument on the wider issues raised in the pleadings.
Erle C.J. stated:

I am of opinion that the declaration which charges the deft. by reason of
his negligence with damaging the cable of the plts. is good. I assume, for
the purpose of this action, that the bottom of the sea may be used for
lawful purposes as well as the surface, and the court may, I think, take
judicial notice of there being submarine cables, as they are named in
Acts of Parliament, and are known by everyone, to be lying at the bottom
of the sea. The plts., in my opinion, had a right to use the bottom of the
sea, and to place cables there for the purposes of telegraphic communication, and the deft. had also a right to traverse the surface of the sea for
the ordinary purposes of navigation, and to let go his anchor if the need of
navigation required it.[41]

[40] (1864) 10 L.T. (N.S.) 32. See also 33 L.J. C.P. 139, 10 Jur. 129, 12 W.R. 384. The
reports differ considerably.
[41] Ibid., 32–3

The final case during the period presently under review which touched on the question of the legal status of the seabed was *Corporation of Hastings* v. *Ivall* decided in June 1874.[42] In the course of his judgment, Malins V.C. stated:

> There was an Act of Parliament obtained for the establishment of a pier, and it became necessary for the pier company to have the right to erect their pier between high and low-water mark and out to sea. It is perfectly clear that the corporation could have no right below low-water mark. Beyond that point they must rely on the grant from the Crown.[43]

The case concerned a portion of foreshore at Hastings, i.e., land between high- and low-water marks, and so the reference to the seabed below low-water was an *obiter dictum*.

B. Scottish Judicial Decisions

Four relevant cases were decided by Scottish courts during the period under review. In the first, *Officers of State* v. *Smith* decided in 1846, the subject matter was the extension of a wall across the sands of the foreshore. Thus the status of the bed of the sea below low-water mark was not at issue. Nevertheless, the Scottish judge, Lord Cockburn,[44] in deciding against arguments denying the Crown's right as *prima facie* owner of the foreshore, declared:

> All these views go to impeach a principle which is involved both in the prerogative of the Sovereign, and in the paramount right of the King, as feudal superior, over all the land in the kingdom, whether periodically covered with water or not. I know nothing which I should think might be predicated with greater safety, or that less requires formal proof, than that the bed of the British seas belongs in property to the British Crown.[45]

The decision of the Scottish court was affirmed by the House of Lords three years later without mention of the solum below low-water mark. However, Lord Campbell stated:

> Notwithstanding some loose dicta to the contrary, there can be no doubt that by the law of Scotland, as by the law of England, the soil of the sea-shore is presumed to belong to the Crown, by virtue of the prerogative, although it may have been alienated, subject to any easements which the public may have over it.[46]

[42] (1875) L.R. 19 Eq. 558.
[43] Ibid., 584.
[44] Not to be confused with Sir Alexander Cockburn, later Lord Chief Justice of England.
[45] (1846) 8 D. 711, 723.
[46] (1849) 6 Bell 487, 500, *sub nom. Smith* v. *Earl of Stair*.

The second case was *Gammell* v. *H.M. Commissioners of Woods and Forests and the Lord Advocate* which began in the Scottish courts in 1851. The Office of Woods brought a summons in the Scottish first instance court against Gammell, who was the proprietor of the estate of Portlethen in Kincardineshire, claiming that 'the salmon-fishings around the coast of Scotland, and in the navigable estuaries, bays, and rivers thereof, so far as the same have not been granted to subjects by charters or otherwise, belong to the Crown *jure coronae*, and form part of the hereditary revenues of the Crown in Scotland'. At first instance, the Lord Ordinary, Lord Murray, in upholding the claim of the Crown, stated that, 'The Defenders [i.e., Gammell] admit the right of the Crown to make grants of salmon-fishing in all estuaries; but they seem to make a boundary as to what is sea beyond the estuary . . .'.[47]

On appeal, the Inner House, with Lord Justice-Clerk Hope dissenting, affirmed the decision below.[48] Lord Medwyn cited Erskine, a Scottish institutional writer, for the proposition that the Sovereigns were 'lords or *domini* of the British seas which surround this island; in consequence of which only it is that treasures brought up from the bottom of those seas or wreck-goods found floating on their surface, belong to the Crown'. Lord Medwyn continued:

This, of course, does not reach to any great or unlimited distance from the shore, but if they are sovereigns of the seas surrounding our shores, they can grant an exclusive right to the produce which may be found in them, such as salmon, probably not extending beyond a right of grant to the owner of the adjacent lands;—at least I do not know that the exercise of the right has ever gone farther. For, since the sea-shore and bed of the sea belong to the Crown, every produce of it—rocks, oysters, mussels, fish, and the means of catching them—may be granted, provided this does not interfere with the primary uses of the shore. I have no doubt that, if Mr. Gammell could show an express grant of salmon-fishings in the sea *ex adverso* of his lands, the grant would be good.[49]

In his dissenting opinion, Lord Justice-Clerk Hope stated:

But where, I ask, is the authority for this very novel and dangerous doctrine, which obliterates at once the whole doctrine of *jus regale*, and treats not only the whole land, but the bed of the sea, as the private property of the Crown, and the right of fishing in the sea as a source of profit or revenue to the Crown? . . . The foundation of this most extra-

[47] 1851; cited in (1859) 3 Macqueen 419, 423.
[48] *Commissioners of Woods and Forests* v. *Gammell* (1851) 13 D. 854.
[49] Ibid., 873.

ordinary doctrine, as well as of the kindred pretension advanced directly in this action, arises from the novel view taken of a *jus regale*, and from the assumption that *jura regalia* form part of the proper patrimony or hereditary revenues of the Crown.[50]

The case went on appeal to the House of Lords where it was argued twice; the first appeal, in 1853, did not lead to a judgment being given, the second, in 1859, led to the affirmation of the decisions in the courts below.[51] Extracts from the printed Case lodged on behalf of the Office of Woods were set out in the report. It ran in part as follows:

All nations being equal, all seem to have an equal right to use the unappropriated parts of the ocean for navigation. But those parts of the sea which adjoin the land *are appropriated as accessory to the coast that commands them.* The doctrine laid down by Heineccius is that now generally received by the best writers. He maintains that the ocean is incapable of appropriation, but that *parts of the ocean and narrow seas may be appropriated, subject to the right of navigation.*

The sea within cannon shot of the shore, or a distance of three miles, is occupied by the occupation of the coast; and sea fisheries are subject to occupancy, and capable of exclusive possession. Craig lays it down that the property of the sea belongs to those to whom the nearest continent belongs, and that the right of fishing in the adjoining sea belongs to the same parties to whom the property of the sea, so far as it can be appropriated, belongs.

The right of fishing in the sea is totally distinct from the right of maritime dominion. The English have never pretended to have a property in all the seas over which they have claimed maritime dominion by means of their fleets. But all those portions of the sea adjacent to and commanded by the coast, so far as capable of appropriation, are held to form *a part of the national territory.*

. . . the rights which belong to the Crown are of two different kinds: 1st, the *jus publicum*, which belongs to the Monarch in jurisdiction and sovereign right, and which may be held as a mere trust for behoof of the public; and 2ndly, the *jus privatum*, under which the Sovereign possesses the land and sea adjoining the coast as patrimonial property, so far as it is capable of appropriation. . . .

The public rights belonging to the Crown are inalienable, while the private ones, being capable of yielding profit, may be retained or alienated to a subject.[52]

The Crown also stated in its printed Case:

[50] Ibid., 868–9.
[51] *Gammell* v. *H.M. Commissioners of Woods and Forests* (1859) 3 Macqueen 419.
[52] Ibid., 424–5.

All the landed territory in the kingdom, so far as it has not been gifted to a subject, undoubtedly belongs to the sovereign as a patrimonial property, which may be retained or alienated at the pleasure of the Crown. In like manner, the bed of the sea, where-ever it can be appropriated, and has not been made the subject of special grant, is unquestionably the private property of the Crown: and there is no reason, in point of principle, why the right of fishing in the sea, so far as it may be a source of profit, should not also be treated as a patrimonial right belonging to the Crown.[53]

In the course of his speech, the Lord Chancellor, Lord Chelmsford, stated:

. . . it was strongly urged that the sea being common to all, there could be no appropriation of it except in that limited portion which adjoins the shore, and that the right claimed was unreasonable, as it would embrace any fishing whatever in the deep sea at an indefinite distance from the coast. But it appears to me that this is a misapprehension of the claim made by the Crown, and that the limits are not so undefined as alleged, although the right, from its nature, must be to a certain extent indefinite.[54]

Lord Cranworth had similar views:

I confess that, both upon the recent argument and upon that which took place some years ago, I have entertained some considerable doubt, arising from the indefinite nature of the claim, and the great difficulty, if not impossibility, of defining to what extent the claim would go with respect to sea fishings. But upon the whole . . . I dare say those doubts are unfounded; and I think an observation that was made is not unentitled to considerable weight, namely, that if this doubt were well founded, an exactly similar doubt might be raised as to the prerogative right of the Crown, in England at least, to the bed of the sea, because that is undefined; yet nobody doubts that such a right exists.[55]

Lord Wensleydale also considered the ambit of the Crown's claim in the adjacent sea:

. . . it would be hardly possible to extend it seaward beyond the distance of three miles, which by the acknowledged law of nations belongs to the coast of the country, that which is under the dominion of the country by being within cannon range, and so capable of being kept in perpetual possession. It is very true that Lord Coke says, that the right to jetson and flotson, which is part of the prerogative of the Crown, extends over all the narrow seas. But I apprehend it is not necessary to go so far as

[53] Cited in the judgment of Lord Justice-Clerk Hope: 13 D. 854, 868.
[54] 3 Macqueen 419, 453–4.
[55] Ibid., 464–5.

that, but that it is sufficient to say that . . . it may be perfectly true that the right is possessed within the three miles of sea over which the jurisdiction both in Scotland and in England extends.[56]

The third relevant Scottish case during the period under review was *Duchess of Sutherland* v. *Watson* decided in 1868.[57] Unlike the cases of *Gammell* and *Smith*, this did not proceed to the House of Lords. The claim was that the pursuer 'has the sole and exclusive property in and rights to the whole mussel-beds, scalps and fisheries on the shores and sands of Nigg and in the bay of Cromarty', i.e., it appears not to have directly concerned the use of the bed of the open sea. The pursuer stated in argument:

It is necessary to inquire, first, what is the nature of the Crown's right to the sea, and the origin of it. The sea within three miles or cannon shot of the shore is part of the territory. Now, the sea is heritable, and, therefore, it and its solum are vested in the King as superior. This right is evidenced by acts of proprietorship—particularly by making grants of minerals under the shore and the bed of the sea.[58]

In reply, the defenders argued:

By the law of nature, and also by the law of Rome, the sea was *inter res communes*. In process of time, however, the *mare proximum* came to be regarded as capable of appropriation, and as vested in the Sovereign in trust for the inhabitants of the State,—in other words, it became a *res publica*.[59]

The judgments of the Inner House (Lords Cowan, Benholme, and Neaves, Lord Justice-Clerk Patton), given on 10 January 1868, were in favour of the pursuer. Lord Neaves, in particular, said:

. . . we have here at issue, I think, in the first place, that the *solum* or *fundus* of the deep sea—that is, not only the part between high-water and low-water mark, but the sea within such a line as may be reasonably drawn in connection with the shores—belongs in property to the Crown, and does so as a patrimonial right. That it does so belong to the Crown, at least within narrow limits near the shore, such as are here in question, is clear; and that would be clearly seen if a question were raised as to any minerals which might extend under the sea, and which might be worked outwards from the shore to a point under the deep sea. I think that that right is a patrimonial one. It is not a right held by the Crown in trust for

---

[56] Ibid., 465–6.
[57] (1868) 6 M. 199.
[58] Ibid., 203.
[59] Ibid., 206.

Chapter IV

The Cornwall Submarine Mines

A. Practice up to 1856

The nineteenth-century practice over the submarine mines of
Cornwall deserves separate treatment not only for its importance
but because it combined executive, legislative, and judicial
practice. The fact that an Act of Parliament was passed in 1858 to
regulate their exploitation as between the Crown and the Duchy of
Cornwall has been used by judges and writers to support views on
the legal status of the seabed and subsoil in general.[1]

The history of Cornish mining was conveniently set out in a
Case Stated to the Law Officers prepared by the Office of Woods
in 1844.[2] According to this account, the Duchy had since the
seventeenth century demised by lease to various individuals mines
and minerals, mainly tin and copper, located in certain manors in
the county. Mining under the sea commenced only towards the
end of the eighteenth century with the introduction of the steam
engine to drain the mines. In the words of the Case Stated:

On the part of the Duchy of Cornwall, no claim was made to the minerals
got under the Sea until shortly before the expiration in 1840 of the
Lease . . . granted to the Messrs. Williams and Smith, and it is believed
that neither they or the previous Copper Lessees ever made any claim
under the authority of the Duchy Leases.

The first assertion of right on the part of the Duchy itself to Mines and
Minerals under the sea occurred about the year 1837 when the parties
working a copper mine called Wheal Pearce in the Parish of St. Austell
applied for a reversionary grant for liberty to follow the Lode under the
Sea.

Nor had the Crown itself made any claim to the minerals raised
from workings beneath the sea, not even from the Botallack Mine[3]
which was one of the oldest and largest submarine copper mines;

[1] e.g., Lord Coleridge C.J. in *R*. v. *Keyn* (1876) L.R. 2 Ex. D. 63, 157–8; Sir Cecil Hurst,
(1923–4) 4 *BYBIL* 34–5; Gidel, *Le droit international public de la mer*, vol. III, 330, n.2.

[2] CREST 40/52, fos. 91–8.

[3] According to a contemporary writer, this mine extended horizontally 480 feet under
the sea, at a depth of 20 fathoms. (1859) 5 *Law Magazine and Law Review* 111.

the dues for minerals raised from such workings were paid by the lessees to the owner of the land on which the shaft was sunk.

In 1840, the Solicitors to the Duchy called upon the lessees of the Levant Mine to account to the Duchy in respect of the copper and other minerals raised. At first, the persons exploiting the mine denied that either the Duchy or the Crown had any right whatever to the minerals wherever raised, only the owner of the soil where the minerals were finally brought to the surface; later, they were persuaded that this owner had no right to the ores taken from under the sea though entitled to be paid for the use of his shaft. Finally, they agreed to pay dues to the Duchy in respect of the minerals taken below high-water mark. The Duchy and the Crown then came to an understanding whereby those dues were paid into an account with Messrs. Coutts & Co., bankers, in the joint names of the Duchy and the Crown, the latter being represented by one of the Commissioners of Woods. The first payment of royalty for the Levant Mine was made on 16 June 1842.[4]

The persons exploiting the Botallack Mine, together with the owner of the land on which the shaft was sunk, Lord Falmouth, were made of sterner stuff and determined to resist similar claims by the Duchy in respect of the minerals raised from under the sea. The question then arose how legal action could be taken against these persons and, in particular, by which plaintiff, Crown or Duchy, should any such proceedings be undertaken.

The Office of Woods thereupon submitted a Case for the joint opinions of the Law Officers of the Crown and of the Duchy.[5] The Case Stated asked for advice:

As to what steps should be adopted to enforce the rights of the Sovereign or the Duke of Cornwall in respect of the Mines and Minerals under the Sea generally and under Botallack in particular and by and against what parties the same should be taken.

As also, whether a Commission should be applied for or could be obtained to compel the adventurers in Botallack to allow an inspection and admeasurement by competent persons of the Workings under the Sea.

The report of the Law Officers was signed on 27 February 1844 by Sir F. Pollock A.G. and Sir W. Follett S.G. for the Crown, and I. Talbot and E. Smirke for the Duchy.[6] The report read:

---

[4] *Answer on behalf of the Crown to the Statement of the Duchy*, 1866, p. 11.
[5] CREST 40/52, fos. 91–8.
[6] Ibid.

As it does not appear at present that the Mines under the high seas are parcel of the Duchy, it will be expedient that any proceeding adopted for enforcing the right of the Crown or Prince should be taken by and on behalf of Her Majesty.

If it can be shewn that ore brought within the body of the County, has been taken from Mines under the Sea, the proper remedy will be an information in the nature of an action of trespass or trover against the parties who have taken or detained it.

If the Landowners or adventurers working on or near the shore purposely conceal their works and refuse to inform the agents of the Crown as to the extent or direction of their submarine excavation, we apprehend that an information in the nature of an English bill for a discovery or an account, or both, will be founded on the fraudulent concealment and on the evident impossibility of obtaining any other remedy. In *Lord Lonsdale* v. *Curwen* 3 Bligh Rep. 168–171 an inspection was also granted under circumstances less strong than the present.

The precise form of the Bill and the proper parties to it will depend on the facts of the particular case selected. Both the Lord and the adventurers must probably be made defendants.

No action against the adventurers or Lord Falmouth appears to have been taken and in 1847 there was a proposal to grant to the latter a lease of the undersea minerals. An agreement was not reached, however, because of a dispute over the amount of draw-back claimed by him as way-leave for the use of his land.[7] Other landowners were more docile and expressed their willingness to come to terms with the Crown. This raised acutely a further legal problem which was submitted to the Law Officers of the Crown in 1847 by the Office of Woods. The Case Stated set out the problem:

The Mines under the Sea, the Sea Shores and the Shores of Tidal Estuaries and Rivers on the coast of Cornwall are claimed by the Commissioners of Woods on behalf of Her Majesty and they were also claimed by the Council and other proper Officers of His Royal Highness the Prince of Wales as part and parcel of His Duchy of Cornwall.

These Mines have also in several instances been claimed by Lords of Manors and adjoining Land Owners but the Crown and the Prince have by their united exertions succeeded in procuring many of those Parties to attorn and there are various applications for Leases of Minerals situated as above mentioned now pending. The question is ought such Leases to be granted by the Crown or the Prince, or if granted by one how are the rights of the other to be protected in the meantime, the object at present being to compel wrong doers and others to attorn either to the Crown or Prince the question of right as between the Crown and Prince being left

[7] CREST 40/55, fo. 30.

for future consideration and decision. [T]he course which we have suggested is as follows vizt. the question is by whom is the Lease to be granted and to whom is the Rent or Royalty to be reserved and these two questions can only as it appears to us be properly and satisfactorily answered by the Opinion of the Law Officers of the Crown and Prince of Wales. We would in submitting the matter to them humbly suggest that the Leases of Mines under the Sea should be granted by or on behalf of Her Majesty that the Rent should be reserved to Her Majesty but to be paid to some Receiver specially appointed by the Board and the Council of His Royal Highness that such Rent after deducting expenses should as received be from time to time invested in the purchase of 3 percent Consols in the joint names of some two parties to be agreed upon as Stakeholders on behalf of the Crown and Prince until the right shall be determined and that a Deed setting forth with precision the whole arrangement should be executed by or on behalf of the Crown and Prince and be inrolled in the Land Revenue Record Office and in the proper Office of His Royal Highness the Prince of Wales. The Commissioners of Woods concur in the above suggestions provided you see no objection thereto, but inasmuch as the Officers of the Duchy are more peculiarly and extensively conversant with Mineral Property of this description in Cornwall than the Officers of the Crown the Commissioners consider that it might be more convenient that the Leases should be granted by the Prince of Wales if you are satisfied that the rights of the Crown will be sufficiently and properly guarded by means of a Deed of the nature and to the purport above suggested and as a Duchy Council is appointed for Tuesday next the Chief Commissioner of Woods would be obliged by your opinion on this matter in the course of tomorrow that he may signify the same at the Duchy Council on Tuesday next.[8]

The Crown's Attorney-General, Sir J. Jervis, and Solicitor-General, Sir D. Dundas, gave their report on 13 November 1847.[9] It was very brief:

We think that the leases should be granted in the name of the Crown.

This report was not accepted by the Duchy with the result that, with one or two exceptions, e.g., a lease to H. H. Parish of Wheal Ocean Mine, the making of grants was suspended, thus causing detriment to the undersea mining industry.[10]

The Crown, however, did not remain inactive for long. It should be noted that its claim was not only to the submarine mines below low-water mark on the open coast but also to those under the foreshore, and under estuaries and tidal navigable rivers. On 4

[8] CREST 40/52, fos. 263–4.
[9] Ibid., fo. 264.
[10] See *Supplemental Reply on the part of the Duchy of Cornwall*, 1869, p. 5.

April 1854, for example, the Attorney-General of the Crown, Sir Alexander Cockburn, filed an information in Chancery against Lord Vivian and the Attorney-General of the Duchy as joint defendants, praying that Lord Vivian should be decreed to perform specifically a conveyance to him by the Crown of the foreshore of the Truro River adjacent to his estates.[11] The first paragraph of the above information went further than the immediate matter in hand by stating the full extent of the Crown's maritime claim:

The sea adjoining the coasts of this kingdom, and all arms, estuaries, creeks, havens, and ports of the sea, and also all navigable rivers within these realms, where and so far as the tide flows and re-flows, and the soil and ground forming the bottom and bed thereof respectively, as also the shores and soil thereof respectively, lying between high and low water mark, together with all profits arising therefrom, respectively belong, of common right, to Her Majesty the Queen, and have at all times so belonged to Her and Her Royal Predecessors Kings and Queens of this realm, in right of their Crown, subject nevertheless to such grants by Her Majesty, or Her Predecessors, as are now in force.

Meanwhile, the Office of Woods had taken the opportunity to re-open with the new Lord Falmouth the question of the owner-ship of minerals excavated from the Botallack Mine. On 3 Sepember 1853, the latter replied in terms more uncompromising than those expressed by his cousin in the previous decade:

It is true that I was no party to the communications which took place between the Crown and my late Cousin, but I had certainly hoped, from the time that had elapsed since this subject was last brought under the notice of the late Earl of Falmouth in 1847, and from the circumstance of no answer having been returned to the enquiry contained in the Letter of Messrs. Gregory & Co. [Solicitors to Lord Falmouth] in the same year, that the Crown and Duchy had seen reason to give up their intention of disturbing the exercise of rights, which it is clearly proved, had been openly and notoriously enjoyed without the slightest interruption ever since my own family became possessed of the lands in question, or of putting me to the expense of resisting a claim upon a portion of my property, which even previous to the date above alluded to, had been by every indication, for generations in the undisturbed possession of private individuals.[12]

Lord Falmouth concluded, 'I also need hardly add, that I have

---

[11] The information in full and an account of the circumstances of the case were set out by J.W. Pycroft in *Arena Cornubiae*, 3rd ed., 1856, 34–49.

[12] CREST 40/55, fos. 30–1.

ascertained my true legal position by the opinion of some of the first and ablest men of the day practising at the Equity and Common Law Bars and these warrant me in the conviction that the rights which I claim are founded in Law as well as in Justice.'

In 1855, the Office of Woods prepared a Case Stated for the opinion of the Law Officers on whether the claim made by Lord Falmouth should or should not be acquiesced in and, if not, what proceedings should be adopted to test its validity. The Case Stated is noteworthy for the way it set out the legal authorities said to favour the Crown's claim to the soil under the adjacent seas.[13] The authors referred to were Sir Matthew Hale, Bacon, Sheppard, Viner, Selden, Blackstone, Fitzherbert, Chitty, Hall, Callis, and Horne. The decisions cited in support of the claim were *Todd* v. *River Clyde Trustees*,[14] *Attorney-General* v. *Farmer*,[15] *Attorney-General* v. *Oldsworth*,[16] and the *Banne Fishery* case.[17] In the Case Stated, the Office of Woods maintained that the first exercise of the right now claimed by Lord Falmouth was made long after the time when the Crown could make such a grant and therefore no such grant could be presumed. Here the Office cited the statute 1 Anne c. 7, which restrained the Crown from making grants for more than 31 years of land forming parcel of the hereditary possessions of the Crown, and the case of *Goodtitle* v. *Baldwin*.[18] The Office concluded its 'Further Instructions' with the following observations:

It is respectfully suggested that the right of the Sovereign to the bed of the Sea is co-extensive with the territory of England, that within that territory there is not any land which can be called common property for that if there is no other owner, the Land belongs to the Crown. 'A vacant possession is the possession of the Crown' per Abinger C.B. in a case of *Att. Genl* v. *Manwaring* not reported. That this general right of property in the Sovereign in the absence of any other owner is the foundation of the feudal system.

It is further submitted that although it may not be very easy to define the exact seaward limit of the territory of England, it is clear that such territory extends beyond low water mark into the main Sea. The exercise by the inhabitants of the Country within a certain distance from the

[13] Ibid., fos. 29–35. After a consultation with the Law Officers on 13 April 1855, the Office of Woods drew up 'Further Instructions' in which many of the following authorities were set out (ibid., fos. 54–5). The circumstances in which this consultation was made have not been found.
[14] (1841) 2 Rob. App. 333.
[15] (1676) 2 Lev. 172.
[16] (1636–7), see Chapter I above.
[17] (1610) Davis 55.
[18] (1809) 11 East 488.

shore of the right of fishing to the exclusion of Foreigners, a right which they enjoy by virtue of their allegiance to their Sovereign, and subject to his prerogatives, the prerogative right of the Crown to things derelict, jetsam, flotsam, and lagan, which are found in the sea below low water mark, and the power which has been repeatedly exercised of creating ports nearly all of which extend beyond low water mark, and many some distance into the Sea; the right to Royal fish taken in the sea adjoining the Coast all prove that the territory of England and the prerogatives of its Sovereign which are co-extensive with it, are not limited by low water mark.[19]

Sir Alexander Cockburn A.G., Sir Richard Bethell S.G., and James Willes (later Willes J.) gave their opinion on 2 May 1855. It ran:

1. We are of Opinion that the claim made by Lord Falmouth should not be acquiesced in.
2. We advise that an information be filed in the Court of Chancery for a discovery and account. The information should state a Working between High and Low Water Mark and also beyond. To avoid question it will be advisable to make the Attorney General of the Duchy a party as defendant.[20]

The information was filed in Chancery on 10 September 1855 in the name of the Attorney-General, Sir Alexander Cockburn, against Lord Falmouth, Stephen Harvey James, and the Attorney-General of the Duchy. It began:

The sea adjoining the coasts of this Kingdom, and the bed, soil and shore thereof, up to high-water mark of ordinary tides, together with all mines and minerals lying in and under the same, and all profits arising therefrom, belong, of common right, to Her Majesty the Queen, and have at all times so belonged to Her and Her Royal Predecessors, Kings and Queens of this Realm, in right of their Crown, subject, nevertheless, to such grants, by Her Majesty or Her predecessors, as are now in force.[21]

On 22 October 1855, Lord Falmouth filed his answer to the information. It read in part:

. . . I do not know and cannot answer as to my belief or otherwise but I submit to this Honorable Court as a question of Law whether the Sea adjoining the Coast of this Kingdom and the bed soil and shores thereof up to high water mark of ordinary tides does or not and also whether all

[19] The case of *A.G.* v. *Mainwaring and Jones* (1833) is mentioned in Moore, 464.
[20] CREST 40/55, fo. 35.
[21] Chancery Cause A 73 of 1855; C 15/175.

Mines and Minerals lying in and under the same and all profits arising therefrom do or not belong of common right to Her Majesty the Queen and whether they have or not at all times so belonged to Her and Her Royal Predecessors Kings and Queens of this Realm in right of Their Crown subject to such Grants of Her Majesty or Her Predecessors as are now in force.[22]

The Law Officers of the Crown and other counsel acting for the Crown gave their opinion on 18 January 1856 to the effect that as the Duchy of Cornwall was also making a claim to the mines in question it was 'absolutely essential' to make the Attorney-General of the Duchy a party to the suit.[23] This was duly done.

On 9 April 1856, Horace Watson, Solicitor to the Office of Woods, wrote to the solicitor to Lord Falmouth, Gregory, proposing a lease 'of such parts of the veins or beds of minerals in Botallack as are situate below low water mark and thence as far seaward as the working of the mine can or may be extended'. The proposed lease was to be for a term of 31 years from 10 October 1853 and for a royalty of 1/36 of the value of copper raised and 1/48 of the value of tin raised. The granting of the lease was to be delayed until the outstanding question between the Crown and the Duchy had been disposed of.

Lord Falmouth, however, thought that better terms could be arranged. The matter was again referred to the Law Officers who suggested modifications of the proposals originally made by the Office of Woods. They wrote:

Considering the great length of time, 200 years and upwards, during which Lord Falmouth and his predecessors have, as he alleges, exercised the right which he claims, of working the minerals from under the sea adjoining the Botallack Estate; and the possibility of a Jury presuming from such long enjoyment, a grant from the Crown, we think it not unlikely that considerable difficulty may arise in establishing the right of the Crown to relief against him . .[24]

The dispute was compromised by an Order of the Master of the Rolls, made on 20 December 1856, to the following effect:

That as soon as the conflicting claims of the Crown and the Duchy of Cornwall should be settled, a lease should be granted to Lord Falmouth of the minerals under the sea below low water mark as far seaward as the

---

[22] Ibid. See also CREST 40/52, fos. 114–15.
[23] CREST 40/52, fo. 117 (Cockburn, Bethell, Palmer and Hanson).
[24] Ibid., fo. 187.

Botallack Mine could or might be extended for the term of 29 years from the 10th October, 1855.[25]

B. Arbitration before Sir John Patteson, 1856–1858

The report of the Law Officers in November 1847 and the consequent uncertainty over the legal position caused the Crown, in a desultory way, to seek a final solution. In July 1852, probably through the Office of Woods, it prepared a draft Case Stated for the consideration of the Law Officers of the Crown and the Duchy.[26] It was proposed to ask:

1. Whether the mines under the sea shores of the county of Cornwall between high and low water mark belong to Her Majesty in right of Her Crown or to His Royal Highness the Prince of Wales in right of the Duchy of Cornwall?
   and
2. Whether the minerals under the sea below the line of low water round the said county belong to Her Majesty or to his Royal Highness?

Apparently, this Case Stated was never put to the Law Officers.

On 18 February 1856, nearly a year after the question of the unsatisfactory state of the law had been raised in the House of Commons,[27] the Lord Chancellor, Lord Cranworth, and the Chancellor of the Duchy, T. Pemberton Leigh, addressed a joint letter to Sir John Patteson, a judge of the Queen's Bench Division. This letter ran:

Questions of some importance have arisen between the Crown and the Duchy of Cornwall, with respect to the right to mines under the sea, within the county of Cornwall. These questions relate, first, to minerals between high and low water mark; and, secondly, to minerals below low water mark, but won by the extension of workings commenced above low water mark.

It is considered, both by the Queen's Government and by the Council of the Duchy of Cornwall, that it is highly desirable to have these questions set at rest, without adverse litigation between Her Majesty and the Prince of Wales; and that the best mode of proceeding will be to obtain in the first instance, upon the points in difference, the opinion of some gentleman whose eminence as a lawyer, and whose independent character and position, will give such authority to his determination, as

---

[25] The form of the Order was set out in the schedules prepared for the consultation with the Law Officers in March 1878. See Chapter VI below.

[26] This draft was used as the *Preliminary Case on behalf of the Crown*, below.

[27] *147 P. Debs.*, 3rd series, col. 981 (23 March 1855).

to afford satisfactory ground for an Act of Parliament to give effect to it, if such a measure should be found necessary.

It has appeared to us, that there is no individual who combines in so high a degree as yourself, the different qualifications requisite for the performance of this duty, and therefore, with Her Majesty's sanction, we, on behalf of the Queen's Government, and of the Council of the Duchy of Cornwall, have the honour to request that you will undertake it.

From such examination of the matters as we have had an opportunity of making, we think that there can be as little controversy as to matters of fact, and that the rights must depend on principles of law, applied to the construction of Statutes, Resolutions of Parliament and Courts of Law, Charters, and other written documents, with respect to the existence and contents of which no dispute can arise.

It is proposed, however, that the statements on behalf of the Crown, and the Duchy, after being exchanged between the agents, shall be laid before you, and that it shall be left entirely in your discretion to call for any further evidence, either written, or parol, and to require or not the argument by counsel, either of the whole question, or of any particular point which may arise, as you may find expedient; the sole object being to obtain, (without the delay and very great expense of a trial at bar, and other legal proceedings which might follow upon it,) such a deter-mination as may satisfy the Legislature that, if called upon to do so, they may safely act upon it.

If upon both, or either of these questions, there should appear to you to be so much doubt, as to make them, in your judgment, fitter to be the subject of compromise than of decision, it would be desirable that you should state upon what terms you think it reasonable that such com-promise should be effected.[28]

Sir John Patteson accepted the position of arbitrator at a fee of £500. Most of the subsequent proceedings in the arbitration took the form of printed submissions by the two parties.[29] No records of any oral proceedings have been found.

[28] *HCP*, 1857–8 (paper 399, 1) xlvii, 245.
[29] The submissions, in the order in which they were made, were:
(a) *Preliminary Case on behalf of the Crown*
(b) *Preliminary Statement of the Duchy of Cornwall*
(c) *Observations of behalf of the Crown by way of reply to the Statement*
(d) *Remarks of the Officers of the Duchy upon the Observations*
(e) *Reply on behalf of the Duke of Cornwall to the 'Observations' on behalf of the Crown*
(f) *Brief for Counsel. Case of H.R.H. the Duke of Cornwall*
(g) *Further Documents on behalf of the Crown*
(h) *Observations on behalf of the Duke of Cornwall on Further Documents*
(i) *Resumé of the Duchy Case*
(j) *Observations on behalf of the Crown*
Copies of these papers are preserved in the records of the Duchy. Some, but not all, are in CREST 37/253.

The Preliminary Case on behalf of the Crown was nothing more than the draft Case Stated prepared for the opinion of the Law Officers in 1852. That part of it which dealt with the mines below low-water mark ran as follows:

. . . As to the minerals under the bed of the sea below low water mark. The British seas, not only as regards the maritime jurisdiction, but also as to the ownership of the fundum or soil at the bottom of them, are vested in the Crown, 1 Roll, 5 Lib. 15, 2, 168, 170, Lib. 42 and 45. Selden's *Mare Clausum*, Lib. 2, Chap. 2.

The jurisdiction and consequent ownership of the Crown, as Lord of the Sea, has been defined, with respect to the British Channel, to extend midway between England and France, and to the middle of the sea between England and Spain, 3 Leon. 73, 5 Com. Dig. 102.

The jurisdiction and limits of a county bordering upon the main sea terminate at low water mark. Beyond that boundary the jurisdiction of the Sovereign (as exercised by the Court of Admiralty) always exists, and is not dependant upon the flowing of the tide, as it is with regard to land between high and low water mark. *Cross* v. *Diggs*, Siderfin's Report, 158, when it was decided that a suit for the profits of the beaconage of a rock in the sea, near to the coast of Cornwall, was properly instituted in the Court of Admiralty.

A subject may have the grounds of the sea to low water mark by prescription, but no custom can extend the ownership of the subject further. Callis on Sewers, p. 53, and in *Constable's* case, already referred to, it was held that the soil on which the sea ebbs 'and flows, *i.e. between* the high water mark and low water mark, *may* be parcel of the manor of a subject.'

The *Preliminary Statement of the Duchy of Cornwall*, dated May 1855, was largely concerned to show that the Charters granted to the Dukes of Cornwall by the Crown had vested in the Dukes 'the whole territorial interest and dominion of the Crown in and over the entire County of Cornwall'. This interest and dominion, in the opinion of the Duchy, extended to the submarine mines. The *Preliminary Statement* ran:

Before concluding, it may be well to notice the distinction taken by the advisers of the Crown, between *mines under the sea* and *under the sea shore*; and to show that it is entitled to little, if any, weight.

It is clear that land left derelict by the sea, or reclaimed by the labour of man, becomes part of the adjoining County; and it is submitted that there is no substantial distinction between land so reclaimed and minerals reclaimed by means of under-sea workings.

The same reasons which would apply to the case of surface land reclaimed, would equally apply to that of land reclaimed under the water; and it can hardly be doubted that if a murder were committed in one of these under-sea mines adjoining the County of Cornwall, the Coroner of Cornwall would have jurisdiction to hold an inquest, or that the offender might be tried in the County by a Cornish jury.

On referring to the authorities cited by the advisers of the Crown in support of this part of their case, it will be found that these authorities apply only to *surface soil*, and not to under-ground excavations.[30]

The Duchy statement went on to claim that although it followed from the case of *Sir Henry Constable*[31] that the low-water mark was the extreme bounds of the county and of the jurisdiction of the county officers, the possibility of undersea mines or reclamation was there never contemplated because '. . . it is clear from the very nature of Admiralty jurisdiction that it could never be meant to extend to land regions unconnected with the open sea, although those regions might, in fact, be locally situate under the bed of the ocean'; *Cross* v. *Diggs*[32] was in the Duchy's favour since it laid down that every suit relating to a rock in the open sea should be brought in the temporal courts. Finally, the Duchy argued that the submarine mines could be regarded as akin to reclaimed land which, on the authority of Callis, became parcel of the adjoining county.

The Office of Woods then filed a document headed *Observations on behalf of the Crown by way of reply to the Statement*. Two paragraphs only are relevant for present purposes. Paragraph 116 ran:

Before concluding these observations, it should be noticed that the jurisdiction of the Sovereign over the sea, as confided to the Lord High Admiral, or Commissioners of the Admiralty, is now exercised by the Board of Admiralty over the sea adjacent to Cornwall, and under which the mines in question extend, and that the profits from Droits of Admiralty are paid to the credit of the public revenue, under the terms of the Civil List Act. The jurisdiction thus exercised is vested in the Crown by virtue of the same sovereignty as that to which it is entitled to the territorial right to the soil under the sea; and it is indeed difficult to see why the rights of the Crown should not have application in the one case as well as the other, and yet according to the contention in the Duchy Statement the title in the Crown does not extend to the mines covered by the sea, while it does not appear that any active measures have been taken by the Duchy to establish that these prerogatives do extend to the water covering those very mines and the profits received from it.

[30] *Preliminary Statement*, p. 12. Its correct date was probably 1856.
[31] (1601) 5 Co. Rep. 107.
[32] (1663) 1 Siderfin 158.

Paragraph 117 read:

It is suggested, that the mines and minerals worked from the land and under the sea became by a sort of acquisition annexed to the county. The Officers of the Crown are unable to find any authority for this suggestion. What would have to be done with respect to the trial of crimes committed in the deep-sea mines is a matter probably which would require, when the case arises, the interposition of Parliament; but if it is conceded that the bed and soil of the English seas below low-water mark belong to the Crown, it is difficult to conceive how the grantee of a manor, honor, or even county, bounded by low-water mark by extending his works under the Royal property, and so committing a trespass and intrusion thereon, can annex that portion of the property to his own.

The Duchy prepared a substantial document, dated June 1856, in which it set out the Crown's *Observations* paragraph by paragraph, and in parallel columns, in red print, set out its own comments thereon. This document, *Remarks of the Officers of the Duchy of Cornwall upon the Observations on behalf of the Crown*, was, according to a hand-written note inside, not delivered to the arbitrator but was submitted to the Law Officers of the Crown 'in order that they may be aware of the views entertained by the Advisers of the Duchy'.

With respect to paragraph 117 above, the Duchy claimed that, if the shore below high-water mark belonged to it, the extension of mines below low-water mark was in the nature of an accretion which followed, upon the authority of *Scratton* v. *Brown*,[33] as an accessory to the principal. With regard to the nature of the Crown's right to the bed of the sea, the Duchy continued:

It seems to be quite clear that it is not an absolute or an ordinary right of property. The right would appear to be in the Crown more by reason of the absence of any other owner than from any other cause. A conveyance of the shore, being supposed capable of actually passing the legal estate in soil, which at the date of the conveyance was below low water mark, but from which the sea afterwards recedes, seems necessarily to lead to this conclusion—exemplifying more fully the principles previously recognized in Lord Yarborough's and other cases of accretion by slow degrees.

That upon a large tract becoming suddenly derelict by the sea, the property in the soil becomes an absolute property in the Crown, does not, it is submitted, contradict this conclusion. This species of property, like any other vacant possession, would, by the law of nature, belong to the first occupant; but to prevent the inconveniences which would result

[33] (1825) 4 B. & C. 485.

from this, the Laws of the State vest it in the supreme power, and the title of the Crown previously inchoate, becomes absolute and indefeasible.

The Office of Woods then filed a document headed *Observations on behalf of the Crown* dated 22 May 1857. In this document it was claimed that 'no arguable question at all' existed as to the soil of the sea beyond the *littus*. The document went on:

In the absence of evidence to displace the Crown's title, the Crown is, (to use the words of Alderson, B., and Maule J. . . .) clearly entitled according to all the authorities, to the *soil of the sea itself* adjoining 'the coast of England'.

The Duchy Officers contend, that if they are entitled to the shore down to low water mark, they are also entitled to work *below* the low water mark, on the ground that that would be in the nature of what they call an '*accretion*', and that that part of the soil of the bed of the sea which they take possession of becomes a part of the county, and therefore a part of the Duchy property.

The consequences of this argument themselves furnish a sufficient answer.

The bed of the sea is *prima facie*, the property of the Crown, *ub. sup.* This right, according to English law, extends '*ad inferos*'—'*cujus est solum, ejus est usque ad inferos*'. . . .

If then the miners of the Duchy (assuming for the present argument the sea shore to be a parcel of it) drive a shaft beyond the limits of the low water mark, and take the ores below that mark, they unquestionably take the minerals of the Queen; for, if the bed of the sea belongs to the Crown, so do the minerals under it; '*cujus est solum ejus est, usque ad inferos*'.

Then it is said by the Duchy, 'we make the minerals ours by the act of extending the county by mining'. That one man should be able to change his neighbour's property into his own by committing a trespass upon the former, is hardly consistent with the English, or any other law.[34]

The Crown then asked:

When does the bed of the sea *cease* to be the property of the Crown? If minerals from the bed of the sea were, at the distance for example of one quarter of a mile from the shore, removed by diving bells sent down at sea, what pretence would there be for the Attorney-General of the Duchy to interfere?

It is not easy to suggest any reason why the fact that the Duchy lands adjoin the Crown lands should be held to confer a right upon the owner of the former to make use of the latter; and it may be doubted whether there is any authority for the proposition that such a right can be considered to arise *pur cause de vicinage* as it were, without the reciprocity

[34] *Observations*, p. 7. The judicial extract is from *A.G.* v. *Chambers* (1854).

this Bill; it concerned the rights of the Crown and of the Duchy alone, and there was a saving clause most carefully drawn securing the rights of every person except those in dispute between the Crown or the Duchy.[47]

The Bill then proceeded to the Lords where it was debated on 26 July 1858.[48] Lord Wynford said that he hoped some guarantee would be given that, in any claim hereafter on the part of the Crown to land between high- and low-water mark, the present arbitration would not be referred to as a precedent. The Duke of Newcastle replied that no such guarantee could be given on behalf either of the present or any future government. All he could say was there was nothing in the Bill to affect the rights of anybody as to property out of the county of Cornwall. Finally, the Lord Chancellor, Lord Cranworth, declared that it amounted 'merely to a private arrangement between the Crown and the Duchy of Cornwall, and the Bill clearly saved the rights of all other parties'.

On 2 August 1858, the Bill received the Royal Assent as the Cornwall Submarine Mines Act 1858 (21 & 22 Vict., c. 109). The Act 'enacted and declared' as s. 2 that:

All Mines and Minerals lying below Low-water Mark under the open Sea, adjacent to but not being Part of the County of Cornwall, are, as between the Queen's Majesty in right of Her Crown on the one hand, and His Royal Highness Albert Edward Prince of Wales and Duke of Cornwall in right of His Duchy of Cornwall on the other hand, vested in Her Majesty the Queen in right of Her Crown as Part of the Soil and territorial Possessions of the Crown.

Thus the words 'as Part of the Soil and territorial Possessions of the Crown' were added between the drafting of the Articles of Agreement and the presentation of the Bill. The significance of these words, which were not in the award of Sir John Patteson, was to be stressed later by commentators on the Act.

Finally, the definition section, s.8, stated that:

. . . the expression 'Mines and Minerals' shall comprehend all Mines and Minerals, and all Quarries, Veins, or Beds of Stone, and all Substrata of any other nature whatsoever, and the Ground and Soil in, upon, and under which such Mines and Minerals, Quarries, Veins or Beds of Stone, and other Substrata lie.

Once the Act had entered the Statute Book, the Crown lost little

[47] Ibid., col. 1753.
[48] Ibid., cols. 2077–8.

time in profiting from its provisions.[49] On 11 January 1859, the
Commissioners of Woods granted to Viscount Falmouth a lease of
the submarine workings of the Botallack Mine 'below and from
low water mark as far seaward as the Botallack Mine . . . extends'.
The lease was for 29 years from 10 October 1855. The rent
reserved in the lease was a royalty of 1/72 part of the value as sold
of the tin, tin ore, and tin stuff raised, and 1/34 part of the value of
the copper, copper ore and other minerals raised. Other leases of
undersea workings made in the next six years were of the mines
Wheal Margery, Pendeen Consols (800 fathoms seaward), West
Tolvadden, Carnelloc, Wheal Prudence (600 fathoms seaward)
and Cape Cornwall. In May 1859, the joint account of the Crown
and the Duchy at Messrs. Coutts & Co., into which had been paid
since 1842 the proceeds from the undersea mines, in particular the
Levant Mines, was closed, the bulk of the balance going to the
Crown. The Duchy, however, was far from beaten.

E. Arbitration before Sir John Coleridge, 1866–1869

The issue which next arose between the Crown and the Duchy
touching on the legal status of the undersea mines was over the
extent seaward of the county of Cornwall for the purposes of the
1858 Act. A Case Stated was submitted by the Crown for the
opinion of F. S. Reilly of Lincoln's Inn whose reply, dated 11 July
1864, began as follows:[50]

The object is to ascertain the seaward limits of the County of Cornwall
for the purposes of the Act of 1858.
     The Act assigns to the Duchy of Cornwall—
     1. Mines under the seashore between high water and low water mark
        within the county.
     2. Mines under estuaries and tidal rivers and other places (below high
        water mark) even below low water mark, being in and part of the
        county.
     The Act assigns to the Crown mines below low water mark under the
open sea, adjacent to, but not being part of, the county.
     The effect of the interpretation of 'mines and minerals' in Section 8 of
the Act, is to carry with the mines the whole property in the soil.
     The county, for purposes of property, must, it would seem, be iden-
tical in extent with the county for purposes of jurisdiction. The Act draws
no distinction.

[49] The following practice is taken from the *Answer on behalf of the Crown to the Statement of the Duchy*, October 1866.
[50] Reilly's opinion, but not the Case Stated, was printed in Foreign Office Confidential Print No. 2290; FO 881/2290, pp. 6–11.

Reilly considered separately (i) the open seashore, (ii) arms of the sea, (iii) ports. In respect of (i), Reilly concluded, after citing various extracts from Coke and from the case of *Embleton* v. *Brown*,[51] that:

. . . it does not appear to have been ever suggested that the county comprises any part of the bed of the sea.

With respect, therefore, to the open sea shore there seems to be no room for controversy between the Crown and the Duchy. The possessions of the Duchy there, are bounded by the line of low water at the lowest known tides. For to that line, I think, the county, for the purposes of jurisdiction, extends, and not merely to the line of low water at ordinary spring tides.

After considering various cases, in particular *R.* v. *Cunningham*,[52] and a passage in *Fitzherbert's Abridgement*,[53] Reilly concluded in respect of (ii):

In this state of the Authorities, the only conclusion I can arrive at is, that it would be difficult to deduce from them any rule for drawing a line of demarcation in arms of the sea round the coast of Cornwall to separate the Crown property from that of the Duchy.

On point (iii), Reilly recalled the controversy between the views of Coke on the one hand, and Admiralty judges such as Exton and Sir Leoline Jenkins on the other, as to the extent of Admiralty jurisdiction. He remarked:

The question, in short, whether or not a port, as such, is necessarily within the body of the county is involved with the much-controverted question of the extent of the Admiralty jurisdiction.

Reilly summed up the entire problem submitted to him as follows:

On the whole case, I am of opinion that the rights of the Crown and of the Duchy, in respect of the important property in question, cannot be satisfactorily determined without a judicial or other authoritative decision being obtained as to the law; or, at least, without a fuller examination that it has been possible for me to give to the materials for such a decision.

The Crown and the Duchy could well have accepted Reilly's suggestion for on 11 April 1866 tripartite Articles of Agreement were drawn up between the Queen, C.A. Gore as Commissioner of

---

[51] (1860) 30 L.J. M.C. 1.
[52] (1859) 30 L.J.M.C. 66; Bell's Crown Cases 72.
[53] Fitzherbert, *Coron.* 399, quoting a dictum by Stanton J.

Woods, and the Duke of Cornwall. By these Articles it was referred to Sir John Coleridge, a judge of the Queen's Bench Division, as arbitrator to decide between the Crown and the Duchy within the purview of the Cornwall Submarine Mines Act the line of boundary between the seashore, estuaries, tidal rivers, and other places part of the county of Cornwall on the one hand, and the open sea adjacent but not part of the county on the other hand.

As in the earlier arbitration before the late Sir John Patteson, the proceedings took the form mainly of printed documents submitted to the arbitrator.[54] In the first of these, *Statement on the part of the Duchy of Cornwall with reference to the Seaward Extent of the County of Cornwall as between the Crown and the Duchy*, the argument of the Duchy was set out:

. . . it would seem necessary to consider in the present case, whether the language of the first section of the Act, declaratory of the rights of the Duke of Cornwall, is not to be construed as including all such parts of the fundus of the sea, as the Crown could grant *even to an ordinary subject*; or whether it must be considered as confining the rights of the Duchy to the extent of the soil of the sea comprised within the limits of the Ports of the County of Cornwall; or whether it must be construed so narrowly, as to limit the rights of the Duchy, as against the Crown, to an extent analagous [sic] to the supposed limits of the jurisdiction of county officers, or the jurisdiction of the Temporal Courts of the Realm, as against the jurisdiction of the Admiralty.

The *Statement* then set out three alternative propositions for the consideration of the arbitrator:

First, That the extent of the fundus of the sea which, as part of the maritime territories of the realm, (without reference to any supposed boundary of local or other jurisdiction,) was comprised in the Parliamentary Charters of 11th Edw. III, and which was intended by 'The Cornwall Submarine Mines Act, 1858', to be vested in the Duke of Cornwall, as part of the soil and territorial possessions of the Duchy,

---

[54] The submissions, in the order in which they were made, were:
  (a) *Statement on the part of the Duchy of Cornwall with reference to the Seaward Extent of the County of Cornwall as between the Crown and the Duchy*
  (b) *Answer on behalf of the Crown to the Statement of the Duchy*
  (c) *Reply on the part of the Duchy of Cornwall, with Appendix*
  (d) *Supplemental Reply on the part of the Duchy of Cornwall, with Supplemental Appendix*
  (e) *Rejoinder on behalf of the Crown to the Reply on behalf of the Duchy*
  (f) *Remarks by way of reply to the Rejoinder on behalf of the Crown*
  (g) *Final Observations on behalf of the Crown*
  (h) *Concluding Statement and Summary of the Case on the part of the Duchy of Cornwall*
Copies of these papers are preserved in the records of the Duchy and in CREST 37/253.

should be held to be the full limit on the open coast of the fundus below low water-mark, which the Sovereign might grant to an ordinary subject, as part of the maritime territories of the Realm: this limit appearing to extend to three geographical miles off the shores of the Kingdom generally, except in the case of bays or indentations not exceeding ten geographical miles across, when the distance of three miles would be reckoned from a line drawn, from low water-mark off one headland, to low water-mark off another headland: including a similar area of the fundus of the sea contiguous to the Scilly Islands, with their adjacent rocks and islets, as an outlying part of the County of Cornwall; and which Islands, with their shores and intervening sounds and channels, have long been the subject of successive grants, as parcel of the possessions of the Duchy.

Secondly. As an alternative proposition, that the Act of 1858 should be held declaratory of the right of the Duchy of Cornwall, to such portion, at least, of the fundus of the sea, as is comprised within the limits of the Ports of the County. In this view of the case, the rights of the Duchy to the soil of the sea adjacent to the Scilly Islands, which are not within the limits of any legal port, being confined to such parts of the fundus, as have been comprised in Duchy leases.

Thirdly. That if the seaward limit of the County of Cornwall, within the purview of 'The Cornwall Submarine Mines Act, 1858', is to be fixed with reference to the supposed extent, as against the Admiralty, of the jurisdiction of the county officers, or of the temporal Courts of the Realm; the line of boundary should, in the absence of any precise limit for such an extent of a County seawards be drawn in accordance with the precedent afforded by the line of departure from the coast, named in the British and French Fisheries Convention Act, 6 and 7 Vict. cap. 79 (that is to say): it should be a straight line from low water-mark off one headland, to low water-mark off another headland, in the case of bays or indentations of the coast not exceeding ten geographical miles across; and, in the case of all greater indentations, should follow the line of low water-mark. Which line, having regard to the extent of the ancient jurisdiction of the Coroner of a County relative to wreck of the sea, (*vide* 3 Edw. I. cap. 4) would be the line of low water-mark at spring tides. The same principle being extended to all islands, (if any) other than the Scilly Islands, as outlying parts of the County, situate beyond the line of boundary, which, in this alternative, would be drawn around the coast of the mainland. And to all parts of the circumjacent seas around the group of islands, islets and rocks forming the Scilly Islands, as distinguished from the portions of the sea intervening between those islands, comprised in successive grants and leases by the Duchy.

In its *Answer*, which bore the date October 1866, the Crown through the Office of Woods argued that the county of Cornwall within the purview of the Act of 1858 comprised the area which

was the county of Cornwall as between all other persons whatsoever and that the matter was concluded by the award and
further award of Sir John Patteson in 1857 and 1858 respectively.
It agreed with the third proposition of the Duchy to the extent that
the determination of the body of a county should be made on the
basis of the jurisdiction of the sheriff of the county, but continued:

It cannot be admitted that the French Fisheries Act has any legitimate
bearing on this question, as it is impossible to ascertain what were the
political as well as legal considerations which operated on the two
Governments in framing that international contract. Neither has the
ancient jurisdiction of the coroner which is referred to any more legitimate application. The jurisdiction of the coroner extended beyond the
sea coast, the *littus maris*. In like manner it is to be observed that there is
not now any question as to the extent or limits of the custom's ports. The
jurisdiction of a custom's port is as independent of the territorial limits of
a county as it is of the seashore between high and low water mark.[55]

In its *Reply*, the Duchy further developed the three alternative
positions advanced in its *Statement*. It claimed that the Crown
appeared 'to lose sight altogether of the object of the Parliamentary Charters relating to the Duchy of Cornwall . . . and of the
exceptional position in which the property passing under those
Charters, with all its incident Regalities and territorial rights, is
placed, by their peculiar limitations; which effect a setting apart of
a portion of the Hereditary Possessions of the Crown for a specific
purpose.'[56] Consequently, the Duchy argued, the Charters should
be construed as passing to it every territorial right capable of being
passed by the Crown. The Duchy conceded for the sake of argument that the Act of 1858 recognized some territorial right in the
Crown in respect of the seabed. Its *Reply* continued:

. . . it becomes necessary to consider, what is the limit of the maritime
territory, or of the bed and soil of the sea, which has been considered to
be vested in the Sovereign of this country, as part of the Realm of
England; and thus, as a part of the territorial possessions of the Crown,
capable of passing, as parcel of a Section of the Realm, under the Duchy
Charters, in the rendering proposed for them, as between the Crown and
the Duchy, by the First Proposition.[57]

Then followed citations from authorities such as Callis, Hale,
and Angell, and of cases including *Duke of Beaufort* v. *Mayor of*

---

[55] *Answer*, pp. 7–8.
[56] *Reply*, p. 1.
[57] Ibid., 3.

Swansea,[58] *Free Fishers of Whitstable* v. *Gann,*[59] and *Attorney-General* v. *Tomsett.*[60] These authorities were summed up by the Duchy as follows:

. . . it is submitted that a solution is afforded, to some confusion, which may have existed, with reference to the *maritime jurisdiction* or dominion, and the *maritime propriety* or territorial ownership of the Crown, in and over the sea around the coasts of this country; and that the extended authority and interest given by the older text writers to the Sovereign of these realms in and over the adjacent seas, as, for instance, the sea between Britain and France, was not, in strictness, proprietary or territorial over the whole extent of that area; but simply an authority arising from the dominion and jurisdiction which a powerful nation exercised over it, for the more peculiar and perfect protection of its own rights and interests.[61]

The Duchy *Reply* then went on to consider the effect of this view in municipal law:

This limit of the territorial ownership of the sea, as part of the Realm of England, and which may be granted by the Sovereign, and, therefore, in point of territorial division most probably 'within some county, as all the Realm of England is within some county', (Per Wightman, J., *Reg.* v. *Musson*, 4 Jur. N.S. 111), would, moreover, bear a greater analogy to what Lord Hale speaks of as a 'districtus maris'; an expression applied, as descriptive of the three mile limit, by Chief Justice Erle . . .

The high authority of Chief Justice Erle, in the Whitstable Case, is considerably strengthened by the fact of only one, (Lord Chelmsford) out of the many judges before whom the case came, expressing any dissent to the proposition of a transfer by the Crown of the soil of the sea to the extent under consideration; and the reasoning upon which Lord Chelmsford's views were founded appears, it is submitted, to be evidently incapable of support, being based on a negation of the Crown's territorial right to the fundus of the sea below low water-mark.

It appears from this latter passage that the Duchy had completely renounced any doubts it might have once entertained on the Crown's right to any part of the seabed. Its view on this point was indeed expressed thus:

The reasoning in modern times, which might lead to the inference that the soil below low water mark could not form part, or be included in a grant, of all the territorial rights of a maritime county, would thus seem

[58] (1849) 3 Exch. 413.
[59] (1865) 11 C.B. (N.S.) 387.
[60] (1835) 2 C.M. & R. 170.
[61] *Reply*, p. 9.

alone to rest upon the supposition that the Crown has no territorial interest in the soil of the sea, beyond low water-mark, and that it forms no part of the Realm.

There can however, be no question raised, on the part of the Officers of the Crown, in the present case, with regard to the right of the Crown to the fundus of the sea being a territorial right, and therefore part of the Realm, and consequently capable of being included in any grant of a particular portion of the maritime territories of the Realm, like the county of Cornwall; such territorial right of the Crown being the foundation of their claim . . .[62]

The *Reply* next attempted to urge that the limits of a county could not be determined along the usual lines of division between Admiralty and common law jurisdictions since these jurisdictions were incapable of precise definition; sometimes, indeed, shifting with the tide.

It will be borne in mind in addition, that there appears to be no original jurisdiction vested in the Admiralty, for trying questions connected with the title to land. Callis states, and it is a universally received principle, that the soil of the sea belongs to the Sovereign by the Common Law of England, 'for no law gives the King any soil but only the Common Laws of England', and this being so, it would be hard to maintain that questions with regard to the soil, so given to the Crown by the Common Law, were not within the jurisdiction of the Temporal Courts of the Realm, (as distinguished from the Admiralty Court) administering the Common Law . . . and if the action were real, to try the title to the soil, as well in the case of the Crown, which has no peculiar prerogative with regard to informations in the Exchequer for intrusion or suits in the nature of a real action . . . as in the case of a subject, the venue would have to be laid in the locality or 'County' where the cause of action arose, as a venue must be laid in some County, and cannot be indefinite.[63]

The Duchy argued that the Crown, by laying informations in Chancery in respect of the soil below low-water mark, proceeded on the basis that the seabed was within the counties, since the jurisdiction of the Chancery Courts could only be co-extensive with that of the common law courts. It repeated the argument which it had used in the proceedings before Sir John Patteson to the effect that land reclaimed by the labour of man 'becomes at once "manoriable", whether such reclamation arises by the extension of mineral workings below the surface of the bed of the sea, or by inclosures of the surface, or erections upon it, such as

[62] Ibid., 10.
[63] Ibid., 13.

piers and harbours [and] must, it is submitted, be treated as becoming parcel of a County; following the maxim enunciated by Mr. Justice Holroyd in *Scratton* v. *Brown*, 4 B. & C. p. 502 "the accretion follows as an accessory to the principal" '. In the opinion of the Duchy, the fact that local Acts of Parliament usually provided specifically for reclaimed land to be parcel of the adjacent county was due to abundant caution.

In support of the second alternative proposition advanced in its *Statement*, the Duchy argued that as the ancient Parliamentary Charters had granted to it the profits of the ports in Cornwall, these Charters had transferred to the Duchy every territorial right of the Sovereign to the soil of those ports. These territorial rights included anchorage, stated by Lord Hale in his treatise *De Portibus Maris* to 'arise from or in respect of the propriety of the soil, and as an evidence of it'. The extent of the various ports, moreover, was laid down in a commission issued from the Exchequer in 1677–8 under the statute 13 & 14 Car. 2, c. 11, s. 14, and included areas of sea below low-water mark. On the authority of Coke, every port or haven was within a county. Therefore, concluded the Duchy's argument:

. . . if the soil of the sea, around the mainland of Cornwall to the extent of the three mile limit, which appears to form the extreme seaward boundary of the territory of the realm, cannot be considered as comprised within the territory passing under the Parliamentary Charters relating to the Duchy of Cornwall; all such soil of the sea lying within the extreme seaward limits of the Ports of the County . . . must be held to have passed to the Duke of Cornwall, and become parcel of the Duchy, as part of the territory of the County by virtue of those Charters: such an extent of the soil of the sea, being at least analogous to that part of the maritime territory of the State . . .[64]

With regard to the third alternative proposition, the Duchy conceded that it was founded on a narrow and uncertain ground, namely the extent of the jurisdiction of the temporal courts relative to that of the Admiralty. The problem of the jurisdictional nature of bays, which had caused concern to Reilly, was discussed in the context of citations from Coke, Hale, Rolle, and Angell. The Duchy's argument on this point concluded:

In this apparent conflict of the authorities as to the distance which might prevail between the 'fauces terrae', the only tangible guide for fixing the seaward limit of the County of Cornwall in the present case, if it should

[64] Ibid., 20.

be considered that a line of boundary of so doubtful propriety as to bear any analogy to the presumed jurisdictional limit of a county, is at all desirable to be adopted, in making a final settlement of the present question, seems to be that mentioned in the 3rd proposition, as afforded by the legislature in the British and French Fisheries Convention Act, 6 & 7 Vict., cap. 79, sec. 2, (et vide Sched. Article II.).[65]

The Duchy next submitted a *Supplemental Reply* in which further supporting evidence was set out. One of the principal arguments here was that the Crown could vest in any grantee portions of the bed of the sea below low-water mark; in support of which the Duchy cited *Attorney-General* v. *Chambers*,[66] the preamble of the Thames Conservancy Act 1857, the amended information filed by the Crown in 1855 relative to the Botallack Mine, and the two Whitstable cases.[67] These latter cases were stated by the Duchy to show that

. . . the jurisdiction of the Common Law Courts of this Realm, every part of which is divided into counties; and, therefore, the jurisdiction of every ministerial officer of the Common Law extends to the distance mentioned by Chief Justice Erle in the first of the two cases . . . viz., a distance of three miles from low-water mark, in all questions touching the soil.

The Supplemental Reply also cited a local Act of Parliament of 1844 concerning the port of Padstow[68] which 'affords another Proof . . . of the assertion and recognition of the rights of the Duchy over the deep sea around the mainland of the county. And as it does not contain, contrary to the usual practice in all local Acts, any mention of the Crown in the general saving clause, it seems to offer a remarkable instance of the Duchy, and the Duchy alone, being entitled to the deep sea, within the limits of its provisions, described as being within the county of Cornwall.'[69] In an appendix to the *Supplemental Reply*, the Duchy set out documents, dated between 1615 and 1649, concerning the recovery of silver bars from the bed of the sea below low-water mark beyond the Lizard. These documents were claimed to be evidence that the

[65] Ibid., 23.
[66] (1854) 4 De G. M. & G. 206.
[67] *Gann* and *Foreman*. See Chapter III above.
[68] 7 & 8 Vict., c. xxiv. This defined the limits of the port to include certain waters within lines drawn from various points up to a mile and a half below low-water mark and recited that the Duke of Cornwall claimed to be entitled to the *fundus* of the port as part and parcel of his possessions in the county.
[69] *Supplemental Reply*, p. 4.

the Botallack Mine, the court would have ordered his arrest through a serjeant-at-arms, even though the sheriff of Cornwall would have had to endorse the writ of *capias* 'non est inventum'.

In its *Remarks by way of Reply*, the Duchy sought to distinguish the cases cited by the Crown on the ground that they concerned the division between the Admiralty and common law jurisdictions and 'Admiralty jurisdiction has nothing to do with the territorial or proprietary rights of either the Sovereign or the Duchy, in any portion of the sea's bed, but proceeds from the general empire or authority vested in the Sovereign for the protection of the Realm.'[77] The Duchy's *Remarks* then went on to assert that 'there cannot be lands which do not lie within some county'.

In support of this proposition, it cited a charge delivered to the Grand Jury of Sligo in the spring of 1868 by Fitzgerald J. The occasion was the preferment of a bill of indictment for treason felony against one William T. Nagle in respect of certain acts alleged to have been performed by him on board the American ship *Jacknall*. The Grand Jury was summoned under the commission of oyer and terminer and therefore, according to the Duchy, it was necessary that overt acts should have been committed by Nagle 'within the county of Sligo'. The *Remarks* set out[78] a lengthy extract from the charge of which certain parts follow:

. . . [Y]ou must remember that the Queen's dominions are not limited to the actual land of Ireland, but include certain parts of the adjoining high seas. For instances, the sovereignty and dominion of the Queen extend over all arms of the sea, estuaries, and bays within the headlands, and all ports and harbours in the kingdom, and also extend into the high sea adjoining the shores of the kingdom so far as a cannon shot will reach, and that is generally or used to be estimated at a marine league [Here Fitzgerald J. mentioned supporting American practice since Nagle was a United States' citizen] . . . If, therefore, any acts of the prisoner on the high seas shall be offered in evidence, you will have to inquire whether the 'Jacknall' was then within *the headlands of any bay or estuary or within the three miles of the shore*, and I direct you, for the purpose of your inquiry, to consider and deal *with such acts as if actually committed on the adjoining shore*. It is not improbable that some questions of novelty and difficulty may arise on this branch of the case, as it is by no means clearly defined for what purpose the sovereign jurisdiction of the Queen over the adjoining precincts of the high seas, not being within the body of a county, is admitted by foreign nations, or can be maintained in law, or whether an alien whilst on a ship of his own country on the high seas, and

[77] *Remarks*, p. 7.
[78] Ibid., 9–11.

not within the body of a county, can commit any overt act of high treason or treason felony . . . our jurisdiction under the present commission depends on some overt act being satisfactorily proved to have taken place *within the body of the county of Sligo*. The acts relied on to found the jurisdiction may probably be the transaction on board the 'Jacknall' *when within the headlands of Sligo bay or within three miles of the coast of Sligo; and in either case I direct you to consider such acts as if done in the county of Sligo*. As to acts done on the high seas within the three miles limit some question may be raised hereafter, inasmuch as that portion of the high seas, although within the Queen's dominions, may not, for the purpose of sustaining the jurisdiction of this court to try this case, be considered as being part of the body of the county of Sligo. But anything of that kind will be matter for us hereafter, and you will act on the direction I have given you with respect to the locality of these offences.

The Duchy maintained, on the strength of this charge, that Fitzgerald J. had considered the three mile belt to be 'parcel of the United Kingdom'; consequently it would be within some county on the basis of the dictum of Wightman J. in *R.* v. *Musson*. Furthermore, according to the Duchy's interpretation of the charge, the water within the headlands of a bay was 'as unquestionable matter of law' within the body of the adjoining county.

The Crown, in its *Final Observations*, maintained in reply that while the ship was lying in Sligo Bay it was 'within the realm of Ireland' though out of the county of Sligo, and consequently Nagle was 'within the peace of our lady the Queen'. If it could be shown that he had committed one overt act within the county of Sligo, other acts of treason committed on board the ship while it was in the bay could be given in evidence against him on the trial.[79]

In its *Concluding Statement and Summary of the Case*, the Duchy summed up the first proposition as follows:

That the County of Cornwall, conferred by the Crown in Parliament on the Dukes of Cornwall, should be held to comprise, what is termed, the three miles limit of the sea from the shore, on the ground of that being the extent to which the Crown may grant the soil of the sea even to an ordinary subject . . . Which limit, as part of the realm capable of being granted by the Crown, like any other Crown lands within the kingdom, should be held to be within the county, 'as all the realm of England is within some county'. *Reg.* v. *Musson*. . . . And which limit is stated by Mr. Justice Fitzgerald, in the case of the Jacknall . . . to be *prima facie* within a county.

[79] *Final Observations*, p. 4. The jury at Sligo found a true bill (*The Times*, 2 March 1868) but Nagle was later acquitted on grounds of evidence (*The Times*, 4 March 1868). See also the letter by 'Historicus' in *The Times*, 4 March 1868.

amply shown, by ancient records, to have been parcel of the earldom or 'comitatus', and having been, in respect of soil, as parcel of the earldom or 'comitatus' conferred upon the Dukes of Cornwall by the Act of 11 Edward III . . . to which soil all interest, in respect of franchise, which might have been previously severed from the 'comitatus', was again annexed inalienably by the subsequent parliamentary charter of 17th March 11 Edward III, together with various regal rights, which afford the highest evidence of an intention to make the Dukes complete maritime Lords of Cornwall. The seaward limits of the ports of the county are, apparently, best ascertained by the earliest complete survey or definition seawards of the Cornish ports on record . . .[87]

(iii) THE 'HEADLANDS' THEORY

In its *Rejoinder*, the Crown dealt only cursorily with the third Duchy proposition:

The reasons of State which guided the legislature in defining the boundaries of the British fisheries, in the British and French Fisheries Convention Act, can have no bearing on the question what part of the sea around Cornwall is within the county.[88]

In its *Concluding Statement and Summary of the Case*, the Duchy thus summarized the third proposition:

That, at the least, such portions of the sea's bed should be held to be within the county as might be considered to be within the jurisdiction, by the common law, of county officers, or of the inquest and courts held for a county. With reference to this proposition the officers of the Duchy have adduced the various readings of 8 Edward II, Tit. Coron., 399 . . . also various instances of the extent of the sheriff's ancient jurisdiction as to wreck, and the authority of 5 Rep., page 107, to the effect that such jurisdiction extended by the common law to 'flotsam, jetsam, and lagan'; and they have also quoted the authority of Mr. Justice Story in *United States* v. *Grush* . . . as to the extent of the county of Suffolk in the State of Massachusetts, and the authority of Mr. Justice Fitzgerald, in the case of the 'Jacknall', as to Sligo Bay being undoubtedly part of the county.[89]

As the point in issue in the present proceedings had arisen over the statement in the further award of Sir John Patteson of 25 February 1858 according to which there were 'other places in and part of the county of Cornwall, even below low water mark', it was not surprising that the Crown in conclusion attempted to give meaning to this part of the further award in a form which would be

[87] *Concluding Statement*, p. 2.
[88] *Rejoinder*, p.74.
[89] *Concluding Statement*, p. 2. *Grush* (1829), 5 Mason 298.

consistent with its claim. The *Rejoinder* therefore concluded as follows:

What then are the 'other places even below low-water mark being in and part of the county', the minerals under which are by the Act given to the Duchy? It is submitted that they are to be read as *ejusdem generis* with estuaries and tidal rivers, and are those narrow creeks which are to be found on the Cornish coast, and of which the creek of Boscastle may be cited as an example. These little creeks come strictly within the rule as laid down in the Year Book, 8 Edward II, for in them 'one may see what is done of the one part of the water and of the other, as to see from one land to the other'. This is the rule adopted by Lord Hale, *De Jure Maris*, p.10, and it is submitted that the red line which has been drawn by the officers of the Crown on the map originally submitted to the arbitrator adheres closely to this rule, and carries out the letter and spirit of 'The Cornwall Submarine Mines Act, 1858'. A great part of which Act, and of Sir John Pattison's [sic] Award, would become waste paper if the arguments used on behalf of the Duchy were to prevail. But to those arguments, it is, with much confidence submitted, that a sufficient answer has been given.[90]

F. The Coleridge Award

Sir John Coleridge delivered his award, which contained no reasons, on 28 October 1869.[91] The first paragraph ran:

First as between the Crown and the Duchy of Cornwall and within the Purview of the Cornwall Submarine Mines Act 1858, the line of boundary between the Sea shore in and part of the said County from Penleigh Point aforesaid to Marshland Mouth aforesaid and the open Sea adjacent to but not being part of the said County I decide and determine to be the Low Water mark at the Highest ordinary Spring Tides; But from this decision I exclude the Estuaries, tidal Rivers and other places in and part of the said County, for which I make provision in what follows. . . .

The award then delimited various estuaries and river mouths, using lines joining headlands or other points where, in the opinion of the arbitrator, the estuary or river mouth terminated. A map accompanied the award.

---

[90] *Rejoinder*, p. 76.
[91] Duchy of Cornwall records.

G. The Reaction to the Award

On 18 November 1869, a memorandum setting out the text of the award was prepared in the Office of the Duchy.[92] It also set out three points of criticism of Sir John Coleridge's findings:

(i) THE SCILLY ISLES

The eighth paragraph of the award was as follows:

Eighth as between the Crown and the Duchy and within the purview of the said Act I find and determine that the line of boundary in respect of each and all of the several Isles and Rocks known by the name of the Scilly Isles, between the Sea Shore in and part of the County of Cornwall and the open Sea adjacent thereto, but not in or part of it is the Low Water Mark at the Highest ordinary Spring Tides.

According to the Duchy memorandum, the Crown had earlier recognized, through an opinion of the Law Officers in 1833, the validity of the Duchy's title to the Scilly Isles under leases from the Crown. These leases, however, included the sounds and harbours within the definition of the area under lease. During the course of the arbitration before Sir John Coleridge, the Duchy had reaffirmed its title to the soil of the havens, sounds, and channels intersecting the islands though without considering such title to be in question in the arbitration. It therefore considered that the eighth paragraph of the award was *ultra vires*. The memorandum concluded in respect of this point:

It may be that in the opinion of Sir John Coleridge the Sounds between the Scilly Islands could not be parts of the County of Cornwall but that is immaterial so far as the Duchy is concerned. The Title of the Duchy to the property rests upon the assertion of right by demise referred to and admitted by the Law Officers of the Crown in 1833.

(ii) THE 'PORTS OF THE SEA'

In the memorandum, the Duchy stated that the legislature had recognized the title of the Duchy to the ports of Cornwall by an Act passed in 1860, namely 23 & 24 Vic., c. 53, which had declared in s. 86 that the provisions for quieting titles within the county of Cornwall as against the Duchy, contained in 7 & 8 Vic., c. 105, did not apply to any 'property, right, claim or question concerning navigable rivers, estuaries, ports or branches of the sea or the

[92] The following material is in the Duchy records and on File 21369, retained at the Crown Estate Office.

fundus or soil thereof or the shores between high and low Water mark thereof respectively.'

The memorandum went on to claim that the Crown had never successfully controverted the argument based on the Padstow Local Act of 1844, 7 & 8 Vic., c. xxiv, and that the award of Sir John Coleridge, being confined in respect of this area to a definition of the tidal River Camel and its estuaries, did not affect the limits of this port. The memorandum summed up the argument relating to the ports of the county as follows:

On the whole it is submitted that the Title of the Duchy to the Ports of Cornwall is not affected or determined by the Act of 1858 and the award made under it: but that the right of the Duchy to the Soil of those Ports will be a fitting subject for arrangement with the Board of Trade in whom the interest of the Crown in the Bed of the Sea (excepting Minerals) would appear to be now vested under 'The Crown Lands Act 1866'.

(iii) THE ESTUARIES

The memorandum stated that around the coast of Cornwall there were many small creeks and inlets which could not be considered to be 'open sea being no part of the county of Cornwall'. The award of Sir John Coleridge, however, had made specific provision for only seven of the larger estuaries and in respect of the others 'the award is indefinite'. The memorandum submitted that '. . . if the attention of Sir John Coleridge were to be drawn to the smaller Creeks and Estuaries adverted to he would probably not object to make an alteration in his award, which would seem to be necessary for its logical correctness,'

The above memorandum was laid before the Attorney-General of the Duchy prior to the Council meeting of 30 November 1869, but it does not appear that anything more was done than to make a complaint to the Office of Woods to the effect that the Scilly Isles were outside the scope of the award, a complaint which seems to have been rejected.

The next development took place in 1889 but for the sake of continuity will be treated in this chapter. In that year, the occupier of the pier at St. Mary's, Scilly Isles, wished to lengthen it and was informed that the Board of Trade required him to take from the Crown a lease or conveyance of the foreshore and seabed on which the proposed extension was to rest. The Duchy objected to this demand on the ground that the opinion of the Law Officers, Horne A.G. and Campbell S.G., with Bellenden Ker, given on 4

January 1833 had declared, '. . . upon the whole that the Scilly Islands are to be considered as part of the possessions of the Duchy of Cornwall, and that they do not belong to the Crown *jure coronae*.'

The Board of Trade referred the matter to the Law Officers, Webster A.G. and Clarke S.G., together with Henry Sutton, and the reply, dated 13 April 1892, was given as follows:

We are of opinion that so much of the bed of the sea and the minerals thereunder between the several Isles known as the Scilly Isles as lie below low water mark and are outside the red line drawn by Sir John Taylor Coleridge on the Map referred to in his Award dated 28th October 1869, are as between the Crown and the Duchy vested in the Crown.

We may add that as regards the site of the proposed extension of the pier it follows that providing the site is below low water mark of the highest ordinary spring tides and is outside the red line above referred to, it is as between the Crown and the Duchy vested in the Crown.

The dispute ended on 2 December 1892, when the Duchy in a letter to the Board of Trade acquiesced in the award of Sir John Coleridge as it referred to the Scilly Isles.

Chapter V

The Queen v. *Ferdinand Keyn* : the *Franconia* Case[1]

A. Introduction

At about 4 p.m. on 17 February 1876, the German steamship *Franconia* and the British steamship *Strathclyde* collided in the Straits of Dover. The *Strathclyde* sank and in consequence thirty-nine persons on board lost their lives. The collision took place one and nine-tenths of a mile from the head of the Admiralty Pier at Dover and within two and a half miles of Dover beach. The *Franconia* was on a voyage from Hamburg to the West Indies, having called at Grimsby to pick up a pilot whom it was to land at Le Havre, while the *Strathclyde* was bound from London to India.

The victims of the disaster were picked up by passing vessels and their bodies landed at various ports. The *Franconia* proceeded to Dover. On 24 February 1876, the Coroner's jury at Deal in Kent returned a verdict of manslaughter against the German master of the ship, Ferdinand Keyn, in respect of the deaths of three persons whose bodies had been landed at that port.[2] On 9 March 1876, the East Middlesex Coroner's jury, sitting at Poplar, returned a similar verdict in respect of the death of Jessie Dorcas Young, who had drowned following the collision and whose body had been brought to London Docks.[3]

The inquisitions found by the Deal Coroner's jury came before Lord Coleridge C.J. on 13 March 1876 at the Kent Spring Assizes at Maidstone.[4] He told the Grand Jury that if the collision had taken place within three miles of the shore on the coast of Kent then the Court would have jurisdiction, otherwise not. In fact, the Crown did not prefer a bill of indictment against Keyn at Maidstone.

The Treasury Solicitor thereupon submitted a case for the opinion of the Attorney-General, Sir John Holker, the Solicitor-

---

[1] For a fuller description of the background to the case, see Marston, (1976) 92 *LQR* 93.

[2] The transcript of the Deal proceedings is in DPP 4/9.

[3] The transcript of the Poplar proceedings is in DPP 4/10.

[4] The transcript of the Maidstone proceedings is in DPP 4/10; see also *The Times*, 14 March 1876.

He argued that the Admiral had an original jurisdiction in the waters adjacent to the English coasts which in former times was exercised by the King's Bench as the court entitled to try all crimes committed within the realm. The following exchange then took place:

SIR R. PHILLIMORE Is your contention that within the space of three miles the Sovereign has the same right of property as on land?

SOLICITOR-GENERAL Yes. If it is necessary for me to contend that I shall contend that: but, I say, even if she has not the right of property, she has the right of jurisdiction, which is a totally different thing—not necessarily the right of property.

KELLY C.B. If there exists jurisdiction because it is British territory, how can you say that the prerogative of the Crown does not extend over it for all purposes?

SOLICITOR-GENERAL I say it does, my Lord.

KELLY C.B. Then why not for the purposes of property?

SOLICITOR-GENERAL The question of property may be a totally different one.

KELLY C.B. Of course.

SOLICITOR-GENERAL It may be, that there has been no such appropriation (to use plain language) of the bottom of the sea that would enable to Sovereign to take possession of it, and in that sense to make it property; and I believe that if it comes to be analysed, the whole rule of the three miles, which is a very elastic one and has only been settled in modern times . . . is governed by, and will be found to turn upon one very plain and common principle; it is, that portion of the land covered by water, over which the particular country exercises occupation and dominion and it is just as if you were trying in this country what is the right of this or that particular territory. Among nations it has been ascertained that there is a right of exercising and a power of exercising a kind of occupation and dominion over that portion of the Sea which washes the shore; or, to speak still more strictly perhaps, over that portion of the land covered with water in the immediate neighbourhood of the land.[13]

The Solicitor-General went on to argue that Dover Harbour had been built far beyond the low-water mark 'and unless this space be within our jurisdiction, and within our right, what right have we to carry out Dover Harbour a single foot'.[14] He concluded

[13] Ibid., 116–18.
[14] Ibid., 147.

the day's argument by drawing a distinction between the concept of the territorial belt as derived from municipal law and as derived from international law:

But if it is said that the existence of this territory of England is a matter of international law, I respectfully say that it is not so, that in the claim of this country (which was a far wider claim than it is now) was to exercise a territorial dominion over it because it was part of this country; and was what this country claimed to be part of its own territorial dominion, and that other nations have conceded to the extent of the three miles. It is known historically that it was claimed to a much wider extent, and for this purpose it is enough for me to contend for what is the international limit. But I should protest against saying that the existence of this band is only a question of international law. It is a question of user or power to hold, it is the right of each nation to hold within its power that amount of land which is covered with water immediately adjacent to its own coast.[15]

The Solicitor-General here was stating in different words what he had emphasized earlier in the day:

. . . it puts the case upon a very plain and common sense ground to say that it is the power of occupation and dominion of the particular State. It does not rest upon any very abstruse principles, but upon common sense principles—it is, that they have the power of occupying by force of arms, and laying claim to that particular piece of water.[16]

On resuming his argument a week later, the Solicitor-General cited at length from *Gammell* v. *The Lord Advocate* which he considered supported the right of royal property and privilege in the three-mile belt. Once again he drew a distinction between municipal law and international law:

I certainly should be sorry in an English Court of Justice to admit that the right of the Crown to those three miles is dependent upon the actual or presumed consent of foreign nations. Certainly it would be giving up that which the greatest lawyers in England from early times down to the present have contended against.[17]

The argument of the Crown on this and succeeding days concentrated more on the exercise of the alleged 'right' than on the existence of the right itself. In particular, the question of which court had the power to adjudicate upon crimes committed on the adjacent waters was raised. The Solicitor-General argued, on the

[15] Ibid., 173–4.
[16] Ibid., 121–2.
[17] Transcript, 13 May 1876, 161–2.

strength of passages from Hale's *Pleas of the Crown*, that the Court of King's Bench historically had cognizance of felonies and treasons done upon the 'narrow seas' outside the bodies of counties and that the cases were presented and tried by men drawn from the adjacent counties.[18] He denied, however, that the word 'port' automatically implied that jurisdiction was vested in the local courts:

. . . if the port is supposed to give jurisdiction by reason of its being a particular port, I think I can show that the port comprehends sometimes so much of the high seas that no part of it would be in England.[19]

The Solicitor-General then argued that the three-mile belt, which he took to be the modern version of the 'four seas', was subject to the common law. At this point Lush J. asked a question which went unanswered:

Can it be contended that the common law of the country without the aid of the legislature, can take cognizance of any offence committed within the three miles?[20]

In his reply, Benjamin emphasized what he considered to be the point at issue:

Is that territorial jurisdiction and dominion over the seas absolute or not? Is there a limitation or does it exist to the same extent as Her Majesty and Parliament have jurisdiction over the City of London? Is the jurisdiction and dominion of the same quality and extent and of the same unlimited character?[21]

After attacking the authority of the works of Selden, Grotius, and Hale cited by the Crown, Benjamin continued:[22]

. . . has Parliament by international law the right to pass such a statute, and whether it has the right or not, has it ever passed such an Act—has the jurisdiction in point of fact been exercised by Great Britain—the particular jurisdiction here asserted?

Lush J. There is no point about that, it there? There is no Act of Parliament.
. . . If the defendant is responsible, he is responsible by the common law.

Benjamin QC Yes, by the common law; and by the common law no authority is shown for these dicta that have been cited.

[18] Transcript, 19 May 1876, 101.
[19] Ibid., 143.
[20] ibid., 174.
[21] Ibid., 240–1.
[22] Ibid.

During the final part of Benjamin's reply, the following exchange took place:

LUSH J. Dominion and territory are not the same.

BENJAMIN QC They are not. My friend says that is territory and I say it is dominion.[23].

C. Court for Crown Cases Reserved—Second Hearing, June 1876[24]

The six judges present at the first hearing were divided on the issue. The legal reporter of *The Times* suggested on 24 June 1876 that Field and Lindley JJ. had favoured the Crown while the other four had favoured the defendant. There appears to have been a weight of opinion against the Crown which on 20 May 1876 provoked the Attorney-General, Sir John Holker, to remark in a letter to Lord Tenterden, Permanent Under-Secretary at the Foreign Office, that 'the judges, who form the court seem inclined to be very stupid in dealing with the question before them, which to my mind is perfectly clear in favour of the jurisdiction of our court'.[25]

Lord Cairns, the Lord Chancellor, then declared his intention of sitting on the augmented Court, an intention which was withdrawn after a 'strong expression of surprise' had been communicated to him by Cockburn C.J.[26] In the event, fourteen judges sat at Westminster Hall on 15 June 1876; the six who had sat in May, with the addition of Sir Alexander Cockburn (Lord Chief Justice of England), Lord Coleridge (Chief Justice of Common Pleas), Bramwell and Amphlett BB., Brett, Grove, Denman, and Archibald JJ.

During the opening speech of Benjamin, some of the judges stated which issue seemed to them to be involved. There was a drastic difference between the problem as seen by Cockburn C.J. and by Lush J.

COCKBURN C.J. If this is British territory for all purposes that territory is within the jurisdiction. It does not matter whether it is on the sea. It all comes to the question really and truly whether the three miles is

[23] Transcript, 20 May 1876, p. 32.
[24] The transcript for the second hearing, apart from that for 22 June 1876 which is missing, is in DPP 4/13. This is in a format similar to DPP 4/12 above. See also the summary of argument in 13 Cox Criminal Cases 403.
[25] FO 64/873.
[26] Cockburn to Cairns, 9 June 1876; PRO 30/51/10.

British territory, whether the British law, civil and criminal, and British jurisdiction applies to these three miles, as British territory.[27]

Lush J. Does the Court which tried him at the Old Bailey possess any criminal jurisdiction over vessels on the High Seas beyond what it possessed before in the Court of Admiralty, and, secondly, whether the Court of Admiralty ever possessed any criminal jurisdiction over a foreign ship—is not that the law?[28]

It was Lord Coleridge who first raised the problem of the bed of the sea. He stated:

. . . as far as I know, there have been repeated conflicting assertions of property over the soil at the bottom of the sea far below low water mark; and if so, I do not at present see where the line is to be drawn unless certainly within the three mile limit. And if the land at the bottom of the sea is the subject of property, I do not see myself on what we can stand except the dominion of the country extending for all purposes to that line.

Cockburn C.J. We are going to make a tunnel under the Channel all the way to France. Whose property is it?

Solicitor-General It will be provided for by Statute.[29]

Grove J. then raised the question of oyster beds, to which Benjamin replied that this was included in one of the four purposes for which jurisdiction could be exercised. He further pointed out that Grotius had said that a Sovereign could build piers, constructions or edifices of any sort for the purposes of navigation provided they did not interfere with the peaceful passage of the vessels of other nations.

The question of venue, which had been rather submerged during the latter part of the argument before the six judges in May, was now raised in a critical form:

Bramwell B. Let me ask at this pause, where was the indictment found, in Kent, or at the Old Bailey?

Solicitor-General At the Old Bailey. . . .

Bramwell B. It must be Admiralty then, otherwise the venue is wrong.

Benjamin QC Undoubtedly.

Solicitor-General If your Lordship means it is not county it is so. I

[27] Transcript, 15 June 1876, pp. 54–5.
[28] Ibid., 65–6.
[29] Ibid., 109–10.

concede that. If this were within the county, then the venue would be wrong.

Lush J. It must be on the high seas, not within the body of the county.

Solicitor-General If your Lordship will allow me, I rather contest that part of it. If it is within the county then the venue and the indictment are wrong.

Lush J. If it is within the county, then it is not within the Admiralty.

Solicitor-General Certainly.

Bramwell B. If it is on the high seas, it does not matter whether it is within three miles or three hundred miles.

Solicitor-General That is what I shall venture to contest most strenuously.[30]

Cockburn C.J. took up the same point:

Supposing Parliament were to pass a law that the three miles from the shore should henceforth be part of the soil or territory of England; that would make British law, I take it, applicable to that extent, civil and criminal.

Benjamin QC Yes.

Cockburn C.J. And then, if a murder were committed, or any other offences, within that three miles, you would not want a special Act of Parliament to say who should or who should not be the subject of the indictment.

Benjamin QC I would not concede that last proposition, to that extent, for this reason—

Cockburn C.J. No doubt there would be technical difficulties which would have to be got over. In the first place, it would be no part of any county or parish. I do not know what you would do with the venue either formerly or what you would do with the venue now.[31]

In opening the case for the Crown, the Solicitor-General stated his argument with more clarity than had appeared from the transcript of the first hearing in May:

. . . in the first instance one must meet the larger and wider question whether it is within English jurisprudence at all, because if I satisfy your Lordships that it is within English jurisprudence, it then, of course, becomes necessary for the purpose of this particular case, to show that

[30] Ibid., 204–5.
[31] Ibid., 250–1.

the venue here is properly laid, and that it is properly charged to be within the jurisdiction of the Central Criminal Court . . .[32]

He cited Hale for the proposition that England had a certain maritime territory, to which Cockburn C.J. replied that the claims of the early English writers in respect of maritime areas were vast:

As to the jurisdiction claimed by Selden, I confess that I do not value his authority very highly. I do not say that as a Judge, but generally speaking. Anybody who contended that the dominion of this country extended over to the coast of Norway, why one could only smile at it.[33]

Lord Coleridge at this point made the comment, with which the Solicitor-General agreed, that because a claim was exaggerated did not mean that it was without foundation. The Solicitor-General went on to argue that England had the marine belt for all purposes and that the English common law applied to it just as it did to the centre of the county of Middlesex. He continued:

Now it does not at all follow that that part of the three mile zone which is always covered up with water is part of the county. On the contrary, I think it will be found it is out of the body of the county, and yet it is part of the sea of England.[34]

He then urged that the territorial belt was part of the realm of England on the authority of Coke's statement that 'if a man be upon the sea of England, he is within the kingdom or realm of England, and within the ligeance of the King of England, as of his Crown of England. And yet *altum mare* is out of the jurisdiction of the common law, and within the jurisdiction of the Lord Admiral, whose jurisdiction is very ancient, and long before the reign of Edward III.'[35] He relied also on Hale's view that 'the narrow sea, adjoining to the coast of England, is part of the waste and demesnes and dominions of the king of England, whether it lie within the body of any county or not.'[36]

The Solicitor-General then turned to the question of property in the subsoil:

. . . probably it will be familiar to your Lordships that under the sea far below low water mark on the coast of Northumberland there are several mines. There is the Botallack mine in Cornwall which goes, I think, some

[32] Transcript, 16 June 1876, pp. 161–2.
[33] Ibid., 171–2.
[34] Ibid., 182.
[35] Coke, *Commentary upon Littleton*, s. 439.
[36] Hale, *De Jure Maris*, ch. 4.

miles under the sea, and there, I think the persons who are there are under the protection of the English law.[37]

Although the Lord Chief Justice immediately expressed a doubt on this last assertion, the discussion on the particular mines was never taken further as the Solicitor-General was here diverted into another line of argument. The status of the subsoil, however, continued to be discussed. The Solicitor-General, in answer to a question from the Bench, stated that he did not think that more soil than was necessary for the construction of the Channel tunnel could be appropriated since there was no power of dominion over the adjoining soil.[38] At this point, Cockburn C.J. drew a distinction between the appropriation of the subsoil and the appropriation of the surface:

I take it, Mr Solicitor, that a man might encroach on the property of his neighbour by pushing his mine too far, and although he may be liable to the defendant in his attempt if an action were brought to restrain him, yet if he succeeded in undermining the surface and the soil of his neighbour and to do that for a sufficient length of time to give him a title by prescription he would maintain his right to what he got below the surface, but that would not give him the right to the surface of the ground.[39]

A little later, he stated the same argument in terms of international law:

Supposing the nations at large have a right to pass over the surface. You may still appropriate that which is below it without appropriating the surface. That is all it amounts to. It does not follow that because you are undermining the sea that therefore the soil above is within the Crown of England at all.[40]

The Solicitor-General was not diverted from his argument by these critical comments. He argued, 'I propose to show that with reference to property and property in the sea and in the soil below the sea within that limited area the English courts and the English Legislature have recognized a right of property in the Crown.'[41]

The examples he cited were attacked by some of the Bench. Kelly C.B. remarked pertinently that the power to legislate could not be the test for ownership; the legislation regarding the

[37] Transcript, 16 June 1876, p. 259.
[38] Ibid., 260–1.
[39] Ibid., 261–2.
[40] Ibid., 265.
[41] Ibid., 266.

Admiral's jurisdiction extended to seas the world over. The principal judicial decision cited by the Solicitor-General, *Gammell* v. *Commissioners of Woods and Forests*, was doubted by Cockburn C.J. as authority for the proposition advanced by the Crown. In this case, which concerned salmon fisheries in Scotland, Lord Cranworth had said about the vagueness of the extent of the fishery 'an exactly similar doubt might be raised as to the prerogative right of the Crown, in England at least, to the bed of the sea, because that is undefined, yet nobody doubts that such a right exists.'[42] Lord Wensleydale in the same court had added that it would hardly be possible to extend the fishery beyond three miles 'which by the acknowledged law of nations belong to the coast of the country'. Cockburn C.J., however, took the view that the case did not involve any question of a proprietary right since the 'right of taking fish is not property'.[43]

The problem of venue reappeared later when the Solicitor-General, citing Hale's *Pleas of the Crown*, argued that the King's Bench exercised a concurrent jurisdiction over treasons and felonies committed on the 'narrow seas'. Lord Coleridge then summed up the Crown's argument as follows:

> As I understand your argument (we must go by steps) it is this. You say that there was the English jurisdiction exercised in the same way over these seas in cases of felony—that before that time—and I am now talking of King Edward III—that it was exercised by the King's Bench. Then there was a dispute between the common law courts and the Admiralty Courts, and that there was first of all an order which may have been altogether beyond the powers . . . in the King's Council; and that subsequently there were Acts of Parliament regulating the exercise of that jurisdiction, and making over to the Admiralty certain powers which were therefore exercised by the King's Bench.

SOLICITOR-GENERAL That is precisely what I am endeavouring to show.[44]

---

[42] (1859) 3 Macqueen 419, 465.

[43] Transcript, 16 June 1876, p. 284. The report in *The Times* of 17 June 1876 contains at this point the following exchange which does not appear in the transcript:

Lord Coleridge said certainly the Law Lords in that case seemed to lay it down that the Crown had the right of property within the three miles; and if there was property it would seem there was dominion, and if dominion, then apparently jurisdiction.

The Solicitor-General said he certainly understood that all jurists agreed that where there was dominion there was sovereign jurisdiction, including criminal jurisdiction.

[44] Transcript, 21 June 1876, pp. 245–6. The Crown relied on Hale, *Pleas of the Crown*, Part II, ch. III.

On 23 June 1876, Benjamin began his reply. He continued to insist that the Admiral never had jurisdiction over foreign ships. The following exchange then took place:

COCKBURN C.J. Then I understand you to make two points; firstly, that [the *locus in quo*] is not within the realm of England, and, secondly, if it is, that the common law does not apply to it.

BENJAMIN QC Yes, my Lord, it requires an Act of Parliament.

LUSH J. It seems that originally five hundred years ago, it was not within the realm, and I do not know how it can become so by the consent of foreign nations.

BENJAMIN QC Richard II says it is not a part of the realm in the statute. The statute says the high seas are out of the realm of England.

COCKBURN C.J. . . . Supposing a general consensus of nations arising in modern times to allow every State which borders on the high seas to treat that belt of three miles which otherwise would be common to all nations as its own as far as it thinks proper. Then we come to the consideration of whether that consent at once annexes the three miles so as to make it part of the territory of the realm, or whether it simply amounts to this, the legislature of the country—the legislative portion of the government—may deal with that three mile belt as it pleases, without any reference to international law. The question is, has it done so?[45]

Benjamin sought to draw a distinction between the waters of the territorial belt and the soil beneath. He argued that the case of *Gann* v. *Free Fishers of Whitstable*, rather than being a decision against his client, in fact was in his favour since the House of Lords had held that although the Crown owned the land under the water, it did not own the water itself. He continued:

But what I say is that British territory *qua* territory may be the ground. The water is not British territory and does not belong to Great Britain. . . .

LORD COLERIDGE C.J. Do you admit that the soil is in the Crown of England?

BRETT J. The three miles.

BENJAMIN QC Everybody can go down there; it belongs to nobody on earth.

BRETT J. Do you admit the soil to be in the Crown of England for these three miles?

[45] Transcript, 23 June 1876, pp. 99–100.

BENJAMIN QC I do admit it, if you can go three miles below the ground that it is in the Crown of England. What is called the foreshore belongs to the Crown.

COCKBURN C.J. We are dealing with the three miles.

GROVE J. Do you admit that below low water mark it is in the Crown?

BENJAMIN QC Yes.

GROVE J. Where to?

BENJAMIN QC I admit that the Crown can take the land below low water mark as long as it takes possession for building piers, and so on, or mining under it. . . .

DENMAN J. It really seems to come to this. The writers on the law of nations and the cases that have been decided on the law of nations only contemplate practically daylight and do not contemplate the visionary assertion of things at the bottom of the sea. They speak first of the surface of the water as that which is for the common use of all mankind. They speak of the common surface of the soil being used by man. It never occurred to them that the bed of the Atlantic belonged to any man yet we are occupying it by cables and I suppose to the extent of our occupying it by cables it is to that extent liable to our jurisdiction, and that no nation can encroach upon that spot where we have laid our cables, because we laid the first cable and nobody ever dreamt before of laying their cables there.

BRETT J. Do you admit that below high water mark it belonged to the party who is the first possessor or do you admit that it belonged to the sovereign of England?

BENJAMIN QC If it is question of property I really do not know. I only know that there are mines which have extended out below the sea and which do belong to private individuals, but whether according to feudal tenure or a fact those mines underground in former times could be claimed by the Crown after being opened and the subject ousted on the ground of the paramount right of the Crown I cannot undertake to say.[46]

Benjamin next attempted to turn the argument towards the implications of the word 'dominion', which, he said, did not mean 'property'.[47] The Bench, however, was still keen to discuss the bed and subsoil of the sea:

GROVE J. Supposing an adjacent landowner has a mine under the sea but no grant of what is commonly called the foreshore; he drives his mines

[46] Ibid., 136–40.
[47] Ibid., 141.

under the foreshore. How would you claim that then if he goes further on?

BENJAMIN QC I say I do not know as to that.

GROVE J. That has been constantly discussed in the case of *Attorney-General* v. *Chambers* and other cases. . . .

If the Crown has the sea shore down to low water mark and then the person proceeds beyond it without licence from the Crown—

COCKBURN C.J. It depends upon whether the Crown has any right to territory beyond the foreshore. . . .

It is admitted on all hands that the foreshore where not granted away belongs to the Crown. If a subject undermines this foreshore he is committing an encroachment upon the rights of the Crown and can be restrained from doing so. But supposing he has got the licence from the Crown to go to the limit of the foreshore and then he goes beyond that limit and then the Crown were to claim as against him? Surely the decision would depend on whether the Crown had any right to go beyond the foreshore.

BENJAMIN QC Yes.[48]

Benjamin, supported by Bramwell B. from the Bench, here took the view that the present discussion was irrelevant to the question at issue in the case, which, according to him, was whether the admiral had jurisdiction over the crime. Brett J., however, thought that the discussion was relevant to those who did not hold the view that the case turned simply on a point of venue. Cockburn C.J. was clearly reluctant to leave the subject of the seabed:

Supposing that the land at the bottom of the sea is territory of England according to English law, whoever has land covered by water is the owner of the water that covers the land—does that apply to the sea? . . .
On the high sea the ship does not touch the bottom. It is floating on the water, and unless the property in the water passes or attaches itself as a necessary accessory to the property in the land, the ship in the water is not on the land.[49]

The discussion then turned to the question whether the sea could be the subject of property and whether there could be property in the fish swimming in the open sea. It is clear from Benjamin's closing remarks that such questions were irrelevant to his main argument:

[48] Ibid., 141–4.
[49] Ibid., 146.

Then, my Lords, I say further, that it is perfectly indifferent to me what may be the nature or extent of the rights of the Crown in the present case or what may be the law of nations upon the subject of the rights of the Crown, or the dominion of the country over three miles of sea . . . I adhere to this proposition as the sheet anchor of my cause, that whatever be the power of England over these three miles, it is for the Government of England to exercise that power, and until the Government exercises that power, the Courts should hold their hands.[50]

D. Summary of the Arguments

(i) FOR THE ACCUSED

His principal argument claimed that the Admiral, in whose jurisdiction the crime was averred to have been committed, had never had the power to adjudicate upon crimes committed on board foreign ships on the high sea. Neither had the King's Bench ever exercised such a jurisdiction. Even if the three-mile belt were part of the realm of England by virtue of the common law or, alternatively or cumulatively, by virtue of the incorporation into English law of a rule of public international law, there was no jurisdiction in any English court to try crimes committed on board foreign ships in these waters since the Admiral was restrained by ancient statutes from adjudicating upon crimes committed within the realm. On the other hand, it was admitted by the Crown that the local courts administering common law had no power of adjudication over crimes committed below low-water mark on the open coast, i.e., outside the counties. Legislation was required to confer such jurisdiction and none had been passed which applied to the facts of the present case. In any event, the authorities supporting the claim of the Crown to the property in the seabed and subsoil of the belt were of no relevance to the right of property or jurisdiction in the waters above.

(ii) FOR THE CROWN

The three-mile belt, as the modern version of the 'four seas', was part of the realm of England. Consequently, English law applied to all persons and vessels therein. This conclusion was based both on common law authorities, who claimed that the seabed and subsoil adjacent to the coasts of England, as well as the waters above, were the dominions and property of the Crown, and also on

[50] Ibid., 241–2.

public international law authorities. It followed that English courts had the power to try crimes committed in the belt whether on board British or foreign ships and irrespective of the nationality of the accused. The Court of King's Bench at one time exercised this power but the belt was within the Admiral's area of adjudication, being 'high seas'. The ancient statutes restraining the Admiral from exercising jurisdiction within the realm were inapplicable to the present case since the word 'realm' in those statutes must be interpreted as being confined to the counties. Alternatively, there was a concurrent jurisdiction over the belt in the same way as this existed to some extent over certain inland waters.[51]

E. The Judgments[52]

The judgments, which took two days to deliver, were read on 11 and 12 November 1876 in open court. As Archibald J. had died between the second hearing and the delivery of judgment, thirteen judges participated in the decision. By seven to six, the Court resolved to quash the conviction of Keyn at the Central Criminal Court in the previous April. Cockburn C.J., Kelly C.B., Bramwell J.A.,[53] Lush and Field JJ., Sir Robert Phillimore, and Pollock B. formed the majority; Lord Coleridge C.J., Brett and Amphlett JJ.A., Grove, Denman, and Lindley JJ. dissented. In view of the controversy to which the decision has given rise, the individual judgments will now be summarized with the object of setting out the *ratio decidendi* of each. In this way it may be possible to ascertain the *ratio decidendi* of the case itself, which, according to orthodox legal theory, is the only part of the case which possesses any binding force within the hierarchy of English courts.

(i) THE MAJORITY JUDGES

Sir Robert Phillimore first considered the position in municipal law. The high seas began at the low-water mark, which was the seaward limit of the county. There was no sufficient authority for the conclusion that the high seas were ever considered to be within the realm or that the realm of England extended beyond the

[51] Transcript, 16 June 1876, p. 183. The last point was never developed.
[52] (1876) L.R. 2 Ex. D. 63.
[53] Bramwell, Brett, and Amphlett JJ.A. had recently been promoted to the rank of 'Justices of Appeal'.
[54] (1876) 2 Ex.D. 63, 65–86.

seaward limits of the county. There was no instance of the exercise of criminal jurisdiction over a foreign vessel for an offence committed outside inland waters of the realm.

He then considered the position in international law. Although a State was entitled to a certain extension of territory beyond low-water mark, this was for the attainment of particular objects only. It did not mean that the State was competent to exercise within this area the same rights of 'jurisdiction and property' which appertained to it in respect to its lands and ports. This conclusion seemed to be that favoured by the legislature since criminal legislation which applied to ships below low-water mark was framed exclusively for British subjects and ships or related to the protection and peace of the State.

Bramwell J.A.[55] took what he called a 'very narrow-minded view' of the matter. There was no authority to support the argument that the Admiralty ever had a criminal jurisdiction in matters occurring within a distance of three miles which it would not have had if they had occurred beyond that distance.

Kelly C.B.[56] agreed 'substantially' with the judgments of both Sir Robert Phillimore and Cockburn C.J. He remarked that a treaty, or express agreement or a uniform, general, and long-continued usage acquiesced in by the foreign State affected would be required for England to exercise criminal jurisdiction over foreign ships at sea. The authority of writers was not enough to confer this jurisdiction on English courts.

Cockburn C.J.[57] delivered the longest of the majority judgments. Like Sir Robert Phillimore, he discussed both international and municipal law, and he frequently moved from one to the other in the course of his judgment. He held first that the place where the collision occurred was high seas, out of the body of any county and outside the jurisdiction of the common law courts. The old cases mentioned by Hale did not support a contrary conclusion. The place was thus within the area over which the Admiral had jurisdiction, a jurisdiction which had been transferred unchanged to the common law courts including the Central Criminal Court. However, the Admiral's jurisdiction was in practice confined to English ships, except in cases of piracy.

The Lord Chief Justice then turned to the argument that the adjacent waters formed part of the 'realm or territory of the

[55] Ibid., 149–50.
[56] Ibid., 150–1.
[57] Ibid., 159–238.

Crown'. He rejected outright the views of writers such as Hale and Selden on this matter. He pointed out that the Crown's argument in the case had been presented in different and conflicting ways. At one time it was argued that the sea and its bed formed part of the territory or realm as though it were so much land; at another time it was argued that sovereignty simply attached to the sea. However, it followed from the terms of the statutes of Richard II[58] that the realm was coterminous with the counties; no subsequent statute had changed this fundamental position. Cockburn C.J. considered that the assertions of ancient writers claiming the bed of the sea to be part of the realm of England and of the territorial possessions of the Crown belonged to the 'wild notion of sovereignty over the whole of the narrow seas'; Hale himself, moreover, had stopped short of saying that the seabed was part of the realm. The Lord Chief Justice rejected the early authorities: 'It seems to me to follow that when the sovereignty and jurisdiction from which the property in the soil of the sea was inferred is gone, the territorial property which was suggested to be consequent upon it must necessarily go with it.'[59] He conceded that where the sea or the bed on which it rested could be physically occupied permanently it might be made subject to occupation in the same way as unoccupied territory. The Cornwall Submarine Mines Act 1858 was not authority for a general assertion that the Crown held the property in the bed of the sea as it was merely the settlement of a dispute between the Crown and the Duchy.

Cockburn C.J. then turned to the legislation applying to ships at sea. By applying the rule of statutory construction that the British Parliament could not be assumed to intend to legislate as to the rights and liabilities of foreigners, he concluded that there had been no assertion of legislative authority with respect to the general application of the penal law to foreigners within the three-mile belt. None of the special cases, such as revenue and pilotage, showed how far without legislation the law could apply to foreign ships.

He discussed in detail the position in international law, admitting that 'it is out of this extravagent assertion of sovereignty that the doctrine of the three mile jurisdiction, asserted on the part of the Crown, and which, the older claim being necessarily abandoned, we are now called upon to consider, has sprung up'.[60] After a

[58] 13 Rich. 2, c. 5; 15 Rich. 2, c. 3.
[59] (1876) 2 Ex. D. 63. 196.
[60] Ibid., 176.

review of the writers, both British and foreign, he pointed out that every shade of opinion existed regarding the extent and legal nature of the rights possessed by a State over the adjacent belt of sea. Even though all writers appeared to be agreed that the power of the littoral State to deal with the three-mile zone existed, it did not follow that, in the absence of legislation, the 'ordinary law of the local state will extend over the waters in question'.[61] Writers could not make law and there were no treaties or even usage accepting such powers.

Finally, he declared that even if the three-mile belt formed part of the 'territory or realm' of England, 'so that jurisdiction has been acquired over it', there was no court competent to deal with the present case:

> To put this shortly. To sustain this indictment the littoral sea must still be considered as part of the high seas, and as such, under the jurisdiction of the admiral. But the admiral never had criminal jurisdiction over foreign ships on the high seas. How, when exercising the functions of a British judge, can he, or those acting in substitution for him, assume a jurisdiction which heretofore he did not possess, unless authorized by statute? On the other hand, if this sea is to be considered as territory, so as to make a foreigner within it liable to the law of England, it cannot come under the jurisdiction of the Admiralty.[62]

Lush J.[63] agreed entirely in the conclusions of Cockburn C.J. and 'in the main' with his reasoning. He wished, however, to deny that Parliament was incompetent to legislate for the belt of sea termed 'by a convenient metaphor' the territorial waters of Great Britain. But until Parliament had so legislated, the waters in question were outside the realm and the extent of the common law. They were high seas and on the high seas the Admiralty jurisdiction was confined to British ships.

Pollock B. and *Field J.* concurred in the judgment of Cockburn C.J. without delivering separate judgments.

(ii) THE MINORITY JUDGES

Lindley J.[64] held that the statutes 28 Hen. 8, c.15 and 39 Geo. 3, c.37 had extended the criminal law over the high seas so far as it was competent for Parliament to do so. It was not necessary to decide whether the adjacent seas were part of the realm. In view of

[61] Ibid., 193.
[62] Ibid., 230.
[63] Ibid., 238–9.
[64] Ibid., 86–99.

the international law rule that 'every state has full power to enact and enforce what laws it thinks proper for the preservation of peace and the protection of its own interests' in the three-mile belt, it followed that these statutes made punishable by English law all offences within this belt. There was no principle or authority for holding that the Admiralty had no criminal jurisdiction over persons on board foreign ships on the high seas within this distance of the coasts.

Denman J.[65] based his judgment on a second point in the case, which was rejected by the majority judges, namely that the crime had in law taken place on board the British ship. On the principal point, he entirely agreed with the judgment of Brett J.A.

Grove J.[66] concluded, after a review of decisions, statutes and the views of writers, that there was a 'jurisdiction' for certain purposes in tribunals of the country within the three miles. The dominion over the belt was absolute and there was no distinction between a ship in passage and a ship at anchor. In the latter case, he stated, the ship was availing itself of the soil, which, to give the country a right of interference, must be assumed to be a part of the territory of that country. If so, said Grove J., the water over that soil must also belong to that territory: *cuius est solum eius usque ad caelum.* As the Admiral had concurrent jurisdiction with the common law courts in a port or haven, as illustrated by *R.* v. *John Bruce,*[67] so therefore, according to Grove J., there must be a similar jurisdiction over the three-mile belt. He did not deal with the second point in the case.

Amphlett J.A.[68] considered that the question was whether the locality of the offence was within the dominion or sovereignty of England. If so, the law of England would attach thereto without the necessity of legislation. He took the view that the House of Lords in *Gammell* v. *Commissioners of Woods and Forests* had decided that not only was the three-mile zone within the territory of England, but that the actual property therein was vested in the Crown. The last point was confirmed by the legislature in the Cornwall Submarine Mines Act 1858. By international law the position was the same. As the locality was within English territory, Amphlett J.A. considered that it was clearly within the former jurisdiction of the Admiralty. He rejected, however, the Crown's

[65] Ibid., 99–108.
[66] Ibid., 108–17.
[67] (1812) 2 Leach 1093.
[68] (1876) 2 Ex. D. 63, 117–24.

argument that the crime had been committed on board the British ship.

Brett J.A.[69] opened his judgment by emphasizing the point made in argument by Benjamin QC, namely, that even if the three-mile belt were part of the territory of England, the Central Criminal Court, or indeed any Court hitherto constituted, did not have jurisdiction to apply the criminal law to such a case. Brett J.A. considered that the question what was or what was not a part of the realm did not fall to the judges to decide but to Parliament. However, in respect of the open seas there had been no such declaration; the Court must answer the question. After examining a number of writers on international law, Brett J.A. concluded that substantial agreement existed that the coastal State had sovereignty and dominion over the adjacent sea, and, where these were found, jurisdiction was necessarily given or imported.

Once let it be fixed what is the sea of England—and this is high authority that such sea is within the kingdom, and realm, and dominion of the sovereign—that is to say, once agree that the three miles are the sea of England, and then it follows that the rights of England within that sea are as if it were land territory, and are the same as in any other part of the kingdom, and realm, and dominion of the sovereign.[70]

'Brett J.A. held that by the law of nations, made by the tacit consent of substantially all nations, the open sea within three miles of the coast was a part of the territory of the adjacent nation, as much as and completely as if it were land constituting a part of the territory of such a nation.

He then turned to the question whether the Central Criminal Court had jurisdiction in the case, which, he said, was a strictly municipal question and had no regard to international law. He proceeded on the presumption that there was some Court appointed to adminster law in that part of the national territory. The ancient authorities were consistent with a criminal jurisdiction over all ships being vested in the Admiral, at least in the seas adjacent to the English coasts. The word 'realm' in the statues of Richard II meant that part of it within counties.

Brett J.A., however, rejected the Crown's contention that the crime was committed on board the British ship.

Lord Coleridge C.J.[71] declared that on the first point in the case he

[69] Ibid., 124–49.
[70] Ibid., 140. Brett J.A. cited Coke, *Commentary upon Littleton*, s. 439.
[71] Ibid., 151–8.

agreed without qualification with the reasoning of Brett J.A. and Lindley J., and on the second point with the reasoning of Denman J. though not without some doubt. In his opinion the crime was committed within the realm of England and there was jurisdiction to try it. He asserted that the 'realm of England, the territory of England, the property of the State and Crown of England over the water and the land beneath it, extends at least so far beyond the line of low water on the English coast as to include the place where this offence was committed'.[72]

This conclusion was supported by the legislature when it enacted the Cornwall Submarine Mines Act 1858. This was passed after an arbitration before Sir John Patteson between the Crown and the Duchy of Cornwall. Lord Coleridge was of the opinion, having studied the documents in this arbitration and in the later arbitration before his father, Sir John Coleridge, that the whole argument of the Crown was founded on the proposition that the *fundus maris* below low-water mark, beyond the limits of the county of Cornwall, belonged in property to the Crown, and not to the first occupant. According the Lord Coleridge, the legislature, in enacting the Cornwall Submarine Mines Act 1858, had accepted this view, since this Act declared and enacted that the mines and minerals under the open sea were 'part of the soil and territorial possession of the Crown'. This could not be limited to the seabed adjacent to Cornwall. He added:

We have therefore it seems the express and definite authority of Parliament for the proposition that the realm does not end with low-water mark, but that the open sea and the bed of it are part of the realm and of the territory of the sovereign. If so it follows that British law is supreme over it, and that the law must be administered by some tribunal. It cannot, for the reasons assigned by my Brother Brett, be administered by the judges of oyer and terminer; it can be, and always could be, by the Admiralty, and if by the Admiralty, then by the Central Criminal Court.[73]

The judge also held in favour of the Crown on the second point in the case.

(iii) THE RATIO DECIDENDI OF R. V. KEYN

It is not proposed to discuss in this work the complexities of the concept of *ratio decidendi*. It is sufficient to determine, on orthodox

[72] Ibid., 155.
[73] Ibid., 157–8.

grounds, which proposition of law in the case has binding force on later courts.[74] In order to do this, the following premises are adopted:[75]

(a) The *ratio decidendi* of a case is the rule of law acted on by the court in arriving at its final order.

(b) In multi-judge courts, where there are judges who dissent from the order, the *ratio decidendi* of a case is the rule of law acted on by the majority of the assenting judges, this majority also comprising a majority of the whole court.

(c) In determining the *ratio decidendi* of a case, account cannot be taken of the judgments of those who dissent from the final order of the court.

(d) Where some assenting judges act on a certain rule and other assenting judges act on a narrower version of the same rule, the *ratio decidendi* of the case may be constructed from the lowest common denominator, i.e., the narrower rule.

In *R.* v. *Keyn*, thirteen judges took part in the decision, six of whom dissented from the order made; thus, according to premise (b) above, the *ratio decidendi* of the case, if there is one, must be a rule acted on by all seven assenting judges. Bramwell J.A., however, delivered a judgment which was narrower than those of the other majority judges. He held that Keyn's conviction should be quashed on the ground that the Admiral never had a criminal jurisdiction over foreign ships anywhere on the open sea. It cannot be assumed that he agreed or disagreed with the view of Cockburn C.J., concurred in by Kelly C.B., Pollock B., Lush and Field JJ., to the effect that the adjacent sea and its bed were not part of the realm of England. On the other hand, these judges, together with Sir Robert Phillimore, must have agreed with the narrower view of Bramwell J.A.

On this analysis, the *ratio decidendi* of *R.* v. *Keyn* is confined to the extent, *ratione materiae*, of the Admiral's power of adjudication; thus a later court, though bound by this *ratio*, might still hold consistently with theory that the adjacent sea, seabed and subsoil, or any combination of them, are part of the realm of England, or, *a fortiori*, territory of the Crown lying outside that realm.

---

[74] *Keyn* is binding on courts lower than the Court of Appeal and probably on the Court of Appeal itself. It is not, of course, binding on the House of Lords.

[75] See Rupert Cross, *Precedent in English Law*, 3rd ed., 1977, ch. 2 for a general discussion of *ratio decidendi* and *obiter dictum*.

Chapter VI

The Reaction to *R*. v. *Keyn*

A. The Events of 1877

The decision of the Court for Crown Cases Reserved came as a shock to many in Whitehall and Westminster. W. Malcolm minuted in the Colonial Office in October 1877 that the case 'seems to have sent people mad'.[1] The Lord Chancellor, Lord Cairns, in a letter to the Secretary of State for the Colonies, wrote:

I do not concur with the opinion of the majority of the Judges in the 'Franconia' case, and, whether that opinion be right or wrong, I have no doubt that there is legislative power for the purpose of repressing criminal acts within the three mile limit round the coasts.[2]

Similarly, the Secretary of State for Foreign Affairs wrote in a letter to the German Ambassador that 'the prosecution was instituted in perfect good faith, no one imagining that there was any want of jurisdiction'.[3]

The Law Officers themselves, who had been responsible for arguing the case in the courts, at first expressed some caution about its effect. In an opinion given to the Foreign Office on a draft Order in Council for the regulation of the exercise of the Crown's jurisdiction over British subjects in Western Polynesia, Holker A.G. and Giffard S.G., together with Parker Deane as unofficial legal adviser on international law, stated on 3 January 1877:

That if the judgment in the 'Franconia' case is to be taken to decide that the sea washing the shores of a State to the distance of three miles is not part of such State, we should, in deference to such decision, come to the conclusion that under the Pacific Islanders Protection Act, 1875, s. 6, Her Majesty had no power to make by Order in Council laws which should affect British subjects on board British or foreign ships whilst on such portion of the sea.[4]

On 26 January 1877, F.S. Reilly, who was acting as *ad hoc*

[1] CO 23/217, fo. 448.
[2] Cairns to Carnarvon, 3 May 1877: CO 83/15.
[3] Salisbury to Munster, 10 June 1878: FO 83/732.
[4] CO 885/12; Law Officers' Opinions to the Colonial Office, vol. III, No. 121.

parliamentary counsel in the above matter, commented on this
report:

It is, I conceive, the established rule in English law that legislative power
exercisable on land is exercisable for a distance of three miles out to sea;
and, I think, there is nothing in the decision in the *Franconia* Case to
shake this rule[5]

Reilly's precision was not shared by the Law Officers who, on 16
March 1877, in a further report to the Foreign Office on the draft
Order in Council, used the ambiguous word 'jurisdiction'. They
wrote: 'That the case of the 'Franconia' seems to us to place limits
upon the exercise of any jurisdiction on board foreign ships below
low-water mark, and to show a distinction between land and the
sea below low-water mark, though within the three mile zone.'[6]

Meanwhile, the courts were soon obliged to consider the
implications of *Keyn*. On 13 January 1877, in the Common Pleas
Division, the case of *Harris* v. *Owners of the 'Franconia'* came before
Lord Coleridge C.J., Grove, and Denman JJ., all of whom had
dissented in *Keyn*. This was a civil action to recover damages for
the death of one of the persons on board the *Strathclyde*. The plaintiff
had obtained an order for service of the writ of summons on the
defendants in Hamburg. Benjamin QC, on behalf of the defendants, argued that the cause of action had not arisen within the
jurisdiction of the English courts and that therefore the order
should not be made. In upholding this argument, Lord Coleridge
C.J. said:

It seems to me to be quite plain that the decision in *R.* v. *Keyn* is binding
upon all the Courts. The ratio decidendi of that judgment is, that, for the
purpose of jurisdiction (except where under special circumstances and
in special Acts parliament has thought fit to extend it), the territory of
England and the sovereignty of the Queen stops at low-water mark.[7]

The other two judges agreed, Denman J. remarking, 'The case
of *R.* v. *Keyn* clearly goes the length of holding that, for all
purposes, apart from any express statutory provision, the moment
you get beyond low-water mark you get beyond the jurisdiction
within which the Queen's writs run.'[8]

Two weeks later, on 29 January 1877, Lord Coleridge C.J. and

[5] CO 83/15.
[6] CO 885/12; Law Officers' Opinions to the Colonial Office, vol. III, No. 129.
[7] (1877) 2 C.P.D. 173, 177.
[8] Ibid., 178.

Grove J. decided the case of *Blackpool Pier Co. Ltd. & South Blackpool Jetty Co. Ltd.* v. *Fylde Union Assessment Committee.*[9] The question was whether the appellants were rateable in respect of their occupation of that part of a pier which projected below low-water mark. The structure in question, Blackpool North Pier, commenced at Talbot Square and extended 540 feet into the sea beyond low-water mark by means of an iron frame resting on piles driven into the bed of the sea. The land below low-water mark had been acquired by the company 'by purchase, grant, or otherwise from the Crown dated the 23rd day of July, 1862'. Lord Coleridge C.J., clearly on the basis of *Keyn*, held that the part of the pier below low-water mark lay 'beyond the realm of England'; it was not an artificial accretion from the sea within the meaning of s. 27 of the Poor Law Amendment Act 1868[10] so as to be included within the adjoining parish. Grove J. concurred, stating that the part in question was 'out of the jurisdiction of the realm of England'.

This case was followed on 14 February 1877 by the opinion of the Judicial Committee of the Privy Council in *Direct United States Cable Co. Ltd.* v. *Anglo-American Telegraph Co. Ltd.*[11] on appeal from the Supreme Court of Newfoundland. The point at issue was whether the Newfoundland legislature could validly exercise authority over the laying of a cable on the bed of Conception Bay at a spot more than three miles from the nearest point on the shore. Benjamin QC, as counsel for the respondents, argued successfully that this could be done. His main argument was that the spot in question was situated within a bay, and bays were within the national territory. In answer to the objection that *Keyn* had prohibited the exercise of jurisdiction beyond three miles, Benjamin replied that 'all that the *Franconia* case decided was that the realm of England in its external coast ceased at low-water mark; that beyond that point there was a limited authority which Parliament and not the courts *ex proprio motu* could exercise if it wishes.'[12] Lord Blackburn, who delivered the advice of the Judicial Committee, declared that the case did not call for an opinion on the questions discussed in *Keyn*.

The decision in *Keyn* caused an immediate reaction at Westminster. On 9 February 1877 the House of Commons

---

[9] (1877) 41 J.P. 344.
[10] 31 & 32 Vict., c. 122.
[11] (1877) L.R. 2 App. Cas. 394.
[12] Ibid., 408.

ordered the printing of a private Members' Bill[13] prepared and brought in by three government members, John Gorst, Charles Ritchie, and Sir Henry Wolff. The long title of the Bill stated that its purpose was 'to declare that the power and jurisdiction of Her Majesty extend to a distance of three miles seawards from the sea coasts of her dominions and to make better provisions for the administration of justice'.

The Bill had only two clauses; the first read:

That portion of the high seas which lies within a distance not exceeding three miles from the sea coast of any territories which are now or may hereafter become subject to Her Majesty, her heirs or successors, constitute part of the dominions of Her Majesty, except where the limits of Her Majesty's dominions are or shall be otherwise defined by some express law or treaty.

The second and final clause read:

All courts, judges, magistrates, sheriffs, constables, officers, and ministers of Her Majesty who exercise any power or jurisdiction at any place upon the sea coast of Her Majesty's dominions shall exercise a like power and jurisdiction over such portion of the high seas as lies at a distance not exceeding three miles from such place as aforesaid, and is not nearer to some place on the sea coast at which such court, judge, magistrate, officer, or minister has no power or jurisdiction.

Provided always, that nothing herein contained shall take away the power and jurisdiction of Her Majesty's High Court of Admiralty or any power or jurisdiction of Her Majesty over any part of the high seas.

During the second reading of the Bill on 18 April 1877, Gorst, referring to passages in the judgments of Cockburn C.J. and Lush J. in *Keyn*, concluded:

It was thus evident that the question whether the territorial waters were part of the Queen's dominions had, in the *Franconia* case, not been decided at all.[14]

The Attorney-General, Sir John Holker, then suggested that the Bill be withdrawn so that the Government itself could introduce an official measure to deal with the undoubted problems raised by the decision of the Court for Crown Cases Reserved. He remarked:

When that case was examined, it would be found that the great bulk of

---

[13] *HCP*, 1877 (Bill 10) vii, 9.
[14] 233 *P. Debs.*, 3rd series, col. 1381.

the Judges who decided it were of opinion that the belt of ocean . . . was the territory of the State whose shores it adjoined.[15]

Gorst thereupon withdrew his Bill. Two points of significance arising from the incident should be noted: first, there was no attempt in the Bill to make the belt part of the realm of England, it was apparently assumed without question that the law of England would automatically extend to the belt if it were constituted part of the dominions of the Crown; secondly, the discussion was confined to the 'high seas', no mention being made of the seabed and subsoil.

This latter point, however, was causing anxiety to a Crown lessee of submarine minerals off the coast of Durham. On 8 June 1877, the following letter was written to Charles Gore at the Office of Woods:[16]

> 19 Surrey Street,
> Strand, London.
> 8th June 1877.

Dear Sir,

We have to trouble you upon a very important point, which has been suggested in reference to the Law, which seems to have been laid down by Lord Chief Justice Cockburn when giving judgment last year in the case of *Regina* v. *Keyn* (2 Law Reports Exchequer Division page 201) in reference to the Title of The Crown of Great Britain to Minerals *beyond low water mark*. We are aware that the main issue in that case was with respect to the ship Franconia being subject to the *Criminal* laws of Great Britain, when navigating the Seas at a point below low water mark, and that therefore the Law so laid down by that learned Judge as to the right of the Crown to such Minerals was a dictum, rather than a deliberate enunciation of the Law on the Civil point *after due discussion*.

Nevertheless even the dictum of Lord Chief Justice Cockburn, more especially when in express opposition to a view of the same law previously propounded by Chief Justice Coleridge, may be considered to give to the enunciation of the declared Law a force almost beyond that of an incidental dictum. We are interested in this view of the Law on behalf of Viscount Castlereagh with reference to certain Leases granted by the Crown to the Marquis of Londonderry (then Lord Vane) in 1866 of certain minerals under the sea to the distance of 2 miles beyond low water mark, and another Lease of other minerals similarly situated and which was granted to the Marquis and others in 1868. A very large family arrangement is now being carried out between the Marquis and his Son, and the interests of the Marquis in these Leases are dealt with in that arrangement.

It is most important therefore to the Viscount that no doubt exist as to the validity of the Leases, and that they really are properties of value.

While therefore on the one hand we are by no means prepared to admit that, if the Law be as laid down by Chief Justice Cockburn, the Leases in question are not perfectly good, on the ground amongst others that the grant of such Leases operated as acts of appropriation by the Crown, and thereby establishes its title to the same, yet we feel assured that you will at once admit that the Crown as the Lessor and Landlord of the Minerals in question should do everything within its power to dissipate all possibility of doubt, as to the efficiency of the Leases referred to.

It was acknowledged by Lord Chief Justice Cockburn (page 198) and also by Justice Lush (page 239) that Parliament could by legislative Enactment determine all doubt on the question. If this be so we certainly do request that you will be pleased to lay this letter before the proper authorities with a view to obtaining for the Lessees that Parliamentary protection and security which they are certainly entitled to request at the hands of the Crown, having incurred very considerable expenditure in developing the Mines in question, and bringing them into working order.

Requesting the favor of a reply.

Few & Co.

On 15 June 1877 Gore asked his Office for schedules to be prepared of dealings with the surface and the minerals below the surface (exclusive of the beds and minerals under the beds of tidal rivers). The letter was then referred to the Departmental solicitor, T. W. Gorst, together with the schedules, the contents of which will be explained below. On 31 July 1877, Gorst wrote the following minute:

Referring to Mr. Gore's Minute of July 20th, I do not think that the law has been laid down by Lord Chief Justice Cockburn as supposed by Messrs. Few & Co.

The question was as to the jurisdiction of the Central Criminal Court over the sea which washes the Coast of the Country: Lord C.J. Cockburn agreed with the minority of the Judges in thinking that the 3 mile belt of water was by the consent of nations British Territory, though he did not think the law gave the Court the jurisdiction claimed, and he expressed an opinion that the legislature could confer that jurisdiction if it thought fit to do so: and I conclude the reason why it can do so is because the belt is British Territory.

I do not find that the Chief Justice has laid it down as Law either that the belt is not British Territory, or that Minerals below low water mark do not belong to the Crown.

I understand that the Government has been considering what steps should be adopted with regard to the subject, and I suggest that Messrs. Few & Co.'s letter should be submitted to them.

On 1 August 1877 Gore replied that 'it would be advisable in writing to the Treasury to state the number of existing leases of Minerals below low water mark and not within any County and the minimum royalties reserved by such leases.'

Four schedules dealt with the practice in England, and separate schedules set out the practice in Scotland, Wales, Ireland, and the Isle of Man.[17] It is not clear when they were drawn up; the last date mentioned in any of them under the original hand being 31 December 1873. The titles of the schedules in respect of England were as follows:

Schedule No. 1: England—Schedule of Licences to lay down and maintain telegraphic cables affecting land below low water mark exclusive of the beds of tidal navigable rivers upon payment of rents.

Schedule No. 2: England—Schedule of Leases affecting land below low water mark exclusive of the beds of tidal navigable rivers.

Schedule No. 3: England—Schedule of Leases of Minerals under land below low water mark exclusive of Minerals under the beds of tidal navigable rivers.

Schedule No. 4: England—Schedule of Sales of Land below low water mark.

It is not proposed to describe here the contents of these schedules since this has already been done in discussing the pre-1876 practice in Chapter II above.

B. The Events of 1878

The Government Bill[18] designed to overcome the problem posed by *Keyn* was presented to the House of Lords on 14 February 1878 by the Lord Chancellor, Lord Cairns.[19] It had been drafted by the Parliamentary Counsel, Henry Thring, on instructions from Lord Cairns as the Jurisdiction of the Admiral Bill. Thring's last draft, dated June 1877, was substantially similar to the Bill now introduced.[20]

---

[17] These latter schedules are in CREST 37/356.

[18] *HLP*, 1878 (Bill 23) vi, 221.

[19] 237 *P.Debs.*, 3rd series, cols. 1601–14.

[20] No trace of Thring's drafts and memoranda has been found in the public archives. The author is grateful to the First Parliamentary Counsel for permission to examine Thring's papers retained in his Office.

The long title of the Bill—'an Act to regulate the law relating to the trial of offences committed on the sea within a certain distance of the coasts of Her Majesty's Dominions'—indicated that its main purpose was simply to deal with the specific problem arising out of the *Keyn* case rather than to lay down a new regime for the territorial waters, much less for the seabed and subsoil which were not mentioned specifically in the Bill.

The preamble seemed at first sight to have a drastic effect. It proclaimed that 'the rightful jurisdiction of Her Majesty, her heirs and successors, extends and has always extended over the open seas adjacent to the coasts of Her Majesty's dominions to such a distance as is necessary for the defence and security of such dominion'. However, apart from the rule of statutory interpretation that a preamble has no operative force, the term 'jurisdiction' might have meant simply the power to legislate. It was certainly one of the aims of the Government in introducing the Bill to counter suggestions, said by Lord Cairns to have been made in *Keyn* by Sir Robert Phillimore, Cockburn C.J., and Kelly C.B., that the legislature was unable to legislate for the belt without the consent of foreign States.

Lord Cairns maintained that the claim to a jurisdiction over the waters round the Kingdom was as old as Bracton and Selden, and that it had never been departed from. He also inferred that the decision in *Keyn* had been given *per incuriam*, since the Court had not been referred to a Treasury Warrant issued in 1848 which had extended the limits of the port of Dover to cover the spot where the collision had taken place. Lord Cairns implied that the Warrant had made the area of waters covered by it part of the United Kingdom.[21] The only reference to the seabed or subsoil in the speech of the Lord Chancellor came incidentally when he cited, amongst other authorities, the well-known dictum of Erle C.J. in *Free Fishers of Whitstable* v. *Gann* that 'the soil of the sea-shore to the extent of three miles from the beach is vested in the Crown'.[22]

On 8 March 1878, the House of Lords went into Committee on the Bill and a number of amendments were made.[23] Following a

[21] Although the terms of the particular Warrant had not been cited to the Court, the extent of the port of Dover and of ports in general was known to the Court and was declared by the Solicitor-General to be irrelevant to the issue (DPP 4/13; Transcript, 17 June 1876, pp. 136–45). The existence and extent of the Treasury Warrant of 28 February 1848 had been pointed out by a correspondent, 'W', in *The Times*, 29 October 1877. See pp. 281–5 below.

[22] (1865) 11 C.B. (N.S.) 387, 413.

[23] *Journals of the House of Lords*, cx, 77–8: 8 March 1878.

further amendment on Report the amended Bill, which was read a third time in the Lords on 14 March 1878, was then sent to the Commons.

Meanwhile, the unamended Bill was occupying the attention of the Office of Woods. On 2 March 1878, its solicitor, Gorst, wrote the following minute:

It appears to me that the meaning of the first preamble is to declare that the Queen's jurisdiction extends over the open seas which lie next to the margin of the land next the sea of the regions or districts subject to Her Majesty.

In old writings 'coasts' is sometimes used in the same sense as 'dominions' is here, but I find no instance of 'coast' ever used to express the boundary of a region or district not an island. I think therefore that the preamble does not imply that the bed of such open seas is not within the dominions of the Queen, and that a Report to the Treasury is not necessary.[25]

This minute must have stirred the memory of the Principal Clerk, J. Redgrave, for he wrote on it:

It would appear to be desirable that the opinion of the Law Officers should be taken as to the expediency of seeking legislation upon the point raised by Messrs. Few & Co. on June 8, 1877 on behalf of the Marquess of Londonderry, as to the title of the Crown to the minerals beneath the sea below water mark—and an opinion could be asked at the same time in relation to the present Bill. Mr Gorst concurs in this view and I have prepared the annexed memorandum shewing how the rights of the Crown have been exercised.

On 6 March 1878, the Commissioner, Charles Gore, to whom the last minute was probably addressed, referred the matter back to Gorst along with the schedules which had been produced at the time of the 1877 discussions.

By this time, the Bill had passed through its committee stage in the Lords. The print of the amended Bill[26] indicated that an addition had been made on Report to the paragraph in the definition clause which defined the 'jurisdiction of the Admiral'. The addition ran:

. . . and for the purpose of arresting any person charged with an offence declared by this Act to be within the jurisdiction of the Admiral, the territorial waters adjacent to the United Kingdom, or any other part of Her Majesty's dominions shall be deemed to be within the jurisdiction of any judge . . .

This particular amendment caused Gorst disquiet. On 15 March 1878 he wrote:

I transmit a print of this Bill as amended on Report. The definition of 'the Jurisdiction of the Admiral' has been amended, and now speaks of territorial waters adjacent, not to *the coasts* of the United Kingdom, but to *the United Kingdom* itself, an expression which would seem to imply that the bed of the sea adjacent to the sea coasts is not within the United Kingdom.

In pursuance of Mr. Gore's minute of March 6th a case has been laid before the Law Officers, and I have in further papers called their attention to the above mentioned amendment.

The Case stated[27] to the Law Officers, which was based largely on Redgrave's memorandum, first set out the text of the letter received from Few and Co. with, in addition, a tabular representation of the details of the Durham leases in question. Under the heading 'Observations', the Case continued:

If there should be any doubt as to the absolute right of the Crown to the Bed of the open Sea to a distance of a marine league from Low water mark or as to the powers of the Commissioners of Woods to grant sell or demise any portions of such Bed of the Sea or the mines minerals and other substrata it might be advisable to seek legislation upon the subject. The substrata are known to be of great value and they are now becoming of commercial importance.

The Case then described the events leading to the enactment of the Cornwall Submarine Mines Act 1858 and stated that the total sum received by way of royalties since the Act was passed was in excess of £6,500. It went on to describe the workings off the coast of Cumberland, from which royalties valued at £30,000 had been received from the lease made in 1860, and those off the coasts of Durham and Northumberland. The royalties in all had returned nearly £10,000 in the financial year 1876–7. The Case continued:

Other acts of ownership have been exercised by the Crown over the bed of the open Sea within what has been held to be British Territory as follows:

7 Licenses have been granted by the Commissioners of Woods for the deposit of Telegraph Cables.

26 Parcels of Land have been sold as sites for parts of Piers etc.

Similar acts of ownership have been exercised over and Leases of Coal etc. have been granted in Estuaries such as the Firth of Forth the Solent

[27] CREST 40/94, fos. 343–9.

the Mouth of the Thames etc. but no reference is made to them in the preceding statements which are limited to acts of ownership over parts of the Bed of the open Sea.

It has been suggested that if any doubt exists as to the Crown's Title to undersea mines the Bill now before Parliament for regulating the Law relating to the Trial of offences committed on the Sea within a certain distance of the Coasts of Her Majesty's Dominions a copy of which is sent herewith affords a favorable opportunity of obtaining a declaration of Her Majesty's Title to undersea Mines.

It has also been suggested as the word 'Coast' does not always mean 'Sea Coast' the first preamble of such Bill may be taken to imply that Her Majesty's Dominions do not extend beyond the Sea Coast thereof Seaward and may so prejudice the Crown's Title to undersea mines. . . .

The Law Officers of the Crown are requested to advise the Commissioners of Woods

Whether any doubt exists as to the Crown's Title to the bed of the Sea adjacent to the Sea Coasts of the Queen's Dominions and to the minerals therein.

Whether the first preamble of the Bill now before Parliament may be taken to imply that Her Majesty's Dominions do not extend beyond the Sea Coasts thereof Seaward and may so prejudice the Crown's Title to the bed of the Sea and the minerals therein.

Whether any and if so what steps it is advisable to take in the interest of the Crown either as regards the Bill now before Parliament or otherwise.

The reply of the Law Officers, Sir John Holker A.G. and Sir Hardinge Giffard S.G., was given on 16 March 1878.[28] It read as follows:

1. We do not think any doubt really exists as to the Crown's Title to the bed of the sea adjacent to the Sea Coasts of the Queen's Dominions and to the minerals therein. But apart from that abstract proposition we think the Crown's title to the mines in this case described is conclusively shewn the mere occupation of them if they had not been part of Her Majesty's dominions and even if without her previous authority that occupation had been by a subject such occupation would at Her Majesty's pleasure have vested the newly occupied territory in her in right of Her Crown and by this we mean not only the right of dominion but the right of property.
2. We do not think the preamble of the bill before Parliament implies anything which can prejudice the Crown's title to the Bed of the Sea referred to and the minerals therein.

[28] Ibid. According to a note by Gorst on the file, the report was written by the Solicitor-General, Sir Hardinge Giffard.

3. We do not recommend any steps to be taken with the view suggested in the question.

Accordingly, the Office of Woods replied to Few & Co. on 10 April 1878 as follows:

I am to inform you that your letter of 8th June last has been submitted to the Law Officers of the Crown.

They are of opinion that no doubt really exists as the Crown's title to the bed of the sea adjacent to the Queen's Dominions and they do not recommend that any application should be made to Parliament upon the subject as suggested in your letter.[29]

The Bill was debated on two occasions in the House of Commons. On the second occasion, on 15 August 1878, the Solicitor-General declared:

By the decision in the *Franconia* case, which must now be accepted as the law of England, the waters washing the shores of this country below low water mark must be taken to be out of their jurisdiction, and consequently the life and honour of any British subject bathing at the sea side—say, of a schoolgirl at Brighton or elsewhere—would be at the mercy of any foreigner on board a foreign ship who chose to take it . . . Anyone who paid attention to the decision in the *Franconia* case would see that a foreigner committing a crime one inch below low water mark was out of the jurisdiction of this country.[30]

No references to the seabed and subsoil were made in the course of these debates and the Bill became law on 16 August 1878 as the Territorial Waters Jurisdiction Act 1878.[31]

C. The Events of 1880–1

The effect of the decision in *Keyn* was discussed in connection with the protracted dispute between Britain and Portugal over the collision in 1875 between the British ship *City of Mecca* and the Portuguese vessel *Insulano* which had taken place about ten miles off the Portuguese coast. The Portuguese courts had assumed civil jurisdiction over the collision and on 30 January 1880 the British Minister in Lisbon, Robert Morier, addressed a note of protest to

[29] CREST 37/356.

[30] 242 *P.Debs.*, 3rd series, col. 2035. Harry Poland, one of the Crown's junior counsel in *Keyn*, is said to have written to Sir Hardinge Giffard following the decision: 'It is too absurd to say that all Her Majesty's subjects bathing or boating below low-water mark are not in the United Kingdom, and under the protection of the English law.' A. Wilson Fox, *The Earl of Halsbury*, 1929, p. 109.

[31] 41 & 42 Vict., c. 73.

the Portuguese Foreign Minister, Braamcamp, in which he discussed both the decision in *Keyn* and the Territorial Waters
Jurisdiction Act. In respect of the latter, Morier wrote:

The Preamble declares 'that the *rightful* jurisdiction of Her Majesty, her
heirs and successors, extends and has always extended over the open
seas adjacent to the coasts of the United Kingdom to such a distance as is
necessary for the defence and security of such dominions', *i.e.*, it makes
no claim on behalf of Her Majesty to the *absolute* proprietary rights and
rights of jurisdiction of the publicists, but only to the *rightful* jurisdiction
over these waters to such distance as is necessary for the security of her
dominions; in other words, it gives Parliamentary sanction to the international doctrine, 'Terrae dominium finitur ubi finitur armorum vis',
without either defining what the *dominium* consists in, or the exact
distance to which it extends.[32]

Morier's action in complaining of the finding of the Portuguese
Court was criticized by the Law Officers, James A.G., Herschell
S.G., and Deane, in a report given to the Foreign Office on 8 July
1880,[33] but his interpretation of the law was not commented upon
except that his criticism of the Portuguese reasoning was
described as 'able and minute'.

A year later, the Law Officers were again called upon to advise
on matters relevant to *Keyn* when they were asked by the Board of
Trade whether s. 432 of the Merchant Shipping Act 1854, which
dealt with wreck enquiries, applied to foreign vessels. On 20 July
1881, James, Herschell, and A. L. Smith (later A. L. Smith L.J.)
replied:

We are of opinion that section 432 of the Merchant Shipping Act, 1854,
applies to foreign ships while they are within the limits of British jurisdiction, that is to say, in this case the United Kingdom, and that the
powers of that and subsequent sections may be put in force if the loss,
abandonment, damage, or casualty occurred within these limits. Since
the case of *Reg.* v. *Keyn* and the Territorial Waters Act, 1878 [sic], the
United Kingdom must be held to terminate at low-water mark (see
Harris v. *Owners of 'Franconia'*), including, however, all ports, harbours,
estuaries, bays, and waters which are situate *inter fauces terrae*.[34]

The Board of Trade then drew up a broadsheet[35] to compare
and contrast its practice with the above report of the Law Officers.
The broadsheet showed that it was the practice of the Board to

[32] FO 881/4243, p. 130.
[33] FO 881/4781*, pp. 4–5.
[34] CO 885/12; Law Officers' Opinions to the Colonial Office, vol. III, No. 262A.
[35] MT 9/195.

inquire into wrecks of foreign ships taking place within three miles of the shore or within any estuary or firth. However, in the light of the Law Officers' report, a Board of Trade official wrote on the above broadsheet, 'I presume that any part of the sea between England and Ireland which is below low water mark, or not *inter fauces terrae* is outside British Jurisdiction.'

The Board of Trade was prepared to be more restrictive than the Law Officers, who later in their report interpreted the words 'on the coasts' in s. 228 of the Act as extending to 'a reasonable distance' from the shore, in line with the decision of Dr. Lushington in *The Leda*.[36] The Board official wrote on the broadsheet, '. . . the decision was given by Dr. Lushington before the decision in *Reg.* v. *Keyn* and was declared by Lord Chief Justice Cockburn to have no application to Foreign vessels.'

D. Conclusion

The official British view of *Keyn*, expressed in the years immediately following the decision, can be summarized in three conclusions:
  (i) the realm of England (or the United Kingdom) ended with the counties at the low-water mark on the open coast;
 (ii) English common law courts had no power of adjudication over acts committed below this mark unless such a power had been specially conferred upon them;
(iii) notwithstanding the above two conclusions, the decision did not affect the claim of the Crown to full property rights in the seabed and subsoil adjacent to the Crown's dominions.

This claim was still considered by the British Government to be well-founded, as will now be demonstrated by the history of a matter which was running a parallel course with the events described in this chapter, namely the plans to construct a tunnel under the English Channel to link England and France.

---

[36] (1856) Swa. 40.

Chapter VII

The Channel Tunnel Scheme 1874–83[1]

A. The Negotiations

During the first seventy years of the nineteenth century, various schemes were put forward, mostly in France, for constructing a tunnel to link England and France.[2] These schemes caused some discussion of the status of the subsoil of the Channel in international law, but it was not until 1874 that the municipal law status of the submarine land below low-water mark began to concern the British executive.

The occasion for concern was the passing of the South Eastern Railway Company Act 1874[3] which authorized the Company to spend £70,000 on borings and other works with the aim of constructing a Channel tunnel. This Act, promoted by the Company's chairman, Sir Edward Watkin, MP, was not the only Parliamentary activity of its kind. In late 1874, the Channel Tunnel Company, an Anglo-French consortium, gave notice in Parliament of a Bill in which it sought approval for the power to acquire lands for the purpose of carrying out preliminary experimental operations. A chart annexed to the Bill showed that the lands included an area below low-water mark in St. Margaret's Bay, Kent. On 15 January 1875, the Commissioner of Woods, Charles Gore, wrote to the Treasury about the latter scheme:

Foreshore is ordinarily understood to mean the land lying between high water mark and low water mark and land so situated is often claimed by subjects under Grants from the Crown. But the greater part of the Works of the Company if carried out as designed will be executed under the bed of the Sea below Low water mark which as far as the territory of England extends in the direction of France is indisputably the property of the Crown. It may be open to question what is the exact limit seaward of the

---

[1] The substance of this chapter has appeared in (1974–5) 47 *BYBIL* 290.

[2] See, e.g. the summary set out in a letter of 17 November 1871 from the Channel Tunnel Committee to the Secretary of State for Foreign Affairs: 68 *British and Foreign State Papers* 657–8.

[3] 37 & 38 Vict., c. ciii.

Territory of England. The area of Coal adjacent to Durham which has been already let by this Department on behalf of the Crown to the Marquis of Londonderry and other Lessees extends seawards to a distance of two miles from high water mark. Such distance not being fixed as the limits of the Crown's right to Coal but only as the extent to which that right is demised. And the Cornwall Submarine Mines Act 1858 does not mention any specific distance from low water mark as the limit of the Crown's right to Under-Sea Mines. So also the Licenses granted by me to Submarine Telegraph Companies authorize the laying of Cables on the bed of the Sea from low water mark as far as British Territory extends without any definition of seaward limits. With respect to the Water space of the Sea the right of British subjects to an exclusive right of fishing is so far as France is concerned governed by a Convention between the two Countries which was confirmed by the Act 31 & 32 Vic. c. 45 and which (with some exceptions) fixes 3 miles from low water mark as the distance within which the exclusive right of fishing of the subjects of each Country is to be exercised. But that provision is only a matter of treaty regulation made for a limited period (10 years from 1868) and is in no way binding as to the right to the soil of the bed of the Sea. In the case of a Mine worked under, or an Island newly formed in, the Straits of Dover, it is difficult to see that any limit could be justly assigned as the end of British Territory short of the medium filium aquae between England and France . . .

Whatever may be adopted as the line of frontier under the Sea between England and France it is clear that for 3 miles at the least the Tunnel will be constructed through sub-strata belonging to the Crown of England and the question at once presents itself on what terms if at all the consent of the Crown should be given to the execution of the Work in question.[4]

The Permanent Under-Secretary to the Board of Trade, T. H. Farrer, was less pessimistic about the legal problems. On 20 January 1875 he wrote to the Foreign Secretary, 'The Bill merely proposes to empower the Company to acquire for the purpose of preliminary experiments certain lands (including foreshore and bed of the sea within the British territorial limits) at St. Margaret's Bay, Dover.'[5]

The Treasury then suggested that a joint Anglo-French commission be set up. This was agreed to by the Foreign Office and the French Government. The British members of the Joint Commission were C. M. Kennedy of the Foreign Office, Captain

[4] CREST 37/318.
[5] Farrer to Tenterden: C. 3358, p. 40. The main published official source is the above Command Paper, 'Correspondence with reference to the proposed construction of a Channel tunnel', *HCP*, 1882, liii, 1. Some additional inter-departmental and diplomatic correspondence is in seven Foreign Office case volumes, FO 27/2214–19, 2901.

Tyler of the Board of Trade, and Horace Watson, Solicitor to the Department of Woods.[6] They heard evidence in April and May 1875, and presented their preliminary report to the Treasury on 10 May 1875. This report contained the following passage:

Article 5. Limits of Nationality and Jurisdiction. In the Report dated the 13th July, 1874, of a French Commission on the subject of the Submarine Railway, it is stated that the question of the right of property in the bed of the sea is one which has only a theoretical interest. But it may be doubted whether, on the present occasion, it will not be necessary to deal with that question as being one of practical importance. It is presumed that, by the law of France, the right of property in all unappropriated soil is vested in the State, as it is in this country in the Crown, and that such right includes the soil of the bed of the sea, to the distance seaward to which the country extends, subject, of course, to any public rights of navigation, anchorage, fishing, etc. In England this right of the State or the Crown is now the source of a substantial revenue derived from mines worked under the sea adjacent to Cumberland, Cornwall, Durham, etc.; and for the working of mines under the sea adjacent to Cornwall, facilities have been provided by Parliament in 'The Cornwall Submarine Mines Act, 1858'. It is apprehended that the jurisdiction of the Legislature of Great Britain is, as regards foreign nations, not less extensive than the Crown's right of property in the soil of the bed of the sea, and that such jurisdiction extends to a distance of 3 miles, at least, from the English coast. If a mine or tunnel were driven under the sea towards France to a greater distance than 3 miles, it is apprehended that, to the extent of the space comprised in the mine or tunnel, the work would be situate in England, and would belong to the Crown (and become subject to the jurisdiction of the British Parliament), if by no other title, at all events by the title which would be derived from the first occupancy and possession of that which would be practically a prolongation of, or an addition to, the territory of the country from or in which the mine or tunnel was driven. The right would, of course, be limited to the space actually occupied and possessed, and would not be in any way antagonistic to, or an interference with, any rights of other nations to navigate, to cast anchor, and to fish in the high sea (outside the natural territorial limits of the country), above the mine or tunnel. It is doubtless possible to suppose a case which might give rise to a question by the foreign State on the opposite coast, as, for instance, if the proposed tunnel were driven from the English coast until it got beyond the mid-channel, or even to the limit of 3 miles from France. But no such question could arise if a preliminary Treaty were made defining the limits of the respective ownerships and jurisdictions of the two countries, and it seems to be desirable that such a course should be adopted on the present occasion.

What, then, must be the common boundary of England and France in the Submarine Tunnel?

It is apprehended that this question can receive only one satisfactory answer, viz., that the boundary must be half-way between low-water mark in France and low-water mark in England. This boundary could be readily ascertained and marked out under the direction of the Mixed Commission.

It is proposed, therefore, to recommend that the boundary between England and France in the Channel Tunnel shall be so ascertained before the railway is opened for public traffic; and shall be half-way between low-water mark (above the tunnel) on the coast of England, and low-water mark (above the tunnel) on the coast of France.

This definition of boundary will be for the purposes of the tunnel and railway only, and will not, as regards the sea over the tunnel, in any way affect any question of nationality, or any rights of navigation, fishing, or anchoring, or other rights.[7]

The French members of the Joint Commission then delivered a report dated 12 October 1875[8] in which they commented on the preliminary report of the English members. After referring to the construction of international railways, they continued:

A la vérité, la situation n'est pas exactement la même dans le cas d'un chemin de fer sous-marin, parce que, au delà du territoire propre à chaque nation et défini par la ligne du niveau de plus basses eaux, il existe un espace à l'égard duquel les droits de propriété peuvent sembler incertains.[9]

The British members then revised their draft. The new version began:

Article 1. The boundary between England and France in the tunnel, when constructed, shall be half-way between low-water mark (above the tunnel) on the coast of England, and low-water mark (above the tunnel) on the coast of France. . . . The definition of the boundary provided for by this Article shall have reference to the tunnel and [submarine] railway only, and shall not in any way affect any question of the nationality of, or any rights of navigation, fishing, anchoring, or other rights, in the sea above the tunnel, or elsewhere than in the tunnel itself.[10]

This Article was accepted, with the addition of the word

[7] C. 3358, pp. 87–8.
[8] Ibid., 132–6.
[9] Ibid., 133.
[10] Ibid., 139.

'submarine' as indicated above, as part of a Protocol *ad referendum* which was signed by all the Joint Commissioners on 5 February 1876.[11] This Protocol was designed to regulate as between Britain and France the construction and operation of the tunnel. It envisaged the establishment of an international commission.

The next stage foreseen by the Foreign Office was that a treaty, preceded by legislation, should be concluded on the basis of the Protocol. On 15 May 1876 the Protocol was submitted to the Law Officers, Sir John Holker A.G., Sir Hardinge Giffard S.G., and Parker Deane, the Foreign Office consultant on matters of international law. Their reply, dated 18 May 1876, endorsed the steps proposed but made no observations on the Protocol except to point out that no provision had been made for jurisdiction over and punishment of offences before the time the tunnel was in working order.[12] As Holker and Giffard were engaged at this very time in arguing the Crown's case at the first hearing of the Court for Crown Cases Reserved in the appeal of Ferdinand Keyn, it is perhaps not surprising that the report was short.

The means to be used to overcome this deficiency of jurisdiction caused a divergency of views among the British Commissioners. Horace Watson objected to the idea of an agreement to control the works before they had met in the middle of the Channel. In words which suggest that he was the author of Article 5 of the Report already quoted, he wrote on 25 May 1876:

The boring from each shore will, as it progresses, become part of the soil and territory of the country from which it has been driven, if by no previously existing title, at all events by the law of first occupation and possession.[13]

On 12 July 1876, Holker, Giffard, and Deane gave a further opinion to the Foreign Office[14] stating that they had not intended in their first report to recommend that an 'international contract' be made, but only that provision should be made in England for offences committed during the progress of the works.

B. The Excavations

Meanwhile, the Channel Tunnel Bill passed through Parliament

[11] Ibid., 151–4 for the full text of the Protocol.
[12] FO 881/4028, p. 27.
[13] C. 3358, p. 163.
[14] FO 881/4028, p. 28.

and received the Royal assent on 2 August 1875 as the Channel Tunnel Company (Limited) Act 1875.[15] During its Parliamentary progress, the Board of Trade secured the insertion of a clause which became s. 9 of the Act. This read:

Nothing contained in this Act shall authorize the Company to take, use, tunnel under, or in any manner interfere with any portion of the shore or bed of the sea, or of any river, channel, creek, bay or estuary, or any right in respect thereof belonging to the Queen's Most Excellent Majesty in right of Her Crown, and under the management of the Board of Trade without the previous consent in writing of the Board of Trade on behalf of Her Majesty (which consent the Board of Trade may give), neither shall anything in this Act contained extend to take away, prejudice, diminish, or alter any of the estates, rights, privileges, powers, or authorities vested in or enjoyed or exerciseable by the Queen's Majesty, Her heirs or successors.

Under s. 7 of the Act, the powers of land acquisition could not be exercised after the expiration of one year from its enactment. These powers in fact were never exercised.

Sir Edward Watkin, in charge of the South Eastern Railway Company, was more active. In 1880, the company made some experimental borings which abutted on the foreshore between high- and low-water marks at Abbot's Cliff, near Folkestone. The bores did not run out below low-water mark. In reply to an enquiry from the Board of Trade, the company asserted that exclusive rights over the foreshore at the spot in question were claimed by the local Lord of the Manor to the exclusion of the Crown.[16]

In 1881, the company presented another Bill to Parliament seeking authority to continue works towards the construction of a tunnel under the Channel. The Bill received the Royal assent on 11 August 1881 as the South Eastern Railway Company Act 1881.[17] The Office of Woods and the Board of Trade succeeded in procuring the insertion of saving clauses under which their permission was required before borings could take place below high-water mark. Under powers given in the Act, the company purchased from the local Lord of the Manor three miles of fore-shore between Folkestone and Dover. The scene was now set for a confrontation. On 14 September 1881 Sir Edward Watkin wrote to Joseph Chamberlain, President of the Board of Trade: 'We are

[15] 38 & 39 Vict., c. cxc.
[16] C. 3358, p. 307.
[17] 44 & 45 Vict., c. cxcv.

about to make a new start, and I hope before Christmas the boring will be far under the sea.'[18]

In order to promote the scheme, the South Eastern Railway Company formed a new entity, the Submarine Continental Railway Company Limited, with Watkin as Chairman. This enterprise, which was incorporated on 8 December 1881, commenced boring operations at a spot above the foreshore between Folkestone and Dover near the western end of the Shakespeare Cliff railway tunnel.[19] The Board of Trade was not slow in reacting. In a letter addressed to Watkin on 13 January 1882, it warned:

The Board of Trade desire me to point out to you that their sanction has never been applied for or given to these experimental works which are being made through tidal lands *prima facie* the property of the Crown.[20]

In another letter, dated 6 March 1882, it informed Watkin:

. . . the foreshore of the United Kingdom, below high-water mark, are [sic] *prima facie* the property of the Crown, and under the management of the Board of Trade who in the absence of any information or legal evidence to the contrary, are unable to admit that the Crown has parted with any rights or interests in the foreshore through which the works are being made.[21]

It is clear that the Government was not confining its objections to works carried out between high- and low-water marks for on 30 March 1882, in reply to a question in the House of Commons, Chamberlain stated bluntly '. . . the Government claim the bed of the sea below low-water mark and for three miles beyond'.[22]

The Government departments were also clear in stating the Crown's claim to seabed and subsoil below low-water mark. On 6 March 1882, the Postmaster General, in a letter addressed to the Treasury, wrote:

The Telegraph Act 1878, gives to this department a right of way for its telegraphs over works of the kind executed within the limits of this country in pursuance of any special Act of Parliament passed after the 1st January of that year, so that the Post Office would be entitled to such

---

[18] C. 3358, p. 319.
[19] For contemporary photographs and plans of the operation, see, e.g., A. S. Travis, *Channel Tunnel 1802–1967* (1967). Similar excavations were commenced near Boulogne at the same time.
[20] C. 3358, p. 324.
[21] Ibid., 327.
[22] 268 *P.Debs.*, 3rd series, col. 308.

right in respect of the approaches to the tunnel, and probably to a point three miles distant from the low-water mark.[23]

On 1 April 1882, Farrer expressed the opinion of the Board of Trade in a further letter addressed to Watkin:

Whatever might be the title of the foreshore, there is no doubt as to the title of the Crown to the bed of the sea beyond low-water mark, and within the territorial limits of the United Kingdom.[24]

C. The Litigation

Relations between Watkin and the Board of Trade now deteriorated rapidly. On 26 June 1882, the Board wrote to Watkin:

The Board of Trade desire to make an immediate inspection of the works of the Company, in order to satisfy themselves that these works have not been carried below low-water mark, and into the three mile limit, the soil of which is claimed by the Crown . . .

[T]he President has decided to consult the Law Officers with regard to the steps to be taken to protect the rights of the Crown.[25]

(i) THE INJUNCTION

The exact nature of the consultations does not appear from the papers found, but official steps were rapidly taken. On 28 June 1882 a writ was issued and on 5 July 1882 the Attorney-General, Sir Henry James, instructed by the Board of Trade, appeared before Kay J. in the Chancery Division of the High Court to apply for an interim injunction against the South Eastern Railway Company and the Submarine Continental Railway Company to restrain them from proceeding with the boring, which by this time had been driven more than 600 yards beyond low-water mark in the direction of the Admiralty Pier at Dover.

The writ sought an injunction against the defendants to restrain them from boring or tunnelling into, excavating, or in any manner interfering with the bed of the sea below ordinary low-water mark and from taking, using or interfering with any soil or substance in, from or out of such bed of the sea and from continuing in possession of any works or excavations in or under such bed of the sea and from further proceeding with experimental borings or other

[23] C. 3358, p. 329.
[24] Ibid., 331.
[25] Ibid., 352.

works in connection with the construction of the tunnel. The writ also asked the Court to declare the right and title of the Crown to, in, and over the soil and bed of the sea under which the borings extended. Finally, the writ sought inspection of the works.[26]

On the point of the interim injunction, Kay J. was addressed by the Attorney-General on behalf of the Crown and by Judah Benjamin QC on behalf of the South Eastern Railway Company. The latter must have recalled vividly his successful appearance against the preceding Law Officers six years previously in *R.* v. *Keyn* and, perhaps, that part of the argument before the Court for Crown Cases Reserved on 23 June 1876 when the very point presently at issue was canvassed hypothetically.[47]

The Attorney-General was reported to have stated before Kay J.:

. . . in respect to the foreshore, while the rights of the Crown would be supposed to exist as owners, yet the Crown might have given property in it to others. It might be that the South Eastern Company could have shown such a property, though they have not shown it, and we do not know whether they have any property in the foreshore. It was possible that they might have been able to show a grant actually in existence, or rights amounting to a grant, entitling them to access through the fore-shore, but directly their works passed low-water mark and were under the bed of the sea, or the soil forming the bed of the sea, the rights of the Crown in the soil forming the bed of the sea would be at once affected.[28]

Benjamin QC replied:

But what was now asserted was that the Crown was the owner of the bed of the sea below low water mark; and so far as the question of property in the Crown was concerned the company was advised that they could successfully contest the right. Whether or not the Crown owned the bed of the sea or whether, according to the principles of international law, the bed of the sea below low water mark was the property of the first occupant, and stood unappropriated to be taken possession of by mankind at large was a matter upon which authorities had differed. The South Eastern Company desired to say that, in the arrangement to which they had consented, they reserved to themselves all their rights upon these points which would be contested in the progress of the cause, but at the same time they would not deny that there were such *prima facie* rights on the part of the Crown in the bed of the sea as had been asserted by various dicta, and therefore in agreeing that the question should be

[26] Cause No. A 1045 of 1882.
[27] DPP 4/13: Transcript, 23 June 1876, pp. 141–4; see pp. 127–8 above.
[28] The *Daily News*, 6 July 1882. The report in *The Times* is not so full.

decided at a later period, they were willing that in the meantime those rights should be respected.[29]

Kay J. thereupon granted an interim junction in the form of an Order restraining the defendants from proceeding with the operations 'beyond ordinary low-water mark without the consent of the Board of Trade' and also granting inspection.[30]

Further proceedings took place a few weeks later when, on 16 August 1882, the Crown applied to the Vacation Judge, North J., for a commission of sequestration to issue against the personal estate and rents and profits of the defendant companies for disobedience of the Order of Kay J. It was admitted that the works had been carried on for a further thirty-six yards. On the defendants giving an undertaking not to use the boring machine for any purpose whatsoever, unless with the written consent of the Board of Trade, the motion was adjourned *sine die*. On behalf of the Submarine Continental Railway Company, Littler QC was reported to have stated in court that, 'The company had purchased the foreshore, and with respect of any rights of the Crown to interfere with any extension beyond the foreshore, there was obviously since the decision in the *Franconia* case a question for argument at the trial.'[31]

The Crown's Statement of Claim in respect of the merits of the principal cause was delivered meanwhile on 9 August 1882. The first paragraph ran as follows:

The bed of the sea adjacent to the coasts of England below ordinary low-water mark (as well as the foreshore between ordinary high and ordinary low-water mark) belongs to and is vested in Her Majesty Her Heirs and Successors in right of Her Crown as a territorial possession [(except so far as Her Majesty or any of Her predecessors has been pleased to grant limited parts thereof to any person)] and Her Majesty has also by Her royal prerogative the absolute right and power over the same for the purpose of defending the kingdom and coasts from waste incursions of the sea invasion of enemies and other interference.[32]

Paragraph 17 of the same Statement read:

The acts of the Defendant Companies in making and continuing the aforesaid tunnel and works under the bed of the sea constitute a purpresture and encroachment on the soil and freehold of Her Majesty and

---

[29] Ibid.
[30] C. 3358, pp. 353–4 for the text of this Order.
[31] *The Times*, 17 August 1882.
[32] CREST 37/584. The amendment in square brackets was added on 16 June 1883.

an infringement of both the territorial and the prerogative rights of the Crown. Such acts affect the national security and no licence or consent by or on behalf of the Crown to make or continue any such works has been given and no determination has been arrived at with reference to the construction of a tunnel under the English Channel either by Her Majesty's Government or by Parliament.

The Crown also included the request 'that so far as necessary the right and title of Her Majesty to in and over the soil and bed of the sea under which the works commenced by the Defendants extend may be declared'.

The Submarine Continental Railway Company did not deliver its Statement of Defence until 17 May 1883.[33] Its first paragraph ran:

These Defendants do not admit that the bed of the sea adjacent to the coast of England below ordinary low water mark belongs to or is vested in Her Majesty her heirs and successors in right of her crown as a territorial possession or otherwise or that Her Majesty has the absolute right and power over the same by her royal prerogative or otherwise for the purpose of defending the kingdom or coasts from waste incursions of the sea invasions of enemies and other interference.

Paragraph 26 of the Statement of Defence expanded the above argument:

These Defendants deny that the acts of either of the Defendant Companies in making and continuing the experimental tunnel and works under the bed of the sea constitute any purpresture or encroachment on the soil or freehold of Her Majesty or an infringement either of the territorial or the prerogative rights of the Crown the bed of the sea below low-water being (as they submit) unappropriated and no part of the realm or vested in or belonging to Her Majesty or any department of Her Majesty's Government. These Defendants deny that the construction of a permanent tunnel would in any way affect the national security and they deny that any such question is involved in this action.

The Statement of Defence on behalf of the South Eastern Railway Company was also delivered on 17 May 1883.[34] It was drafted differently from that delivered on behalf of the other defendant. Paragraph 1 read:

These Defendants do not admit that the bed of the sea adjacent to the coasts of England below ordinary low water-mark belongs to or is vested in Her Majesty her heirs or successors in right of her Crown as a

[33] Ibid.
[34] Ibid.

territorial possession or that Her Majesty has by her royal prerogative or otherwise without the action of Parliament any absolute right or power over the same for the purpose of defending the kingdom or coasts from waste incursions of the sea invasions of enemies or other interference but if any such right exists they submit that it is not applicable or exercisable under the circumstances of the present case.

The final paragraph of the Statement of Defence, paragraph 21, expanded the above argument:

These Defendants submit that the making and continuing the aforesaid experimental tunnel and works under the bed of the sea do not constitute any purpresture or encroachment on the soil or freehold of Her Majesty the bed of the sea below low water-mark being (as they submit) unappropriated and not part of the realm and they submit that such acts are not any infringement of the territorial or prerogative rights of the Crown. They do not admit or believe that the construction of a permanent tunnel would affect the national security but they deny that any such question is involved in this action.

Both defendants also relied on the various local Acts of Parliament passed since 1874 as providing authority for them to carry on the experimental works.

On 16 June 1883, the Crown delivered an amended Statement of Claim.[35] The main amendment, apart from the addition to the first paragraph of a clause indicated above in square brackets, was the insertion of a new paragraph, 1a, which ran as follows:

In the years 1859 and 1861 the Defendants the South Eastern Railway Company purchased from the Crown certain portions of the bed of the sea of limited extent at Dover and at Folkestone, but no grant has been made by the Crown of that part of the bed of the sea under which the works now commenced by the Defendants extend.

In practice, this was the end of the affair. On 5 April 1883, a Joint Select Committee of both Houses of Parliament was appointed to inquire whether it was expedient that Parliamentary sanction be given to the tunnel scheme. This Committee reported on 10 July 1883, concluding by a majority that such a step was not expedient. The report,[36] though voluminous, contained no discussion of the legal problem. As a consequence of this report, the defendants abstained from delivering an amended Statement of Defence. This cause never reached the stage of a hearing.

[35] Ibid.
[36] *HCP*, 1883 (248) xii.

(ii) THE INFORMATION

The writ seeking an injunction was not the only legal step taken by the Crown against the two companies. On 5 December 1882 the Attorney-General filed an information in the Queen's Bench Division against the two companies and their secretary, John Shaw.[37] The information, in addition to requesting a declaration of the Crown's title to the foreshore, asked that the work under the foreshore be restrained and all encroachments and works carried out in or upon it be abated and filled up. It also sought inspection of the works. The first paragraph of the information was drafted as follows:

The foreshore of the sea between high-water mark and low-water mark around the coasts of this kingdom, including the coast of the county of Kent, and the foreshore between high-water mark and low-water mark of all estuaries and arms of the sea and creeks running into the said county, as also the bed of the sea around the coast of the said county, and the bed of the said estuaries, arms, and creeks have been from time immemorial vested in the Kings and Queens of England in right of their Crown in their demesne as of fee, and are now vested in Her Majesty in right of Her Crown in Her demesne as of fee, except in so far as Her Majesty or Her Royal Predecessors Kings and Queens of England has or have been pleased to grant parts thereof to any person or persons, or corporation or corporations, but no grant has ever been made to the Defendants, or either of them, or to any predecessor in title of them, or either of them, of that part of the foreshore of the sea on the coast of Kent under which the works of the Defendant Companies have been carried on and which is the subject of this information.

The defendants entered an appearance to the information, but, although the preliminary proceedings continued spasmodically until well into the next decade, the cause never proceeded to the stage of a hearing.

[37] CREST 37/584.

Chapter VIII

Executive and Legislative Domestic Practice
after 1876

A. The Seabed

The Law Officers' opinion of 16 March 1878 was given at the request of the Office of Woods, Forests, and Land Revenues which, under s. 21 of the Crown Lands Act 1866, retained responsibility for the management of all beds of stone and other mineral substances under Crown land below high-water mark. The Law Officers, however, did not confine themselves to consideration of the Crown's title to such mineral deposits but stated generally that: 'We do not think that any doubt really exists as to the Crown's Title to the bed of the Sea adjacent to the Sea Coasts of the Queen's Dominions.'

It is not known whether this opinion was made available to the Board of Trade but in any event its practice of selling portions of the seabed for the construction of piers and other works continued, as did the confirmation of Provisional Orders made under the General Pier and Harbour Acts. A principal source of information on these and other dealings with the seabed is the series of Parliamentary papers entitled 'Statement of the particulars of all Cases in which the rights and interests of the Crown in the shores and bed of the sea and tidal rivers have been sold, leased or otherwise dealt with by the Board of Trade under the Crown Lands Act, 1866'.[1] These papers separated the dealings of the Board into sales, leases, and 'cases in which money had been paid to the Board in acknowledgement of the rights and interests of the Crown in the shores and bed of the sea and tidal rivers'. In many of the entries it was specifically stated that a particular transaction dealt with 'seabed only', thereby, it would seem, distinguishing transactions dealing with foreshore properly so-called.

Amongst the works for which 'acknowledgements' were given to the Board were outfall sewers, groynes, licences to search for

---

[1] *HCP*, 1866 (172) lx, 467; 1867–8 (18) lvii, 215; 1872 (61) xxxvi, 209; 1877 (127) lxviii, 441; 1882 (122) lxiv, 179; 1887 (100) lxxv, 853; 1892 (118) lxxii, 135; 1897 (285) lxxx, 141; 1902 (259) xciii, 345; 1907 (269) lxvii, 11; 1912–3 (338) lxviii, 231; 1919 (204) xxxii, 185.

treasure on the seabed, the extension and widening of piers, lifeboat slipways, rails for bathing machines, and the removal of boulders on the seabed. One transaction, interesting in the light of the 1891 case of *Lord Advocate* v. *Trustees of the Clyde Navigation*, was the payment of five shillings by the Tobermory Galleon Salvage Company on 20 March 1912 in respect of the 'deposit of dredgings in connection with treasure hunt' although no indication of the locality of intended deposit was given.[2] From time to time licences were issued to the Congested Districts Board for Ireland to cut and gather seaweed below low-water mark opposite certain areas in western Ireland. Leases or licences to lay or land submarine cables continued to be made, although the entries did not state whether there was a specific seaward extent.

In addition to the practice of the Board of Trade summarized in the above series of Parliamentary Papers, the annual reports to Parliament presented by the Office of Woods continued to contain references to certain types of transactions concerning the seabed as distinct from the subsoil minerals. Thus the 59th Report of the Commissioners[3] recorded the lease on 26 June 1880 of a 'piece of land, being part of the foreshore and bed of the sea, with a portion of a pier thereon, situated at East Southsea' to the South Parade Pier Company Ltd. for a term of 99 years from 29 September 1878 at an annual rent of £10. The 66th Report[4] mentioned the sale to the River Wear Commissioners for £200 on 31 August 1887 of 'two pieces of land 96 acres 1r. 19p. portion of the bed of the sea below low water mark opposite Sunderland and Bishopswearmouth'. In the Seventieth Report[5] was entered the sale on 11 February 1891 of a piece of the bed of the sea below low-water mark at Herne Bay to the Herne Bay Pier Company Limited, and in the Report for the following year[6] there was recorded the sale on 18 May 1892 of part of the bed of the sea below low-water mark in front of the town of Clevedon as the site for a pier. The 77th Report[7] listed the sale on 14 November 1898 for £450 of 'pieces of land being part of the foreshore and bed of the sea at Dover, subject to a reservation of the minerals'. The purchasers were the Commissioners for executing the Office of the Lord High Admiral of the United

[2] Ibid., 1919 (204, p. 32) xxxii, 32.
[3] Ibid., 1881 (307 pp. 16–17) xxx, 752–3.
[4] Ibid., 1888 (251 p. 93) xxxiv, 733.
[5] Ibid., 1892 (355, p. 98) xxvi, 406.
[6] Ibid., 1893–4 (302, p. 81) xxiv, 441.
[7] Ibid., 1899 (257, p. 107) xviii, 665.

Kingdom. On 2 November 1903, a sale was made to the Secretary of State for War of 'a piece of land now or formerly foreshore and bed of sea with the buildings thereon known as Fort Albert and the pier adjacent thereto situate at Cliff End in the Isle of Wight'.[8]

Another convenient review of seabed (and subsoil) practice took the form of four appendices to the First Report of the Royal Commission on Coast Erosion and the Reclamation of Tidal Lands in the United Kingdom, 1907.[9] The appendices were entitled:

Appendix II (C): Schedule of sales of foreshore by the Commissioners of Woods in charge of the land revenues of the Crown in Wales, Scotland and Ireland from 1 January 1867 to 31 March 1906.[10]

Appendix II(D): Schedule of lettings of foreshore by the Commissioners of Woods in Wales, Scotland and Ireland which were in force on 31 March 1906, including letting of undersea mines.[11]

Appendix III(A): Schedule of sales of the foreshore by the Commissioners of Woods in England, between 1 January 1867 and 31 March 1906.[12]

Appendix III(B): Schedule of lettings of the foreshore by the Commissioners of Woods in England, in force at 31 March 1906, including lettings of undersea mines.[13]

Further indication of the official view towards the seabed was set out in the evidence in 1902 to the Royal Commission on Salmon Fisheries. The Solicitor to the Board of Trade, Robert Ellis Cunliffe, stated in a paper presented to the Commission that

[a] distinction must be drawn between the sea properly so called, *i.e.*, the 'open sea' and the territorial waters or 'mare clausum', *i.e.*, the sea within the three mile limit of the shore. . . .

The right to fish in territorial waters and in all the tidal parts of rivers in England belongs *prima facie* to all the public of the United Kingdom. The soil *prima facie* is still now, and the right of fishing was originally vested in the Crown . . .[14]

Cunliffe was then questioned about his paper:

Q.62: You say that in your statement you deal with the waters of a river from the sea to the source?

[8] Ibid., 1904 (237, p. 123) xvii, 563.
[9] Ibid., 1907, xxxiv, 1; Cd. 3683.
[10] Cd. 3683, Evidence, Appendices, pp. 8–14.
[11] Ibid., 15–32.
[12] Ibid., 39–54.
[13] Ibid., 55–74.
[14] *HCP*, 1902, xiv, 79; Cd. 1280, p. 73.

CUNLIFFE Yes.

Q.63: Does that include the seacoast outside the rivers?

CUNLIFFE In what we call the territorial waters, yes; but the general principles as regards the law do not afford very much information on that head.

Q.64: Perhaps that is a more important question to Scotland than to England?

CUNLIFFE I imagine it is a great deal more so. I understand that it may be a question whether it may not be further extended to English waters, but I do not think we get much question of English law outside the coast at present.[15]

In 1907, the Hon. T. H. W. Pelham, Assistant-Secretary to the Board of Trade, gave the following evidence to the Royal Commission on Coast Erosion and the Reclamation of Tidal Lands in the United Kingdom:

As a general principle it may be stated that the foreshore and bed of the sea within the three miles limit of jurisdiction, and of every channel, creek, bed, estuary, and of every navigable river as far up the same as the tide flows, were originally vested in the Crown, but in certain parts of the coast the Crown has parted, or is alleged to have parted, with its right in favour of lords of the manor and owners of adjoining property. Strictly speaking, 'foreshore' means the land lying between high water mark and low water mark, but in the Crown Lands Act, 1866, the word foreshore is used as meaning the bed of the sea as well as the foreshore proper.[16]

There is every reason to assume that the practice described above has been continued to the present day in much the same way. The Report of the Committee on Crown Lands in 1955 (Cmd. 9483, p. 17) stated that included in the Crown estate was 'the bed of the sea around the United Kingdom (generally up to the three mile limit) and all foreshore (between high and low water marks) of the sea and tidal waters, except where adverse title has been established. The major part of the foreshore in the United Kingdom remains with the Crown.' Similarly, in an introductory note dated December 1970 to the records which the Crown Estate Office released to the Public Record Office in that year, it is written:

In addition to the foreshore virtually all seabed lying below low water mark of medium tides (or low water mark of ordinary spring tides in Scotland), including that off Cornwall and Lancashire, is Crown Estate

---

[15] Ibid., xiii, 87; Cd. 1269, p. 5.
[16] Ibid., 1907, xxxiv, 17; Cd. 3684, Minutes of Evidence, p. 1.

property and the Crown's proprietary jurisdiction extends to the limit of territorial waters . . . The main source of income is the seabed on which royalties are payable in respect of dredging for sand and gravel.[17]

In an article written in 1951 when he was an Assistant Legal Adviser at the Foreign Office, D. H. N. Johnson described the contemporary seabed practice as follows:

All lands belonging to the Sovereign in right of the Crown are placed under the management of the Commissioners of Crown Lands, who are empowered to lease any Crown land, or any easement, right or privilege thereover, for any term not exceeding 100 years. In granting leases of the sea-bed and the subsoil the Commissioners of Crown Lands are guided by the following principles;

   (i) Sites required for permanent substantial works such as reclamation, piers and jetties are leased at a rent assessed by the Chief Government Valuer.

 (ii) Sites required for sea defence works or outfall sewers are made the subject of an easement or a licence at a nominal rent.

(iii) Licences for dredging materials such as sand, gravel or shingle from the sea-bed are granted at a rent of £1 per annum plus a royalty per ton assessed by the Chief Government Valuer.[18]

Later in the same article, he wrote:

No charge is made by the Minister of Agriculture and Fisheries for the grant of a right of several fishery, but the grantees are required to obtain the consent of the Commissioners of Crown Lands before using or in any way interfering with any portion of the seabed belonging to the Crown.[19]

Apart from the enactments relating to the subsoil, which will be considered below, there are a few public and general Acts passed after 1876 which from their terms can be construed to apply specifically to the bed of the marginal sea.

S. 4 of the Government of Ireland Act 1920 made reservations from the power of the Parliament of Northern Ireland in respect of certain matters, including navigation, submarine cables and lighthouses, buoys and beacons. S. 9(1) of the Northern Ireland (Miscellaneous Provisions) Act 1932, however, provided in part:

[17] CREST 37. The manuscript indexes of the Crown Estate Commissioners in respect of foreshore, seabed, and subsoil, which were transferred to the custody of the Public Record Office at the same time, contain references to many documents not themselves transferred. For example, they contain a reference to an agreement dated 30 April 1935 for the compromise of a claim by the Duchy of Lancaster to the bed of the sea off the coast of Lancashire. This document has not been transferred to the Public Record Office.

[18] (1951) 4 *International Law Quarterly* 445, 448.

[19] Ibid., 453.

The restrictions contained in section four of the principal Act shall not extend so as to prevent the Parliament of Northern Ireland making laws with respect to—

    (a) the construction, carrying out or alteration of any works on or under or over any part of the shore or bed of the sea whether or not vested in the Crown; or

    (b) the carrying out of dredging operations in the sea; or

    (c) the deposit or removal of materials on or from the shore or bed of the sea whether or not vested in the Crown; or

    (d) ferries across tidal waters in Northern Ireland,

if the consent of the Board of Trade and, in a case where any foreshore the management whereof is vested in the Commissioners of Crown Lands is affected, also the consent of those Commissioners, has been obtained.

S. 49 of the Coast Protection Act 1949 defines the term 'seashore' for the general purposes of the enactment as being 'the bed and shore of the sea, and of every channel, creek, bay or estuary, and of every river as far up that river as the tide flows'. No indication is given of the extent seawards of such 'sea'.

S. 34 provides that any person who has not obtained the consent in writing of the Minister (now the Minister for Trade and Industry) is prohibited from carrying out various operations in such a way that 'obstruction or danger to navigation is caused or is likely to result'. One of these operations, specified in s. 34(1) (c), is to 'remove any object or any material from any part of the seashore lying below low water mark of ordinary spring tides'. Under s. 36(1) of the Act such a person is guilty of an offence, which by virtue of s. 43 is a summary offence. S. 18(1) furthermore makes it unlawful 'to excavate or remove any materials (other than minerals more than fifty feet below the surface) on, under or forming part of any portion of the seashore'. The Act nowhere provides for the power of adjudication in respect of these offences to be exercised by any specific court or courts.

Part III of the Coast Protection Act provides for the transfer to the management of the Commissioners of Crown Lands 'so much of the Crown foreshore as immediately before the appointed day was under the management of the Minister of Transport'. The expression 'Crown foreshore' is defined for the purposes of this Part of the Act to mean 'so much of the bed and shore of the sea as belongs to His Majesty in right of the Crown, and includes any right or interest in Crown foreshore'.

The Protection of Wrecks Act 1973 applies to certain types of wreck lying on or in the sea bed within United Kingdom waters. The latter term is defined by s. 3(1) as 'any part of the sea within the seaward limits of United Kingdom territorial waters and includes any part of a river within the ebb and flow of ordinary spring tides'. 'Sea' is defined as including any estuary or arm of the sea.

The Petroleum and Submarine Pipe-lines Act 1975 applies to pipe-lines in 'controlled waters', defined in s. 20(2) as 'the territorial sea adjacent to the United Kingdom and the sea in any designated area within the meaning of the Continental Shelf Act 1964'.

The Ancient Monuments and Archaeological Areas Act 1979 provides in s. 53(1) that a monument 'situated in, on or under the sea bed within the seaward limits of United Kingdom territorial waters adjacent to the coast of Great Britain' may be included under the provisions of the Act. S. 53(7) provides that 'references in this section to the sea bed do not include the seashore or any other land which, though covered (intermittently or permanently) by the sea, is within Great Britain'.

Several Acts passed in the period acknowledge the possibility of legal rights in sedentary fisheries on the bed of the sea outside inland waters. Thus the Sea Fisheries (Clam and Bait Beds) Act 1881 controlled beam trawling injurious to any clam or other bait bed in any area being 'part of the sea adjoining the United Kingdom, and within the territorial waters of her Majesty's dominions, within the meaning of the Territorial Waters Jurisdiction Act, 1878'. S. 1(1) of the Sea Fisheries (Shellfish) Act 1967 provides that the appropriate Minister may by order provide for the establishment, etc., of a fishery for oysters, mussels or cockles 'on any portion of the shore and bed of the sea, or of an estuary or tidal river, above or below, or partly above and partly below, low water mark and within so much of the exclusive fishery limits of the British Islands as is adjacent to Great Britain . . .'. By s. 1(2) of the Act the Ministerial order may confer a right of several fishery on specified persons for not longer at one time than sixty years. The area covered by an order shall by s. 10 'for all purposes of jurisdiction' be deemed to be within the body of the adjoining county, borough or burgh, so far as it is not already within it. By virtue of the Fishery Limits Act 1976, the exclusive fishery limits have been extended to a distance of 200 miles from the baseline of the territorial sea. Schedule 2, paragraph 15 of this Act, however, provides that the seaward extent of s. 1(1) of the 1967 Act above be amended to cover 'waters adjacent to Great Britain to a distance of six nautical miles measured from the baselines from which the breadth of the territorial sea is measured'.

Lastly, there is a recent Act applying to Scotland which deserves mention. The Offshore Petroleum Development (Scotland) Act 1975, which provides for designated sea areas 'in part of the sea surrounding Scotland which is within United Kingdom waters', can be construed as accepting the possibility, by s. 5(3), that there are in such areas 'public or private rights in the sea or sea bed' other than those of navigation or fishery.

Furthermore, there are numerous local Acts dealing with piers and harbours which have made reference to the bed of the sea. Usually, these Acts contain a 'saving clause' in respect of the rights of the Crown. A typical example is s. 50 of the Schedule to the Pier and Harbour Order (Redcar) Confirmation Act 1948[20] which runs:

Nothing in this Order affects prejudicially any estate right power privilege or exemption of the Crown and in particular nothing herein contained authorises the Corporation [of Redcar] to take use or in any manner interfere with any portion of the shore or bed of the sea or of any river channel creek bay or estuary or any land hereditaments subjects or rights of whatsoever description belonging to His Majesty in right of His Crown and under the management of the Commissioners of Crown Lands or of the Minister respectively without the consent in writing of the Commissioners of Crown Lands or of the Minister as the case may be on behalf of His Majesty first had and obtained for that purpose.

These local Acts empower local authorities to use part of the bed of the sea, thus raising the inference that without such power specifically conferred there would be no right to do so. An example of many such provisions is set out in the preamble to the Whitley Bay Pier Act 1966[21] as follows:

And whereas it is expedient that the Company should be authorised to use part of the bed and foreshore of the sea at Whitley Bay and to acquire lands by agreement . . .

[20] 11 & 12 Geo. 6, c. xxii.

[21] 1966, c. xxxv. These local pier and harbour Acts often provide that the pier shall be deemed to be within the local administrative area. Thus, for example, the Pier and Harbour Orders (Blackpool Pier and Great Yarmouth New Britannia Pier) Confirmation Act 1966 (1966, c. xxxiv) provides that so much of the pier at Blackpool as is not within the county borough of Blackpool shall be deemed for all purposes to be within the said county borough, and so much of the Britannia Pier as is not within the county borough of Great Yarmouth shall be deemed for all purposes to be 'within the said county borough and the petty sessional area of Great Yarmouth' (Schedules).

B. The Subsoil

The general flow of executive and legislative practice in this period will now be described, followed by some specific aspects thereof.

(i) EXECUTIVE AND LEGISLATIVE PRACTICE IN GENERAL

The Office of Woods, Forests, and Land Revenues had no need to wait for the reassurance of the Law Officers, Before the date of the March 1878 opinion it had acquiesced in the wishes of lessees of submarine coal mines, including the Marquis of Londonderry in Durham, for an extension of the duration of the leases from thirty-one to sixty-three years and, at the same time, an extension of the area covered from two to three miles from the shore in order to provide sufficient minerals for the longer period of working. Thus Treasury Warrants were issued on 8 November 1877 for the Seaham and Dawdon mines (three miles from low-water mark),[22] 23 April 1878 for the Ryhope mine (three miles from high-water mark),[23] and 18 September 1878 for the Monkwearmouth mine (three miles from low-water mark).[24] The leases, each of 63 years, were expressed to run from 1874. It appears that at the time of such extensions the lessees had not penetrated beyond the two miles stipulated in the original lease of undersea minerals. The lease of the additional mile, therefore, was of unworked minerals *in situ*.

The issue of new leases went on undiminished. The annual Reports of the Commissioners continued to list details of leases of submarine mineral strata adjacent to the coasts of Cumberland, Durham, Northumberland, and Cornwall, while the summaries in the appendices to the *First Report of the Royal Commission on Coast Erosion and the Reclamation of Tidal Lands* gave a good indication of the position in 1906.[25]

In the 1888/9 financial year, the royalties received by the Crown from collieries and mines under the sea were:[26]

Cornwall	£1,107	16	9
Cumberland	£714	15	6
Durham	£5,029	1	7
Northumberland	£2,630	17	7

[22] CREST 10/29, pp. 60–1.
[23] Ibid., 81–2.
[24] Ibid., 91–3.
[25] For an account of undersea workings, see the evidence of 12 July 1889 given by the Crown Mineral Agent, Sir Warington W. Smyth, to the Select Committee on Woods, Forests, and Land Revenues of the Crown (*HCP*, 1889 (284, pp. 129–31) xvi, 301–2).
[26] *HCP*, 1889 (224, pp. 71–5) xxviii, 717–21.

The royalties received from submarine mines in 1896 were:[27]

Cornwall	£682	7	1
Cumberland	£671	13	1
Durham	£10,023	17	11
Northumberland	£3,178	17	1

A later Report recorded the lease of 'coal, culm, ironstone and fireclay under foreshore and bed of the sea near Deal' executed on 20 January 1914 in favour of the Betteshanger Boring Co. Ltd. for a term of three years from 29 September 1912 at an annual rent of £100, while on 28 February 1914 a similar lease was made to R. T. Smith of minerals near Dover.[28]

Meanwhile, the subject of submarine mines was raised on several occasions in the House of Commons. On 30 April 1907, the Financial Secretary to the Treasury, Walter Runciman, stated in answer to a question:

Minerals under the sea belong to [the] Crown and are under the management of the Commissioners of Woods. It is the usual course for persons desiring to carry on mining operations under the sea to apply to the Commissioners for a lease, and many such leases have been granted reserving rents and royalties to the Crown.[29]

Three years later, on 5 July 1910, Keir Hardie asked how far the workings of the Wellington Pit at Whitehaven extended under the sea beyond the low-water mark. The Home Secretary, Winston Churchill, replied that the distance was 'rather less than three and a half miles'.[30] Later on the same day, Hardie asked the following question:

. . . whether the Crown right to the sea beyond the three-mile limit extends to the minerals under the sea; and whether the rights of the Crown to mineral royalties have been protected in the case of mines working minerals beyond the three-mile limit?

The Solicitor-General, Sir Rufus Isaacs, replied:

The rights of the Crown to the minerals under the sea are co-extensive with its rights to the bed of the sea. I am informed that the rights of the Crown were fully protected in the only case of minerals under the sea beyond the three-mile limit which has hitherto been dealt with.[31]

[27] Ibid., 1896 (266, pp. 72–80) xxiv, 647–54.
[28] Ibid., 1914 (311, p. 76) xlix, 794.
[29] 173 *P. Debs.*, 4th series, col. 704.
[30] 18 *HC Debs.*, col. 1496.
[31] Ibid., col. 1503. See pp. 179–82 below.

Hardie was not content to leave the matter and on 7 July 1910 he asked the Chancellor of the Exchequer the following question:

. . . what is the amount of royalty per ton paid by the Whitehaven Coal Company now being worked by that company; and (2) whether he has claimed or obtained payment of royalties on the coal which has been worked under sea beyond the three mile limit at the Wellington Colliery, Whitehaven; if not, what action he proposes taking to recover the same?

The Financial Secretary to the Treasury, C. E. Hobhouse, replied as follows:

. . . The interest of the Crown in the mineral substances down to the bottom of the coal measures under the bed of the sea and below low water for a distance of ten miles from the lighthouse on St. Bees' Head was sold to the Earl of Lonsdale in 1881. In consequence of this sale no royalties are received or could be claimed by the Crown in respect of workings by the Whitehaven Coal Company.[32]

Hardie then asked for the 'terms of the document by which the rights of the Crown to mineral royalties for coal or other minerals being worked under the sea beyond the three-mile limit are protected, and the mines which are at present paying royalties to the Crown under the terms thereof'. Hobhouse replied:

In no cases up to the present have the Commissioners of Woods, etc., granted leases beyond the three-mile limit. In all leases of under-sea mines they require the lessees to leave a barrier on the seaward boundary so they cannot work beyond the three-mile limit without committing a breach of covenant for which the lease would be forfeitable. The workings in under-sea leases granted by the Commissioners of Woods are usually inspected at least once a year by the Crown mineral inspector.[33]

Several public and general Acts govern the exploration and exploitation of minerals, though it is not always clear that they apply to minerals under the marginal sea.

The Coal (Registration of Ownership) Act 1937 applied to 'proprietary interests that subsist in coal and mines of coal in Great Britain'. No definition of Great Britain was given. It is clear that the term was inserted to reflect the exclusion of Northern Ireland from the operation of the Act. By virtue of the Coal Act 1938, which again did not apply to Northern Ireland, the fee simple

[32] Ibid., col. 1782.

[33] Ibid. See also the written reply of the Secretary of State for Mines giving the names and situation of coal mines worked under the sea in the United Kingdom (220 *HC Debs.*, cols. 237–8: 17 July 1928).

in all coal and mines of coal, together with such property and rights annexed thereto, was vested in the Coal Commission as from 1 July 1942. No specific mention was made of minerals situated below low-water mark. By s. 42 the above provisions were declared to bind the Crown 'and shall accordingly apply to land belonging to His Majesty or forming part of the possessions of the Duchy of Cornwall'. On 1 January 1947, the fee simple ownership became vested in the National Coal Board by virtue of the Coal Industry Nationalisation Act 1946. S. 1(1) of this Act charged the National Coal Board with the duty of 'working and getting the coal in Great Britain, to the exclusion (save as in this Act provided) of any other person'. Again, no definition of 'Great Britain' was given.

On 11 May 1964, the United Kingdom ratified the 1958 Convention on the Continental Shelf, which came into force on 10 June 1964 for those States which had deposited instruments of ratification or accession. Already, on 15 April 1964, the Continental Shelf Act 1964 had come into force for the whole of the United Kingdom. S. 1(1) of this Act provides that:

Any rights exercisable by the United Kingdom outside territorial waters with respect to the sea bed and subsoil and their natural resources, except so far as they are exercisable in relation to coal, are hereby vested in Her Majesty.

S. 1(2) provides:

In relation to any coal with respect to which those rights are exercisable the Coal Industry Nationalisation Act 1946 shall apply as it applies in relation to coal in Great Britain . . .

S. 1(1) of the Petroleum (Production) Act 1934 states:

The property in petroleum existing in its natural condition in strata in Great Britain is hereby vested in His Majesty, and His Majesty shall have the exclusive right of searching and boring for and getting such petroleum.

The term 'Great Britain' is not defined and once again it is probable that its use was intended merely to reflect the exclusion of Northern Ireland from the scope of the Act. Under s. 2 of this Act, the Board of Trade, now the Secretary of State for Energy, has power to grant licences. The Continental Shelf Act 1964 is also relevant to petroleum. S. 1 (3) reads:

In relation to any petroleum with respect to which those rights are exercisable sections 2 and 6 of the Petroleum (Production) Act 1934 (which relate to the granting of licences to search and bore for, and get, petroleum) shall apply as they apply in relation to petroleum in Great Britain . . .

The administration of licences is now governed by the Petroleum (Production) Regulations 1976[34] which were promulgated under powers conferred both by the 1934 and 1964 Acts above. The Regulations apply to licences to search and bore for, and get, petroleum

  (a) in strata in the areas of Great Britain and beneath the waters adjacent thereto which lie on the landward side of lines drawn in accordance with the provisions of Schedule 1 . . .

  (b) In strata in the islands on the seaward side of the said lines, in the seabed and subsoil beneath waters which lie on the seaward side of the said lines and, where such lines are not the outward limit of territorial waters adjacent to Great Britain, within that limit, and in the sea bed and subsoil within any designated area . . .

Schedule 1 provides that except for certain estuaries, rivers, harbours, bays, and other places specified in the Schedule, the demarcation line between 'landward' and 'seaward' areas 'shall be the low water line along the coast of the mainland of Great Britain, the Isle of Wight, Anglesey and Holy Island'. The Schedule provides for straight base-lines for the estuaries, etc. specified.

It is still open to argument, both in respect of coal and petroleum, that the submarine strata under 'territorial waters' are outside 'Great Britain', whereas the Continental Shelf Act 1964 expressly (s. 1(1)) applies 'outside territorial waters'. If so, the Regulations will be *ultra vires* in so far as they extend to the bed and subsoil of 'territorial waters' outside Great Britain.

The National Coal Board (Additional Powers) Act 1966 is open to less criticism for it specifically mentions the bed and subsoil of the territorial waters of the United Kingdom. S. 1 (1) (a) empowers the Board, subject to the provisions of the Petroleum (Production) Act 1934 and the Continental Shelf Act 1964 '. . . to search and bore for and get petroleum . . . in the sea bed and subsoil of the territorial waters of the United Kingdom adjacent to Great Britain and of any area for the time being designated under section 1(7) of the said Act of 1964'.

No definition is given of 'territorial waters of the United

[34] Statutory Instruments 1976, No. 1129.

Kingdom adjacent to Great Britain'. The Continental Shelf Act 1964 does not expressly designate the geographical extent of the shelf, s. 1(7) providing merely that 'Her Majesty may from time to time by Order in Council designate any area as an area within which the rights mentioned in subsection (1) of this section are exercisable, and any area so designated is in this Act referred to as a designated area.'

Although the Continental Shelf Act 1964 excludes from its purview the submarine soil within 'territorial waters', the latter area is within the scope of the Mineral Workings (Offshore Installations) Act 1971. This Act, which provides for the welfare of persons on installations situated in territorial waters as well as in the waters situated above the 'continental shelf', begins:

This Act shall apply to the underwater exploitation and underwater exploration of mineral resources—
  (a) in or under the shore or bed of waters to which this Act applies, other than inland waters, and
  (b) in or under the bed of such inland waters as may for the time being be specified for the purpose of this paragraph by Order in Council.

S. 2 reads as follows:

In this Act—
  (a) 'waters to which this Act applies' means the waters in or adjacent to the United Kingdom up to the seaward limits of territorial waters, and the waters in any designated area within the meaning of the Continental Shelf Act 1964,
  (b) 'inland waters' means waters within the United Kingdom, other than estuaries and tidal rivers.

Thus the legislature envisages the possibility of 'territorial waters' which are merely 'adjacent to' not 'in' the United Kingdom. This caution is also reflected in Regulation 3(1) (b) of the Petroleum (Production) Regulations 1976—'outward limit of territorial waters adjacent to Great Britain'—and in s. 1(1) (a) of the National Coal Board (Additional Powers) Act 1966—'sea bed and subsoil of the territorial waters of the United Kingdom adjacent to Great Britain'. The Ancient Monuments and Archaeological Areas Act 1979, which has been described in the first part of this Chapter, also assumes that the bed of the territorial sea may not be within Great Britain.

Finally, in a recent written Parliamentary answer the executive gave its opinion of the general position. On 16 January 1979, the

Government spokesman in the House of Lords, Lord Strabolgi, wrote:

The search for and exploitation of off-shore oil and gas resources is conducted under licences granted by the Secretary of State in accordance with regulations made under the Petroleum (Production) Act 1934 and the Continental Shelf Act 1964. . . .

The National Coal Board, by virtue of the Coal Industry Nationalisation Act 1946, is charged with the duty of working and getting the coal in Great Britain (including territorial waters). Rights exercisable by the United Kingdom outside territorial waters in the seabed and subsoil and their resources relating to coal were vested in the National Coal Board by the Continental Shelf Act 1964 and are exercisable by the Board subject to the consent of the Secretary of State. . . .

So far as other minerals within territorial waters and on the United Kingdom Continental Shelf are concerned these in general form part of the Crown Estate and are under the management of the Crown Estate Commissioners who have professional and scientific advisers. Activities, licensed only after careful consideration of the possible impact on other interests, include the winning of tin, salt and potash, but by far the most important activity is the winning of marine sand and gravel from the sea for use as concrete aggregate or for reclamation. This activity comprises some 10 per cent of the national production of that material.[35]

(ii) THE LONSDALE SALE, 1880[36]

In 1880 came a new development, namely the first recorded sale of the Crown's interest in submarine strata, amounting to 72,000 acres. As mentioned in Chapter II above, a lease had been granted by the Crown on 27 August 1860 to the Earl of Lonsdale consisting of 'the mines, veins, seams and beds of coal, culm, ironstone and fireclay under the bed of the sea, below low water mark therefrom, adjacent to the townships or parishes of Moresby, Parton, Preston Quarter, Whitehaven, Sandwith, Rottington and Saint Bees' in Cumberland. This lease was made for a term of 31 years from 5 July 1859 at a fixed rent of £1 and at a scale of royalties on the different minerals extracted. The seaward limit of the area leased was approximately three miles from low-water mark.

In 1863, the agents of the lessee approached the Office of Woods with a view to the purchase of the Crown's freehold interest in the minerals demised by the lease. The reason advanced was that the workings had extended so far to seaward that it was now necessary for the lease-holder to incur a large outlay in the construction of

[35] 397 *HL Debs.*, cols. 931–2: 16 January 1979.
[36] *HCP*, 1881 (307, pp. 69–73) xxx, 805–9: CREST 37/94.

new works on his lands in order to reduce the cost of raising the submarine coal. As the lessee was only the tenant for life of the Whitehaven Estates, it was proposed to provide the necessary funds by means of a family arrangement, for which the purchase of the Crown's interest in the minerals was desirable. The sum offered by the lessee, £12,000, was, however, declined by the Commissioner, C. A. Gore, as 'altogether inadequate'. An increased offer of £25,000 was declined by Gore for the same reason in 1871.

Some years later, the agents made a proposal to the effect that a new lease should be granted for an extended term, although subsequently they renewed their offer to purchase the freehold, offering £50,000 for the purchase of the Crown's interest in the premises currently demised and in the minerals lying to seaward of those included in the 1860 lease. The agents represented that the proposed arrangement would have to be submitted to the Court of Chancery, and also that a private Act of Parliament would probably be necessary.[37] They therefore requested that the purchase might be optional on the lessee's part up to Michaelmas 1880.

Gore, after consulting the Crown Receiver for Cumberland and the Crown Mineral Agent, thereupon concluded an agreement with the Earl of Lonsdale. In a letter dated 30 March 1880 to the Lords Commissioners of the Treasury, he explained the situation as follows:

I have to report the particulars of an arrangment which I have entered into for the grant of a lease to the Earl of Lonsdale, of the coal and certain other minerals [i.e. culm, ironstone, and fireclay] within a tract of land, forming part of the bed of the sea, beyond low-water mark, adjacent to St. Bees' Head, near Whitehaven, adjacent to the county of Cumberland, with option to the lessee to purchase the minerals so to be demised, and all other minerals, if any, in the tract in question, down to the bottom of the coal measures. . . .

The Crown is to grant to the Earl of Lonsdale a lease of all such estate and interest as Her Majesty may possess in the mineral substances in the undermentioned tract of land, being part of the bed of the sea beyond low-water mark, i.e.:

1. The parcel edged dark blue on the enclosed plan, being the land in which the mineral substances are included in the existing lease to the Earl of Lonsdale.

---

[37] This was done by the Lonsdale Settled Estates Act of 9 July 1880 (24 & 25 Vict., Private Acts, c. *3*).

2. The land lying to seaward of the parcel above referred to, and extending to a distance of 10 miles from the lighthouse on St. Bees' Head, and bounded on the north and south by lines drawn in the direction of the light blue lines on the plan.

The proposed lease was to be for a term from 5 July 1890 (the date on which the existing lease would expire) and at an annual rent of £1, with a scale of royalties. The arrangement continued:

The lessee is to have the option, to be exercised by a notice to be given before the 10th of October 1880, of purchasing at the sum of £50,000, the mineral substances agreed to be demised, and also all other mines and minerals within the whole of the tract before referred to, down to the bottom of the coal measures.

In the letter Gore stated that the submarine workings which had already been carried out by the Earl of Lonsdale and his predecessors in title had extended 'from north to south along the coast for a distance of about three miles, and from low-water mark to seaward for a distance of about 2¼ miles'.

On 8 April 1880, the Lords Commissioners, Crichton and Winn, issued a Warrant to Gore on the terms set out above. In their words '. . . For granting to him [i.e., Lonsdale] the option of purchasing at the sum of £50,000, all the Crown's interest in the minerals so agreed to be demised, and in all other minerals down to the bottom of the coal measures, within the said tract; such option to be exercised before the 10th October next.'

The option to purchase was then exercised, the 59th Report of the Commissioners of Woods, Forests, and Land Revenues recording the sale to the trustees of the Lonsdale Estates, William Stuart, Stirling Crawfurd, and the Rt. Hon. James Lowther, on 21 December 1880 for £50,000 of:

The interest of the Crown in the Mineral Substances, down to the bottom of the coal measures, within or under certain tracts of land, part of the bed of the sea, and below low water mark, adjacent to the Townships or Parishes of Moresby, Parton, Preston Quarter, Whitehaven, Sandwith, Rottington and Saint Bees. (Paper 307, p. 42)

It appears that on 9 April 1937, the purchaser, now called Lowther Estates Ltd., granted a lease of undersea coal to the Cumberland Coal Co. (Whitehaven) Ltd., up to a distance of nine miles from the coast.[38]

In 1973, the Earl of Lonsdale instituted proceedings against the

[38] See COAL 17/648.

Attorney-General and a licencee of the Board of Trade in which he asks, *inter alia*, for a declaration that he is entitled to ownership of any oil or natural gas down to the bottom of the coal measures in the area granted in 1880 and that the above licence is not binding on him. The case has not yet come to trial.

(iii) THE BRICKDALE OPINION, 1893[39]

The legal problems raised but not resolved in the Channel tunnel litigation reappeared in the early eighteen-nineties when Sir Myles Fenton, General Manager of the South Eastern Railway Company, made an application to the Crown for a lease of coal under the foreshore and bed of the sea near Dover. On 27 July 1892, the Commissioner of Woods, Sir Nigel Kingscote, agreed to a lease of sixty-three years from 1 January 1893 of all the coal under the foreshore below high-water mark and under the bed of the sea up to two miles below low-water mark. The proposed lease was made subject to the withdrawal of the adverse claims by the South Eastern Railway Company and the Submarine Continental Railway Company to the 'foreshore'. On 2 February 1893, Sir Myles Fenton expressed his agreement to the above terms.

The steps taken so far by the Office of Woods did not commend themselves to Walter Murton, Solicitor to the Board of Trade. In a memorandum dated 11 February 1893 he wrote:

I entirely share the regret which has been expressed that the Office of Woods have not communicated with us before arranging terms with the applicants. These terms it now appears have already been accepted. I see no reference in them to any 'adverse claims' except those relating to the foreshore, whereas the really serious and important claims set up (almost for the first time on the part of any subject) against the Crown to the bed of the sea within territorial limits, by the S.E. Ry. Co. and the Channel Tunnel Company, have apparently been ignored. I wrote a strong Minute on this subject in December 1891 and it was no doubt sent to the Office of Woods. Sir Myles Fenton distinctly claimed on the part of the applicants for the lease the right to extend their works under the bed of the sea and to take coal therefrom without any 'grant or authority of the Crown'. Accordingly I urged that 'the applicants should give or obtain an effectual guarantee' that the two companies in question should upon the granting of the lease make an absolute admission of the Crown's rights and thereby terminate the litigation still pending. The Companies should in fact submit to a decree.

All that the 'terms' shew is that the two companies are only to submit to a decree with respect to the foreshore, which as I pointed out, was

[39] CREST 37/619.

comparatively unimportant.

It may be that the Office of Woods believe that the Board of Trade are content with respect to the bed of the sea to let the question rest upon the Order of 5 July 1882, but I regret that they did not consult us upon this point. The injunction contained in that Order prohibiting 'the working etc. beyond ordinary low water mark' is interlocutory only 'until the trial of the action or further Order'. The Crown's rights to the bed of the Sea are therefore still sub judice. I am glad however to note that 'until the trial or further Order' the consent of the Board of Trade is made necessary to the 'working excavating taking or interfering with any chalk soil or other substance in from or under the bed of the sea of the coast of Kent between Folkestone and Dover'.

Although this Order only binds the Defendant Companies and not the intended lessees, the provision may assist the Board of Trade in obtaining the required decree in the Chancery suit from the Companies themselves. It is clear that some immediate steps should be taken for this purpose, or at least to ascertain why the Office of Woods have not extended their terms to this suit as well as to the Information with respect to foreshore.

The Office of Woods thereupon submitted the case for the opinion of M. I. F. Brickdale, Crown conveyancing counsel of Lincoln's Inn, whose opinion, dated 13 March 1893, read as follows:

Before the negotiations for a lease of the coal under the bed of the sea beyond low water mark are carried any further it seems right to mention a preliminary difficulty which has occurred to me.

Although it seems to be settled that according to our law the bed of the sea for a considerable distance (though undefined) beyond low water mark belongs to the Crown, I doubt very much whether it is part of England; and unless it is part of England the Act of 10 Geo. 4 cap. 50 [i.e., the Crown Lands Act 1829] does not apply to it; nor on the other hand does the restricting Act of the 1st Anne apply to it [i.e., the Crown Lands Act 1702].

According to *Reg.* v. *Keyn* 2 Ex. Div. 63 and *Harris* v. *Owners of the Franconia* 2 C.P. Div. 173 the territory of England ends at low water mark: and I conceive that the word England in a statute must be construed strictly seeing that it was considered necessary to pass an Act (20 Geo. [2] cap. 42) to make it include even Wales.

It is true that as no coal lying under the bed of the sea could be won except by bringing it through the foreshore, a lease or licence might properly be framed in such a form as to secure to the Crown practically in any case the payment and observance of the proposed royalties and covenants: but if my view is correct the question whether, under the circumstances, it would be proper to grant any such lease or licence seems to require consideration: and I submit that the intending Lessees should be apprised of the state of the case, so that they may judge for themselves whether they would be satisfied with such a lease or licence: especially as a surrender of certain claims or alleged claims by parties with whom they are closely connected is made a condition precedent to the granting of it, and it is necessary therefore to preclude any complaint that the full promised equivalent for such surrender cannot be given.

A copy of this opinion was sent to Sir Nigel Kingscote by the solicitor to the Office of Woods, T.W. Gorst. Its receipt caused a series of minutes to be written within that Office. The first, written probably by J. Hellard, the Principal Clerk, asked whether any advice had ever been received on the distance to which English territory extended or to whom submarine mines could be leased by the Office of Woods. The anonymous reply referred to the opinion of the Law Officers given in 1878 and continued:

It was unhesitatingly in favor of the Crown's right to the minerals under the sea below low water mark, but the case submitted limited the question to the distance of a marine league from the shore.

The Whitehaven undersea coal was recently sold to Lord Lonsdale's Trustees to a distance in the Irish sea of 10 miles due west of the Lighthouse on St. Bees Head. It does not appear that Counsel's opinion was taken as to the Crown's right to deal with the minerals so far seaward. The Irish Sea bed was treated as British Territory and the distance limited to 10 miles so as not to interfere with Scotch or Isle of Man minerals.

The author of the earlier minute then composed the following note:

Mr. Brickdale does not appear to doubt but that the Bed of the sea to a certain distance belongs to Her Majesty and on this point the opinion of the Law Officers above referred to is direct and must I think overrule doubt (if any) cast by Mr. B's opinion. It has been the general practice to limit dealings to 3 miles from low water in accordance with the Jurisdiction established by the Territorial Waters Jurisdiction Act 1878 (41 & 42 Vict. c.73) but I do not know why if a British Subject took possession of soil and minerals beyond that distance the English Sovereign should not claim it as part of the English or British Territory. The right of the Crown to soil below low water is recognised by several acts referred to presently but neither they nor the opinion of the Law Officers above mentioned recognise any particular limit.

The point which seems really raised by Mr. Brickdale's opinion is whether or not the Commissioners of Woods can deal with any interest which Her Majesty may possess in the bed of the sea but I submit that this point is one that is now too late to discuss and if it should ever be decided by a court of competent jurisdiction that they could not so deal, it would be necessary to obtain (and I cannot doubt but that it would be obtained) an act confirming past dealings and expressly placing that interest under the charge of this Department and of the Board of Trade respectively.

The point was not directly advised on by the Law Officers in the case referred to above but they were clearly made aware that the Commissioners of Woods had purported to deal with the mines under the bed of the sea and they raised no objection to their power to do so.

The agreement for reference as to the mines under the Foreshore and bed of the sea off Cornwall was entered into by the Commissioners of Woods and is recited in the Cornwall Submarine Act though the Act does not in terms recognise the right of the Commissioners of Woods to deal with the submarine mines.

But the right to deal with the Crown's Interest in land below low water is clearly recognised by the Herne Bay Fishery Act 1864 and the Ham Oyster Fishery Act 1865, and perhaps more distinctly still by the Crown Lands Act 1866, see s. 8 et seq.

And in addition to these statutory recognitions the Commissioners of Woods have for a long series of years dealt with portions of the bed of the sea and with minerals thereunder. The earliest mineral case was I think the Botallack workings of Lord Falmouth which arose in 1840. Differences then arose to it between Lord Falmouth and the Crown and between the Duchy of Cornwall and the Crown but lettings of the Botallack undersea mines was [sic] made by this Department as from 10 October 1855 and of the Levant undersea mines as from 5 July 1854 while as from about 1865 numerous lettings of undersea mines off the coasts of Durham, Northumberland, and Cumberland, and off parts of Scotland and Wales have been effected by this Department.

In the present instance it would be particularly inadvisable to frame the draft lease in any way than in the form of an actual demise as has been done in the previous lettings and the doing so might be likely to raise again the question which the S.E. Railway Company and Sir E. Watkin have raised but which they are now understood to be willing to abandon i.e. as to their right to go under the bed of the sea without any authority from the Crown.

For these reasons I think the Crown's title to the mines proposed to be demised and the power of the Commissioners of Woods to deal with them must be taken for granted for the purpose of settling the Documents which should be so framed as not to cast the slightest doubt upon such title or powers.

On 17 March 1893, Sir Nigel Kingscote added the final minute to the series:

I agree that it is too late now to re-open any question as to the power of this Department to deal with the bed of the sea and in the present case no doubt whatever should be cast on that power . . .

It appears from the papers remaining on the file that the South Eastern Railway Company and the Submarine Continental Railway Company would not consent to a decree in respect of the seabed below the foreshore, although they were willing to take a lease from the Crown even though the case were to go against the latter. In the event, it seems that no lease was concluded regarding either foreshore or seabed.

The last papers on the Crown Estate file dealing with the Dover coalfield contain an exchange of views between Harper Scaife and Morton Evans, Joint Secretary of the Office of Woods. In a note dated 10 July 1916, Scaife drew Evans's attention to *Chelikani's* case, then just decided. Two days later, Evans replied:

Personally I feel confident that whatever may be the rule as to territorial waters (which are a highway) no nation would ever consider itself limited by any other rule as regards soil or minerals than the practicability of maintaining effective possession. The question is never likely to arise except in narrow seas (e.g. straits between two countries) when I suppose mid-channel or some other conventional line would necessarily have to be adopted.

He added as a postscript that 'we have frequently sold parts of the bed of the sea below low water mark'.

(iv) THE EASINGTON LEASE, 1938[40]

On 20 December 1933, the Commissioners of Crown Lands and the Easington Coal Co. entered into a transaction whereby for a period of 60 years the Commissioners

. . . do hereby grant demise and lease unto the Lessees their successors and assigns all those the mines beds and seams of coal culm ironstone and fireclay . . . within and under all that land foreshore and seabed . . . situate and lying adjoining to and below the former high water mark as shown by the blue line on the plan annexed hereto and extending therefrom seawards in front of the Parish of Easington with Thorpe and the Parish of Hawthorn in the County of Durham within the following limits that is to say Bounded on the West side by the said blue line on the North side by a line drawn for three miles seaward from the North end of the said blue line . . . on the South side by a line drawn for three miles seaward from the South end of the said blue line . . . and on the East by

[40] CREST 37/1247; COAL 17/648.

an imaginary line drawn from North to South at a distance of three miles from the said blue line . . .

In 1938, the Easington Coal Co. wished to obtain a lease of minerals in the three miles seaward of the area of the 1933 lease, i.e. to a distance of six miles from the stipulated western boundary. Within the Office of Crown Lands, A. E. Horton drew up a minute dated 21 October 1938 in which he referred *inter alia* to the Patteson arbitration and the Cornwall Submarine Mines Act 1858, the *Keyn* case, the Law Officers' opinion of 16 March 1878, the 1880 sale to the Earl of Lonsdale, the 1893 memorandum by Brickdale, and Sir Cecil Hurst's paper of 1923. He concluded:

Looking at our proceedings it seems that up to 1878 (Territorial Waters Act) there was no limit and we claimed generally that the bed of the sea below low water mark was vested in the Sovereign in right of his Crown. That the Law officers took the view that the Territorial Waters Act did not affect the Crown's position and that the occupation of an undersea mine by a subject would be sufficient to attach the right of property in it to the Crown and that whilst Mr. Brickdale questioned in 1893 whether such a mine would be part of England he accepted the principle that the bed of the sea below low water mark for an undefined distance belonged to the Crown.

If this be so it seems to me that if the Easington Colliery workings ex adverso Durham proceed beyond the 3 mile limit the right of property will still be in the Crown and that the Company will need an extension of their existing Crown Lease to cover these workings; also that they must pay the usual royalties and observe the usual covenants.

There is on the file the draft of a letter dated 25 November 1938 from the Commissioners of Crown Lands to the Easington Coal Co. Ltd. It read in part:

. . . the Commissioners are prepared to grant to you a lease of these minerals for a term of 52 years and one month from 1st December 1938 and otherwise upon the terms and conditions mentioned below.

The demise to include the coal and culm only (ie. not the ironstone and fireclay) within the area of seabed, shown by a brown verge on the plan enclosed with this letter, extending for a distance of 3 miles from the eastern boundary of the existing Lease, (indicated approximately by a green verge on the said plan) and bounded on the north and south respectively by straight lines being extensions of the north and south boundaries of the last mentioned Lease, and on the east by a straight line adjoining the extremities of the northern and southern boundaries.

On 2 December 1938, the Solicitor, A. D. Stocks, minuted, 'In view of the complicated nature of this lease and in the principles involved in the occupation beyond the three mile limit, I propose to have the draft finally approved by Counsel.'

An unsigned internal minute was written on 5 December in response to the above. It read in part:

The Draft has been prepared as a Lease demising the estate and interest of the Crown (if any) in the minerals . . . Actually, I gather, neither the Crown nor anyone else can be regarded as having any estate or interest in the premises until such time as the mines are taken into possession. The circumstances, or accident, of the Crown being in a position to prevent and control workings in the area in question places it, however, in a position to impose terms upon the Company for its consent. In the circumstances it may, perhaps, be a question for consideration whether the proposed arrangement should not, preferably, take the form of an exclusive licence to work the coal taken than a demise of the minerals themselves, or of any assumed estate and interest therein.

Some of the provision of the draft, e.g. the proviso on page 3 that the lessees shall not make roads etc. on the sea bed overlying the mines, hardly seems applicable, also I am not sure what powers the Crown would possess to prevent the deposit of spoil beyond the three mile limit.

If the lessees' operations are restricted to submarine workings through the area they already hold from the Crown, it would be unnecessary to make any provisions against constructions of any kind upon the surface, and no question would then arise how far it is possible to control acts of that nature beyond the three mile limit.

On 31 December 1938 a supplemental lease was made for the additional area of three miles. On 18 January 1939 the Commissioners of Crown lands completed a form for registration of the lease under the Coal (Registration of Ownership) Act 1937. In this form they inserted the entry: '. . . the following proprietary interest constitutes the freehold reversion—an estate in fee simple vested in His Majesty in right of His Crown—'.

Unfortunately, neither the counsel's opinion, the draft supplemental lease nor the lease itself has been found in the public records. The lease is entered in vol. 16 of the Foreshores Lease Book at p. 350. This item has not been transferred to the Public Record Office.

(v) THE COAL COMMISSION PAPERS, 1944[41]

On 26 April 1944, D. F. Smith of the Coal Commission put the

[41] COAL 17/648.

following questions to the Commission's legal adviser, Dr F. A. Enever:

Will you please advise me (a) whether the Commission have the right to grant leases of coal underlying the bed of the sea beyond the three mile limit and (b) if not, what steps a colliery company can take to work such coal.

Two days later, Enever replied in a lengthy minute. After referring to *Lord Advocate* v. *Wemyss*, *Lord Advocate* v. *Clyde Navigation Trustees*, *Attorney-General* v. *Chambers*, *Lord Fitzhardinge* v. *Purcell*, and *Keyn's* case, Enever turned to the Coal Act 1938. He continued:

. . . we find nothing there indicating any territorial limits other than that the Act does not extend to Northern Ireland (s. 58(2)). The Coal (Registration of Ownership) Act, however, (s. 1(1)) refers to 'coal and mines of coal in Great Britain'—again with a reference, in s. 6(2), that the Act does not extend to Northern Ireland. It can, I think, be assumed that the Coal Act, 1938, has the same effect as if the words 'in Great Britain' had been specifically included, and I think, therefore, that the effect is to vest in the Coal Commission all the coal in respect of which either the Crown or a subject had a proprietary interest, which should, therefore, include the Crown's proprietary rights in the minerals under the soil of the sea, but from the authorities I cannot see that any proprietary rights existed beyond the 3-mile limit, except where a proprietary right may have become established by virtue of a possessory right. It may be, for instance, that certain under-sea coal was being worked before the operation of the Coal Act, 1938, in under-sea mines extending beyond the 3-mile limit. If this were so, it would obviously have been under some licence from the Crown, and it may be that the Crown would be regarded as having acquired a proprietary interest by reason of such workings. If so, that coal also became vested in the Commission.

One fact becomes quite clear, namely that no-one can get access to coal under the bed of the sea beyond the 3-mile limit without passing through coal which has become vested in the Commission, and that if the Commission have not that coal vested in them, no-one else has. The point is a very technical one, but if it is thought desirable, in view of what I have said, not to grant an actual lease of coal outside territorial waters because of the grave doubt whether the Commission have, in fact, any rights vested in them in under-sea coal beyond 3 miles from the coast, one way of overcoming the difficulty which occurs to me would be for the Commission to charge a rent for the carriage of coal, gotten from under-sea mines outside the 3-mile limit, through the mines which the Commission do own, such rent being equivalent to the royalty which would have been charged for the getting of coal from the under-sea mines. If this were done, the Colliery Company would not be answerable to anyone for trespass in respect of the under-sea coal, because there would be no-one who could establish a claim to it, and the technical legal difficulties would thereby be overcome.

If you want a precise answer to the two questions, I should feel bound to say—as regards (a), No; unless a proprietary interest had been, before the valuation date mentioned in the Coal Act, 1938, acquired by prescription; and as regards (b), subject to the latter part of the answer to (a)—none.

In a minute dated 4 May 1944, Smith produced references to the Lonsdale and Easington transactions of 1880 and 1938 respectively. He concluded that 'having regard to the vesting provisions of the Coal Act, it seems to me that the Coal Commission are as fully entitled to lease coal outside the three-mile limit as the Crown were'.

On 23 May 1944, Enever minuted in reply:

Shortly, the position is that the Crown were entitled to the minerals under the bed of the sea certainly up to the 3-mile limit and for an undefined distance beyond, and may have become entitled to minerals beyond that distance by mere occupancy. Therefore the Commissioners of Crown Lands had no compunction in granting leases of under-sea minerals, for by doing so their title was perfected by the occupation of their lessees. As I have said in my previous Minute, any workings of under-sea minerals beyond the 3-mile limit must obviously have been under some licence from the Crown, because there was no-one else who could substantiate a claim to them, and by working under the licence the licensee perfected the Crown's title by occupancy.

The somewhat academic point which now arises is whether the Crown can now claim that they, and not the Commission, are entitled to any undersea coal beyond an undefined limit in excess of 3 miles from the coast, on the ground that all that vested in the Commission on the vesting date was what the Crown then had power to grant, i.e., areas in which the Crown had obtained a title by occupancy, and that the Commission cannot show a title to what has since come into occupation. If it is proposed to grant leases of coal in new under-sea areas beyond the 3-mile limit, without some such words as 'so far as the Commission can lawfully grant the same', it might be as well to ascertain first whether the Commissioners of Crown Lands lay any claim to such coal.

The final minutes on the file, exchanged between Smith and A. E. Horton, indicate that the Coal Commission did not regard itself as legally prevented from making such a lease. Horton considered that the property in coal beyond three miles would become vested in the Coal Commission when actual occupation took place.

C. Conclusion

The above account may give the impression that the Crown's activities with regard to the marginal solum are a matter of history. Nothing could be more inexact. The level of activity has increased in recent years with new submarine mineral discoveries, such as potash deposits off Cleveland, and the revival of interest in former undersea workings, such as the Durham offshore coal deposits and the tin mines in west Cornwall. The annual reports of the Commissioners of Crown Estate show an increasing revenue from offshore mineral extraction (mainly sand and gravel dredging) and from leases of various kinds. A substantial proportion of this revenue will come from the area of solum discussed in this work. In an article published in 1977,[42] Professor F. E. Dowrick estimates that on the basis of a three-mile territorial sea measured from the new baselines the surface area of seabed claimed by the Crown is about 13,000 square miles, considerably more than the area of dry land subject to some form of public ownership in the United Kingdom. With a twelve-mile territorial sea the figure would rise to about 40,000 square miles. By comparison, the total area of dry land and non-tidal waters within the United Kingdom is 94,216 square miles.

[42] Dowrick [1977]*Public Law* 10, 22.

Chapter IX

Judicial Practice after 1876

A. English Judicial Decisions

Within a few years of the decision in *Keyn*, Lord Blackburn, who, it
will be recalled, did not sit in that case, twice made remarks in the
course of delivering judgment in the House of Lords which suggest
that he might not have considered *Keyn* to have had a drastic effect.
In *Bristow* v. *Cormican* in 1878, an appeal from Ireland concerning
fishing rights in Lough Neagh, Lord Blackburn remarked:

> The property in the soil of the sea and of estuaries and of rivers in which
> the tide ebbs and flows is *prima facie* of common right vested in the Crown
> . . .[1]

In *Neill* v. *Duke of Devonshire* in 1882, an appeal from Ireland
concerning fishing rights in the tidal River Blackwater, Lord
Blackburn cited with apparent approval extracts from chapter 4 of
Hale's *De Jure Maris* in which that author had referred *inter alia* to
the King as 'owner of this great waste' in the context of what Lord
Blackburn referred to as 'the narrow seas adjoining the coasts'.[2]

The next case in which the legal status of the marginal seabed
and subsoil incidentally arose was *Attorney-General* v. *Reeve* in
1885.[3] According to the report in the *Times Law Reports*, this was
the revival for the first time in the High Court of an ancient
proceeding, namely an information in the Exchequer designed to
establish a right of the Crown.[4] According to the report, it was also
the first case concerning acquisition of land by accretion since the

---

[1] (1878) 3 App. Cas. 641, 665–6.
[2] (1882) 8 App. Cas. 135, 176–7.
[3] (1885) 1 T.L.R. 675. See also the argument of Sir Hardinge Giffard QC in *Overseers of
Woolwich* v. *Robertson* (1881) 6 Q.B.D. 654, 657 where he cited R. G. Hall for the proposition
that the Crown had by law 'the dominion and ownership over British seas'.
[4] The information filed by the Crown on 5 December 1882 against the companies
engaged in the Channel tunnel excavations could, however, have also been such a
proceeding. See Chapter VII above.

litigation concerning Lord Yarborough.[5] The issue concerned permanently dry land which had appeared at Lowestoft as the result of the recession of the high-water mark caused by coastal works. The Crown claimed that the new land vested in it, since the accretion was perceptible; the defendant, who owned the estate abutting on the land in question, argued that accretion was imperceptible and fell to him in accordance with 'the rule in *Attorney-General* v. *Chambers*'. Lord Coleridge C.J. gave judgment for the Crown on the ground that the accretion was perceptible. In the course of his judgment he quoted without adverse comment Hale's *De Jure Maris* where the rationale behind the general rule for accretion was stated to be 'because in truth the soil, where there is now dry land, was formerly part of the very *fundus maris*, and consequently belonged to the King'.[6]

Five years later, in the case of *Jones* v. *Bennett*, Lord Coleridge C.J. referred to the Territorial Waters Jurisdiction Act 1878 in the following terms:

A declaratory Act means to declare the law, or to declare that which has always been the law, and there having been doubts which have arisen Parliament declares what the law is, and enacts that it shall continue what it then is. The thing is very familiar. In this very matter most of the Profession, I daresay, are aware that a great conflict of opinion existed as to the distance to which the territory of the Queen extended beyond low-water mark. I was one of those who thought that it extended a marine league out to sea; the majority—but a majority of one—were of a different opinion. But when Parliament came to declare, when it came to enact upon the matter, it declared and enacted—and declared adversely to the opinion of the majority, that that has always been the law of the country, that the marine league was the limit.[7]

The above Act was not relevant to the case, being used by the judge only to illustrate his concept of a declaratory statute. It should be pointed out, furthermore, that the 1878 Act, unlike the Cornwall Submarine Mines Act 1858, did not contain the formula 'be it therefore enacted and declared' but the conventional 'be it therefore enacted'.

In *Fitzhardinge (Lord)* v. *Purcell* in 1908, the issue concerned the title to the foreshore on the banks of the River Severn at

[5] *R. v. Lord Yarborough* (1824) 3 B. & C. 91 (King's Bench); (1828) 11 Bligh N.S. 147 (House of Lords).

[6] Hale, *De Jure Maris*, Ch. 4, printed in Moore, 380. In the present case, however, the soil in dispute was previously part of the foreshore, not the bed of the sea.

[7] (1890) 63 L.T. N.S. 705, 708.

Slimbridge and to a fishery in the river adjacent. Thus no question of the status of the seabed directly arose. In the course of his judgment, however, Parker J. remarked:

Clearly the bed of the sea, at any rate for some distance below low-water mark, and the beds of tidal navigable rivers, are prima facie vested in the Crown, and there seems no good reason why the ownership thereof by the Crown should not also, subject to the rights of the public, be a beneficial ownership. The bed of the sea, as far as it is vested in the Crown, and a fortiori the beds of tidal navigable rivers, can be granted by the Crown to the subject . . . The whole doctrine of 'incrementa maris' seems to depend on the beneficial ownership of the Crown in the bed of the sea, which in the older authorities is sometimes referred to as the King's royal waste. It is true that no grant by the Crown of part of the bed of the sea or the bed of a tidal navigable river can or ever could operate to extinguish or curtail the public right of navigation and rights ancillary thereto, except possibly in connection with such rights as anchorage when there is some consideration moving from the grantee to the public. It is also true that no such grant can, since Magna Charta, operate to the detriment of the public right of fishing. But, subject to this, there seems no good reason to suppose that the Crown's ownership of the bed of the sea and the beds of tidal navigable rivers is not a beneficial ownership capable of being granted to a subject in the same way that the Crown's ownership of the foreshore is a beneficial ownership capable of being so granted.[8]

The report does not mention whether *Keyn* was cited. A month later, however, in another decision printed in the same volume of Chancery reports, the relevance of *Keyn* to the status of the seabed was discussed and, as far as the issue before the court was concerned, dismissed as irrelevant. In this second case, *Liverpool and North Wales Steamship Co. Ltd.* v. *Mersey Trading Company Ltd.*,[9] a Provisional Order of the Board of Trade, confirmed by a special Act of Parliament in 1892,[10] had authorized a company to construct a pier at Colwyn Bay. In 1893, the company obtained a grant from the Board of Trade, acting on behalf of the Crown, of a portion of the bed of the sea below the foreshore. The pier was then built extending a 'considerable distance' below low-water mark. In 1897, the company having gone into liquidation, the pier was sold. It was then discovered that the pier had been built outside the limits of deviation laid down in the Provisional Order. In 1901, the purchaser of the pier obtained from the Board of Trade, acting

8 [1908] 2 Ch. 139, 166–7.
9 [1908] 2 Ch. 460.
10 55 & 56 Vict., c. xxxiii.

under powers conferred by the Crown Lands Act 1866, a fresh grant from the Crown of the foreshore and bed of the sea on which the pier rested. He then permitted the vessels of the plaintiff company to use the pier in consideration of a fee. In 1907, the purchaser leased the pier to the defendants who wished to raise the fee. The plaintiffs objected to the increase and brought an action to restrain the defendants from excluding them from the use of the pier and also to recover rates paid under protest, claiming that the defendants were not in lawful possession of the pier. Counsel for the plaintiff company argued that although no doubt the Crown could grant the foreshore, subject to existing rights and to the public rights of navigation, it could not grant the bed of the sea below low-water mark. He cited *Keyn* in support of this submission. The defendants on the other hand argued that the Crown was the 'owner of the bed of the sea below the foreshore, at any rate within the three miles limit'.[11] They admitted that the grantee held subject to the rights of navigation but, until it was shown that those rights were interfered with, there was no nuisance 'and *R.* v. *Keyn* does not apply'. Neville J. however, had earlier intervened to state that in his opinion the question whether the bed of the open sea was vested in the Crown or in the purchaser was 'wholly immaterial' in the circumstances of the case.[12] In his judgment no mention was made of the point.

A third case, *Denaby and Cadeby Main Collieries Ltd.* v. *Anson* two year later, raised the question of the ownership of the bed of the open sea, only for it again to be discarded as irrelevant to the issue. This case concerned a right of anchorage in Portland Harbour, an area enclosed by breakwaters and admitted to be *intra fauces terrae*. At first instance, A. T. Lawrence J. stated:

It is not necessary to consider the views of Selden and of Hale as to Crown property in the narrow seas, nor the decision of the Court of Queen's Bench [sic] in *R.* v. *Keyn* as to the limitation to be put upon these authorities and upon the more modern three-mile limit, for whatever may be the true view as to the soil in the open sea below low-water mark, it has never been held, so far as I know, that the property in the soil of harbours and navigable rivers within the realm is not prima facie vested in the Crown.[13]

In the Court of Appeal, Fletcher Moulton L.J. similarly refused

[11] [1908] 2 Ch. 460, 471.
[12] Ibid., 470.
[13] [1911] 1 K.B. 171, 177.

to discuss the point:

> It is . . . unnecessary . . . to discuss the general question of the pro-
> prietorship of soil situated within the three-mile limit and covered with
> water at all times.[14]

The next two cases to come before English courts in which the
status of the seabed was raised each concerned accretion from the
sea. The first of these cases, *Barwick* v. *South Eastern & Chatham
Railway Companies*, concerned an area of 11 or 12 acres of land,
formerly below low-water mark, which had been reclaimed at
Dover for the purposes of building a station. The question was
whether, under s. 27 of the Poor Law Amendment Act 1868, this
area was within a parish for purposes of rating. In the course of his
judgment, Darling J., at first instance, stated his view of the
Blackpool pier case in terms which suggested that he did not have
the Crown's property claim in the forefront of his mind. He
referred to Grove J.'s judgment in that case and continued:

> The learned judge was speaking of land that had not been reclaimed at
> all. He was speaking of land over which the tide below low-water mark
> habitually ran. It was as much part of the ordinary bed of the sea as the
> middle of the Atlantic. The only relation it had to the realm of England
> was that it was within the three-mile limit, and, therefore, within
> territorial jurisdiction for certain purposes.[15]

Darling J. pointed out that in the Blackpool pier case the line of
low-water mark had not been altered by the construction of the
pier whereas in the present case the low-water mark had been
changed by the reclamation. He continued:

> When Lord Coleridge C.J. and Grove J., in *Blackpool Pier Company* v.
> *Fylde Union*, alluded to its being outside the realm of England, it was for
> the simple reason that nothing that was done by the putting up of the pier
> excluded the sea; it was simply the putting up of a number of piles or
> posts in the sea, putting on them a superstructure, and was no more the
> extending of the realm of England than the anchoring of a ship over the
> same place would have been. But when it comes to putting a solid
> structure which keeps out the sea from a definite piece of land, then I
> think the case is wholly different; and for the reasons I have given, I think
> that the soil upon which this pier or breakwater, or whatever it is, rests,
> which supports the refreshment rooms and other constructions—not the
> artificial part, but the natural soil which was there and which was the
> bed of the sea—has become part of the realm of England by the exclusion

[14] Ibid., 197.
[15] (1920–1) 124 L.T. 71, 74–5.

of the sea from it, and has become part of the parish of Dover by the operation of the Poor Law Amendment Act 1868.[16]

The Court of Appeal affirmed the decision of Darling J. that the land reclaimed was an accretion from the sea within the meaning of s. 27 above. Scrutton L.J. remarked of the Blackpool pier case:

I think no one would ever speak of such an erection as land. Whether a stone jetty was such an accretion would depend on the particular facts, but when a plot of land so large as eleven acres with a large station upon it results from the reclamation, the case is clearly within the statute.[17]

In the second accretion case, *Brighton and Hove General Gas Company* v. *Hove Bungalows Ltd.*,[18] the status of the seabed below low-water mark was not in issue but the judge, Romer J., cited Blackstone's view that 'if alluvion or dereliction be sudden and considerable, in this case it belongs to the King'.[19] He considered that this rule was settled 'beyond all question' by numerous authorities. He added, however that 'the reason given by Blackstone for this rule of law is not generally accepted as being the true one'.[20] Romer J. did not state what rule he thought was the true one, nor did he state the reason given by Blackstone. This reason was set out, with a reference to Callis, immediately after the passage in the *Commentaries* cited by Romer J.—'. . . for, as the king is lord of the sea, and so owner of the soil while it is covered with water, it is but reasonable he should have the soil when the water has left it dry.'

In 1926, the case of *The Fagernes* came before the English courts.[21] This case will be discussed again in the context of the delimitation of the Crown's claim to the soil of the marginal sea. The question was whether a spot in the middle of the Bristol Channel, where a collision between two ships had taken place, was 'within the jurisdiction' for the purpose of serving a writ on shipowners in Italy under Supreme Court Order XI. Thus, *prima facie*, no question of the ownership of the seabed need have arisen, especially in view of the well-known dictum of Lord Herschell in *Attorney-General for Canada* v. *Attorney-General for Ontario* in 1898 that

---

[16] Ibid., 75.
[17] Ibid., 78.
[18] [1924] 1 Ch. 372.
[19] *Blackstone's Commentaries*, Book II, 262–3.
[20] [1924] 1 Ch. 372, 381.
[21] [1926] P. 185 (Hill J.); [1927] P. 311 (Court of Appeal). See also TS 27/296.

'there is a broad distinction between proprietary rights and legislative jurisdiction'.[22]

Nevertheless, the argument of the plaintiffs was that the spot in question was within 'inland waters' which involved a discussion of the status of the subjacent soil. At first instance, Hill J. held that the writ could be served. He doubted whether the view of Lord Coleridge C.J. in *Harris* v. *Owners of the Franconia*[23] was still law to its full extent. He continued, 'It has at any rate been decided by the Judicial Committee of the Privy Council that the bed of the sea, at least within the three-mile limit, is the property of the Crown.'[24]

On 9 December 1926, the case was heard before the Court of Appeal which adjourned the hearing until the Crown could be represented. Argument recommenced on 27 June 1927 when counsel for the Italian shipowners maintained that jurisdiction at common law ceased at the low-water mark except in waters *intra fauces terrae*. The Attorney-General, Sir Douglas Hogg, on behalf of the Crown, stated:

In *R.* v. *Keyn* the effect of the decision was that except where Parliament has thought fit to extend it the territory of England stops at low water mark; see the observations of Lord Coleridge C.J. in the succeeding case of *Harris* v. *Owners of Franconia*.[25]

Counsel for the plaintiffs, however, maintained that the preamble to the Territorial Waters Jurisdiction Act 1878 showed that the decision in *Keyn* was wrong if it laid down that the sovereignty of the Crown stopped at low-water mark. He continued:

At any rate, apart from statute, the bed of the sea, at least within the three-mile limit, is the property of the Crown: see *Secretary of State for India* v. *Chelikani Rama Rao*.[26]

At this stage, the Crown, through the Attorney-General, was asked by a majority of the Court whether it did or did not claim the *locus* as being 'within the realm of England'. The Attorney-General replied that

. . . the Secretary of State for Home Affairs instructed him to say that 'the

[22] [1898] A.C. 700, 709. One might add 'and adjudicatory jurisdiction'.
[23] (1877) 2 C.P.D. 173.
[24] [1926] P. 185, 188. He referred to *Chelikani's* case.
[25] [1927] P. 311, 315.
[26] Ibid., 318.

spot where this collision is alleged to have occurred is not within the limits to which the territorial sovereignty of His Majesty extends'.[27]

In unanimously reversing the order of Hill J., the members of the Court of Appeal did not confine themselves to precise language, using variously terms such as 'realm', 'territory', and 'jurisdiction'. Both Bankes and Lawrence L.JJ. doubted the view of Hill J. on the application of the common law test to the *locus*, whereas Atkin L.J., on the other hand, would have followed his view. On the effect of the statement by the Home Secretary, the members of the Court also spoke with divided voices: Bankes L.J. accepted the statement without declaring that he was obliged to do so, Atkin L.J. declared himself to be bound by the statement, and Lawrence L.J. stated that 'this court could not . . . properly do otherwise' than hold that the *locus* was outside the jurisdiction.

The next reported occasion when any mention of the soil below low-water mark was made in English courts was not until 1954. In 1939, the case of *Stephens* v. *Snell*[28] had decided that the limits of a certain fishery were determined by the bounds of the manor of Axmouth in Devon. In 1954, the same plaintiff asked for a declaration to the effect that the fishery extended seaward as far as the line of the mean low-water mark of ordinary tides. In the course of his judgment granting the declaration, Vaisey J. stated:

In Coulson and Forbes on the Law of Waters (6th ed., p. 24) it was stated that the low-water mark of ordinary tides was the legal seaward limit of the Kingdom on the coast; so that the land below such low-water mark, whether at any particular moment it was left bare or covered with water, was not and could not be any part of the Kingdom or of any manor in the Kingdom. *Regina* v. *Musson* supported that proposition which he (his Lordship) accepted.[29]

The more recent case of *Alfred F. Beckett Ltd.* v. *Lyons* in 1967 like its predecessors was not directly concerned with the status of the soil below low-water mark. The plaintiff company, which held an area of foreshore in Durham under a grant from the Crown, claimed trespass against the defendant who maintained that by prescription the inhabitants of the county were entitled to gather coal found on the foreshore. The coal was washed on to the foreshore both from submarine outcrops and from material which earlier had been tipped into the sea. In the Court of Appeal, Winn

[27] Ibid., 319.
[28] (1939) 55 T.L.R. 962.
[29] *Stevens* v. *Snell, The Times*, 5 June 1954.

L.J. was the only judge to mention specifically the soil below low-water mark. He said:

. . . it was, I gather, accepted by counsel in this appeal that the plaintiffs could not restrain anybody from coming in a boat from seaward and taking coal wherever it might be found below low-tide mark. I desire only to comment that I think it does not follow that the Crown might not be entitled to prevent this being done, either by asserting a proprietary right in the soil of the sea or possibly in Her Majesty's capacity as Lord High Admiral of England. It would be outside the proper scope of this judgment to consider the rights of the Crown in the sea adjoining the United Kingdom, and it suffices to say that there is considerable authority that, apart from a few special cases of express grant, the Crown has ever since the Conquest been the owner of the soil of the sea below low-tide mark to a seaward extent which may be somewhat uncertain. Thus Sir Matthew Hale in his Treatise de Jure Maris, chap. IV, states: 'The narrow sea, adjoining to the coast of England, is part of the wast and demesnes and dominions of the King of England, whether it lie within the body of any county or not . . . In this sea the King of England hath a double right, viz., a right of jurisdiction which he ordinarily exerciseth by his admiral, and a right of propriety or ownership.'[30]

About the same time, two cases, arising out of the same facts, came before English courts. Each might have raised the question of the status of the marginal submarine soil if it had been argued differently. Both cases, *R. v. Kent Justices, ex parte Lye* before the Divisional Court of the Queen's Bench in 1966,[31] and *Post Office* v. *Estuary Radio Ltd.* before the Queen's Bench Division and the Court of Appeal in 1967,[32] concerned the use of wireless telegraphy apparatus on Red Sands Tower, a man-made structure resting on the submarine soil at a distance of 4.9 miles from the nearest low-water mark on the coast, namely that of Kent, but within three miles of what was claimed by the Post Office to be a low-tide elevation, Middle Sands, which itself was less than three miles from the nearest low-water mark, again on the coast of Kent.[33]

In *Lye*, the accused were charged with the summary offence of

[30] [1967] Ch. 449, 481.
[31] [1967] 2 Q.B. 153.
[32] [1967] 1 W.L.R. 847 (O'Connor J.); [1968] 2 Q.B. 740 (Court of Appeal).
[33] The Territorial Waters Order in Council 1964 provides in s. 2(1) that for the purposes of measuring the territorial sea of the United Kingdom, the Channel Islands, and the Isle of Man, a low-tide elevation which lies wholly or partly within the breadth of sea which would be territorial sea if all low-tide elevations were disregarded shall be treated as an island. All islands in these territories have a belt of territorial sea measured from the 'low-water line along the coast'. *Statutory Instruments* 1965, Part III (section 2), p. 6452A.

unlawfully using wireless telegraphy equipment contrary to s. 1(1) of the Wireless Telegraphy Act 1949 while being 'within the jurisdiction of the county of Kent'. They were convicted by a magistrate's court sitting at Canterbury after a finding by the bench that the offence had been committed in 'territorial waters' within the meaning of the 1949 Act. On an application by the accused to the Divisional Court for a writ of *certiorari*, the argument largely concerned the meaning of the expression 'territorial waters' as used in the Act and also the power of the magistrates to hear the charge in the absence of a specific 'venue' provision in the Act. Although the prosecution had sought before the magistrates to reserve the question whether the construction known as Red Sands Tower was part of the United Kingdom, it does not appear from the transcript of argument that this point was discussed before the Divisional Court or that any question was raised concerning the status of the bed of the sea upon which the tower rested. Nevertheless, in the extempore judgments, certain remarks were made concerning that status of territorial waters. Lord Parker C.J. considered that the extent of territorial waters was a matter of sovereignty and that 'as such is peculiarly a matter for the Crown from time to time under the prerogative to determine'.[34] Salmon L.J., who dissented on the meaning to be given to the expression in the 1949 Act, agreed that 'territorial waters' were now within the 'territorial sovereignty' of the Crown. He drew a clear distinction, however, between these waters and the concept of the United Kingdom:

It is an essential ingredient of the offence that it has to be committed in the United Kingdom or the territorial waters adjacent thereto. The meaning of the words 'the United Kingdom' are fairly plain; they include all land within the United Kingdom down to the low-water mark; the case turns upon the true construction of the words 'territorial waters'.[35]

Blain J., who reluctantly joined Lord Parker C.J. in dismissing the application, expressed the following view of *R.* v. *Keyn*:

. . . a majority of seven judges to six in effect held that the realm of England extended only to low-water mark, and that all beyond that was high seas. To be more specific, it was held that the courts had no jurisdiction to try a foreigner charged with an offence whilst on a foreign ship which was passing within three miles of the English coast.[36]

[34] (1967) 2 Q.B. 153, 174.
[35] Ibid., 179.
[36] Ibid., 186.

He then remarked that even though 'the usage and common consent of nations which constituted international law had appropriated to the adjacent state certain waters to a limit of three miles seaward of low-water mark of the coast of that state', nevertheless, this development 'did not and could not enlarge the area of municipal jurisdiction of that state'.[37]

In the second case, *Post Office* v. *Estuary Radio Ltd.*, the Post Office, in May 1967, sought an injunction under s. 14(7) of the 1949 Act to restrain the defendants from broadcasting from the tower. It alleged that the structure was part of the United Kingdom since it had been constructed by the United Kingdom authorities during the Second World War and had been occupied by British troops continuously until 1957. The Post Office alleged in the alternative that the tower was within the internal waters of the United Kingdom, or, as a further alternative, that it was within territorial waters. O'Connor J., at first instance, did not discuss the first of these alternatives. He decided, after construing the terms of the Territorial Waters Order in Council 1964 in the light of the 1958 Convention on the Territorial Sea and the Contiguous Zone,[38] that the tower was situated within the closing line of a 'bay' formed by the mouth of the Thames and, consequently, within the United Kingdom's internal waters; if he were wrong on this point, he considered that the tower would be within territorial waters.[39]

In July 1967, the matter came before the Court of Appeal consisting of Sellers, Diplock, and Winn L.JJ. Counsel for the Post Office argued that there was no agreed definition of the extent of the United Kingdom:

The United Kingdom is in fact altering all the time. For example, the sea at Cromer is eroding the United Kingdom year by year, whereas the sea at Southport expands it year by year.[40]

He submitted that whether any particular territory was part of the United Kingdom was a matter of which the courts took judicial notice, and, on the authority of *The Fagernes*, that a statement made by the appropriate government department as to what constituted the territory of the United Kingdom was conclusive.

The reserved judgment of the Court of Appeal was delivered by

[37] Ibid., 188–9.
[38] 516 *UNTS* 205.
[39] [1967] 1 W.L.R. 847.
[40] [1968] 2 Q.B. 740, 749.

Diplock L.J. The decision of O'Connor J. was upheld without pronouncing on the status of the tower itself or of the bed on which it rested. In the course of the judgment, however, Diplock L.J. stated:

The accreting shingle bank at Dungeness is no Alsatia in which a citizen enjoys immunity from the law of the land. The area to which an Act of Parliament of the United Kingdom applies may vary too as the Crown, in the exercise of its prerogative, extends its claim to areas adjacent to the coast of the United Kingdom in which it did not previously assert its sovereignty.[41]

Then, in contrast to the view of Salmon L.J. in *Lye*, Diplock L.J. clearly indicated that the Court of Appeal considered the belt of territorial waters, as well as the internal waters, to be part of the United Kingdom:

. . . it is not disputed that, construing the Order in Council in the light of the Convention and the law as it was before the Order in Council came into operation, the Crown, in the exercise of its prerogative powers, was thereby asserting a claim which the courts are constitutionally bound to recognise, to incorporate within the United Kingdom that area of the sea which lies upon the landward side of the baseline (that is, internal waters) and within three nautical miles on the seaward side of the baseline (that is, the territorial sea).[42]

In *The Putbus* in 1969, a civil action arising out of the sinking of a vessel in Dutch territorial waters, Phillimore L.J. made a passing remark to the Crown's claim to property in the marginal seabed and subsoil, although the point does not seem to have been argued. He stated:

The Crown claims property in the soil of the sea under its territorial waters and also claims to be entitled to the mines and minerals under that soil: see *Halsbury's Laws of England*, 3rd ed., vol. 39 (1962), p. 556. It follows that if through negligence a ship is sunk in British territorial waters as a result of negligence with the result that it impedes access to an important waterway, the Crown would be entitled to remove it as interfering with a right and to recover the cost in damages for negligence.[43]

In *Loose* v. *Castleton*[44] in 1978 the question for the Court of Appeal was whether the defendant was entitled to remove shellfish

[41] Ibid., 754.
[42] Ibid.
[43] [1969] P. 136, 155.
[44] C.A. Transcript 78/356; *The Times*, 21 June 1978.

from what was alleged to be a sole and several fishery and sea-ground the property of Hamon Le Strange upon the foreshore of the Manors of Heacham and Snettisham in Norfolk, and which extended seawards at least to the mean low-water mark of ordinary spring tides. The point where the shellfish were removed by the defendant was seaward of the mean low-water mark of ordinary tides though landward of the mean low-water mark of ordinary *spring* tides. The defendant argued *inter alia* that 'where a several fishery subsists in tidal waters on a stretch of open coast-line, or on a stretch of coastline adjoining such a very large esturial area as the Wash, its extent cannot be further than the mean low-water line of ordinary tides'.

The Court of Appeal found for the plaintiff, who was a lessee of Hamon Le Strange. Having upheld the claim to the existence of a several fishery on the basis of a presumption of a lost grant before Magna Charta, Bridge L.J. cited the House of Lords decision in *Gann* v. *Free Fishers of Whitstable* in 1865 as 'clear authority' for the proposition that a several fishery in private ownership can lawfully subsist in relation to areas seaward of the mean low-water mark of ordinary spring tides.

The area in question, however, like that in *Gann*, was probably within inland waters, being on the east shore of the Wash, near the town of Hunstanton. The case is thus not clear authority for the proposition that a several fishery, and the soil thereunder, located outside the usual seaward boundary of a county, can be held by a subject on the basis of a lost grant from the Crown.

B. Scottish Judicial Decisions

In several Scottish decisions in the period under review, two of which were taken to the House of Lords, the status of the soil of the sea adjacent to the coast of Scotland was discussed. In none of these cases, however, was resolution of the question essential for the decision.

The first case, *Lord Advocate* v. *Trustees of the Clyde Navigation* in 1891, concerned the legality of the action of trustees in dumping in Loch Long the dredgings taken from the Clyde river bed. Although Loch Long ran twenty-four miles up from the Clyde and was nowhere wider than two miles, the Lord Advocate framed his case in terms which extended to a wider class of waters. He alleged that

. . . [t]he narrow seas of that part of Her Majesty's dominions known as the kingdom of Scotland, and the *solum* or bed thereof below low-water mark, belong to Her Majesty *jure coronae*, subject to the public rights of navigation and fishing. The salt water loch or arm of the Firth of Clyde known as Loch Long is part of the said narrow seas.[45]

He went on to plead that the narrow seas surrounding the kingdom of Scotland, and the *solum* or bed thereof, belonged to and were vested in the Crown, subject to the public rights of navigation and fishing.

At first instance, the Lord Ordinary, Lord Kyllachy, pointed out that there was no allegation that the dredgings were being deposited other than in Loch Long. Otherwise, he would have required some further definitions of the term 'narrow seas'. He remarked on this point:

It is an expression which, in the literature of this subject, is used in different senses. It is sometimes used to denote the sea within cannon-shot of the shore, together with the estuaries, bays, etc., within the *fauces terrae*—*The Queen* v. *Keyn*. . . . But it is also used in another and wider sense, viz., as comprising the whole seas and channels around Great Britain, and between Great Britain and other countries on the continent of Europe.[46]

Lord Kyllachy considered that the question before him concerned only waters *intra fauces terrae*. Nevertheless, he expressed his opinion on the wider point:

(1) I hold it to be now acknowledged as matter of international law that the territory of Great Britain does not extend to the narrow seas surrounding the Kingdom in the older and wider sense of that expression. That is to say, the ancient claims of the kings of England to the whole seas and channels between England and other countries on the Continent cannot now be maintained. This I do not understand to be in controversy.

(2) I hold it to be still an open question whether the territory of the kingdom extends, *e.g.*, to those seas and channels along the coast which are outside the *fauces terrae*, and more than three miles from the shore, but which are situated between the mainland and islands forming part of the kingdom, such as *e.g.*, the island of Arran and the Hebrides. This question may possibly become to be material between the present parties in the event of the defenders seeking another place of deposit; but in the meantime it is hardly a question of practical interest.

(3) The more practical question, and that on which alone I heard argument, was with respect to the nature of the Crown's right in what is

---

[45] (1891) 19 R. 174.
[46] Ibid., 175.

now acknowledged to be part of the territory of the kingdom, *viz.*, the strip or area of sea within cannon shot, or three miles of the shore. Is the Crown's right in that strip of sea proprietary, like the Crown's right in the foreshore and in the land? or is it only a protectorate for certain purposes, and particularly navigation and fishing?

I am of opinion that the former is the correct view, and that there is no distinction in legal character between the Crown's right in the foreshore, in tidal and navigable rivers, and in the bed of the sea within three miles of the shore. In each case it is of course a right largely qualified by public uses. In each case it is therefore to a large extent *extra commercium*; but none the less it is, in my opinion, a proprietary right—a right which may be the subject of trespass, and which may be vindicated like other rights of property.

Such I consider is the result of all best authorities—Scotch, English, and foreign.[47]

Lord Kyllachy cited in support of his opinion the Scottish cases of *Officers of State* v. *Smith*, *Gammell* v.*Lord Advocate*, and *Duchess of Sutherland* v. *Watson*, and the English case of *Gann* v. *Free Fishers of Whitstable*. He referred also to a passage from the dissenting judgment of Lindley J. in *Keyn*[48] and to the arbitration between the Queen and the Duke of Cornwall to the extent that this had been mentioned by Lord Coleridge C.J. in *Keyn*.

On appeal to the Inner House, it was agreed by all the judges that the status of the *solum* of the sea within three miles of the shore was not in issue; nevertheless, various dicta were made concerning it. The Lord Justice-Clerk, MacDonald, remarked:

Let it be assumed to be settled law that there is no right of property below low-water mark on the sea-coast—an assumption which, in my opinion, is not sound.[49]

Lord Young went further:

I have no objection to indicate my own view, it is only my individual view, that the Crown has a right of property within the three mile limit. What about the building of piers and jetties? Is it doubtful that piers so built are built on Scottish land, on ground vested in the Crown, and applicable to any purpose which it will serve? There are many such piers. I cannot distinguish between that part of the three mile limit on which these piers are built, the part adjacent to low-water mark, and that part which lies further out.[50]

[47] Ibid., 177.
[48] (1876) 2 Ex. D. 63, 90–1.
[49] (1891) 19 R. 174, 180–1.
[50] Ibid., 183.

Lord Rutherford Clark concurred, seemingly in the judgment of Lord Young, while Lord Trayner specifically declared that the question of the extent and character of the Crown's right to the *solum* underlying external seas to the distance of three miles did not arise and that he found it unnecessary to express any opinion upon it.

The next case, *Cuninghame* v. *Assessor for Ayrshire* in 1895,[51] concerned a proprietor who held under a Crown lease the minerals lying under the sea below low-water mark *ex adverso* of his lands on the coast of Ayrshire. He appealed against an assessment of rent in respect of the minerals on the grounds:

 (i) unwrought minerals under the sea below low-water mark did not belong to the Crown but were *res nullius* until appropriated by himself;

 (ii) assuming that the minerals were the property of the Crown, they were part of the bed of the sea and were not in the parish or county.

The respondent argued that the minerals lay *intra fauces terrae* and not under the open sea, and, in the alternative, that *R.* v. *Keyn* was concerned only with 'jurisdiction'. The Court rejected the appeal. Lord Wellwood held that the appellant by accepting a lease from the Crown had *prima facie* recognized the Crown's right, but, apart from this consideration, the minerals lay *intra fauces terrae* so there was no need to go into the 'larger question of minerals under open sea'.

The third Scottish case, *Lord Advocate* v. *Wemyss* in 1899,[52] concerned submarine strata adjacent to three ancient baronies, West Wemyss, East Wemyss, and Methil, situated on the north shore of the Firth of Forth. For more than forty years coal had been worked from under the sea *ex adverso* of West Wemyss, but there had been no submarine workings from the other two. In April 1875, while the proprietor of the baronies, Wemyss, was still a minor, the Office of Woods concluded a lease with the trustees, leasing to them for thirty-one years from 1 January 1874 'the whole coal, ironstone, and fireclay in or under the bed of the sea' adjacent to the three baronies to a distance of about two miles from the foreshore. Royalties were to be paid to the Crown on the minerals raised. Wemyss attained his majority in July 1879 but it was not until 1893 that he sought a declaration that he was not bound by

[51] (1895) 22 R. 596.
[52] [1900] A.C. 48.

the 1875 lease. He claimed that under a Crown Charter of 1651, confirmed by an Act of the Scottish Parliament of 1661, not only the foreshore but the coal under the adjacent sea passed to the grantee of the barony, at least as far as the mineral could be worked up to the *medium filium aquae* or, in the case of the open sea, the three-mile limit. He also claimed that, in respect of the coal under the sea adjacent to West Wemyss, he had a title based on prescription.

The argument of the Lord Advocate, representing the Crown in Scotland, was set out in the printed Case submitted to the Appellate Committee of the House of Lords. It read in part:

The subject was under-sea coal, the working of which, if not unique, was extremely rare. The letting or working of such coal by the Crown is a matter of very recent date. Indeed, it is well known that whilst the Crown's rights in theory to the foreshore and the territorial waters is laid down in all the ancient texts, the practical assertion of these rights for patrimonial benefit only began about the middle of the present century . . . There is a passage in *Craig* in which he suggests that, whilst in strict theory, under-sea coal must be held to belong to the Crown, yet the working of coal under the sea requires such ingenuity and toil that the coal so raised ought to belong to those by whom it was won; obviously, in his view, acquiescence by the Crown in such working and appropriation did not infer any recognition of proprietary right, and industry was the only title.[53]

After stating that there did not appear to be any presumption or even probability that possession of the submarine areas was exercised under any title, the Crown's case continued:

But even if this difficulty were overcome, and it were held that there is sufficient evidence that the Respondents have possessed below low-water mark as part of the barony for the prescriptive period, the question remains, what is the estate which they have possessed? How far does it extend? . . . Their first position taken up in argument was that their estate in minerals extended *ex adverso* of the barony between perpendiculars to the coast line at either end, across the Firth to low-water mark on the coast of Haddington. At a later stage of the argument their claim receded to the *medium filium* of the Firth, a boundary line novel to the law of Scotland. . . .

It may be sufficient to shew that the estate generally has been possessed. But below low-water mark there is no estate of any limits

[53] Case for the Appellants, pp. 35–6. Records of the Appellate Committee, House of Lords.

known to the law, short of the Crown's estate in the *solum* beneath the whole of the territorial waters of Scotland.[54]

The House of Lords rejected Wemyss' claim. Lord Herschell declared that as the grant of 1651 referred to *'infra fluxum maris'* this was conclusive that the grant transferred only the coal under the land and foreshore down to the low-water mark. Lord Herschell was prepared to find that Wemyss had established a prescriptive right to coal under the sea adjacent to West Wemyss but held that, by reason of the fourteen years which had elapsed between attaining his majority and bringing the action, Wemyss had barred himself from asserting any right to this coal.

Lord Watson opened his speech by declaring:

I see no reason to doubt that, by the law of Scotland, the solum underlying the waters of the ocean, whether within the narrow seas, or from the coast outward to the three-mile limit, and also the minerals beneath it, are vested in the Crown. Whether the Crown could make an effectual grant of that solum or of any part of it to a subject appears to me to be a question not unattended with doubt; but I do not think that the Crown could, without the sanction of the Legislature, lawfully convey any right or interest in it which, if exercised by the grantee, might by possibility disturb the solum or in any way interfere with the uses of navigation, or with any right in the public. The mineral strata below the bed of the sea, in so far as they are capable of being worked without causing disturbance, appear to me to stand in a different position. To that extent, I know of no principle of Scottish law which could prevent the Crown from communicating the right of working to a subject, in the character either of tenant or proprietor. If that be so, it would follow that submarine minerals, if expressly included, might, to the extent which I have indicated, be competently made parts and pertinents of a baronial or other Crown grant of adjacent lands.[55]

Lord Watson then held that the words of the 1651 grant did not carry the right to coal below low-water mark. In respect of the coal adjacent to West Wemyss, Lord Watson appears to have thought that if Wemyss had acted within a reasonable time after his majority to repudiate the lease made on his behalf in 1875 he could validly have repudiated it. However, the delay was fatal to his claim to set aside the lease.

Lord Morris agreed with the speech of Lord Watson without further comment. Lord Shand, who stated that he entirely agreed

[54] Ibid., 37–8.
[55] [1900] A.C. 48, 66–7.

with the speeches of both Lord Herschell and Lord Watson, also held that the 1875 transaction could not be set aside. He continued, '. . . I shall only say for myself, as I think my noble and learned friends have already said, I should have very great difficulty indeed in extending the doctrine applicable to the foreshore to the extent of covering submarine minerals lying outside the foreshore.'[56]

In the *Wemyss* case, the submarine strata themselves were located under the waters of the Firth of Forth and probably, therefore, *intra fauces terrae*. It is significant that the Office of Woods considered that the lease of 1875 applied to areas within an estuary and not under the open sea, since in the Scottish schedule which was prepared in that office prior to the reference to the Law Officers in 1878, this particular lease was endorsed as relating to an estuary.[57]

The fourth Scottish case, *Parker* v. *Lord Advocate* in 1901,[58] concerned the question whether the sole and exclusive property in and right to the mussel beds, scalps, and fisheries in a spot being part of the foreshore and bed of the River Clyde belonged to and were vested in the Crown or in the appellants. Since the House of Lords in 1904 briefly affirmed the judgments in the Scottish courts below, it is to these latter decisions that it is necessary to turn.

In the Court of Session, the Lord Ordinary, Lord Kincairney, preferred the view that, as the Crown owned the solum and as the mussels remained attached to the mussel beds, therefore the mussels were the property of the Crown as *partes soli*. The different theories had been stated as follows by Rankine in his work *Land Ownership*, cited by the judge:

If the scalps on which they lie are situated within the three-mile limit, the Crown has an exclusive right as part of the hereditary revenue on one of two theories—either to the fish themselves as partes soli, in which case the Crown must be regarded as having a right to the ipsa corpora of the fish, or to the incorporeal right of fishing for them on the analogy of salmon fishings.[59]

In preferring the former theory, Lord Kincairney stated that it was the theory relied on by Lord Neaves in *Duchess of Sutherland* v. *Watson* in 1868.[60]

---

[56] Ibid., 80–1.
[57] CREST 37/356.
[58] [1904] A.C. 364. The judgments in the courts below are also here.
[59] Ibid., 373.
[60] (1868) 6 M. 199. See Chapter III above.

On appeal to the First Division of the Court of Session, the Lord President, Lord Kinross, declared:

The nature of the right, if any, which the Crown has in mussel scalps on the shores or within three miles of the territory of Scotland has been much discussed from time to time; but I consider that it must now be taken to be settled, in so far as a series of decisions of this Court not brought under review of the House of Lords can settle a question of Scottish law, that such mussel scalps form parts of the patrimonial property of the Crown, which it can convey or let in lease to a subject, as it can any other patrimonial property belonging to it, and which is not from its nature inalienable.[61]

Later, he remarked:

. . . I think that the right which the Crown possessed, and frequently granted to subjects, in mussel scalps on or near to the shores of Scotland, is a patrimonial right similar to that which, in theory at all events, the Crown originally had in the whole territory of the country.[62]

As mentioned above, the House of Lords, in 1904, briefly affirmed the decisions in the Scottish courts. The Earl of Halsbury L.C. said:

The Lord President has, I think, with great precision, traced the origin and the application of the Crown rights, and I do not think there is any difference in the law applicable to those Crown rights between the law of England and the law of Scotland.[63]

Lord Davey stated:

I do not think that the attempt made by the appellants to explain the grants of mussel fishings by attributing them to the exercise of the prerogative of the Crown over property held in trust for the public in supposed analogy to English law can be maintained; and I think that the better opinion is that which I consider to be now established law in Scotland, namely, that mussel fishings are part of the heritable patrimonial property of the Crown.[64]

In this case, too, the *locus* was under the inland waters of Scotland, although the arguments and authorities used seemed to draw no distinction between waters *intra fauces terrae* and the sea to a distance of three miles.

The Ayrshire litigation of 1895 was recalled in 1908 in *Lord*

---

[61] [1904] A.C. 364, 373–4.
[62] Ibid., 377.
[63] Ibid., 368.
[64] Ibid., 369.

Advocate v. *Glengarnock Iron & Steel Co. Ltd*. The Crown, by leases in
1889 and 1898, had let to Cuninghame the minerals below low-
water mark *ex adverso* his property between Saltcoats and
Stevenston, on the coast of Ayrshire. A dispute then arose between
the Crown and a sub-lessee of Cuninghame. In the course of his
judgment in the Outer House, Lord Johnston stated: 'It was
known with reasonable certainty that the coal measures extended
under the sea, below low-water mark. Of the coal below low-water
mark the Crown were undoubtedly proprietors.'[65]

On appeal to the Second Division of the Court of Session it was
not disputed that the Crown was entitled to grant the leases.[66] In
view of the remarks made in the 1895 case, however, it is possible
that the courts assumed that the *locus* was *intra fauces terrae*.

Two recent Scottish cases have raised the question of the
Crown's rights in the bed of the marginal sea. In *Crown Estate
Commissioners* v. *Fairlie Yacht Slip Ltd*., the issue was whether the
Commissioners had the exclusive right to permit fixed moorings
on the bed of Fairlie Bay, a feature of the Ayrshire coast further
from the open sea than the site of the above undersea mines. It was
admitted that the Crown had a right to its solum. Lord Dunpark,
in the Outer House of the Court of Session, stated:

I am satisfied that the right of the Crown to the seabed in Fairlie Bay is a
right of property, although that right is subject to certain public rights of
user, such as the right of navigation and of white fishing. This accords
with the statement of the law by Craig (I.15.13), Stair (II.1.5),
Erskine (II.1.6), by Bell himself in the 5th Edition of his Principles at
section 639, and with the views expressed *obiter* by the Lord Ordinary
(Kyllachy) in *Lord Advocate* v. *Clyde Navigation Trustees* (1891) 19 R. 174, at
pp. 177–8; also by the Lord Justice-Clerk (MacDonald) at pp. 180–1,
Lord Young at p. 183 and Lord Trayner at p. 184.

The undoubted right of the Crown to work minerals under the seabed
within territorial waters, or to grant that right to another, must be based
upon a patrimonial right to the seabed and everything below it. It cannot
be founded on a fiduciary title *qua* trustee for the public. . . . Now, as I
understand it, the seabed within the territorial limit and the foreshore
are not part of the public patrimony of the Crown but are nevertheless
the property of the Crown (except in so far as the Crown may have made
grants of the foreshore to individuals) as part of the realm and are held by
the Crown for the defence of the realm and the benefit of its subjects. . . .

　[T]he only restriction on the Crown's right of property in the seabed of
territorial waters and in the foreshore is that the Crown cannot permit

any use of the said seabed or foreshore which interferes with the rights of the public.[67]

The second recent case was *Argyll and Bute District Council* v. *Secretary of State for Scotland*. The issue was whether planning permission extended to the construction of oil platforms in Loch Fyne. The Secretary of State had determined that planning control 'does not extend to areas of the sea bed, at least not where the structure in question does not rise above the level of the sea at high-water mark'. Upholding this decision in the Second Division of the Court of Session, Lord Wheatley, Lord Justice-Clerk, observed:

We had a detailed analysis from junior counsel for the appellants on the Crown's proprietary rights in the foreshore and in the sea bed below low-water mark and beyond, whether to the three-mile limit or intra fauces terrae. I find it unnecessary to examine the interesting tract of authority cited to us on this matter, since the area with which we are dealing is within the confines of Loch Fyne, and the Crown's proprietary rights in the foreshore and in the sea bed below low-water mark in this area were not disputed.[68]

C. Opinions of the Judicial Committee of the Privy Council

Although this study is confined to practice in respect of the bed and subsoil of the sea adjacent to the coasts of the United Kingdom, it has been thought necessary to deal with cases from other jurisdictions on appeal to the Judicial Committee of the Privy Council. The personnel of the Committee is largely the same as that of the Appellate Committee of the House of Lords, and its considered opinion, although in theory not binding on any English court, will usually be given great weight by any such court. It must be remembered, however, that the law discussed by the Privy Council in the cases set out below was that of the jurisdiction from which the appeal came. In some of these jurisdictions, particularly those federal in nature, additional complications arise which it is not the task of the present study to elucidate.

The first relevant appeal to the Judicial Committee after the decision in *Keyn, Direct United States Cable Co. Ltd.* v. *Anglo-American Telegraph Co. Ltd.*,[69] has already been mentioned. Ten years later, an appeal from Canada, *Attorney-General for the Dominion of Canada*

[67] [1976] S.C. 161, 163–5 *passim*.
[68] [1977] S.L.T. Reps. 33, 35.
[69] (1877) L.R. 2 App. Cas. 394.

v. *Attorneys-General for the Provinces of Ontario, Quebec and Nova Scotia*,[70]raised the questions of whether 'the beds of all lakes, rivers, public harbours, and other waters . . . situated within the territorial limits of the several provinces, and not granted before confederation, became under the British North America Act the property of the Dominion or the property of the province'. A separate question related to the power of the Dominion to legislate for fishing 'in waters, the beds of which do not belong to the Dominion'.

Although the printed Case or 'Factum' of the Dominion, presented to the Judicial Committee,[71] cited the dictum of Erle C.J. in *Gann* v. *Free Fishers of Whitstable*, to the effect that the soil of the seashore to the extent of three miles was vested in the Crown, the Committee did not seem to discuss the status of the marginal seabed and subsoil although, during argument, Lord Watson remarked that territorial waters were 'a sort of No Man's land on which the adjoining state may legislate so long as it has the power to see that its legislation is carried out'.[72]

The next relevant appeal, *Attorney-General for British Columbia* v. *Attorney-General for the Dominion of Canada* in 1913,[73] raised the problem far more acutely, though it went equally unresolved. The questions put to the Committee were whether the legislature of British Columbia was competent to authorize the lease or licence to fish below low-water mark in the open sea within a marine league of the coast of the Province and, secondly, whether there was a difference between this area of open sea and the gulfs, bays, channels, arms, and estuaries within the Province so far as concerned the above competence.

In the printed Case submitted to the Judicial Committee in this appeal,[74] the Dominion maintained:

The legislature of British Columbia is incompetent to authorise the Government of the Province to grant the exclusive right or any right to fish below low water mark in any part of the open sea within a marine league of the coasts of the Province, because the Crown is not entitled to the ownership of the soil beneath the sea within the said limit, nor has the Crown any other right or interest which would enable it to grant the fisheries.

[70] [1898] A.C. 700.
[71] Records of the Judicial Committee.
[72] Printed transcript (Government Printer, British Columbia) p. 145.
[73] [1914] A.C. 153.
[74] Records of the Judicial Committee.

It then added that 'the question appears to be finally settled by *Regina* v. *Keyn*'.

On the other hand, the printed Case or Factum on behalf of British Columbia claimed that the territory of the Province included the open sea 'within at least a marine league of the Coast of the Province'. It cited in support the Cornwall Submarine Mines Act 1858.

During the argument of Sir Robert Finlay KC, for the Province, the following exchange took place about the decision in *Keyn*:

SIR ROBERT FINLAY Your Lordships will recollect that directly after that decision Parliament proceeds to fill up the gap by legislating.

THE LORD CHANCELLOR (VISCOUNT HALDANE) Not as to property. Parliament was most cautious to take care not to assert any right of property.[75]

The Lord Chancellor then indicated that the Committee did not propose to deal with the question as to whether the property in the soil of the sea under territorial waters vested in the Crown.

In delivering the advice of the Committee, Viscount Haldane L.C. held that the right of fishing in the sea was a right of the public in general which did not depend on the existence of any proprietary title in the subjacent land. Thus, their Lordships were relieved from expressing any opinion as to the existence of a right of property in the Crown over the bed of the sea up to three miles from low-water mark. He continued:

They desire, however, to point out that the three-mile limit is something very different from the 'narrow seas' limit discussed by the older authorities, such as Selden and Hale, a principle which may safely be said to be now obsolete. The doctrine of the zone comprised in the former limit owes its origin to comparatively modern authorities on public international law. Its meaning is still in controversy. The questions raised thereby affect not only the Empire generally but also the rights of foreign nations as against the Crown, and of the subjects of the Crown as against other nations in foreign territorial waters. Until the Powers have adequately discussed and agreed on the meaning of the doctrine at a Conference, it is not desirable that any municipal tribunal should pronounce on it. It is not improbable that in connection with the subject of trawling the topic may be examined at such a Conference. Until then the conflict of judicial opinion which arose in *Reg.* v. *Keyn* is not likely to be satisfactorily settled, nor is a conclusion likely to be reached on the question whether the shore below low water mark to within three miles of the coast forms part of the territory of the Crown or is merely subject to

[75] Printed transcript (Government Printer, British Columbia) p. 82.

special powers necessary for protective and police purposes. The obscurity of the whole topic is made plain in the judgment of Cockburn C.J. in that case. But apart from these difficulties, there is the decisive consideration that the question is not one which belongs to the domain of municipal law alone.[76]

The next relevant appeal, *Attorney-General of Southern Nigeria* v. *John Holt & Company (Liverpool), Ltd.*,[77] concerned accretion, always a topic likely to produce dicta, but no more, on the status of the submarine soil. The question there for determination concerned the rights of the company in a strip of land now above the foreshore but which had been below high-water mark in 1861 when the company took a Crown lease of the land adjacent to the foreshore. The company asserted that the strip of land had been formed by natural accretion, the Crown that it had been formed by artificial reclamation. In delivering the opinion of the Committee on 9 February 1915, Lord Shaw of Dunfermline stated:

. . . if erosion has continued, their Lordships do not doubt that it would have been no defence against the claim of the Crown that the foreshore upon the line of inroad had de facto been transferred to the Crown as owners of the sea and its bed within territorial limits, and of foreshore . . .[78]

Eighteen months later, it was again Lord Shaw who delivered an advice of the Judicial Committee which went much further than any previous judicial pronouncement on the question. This appeal, *Secretary of State for India in Council* v. *Sri Raja Chelikani Rama Rao*.[79] came from the High Court of Madras. It concerned the question whether the appellant could constitute or incorporate certain lands into a reserved forest. The respondents claimed that the lands had been possessed by them and their predecessors since time immemorial. The lands in question were islands built up on the bed of the sea near the mouth or delta of the Godaveri, a tidal and navigable river. The islands were close to the shore, well within three miles of it. The question in the appeal was posed and answered by Lord Shaw:

Are those islands no man's land? The answer is, they are not; they belong in property to the British Crown.[80]

---

[76] [1914]A.C. 153, 174–5.
[77] [1915] A.C. 599.
[78] Ibid., 611.
[79] (1916) L.R. 43 Ind. App. 192.
[80] Ibid., 199.

He went on to assert that the case of *Keyn*, which had been cited in order to throw doubt on the above proposition, 'had reference on its merits solely to the point as to the limits of Admiralty jurisdiction; nothing else fell to be there decided'; however, whenever the dominion of the bed of the sea 'within a limited distance from our shores' had actually been in issue, then the doubt just mentioned had not been supported. He went on to remark that their Lordships would not refer to the 'Duchy of Cornwall case' but to much more recent examples of contested rights in or over land *ex adverso* of the foreshore. He then cited *Lord Fitzhardinge* v. *Purcell* and *Lord Advocate* v. *Trustees of the Clyde Navigation*, together with the dictum of Lord Watson in *Lord Advocate* v. *Wemyss*. None of these cases, however, directly concerned the open seas but rather the bed and subsoil of inland waters, though this was not mentioned by Lord Shaw. He continued:

It should be added, with reference to the suggestion that the territory of the Crown ceases at low-water mark, and that the right over what extends seawards beyond that is merely of the nature of jurisdiction or the like, that there are manifest difficulties in seeing what are the grounds for this in principle. There is nothing to recommend a local jurisdiction over a space of water lying above a *res nullius*. As to practical results: the confusion that might be produced by leaving islands, emergent within the three-mile limit, to be seized by the first comer is clear beyond controversy. He might be a foreign citizen: he would of course hoist the flag of his own nation, and that nation might proceed to fortify the emergent lands; in short, it is not difficult to figure the anomalies and difficulties which the abandonment of the plain ground taken by Lord Watson would involve to this and to other nations.[81]

After quoting a passage from Lord Stowell's (Sir William Scott) judgment in *The Anna*,[82] Lord Shaw concluded:

Their Lordships do not doubt that the general law, as already stated, is supported by the preponderating considerations of practical convenience, and that, upon the particular case in hand, the ownership of the islands formed in the sea in the estuary or mouth of the Godaveri River is in the British Crown.[83]

In 1920, yet another appeal from Canada relevant to the problem went before the Judicial Committee. This was *Attorney-*

[81] Ibid., 201–2.
[82] (1805) 5 C. Rob. 373, 385c.
[83] (1916) L.R. 43 Ind. App. 192, 203.

General for Canada v. *Attorney-General for the Province of Quebec*[84] in which the question was posed as to the right of the Provincial Government to grant exclusive fishing rights in the 'tidal waters of the Province' either by means of engines fixed in the soil or in any other manner. Viscount Haldane, who delivered the advice of the Judicial Committee on 30 November 1920, remarked:

The Chief Justice [of Quebec], following their Lordships' view, expressed in the British Columbia case, declined to answer so much of any of the questions raised as related to the three-mile limit. As to this their Lordships agree with him. It is highly inexpedient, in a controversy of a purely municipal character such as the present, to express an opinion on what is really a question of public international law. If their Lordships thought it proper to entertain such a question they would have directed the Home Government to be notified, inasmuch as the point is one which affects the Empire as a whole.[85]

The next appeal to the Judicial Committee which touched marginally on the issue of property rights in the bed and subsoil of marginal waters was *Government of the State of Penang* v. *Beng Hong Oon* in 1971.[86] This concerned, *inter alia*, the question whether alluvium formed by gradual and imperceptible recession of the sea belonged to the owner of the adjacent land. In the Malaysian courts, Gill J. at first instance made a statement regarding the accretion rule in terms similar to that of Romer J. in *Brighton and Hove General Gas Co.* v. *Hove Bungalows Ltd.* Gill J. said: 'The reason given by Blackstone for this rule of law is not generally accepted as being the true one, but the rule itself is settled beyond all question by numerous authorities starting with *Scratton* v. *Brown* (1825) 4 B. & C. 485.'[87]

In the Federal Court of Malaysia, Ali F.J. took the less critical view that, 'It seems clear from the words of Lord Hale and Blackstone that, theoretically speaking, the minute particles of earth and sands or accretions, as they are sometimes described, orginally belong to the Crown because they come from the soil under the sea.'[88]

In the advice of the Judicial Committee, delivered on 5 October 1971, no mention was made of the status of the seabed below low-water mark, nor was it mentioned in the dissenting opinion of Viscount Dilhorne.

[84] [1921] 1 A.C. 413.
[85] Ibid., 431.
[86] [1972] A.C. 425.
[87] Records of the Judicial Committee.
[88] [1970] 1 *Malayan Law Journal* 244, 248.

The latest decision of the Judicial Committee relevant to this study is *Pianka and Hylton* v. *The Queen* on appeal from the Court of Appeal of Jamaica.[89] The case involved the prosecution of United States citizens for possession of narcotic drugs on board a United States registered vessel in the territorial sea of Jamaica which by statute was twelve miles in breadth. The alleged offence took place over three miles from shore and the question arose as to the competence of the Resident Magistrate to try the accused. Lord Wilberforce, in delivering the majority opinion of the Judicial Committee, stated that it was clear in 1891, the critical date in the case, 'that the territory of the colony extended to include a three mile belt of territorial waters'.[90] As there were no special provisions in the constitutive instruments of the colony of Jamaica at that time which could be construed as an express claim by the Crown to such a belt, it seems that Lord Wilberforce was prepared to assume that the three mile belt was *ipso jure* part of the colony. If so, then the corresponding belt around the United Kingdom should equally have been regarded as 'territory', if Lord Wilberforce had addressed himself to this question.

[89] [1979] A.C. 107.
[90] Ibid., 123.

Chapter X

Executive External Practice After 1876

It is proposed to discuss the relevant practice of the United Kingdom executive in its external relations (including colonial) to the extent that this practice throws light on its attitude towards the legal status of the solum adjacent to the coasts of the United Kingdom.

A. The Fisheries Arbitrations

The three great fisheries arbitrations in which the United Kingdom was involved after 1876, namely the Halifax Arbitration of 1877, the Behring Sea Arbitration of 1893, and the North Atlantic Fisheries Arbitration of 1910, did not put directly in issue the legal status of the solum. Nevertheless the subject drew some passing remarks.

In the Behring Sea Arbitration, the British Case advanced the thesis that occupation was the basis of dominion over the bed of the sea whether it lay within 'territorial waters' or not. Indeed, the British Government seems to have by implication rejected the idea that the bed of 'territorial waters' was, as a matter of public international law, *ipso facto* under the dominion of the coastal State. The Case advanced the view that

. . . international law recognizes the right of a State to acquire certain portions of the waters of the sea and of the soil under the sea, and to include them within the territory of the State. . . .

The territory of the nation extends to low-water mark; but certain portions of the sea may be added to the dominion. For example, the sea which lies *inter fauces terrae*, and, in certain exceptional circumstances, part of the sea not lying *inter fauces terrae*.

The claim applies strictly to the soil under the sea. Such claim may be legitimately made to oyster beds, pearl fisheries, and coral reefs; and, in the same way, mines within the territory may be worked under the sea below low-water mark.

Isolated portions of the high seas cannot be taken by a nation unless the bed on which they rest can be physically occupied in a manner analogous to the occupation of land.[1]

In his oral argument, the British counsel, Sir Charles Russell A.G., claimed that by virtue of this principle lighthouses built on submerged rocks or on piles driven into the bed of the sea even beyond three miles from the nearest coast became part of the territory of the State which built them.[2]

An article written by an anonymous 'Legal Correspondent' published in the *Morning Post* of 21 May 1923,[3] threw some light on the attitude of the British Government in this arbitration. According to the correspondent, who had been present at the delivery of the judgments in *Keyn* and also had been concerned in the preparation of the British case in the arbitration, Sir Charles Russell was 'deeply impressed' by the 'profound learning' of Cockburn C.J. in *Keyn* and 'so far as this branch of the case was concerned the judgment became our Bible. Russell adopted it in its entirety, save for one or two minor points not fully worked out.' According to the correspondent, the Cockburn judgment supported the proposition

. . . that international law does recognise the right of every State with a sea-board to claim jurisdiction over a belt of waters contiguous to its coasts, which is called its 'territorial waters'; but that without evidence of a claim made such territorial waters do not exist.

B. Law Officers' Opinions to the Colonial Office

During the period 1886 to 1899 three opinions were given to the Colonial Office by the Law Officers of the Crown concerning the legal status of the submarine soil adjacent to the coasts of certain British colonies. Although the status of such areas is outside the scope of the present work, these opinions will be mentioned here since two at least made specific reference to the common law of England.[4]

In the first incident, the Law Officers, Russell A.G. and Davey S.G., were asked whether Her Majesty was competent to assume possession, by Letters Patent or otherwise, of the bed of the sea within the 'boundaries' of the colony of Western Australia as these had been defined by an instrument under the Great Seal in 1830.

[1] H. A. Smith, *Great Britain and the Law of Nations*, vol. II, 419.

[2] J. B. Moore, *International Arbitrations*, vol. I, 900.

[3] See FO 372/1997, fo. 53.

[4] For an account of British colonial practice, see Marston, (1976) 50 *Australian Law Journal* 402.

The opinion, dated 4 August 1886, ran in part as follows:

We are of opinion that it would not be competent for Her Majesty to assume possession by Letters Patent or otherwise of the bed of the sea beyond the three-mile limit, although within the boundaries of the Colony as mentioned. . . [5]

The next opinion relevant to the seabed was given in 1895. The question had arisen in the colony of Bermuda whether or not the Crown could by its prerogative authorize the erection of wharves below high-water mark of the navigable rivers of the Colony. The Attorney-General of Bermuda considered that grants already made by the Crown of land situated below high-water mark were in derogation of the rights of the subjects at large and therefore *ultra vires*. He appeared to found this view on the House of Lords decision in *Gann* v. *The Free Fishers of Whitstable*. The Colonial Office referred the question to the Law Officers, Webster A.G. and Finlay S.G.,[6] whose reply, dated 28 October 1895, ran in part as follows:

. . . upon the information before us we are of opinion that the rights of the Crown in the foreshores and lands below high-water mark in the Bermudas are the same as under the common law in England unaffected by statute. It follows that the Crown can by its prerogative make grants of the soil below high-water mark, and within three miles of that mark under the sea adjoining the Islands of Bermuda, and under navigable creeks of the Colony, but such a grant cannot authorize the construction of any works which would substantially prejudice the public rights of navigation thereby occasioning a public nuisance. . . .

The question is therefore purely one of fact: Will the structure erected pursuant to the grant be a nuisance, i.e. a substantial prejudice to the public right of navigation. (*A.G.* v. *Johnson*, 2 Wils. Ch. Cases, 101; *A.G.* v. *Burridge*, 10 Price, 369). If it will be such a nuisance, the Crown cannot license or authorize the structure.[7]

The opinion went on to declare that there was no difference between the case of wharves projecting from the shore and that of isolated structures.

[5] CO 885/13; Law Officers' Opinions to the Colonial Office, vol. IV, No. 73; CO 18/207, fos. 752–6.

[6] The later career of each of these officers touched more than usually on questions of international law of the sea. Webster (later Lord Alverstone C.J.) was second counsel for the United Kingdom in the Behring Sea Arbitration in 1892–3, and a member of the Alaska Boundary Tribunal in 1903; Finlay (later Lord Finlay, judge of the Permanent Court of International Justice) was leading counsel for the United Kingdom in the North Atlantic Fisheries Arbitration in 1910.

[7] CO 885/14; Law Officers' Opinions to the Colonial Office, vol. V, No. 96; CO 37/226.

The third opinion concerned an application by a dock company at Singapore for a grant of land adjoining their premises, such land consisting partly of foreshore and partly of the bed of the sea below low-water mark. The Law Officers, again Webster A.G. and Finlay S.G., were asked, *inter alia*, 'whether the common law of England as to (a) foreshore, and (b) open sea within territorial limits applies to the Straits Settlements?' The opinion, dated 11 November 1899, read in part:

> . . . We think that it would be held that the Common Law of England as to foreshore and open seas within the territorial limits applies to the Straits Settlements, subject to modifications required by local customs. . . . the question whether these alienations could be impeached would turn on the question whether there is any substantial interference with public rights. The property of the Crown in the foreshore, and in the soil of territorial waters, is subject to the rights of the public, but it does not follow that every reclamation of the foreshore, or of territorial waters, would constitute a public nuisance.[8]

C. The Views of Sir Cecil Hurst

In the first half of the nineteen-twenties, Hurst, while legal adviser to the Foreign Office, published two articles in the newly-founded *British Year Book of International Law* which touched the subject matter of the present work. The first to appear, 'The Territoriality of Bays', published about 1922,[9] was largely concerned with the problem of the delimitation of inland (or internal) waters. It will suffice here to cite Hurst's view of the decision in *Keyn*:

> In 1876 came the case of *R.* v. *Keyn*, a case which shows . . . clearly that the waters within the three-mile limit, the marginal belt which is usually designated as 'territorial waters', are not part of the national territory. If they were, there could have been no question but that an offence committed at sea within those waters would be within the common law jurisdiction of the courts, and if within the common law jurisdiction, Keyn could and should have been tried at the Kent Assizes.[10]

Hurst went on to assert that by the Territorial Waters Jurisdiction Act 1878 '[n]o attempt was made to constitute these waters part of the national territory'.[11]

The second article, 'Whose is the Bed of the Sea? Sedentary

8 Ibid., No. 241, CO 273/254, fos. 68–72.
9 (1922–3) 3 *BYBIL* 42.
10 Ibid., 45.
11 Ibid., 46.

Fisheries outside the Three-Mile Limit', published in late 1923, is more relevant to the present subject. In it, Hurst analysed the status, not only of the submarine areas situated more than three miles from the coasts, but also the 'territorial' seabed and subsoil. He carried out his analysis in respect of both English common and statute law on the one hand, and public international law on the other, although often it is difficult to distinguish which aspect he was discussing in any particular passage. As far as English municipal law was concerned, Hurst took the view that the property in the bed of the sea below low-water mark, at least within the 'three-mile limit', was vested in the Crown. He based this conclusion in particular upon s. 2 of the Cornwall Submarine Mines Act 1858 by which, he considered, Parliament had committed itself to the proposition that the bed of the sea below low-water mark was vested in the Crown.

Hurst maintained that the words 'as part of the soil and terri-torial possessions of the Crown' in that section represented in the eyes of the draftsman a necessary element in Sir John Patteson's award. After quoting those passages from the judgment of Lord Coleridge C.J. in *Keyn* in which Lord Coleridge described what he thought were the rival contentions in the Patteson arbitration,[12] Hurst continued:

> If in face of these two respective contentions Sir John Patteson decided that minerals won from workings below low-water mark belonged to the Crown, it is difficult to reconcile his award with anything but an intention to maintain that the right of the Crown to these minerals was a territorial right, *i.e.* that the property in the bed of the sea and not merely sovereignty and jurisdiction over it was vested in the Crown. The recitals of the Act also show that he had himself suggested that the Bill should make provision for giving to persons working these minerals below low-water mark in right of leases, etc., from the Crown, facilities to extract them upon terms to be agreed between the Crown and the Duchy. Such a recommendation is inconsistent with any view that the right to minerals won from below low-water mark is based on seizure or occupation of a 'res nullius'.[13]

Hurst referred also to local Acts of Parliament passed for the purpose of enabling lands below low-water mark to be reclaimed. He pointed out that their preambles usually recited the claim of the Crown to the land reclaimed and that their operative sections

---

[12] (1923–4) 4 *BYBIL* 34, 35.
[13] Ibid., 36.

contained a provision awarding compensation to the Crown for giving up the land.[14] He then maintained that most of the cases which threw light on the nature of property in the bed of the sea were either fishery cases, or concerned a claim by a subject to establish, by prescription or by presumption of a lost grant, a right which could not be good against the public unless derived from the Crown. He continued:

An exclusive right on the part of a private person to the fishing in any area below low-water mark would constitute a 'several fishery', and the right of the Crown to make a grant of a several fishery disappeared with Magna Charta. As it is admitted in these cases that the rights claimed must have been derived from the Crown, it follows that the rights of the Crown in the bed of the sea must have been fixed at least as early as the thirteenth century.[15]

Hurst declared that *Chelikani's* case 'definitely lays down the rule that the Crown is the owner of the bed of the sea'.[16]

He then turned to the question of the extent geographically of the Crown's property rights in the sea and seabed. After discarding as excessive the argument of Plowden to the effect that the interest of the Crown extended half way to Spain and over the whole of the seas between England and France, he concluded:

The wide claims to jurisdiction over the narrow seas which this country made in the past have fallen into desuetude. There has been no formal renunciation of them and it is merely by disuse that they have lapsed. If the rights of the Crown to the ownership of the bed of the sea are now more restricted than they were at the time at which Lord Hale was writing, it can only be that they also have been narrowed by disuse.[17]

It was on the basis of use or occupation that Hurst advanced his argument that Crown ownership still continued over portions of the bed of the sea situated beyond the three-mile limit where there was such effective occupation. He concluded his article as follows:

. . . so far as Great Britain at any rate is concerned, the ownership of the bed of the sea within the three-mile limit is the survival of more extensive claims to the ownership of and sovereignty over the bed of the sea. The claims have become restricted by the silent abandonment of the more

[14] He specified only two: the Norfolk Estuary Act 1846 and the Lincolnshire Estuary Act 1851.

[15] 4 *BYBIL* 34, 36–7. He referred to *Free Fishers of Whitstable* v. *Gann, Attorney-General* v. *Chambers, Lord Advocate* v. *Wemyss, Lord Fitzhardinge* v. *Purcell,* and *Lord Advocate* v. *Trustees of the Clyde Navigation.*

[16] Ibid., 37–8.

[17] Ibid., 39.

extended claims. Consequently, where effective occupation has been long maintained of portions of the bed of the sea outside the three-mile limit, those claims are valid and subsisting claims, entitled to recognition by other States.[18]

In this second article, Hurst did not expound the opinion in respect of *Keyn* which he had set out in his first article, nor did he give any reason for assuming, as he must have assumed, that the Crown's claim to the bed and subsoil within the 'three-mile limit' was valid *ipso facto*, irrespective of effective occupation.

In view of the authoritative position held by Sir Cecil Hurst at this time, it is relevant to examine the *travaux préparatoires* of the second article. On 23 November 1922, Hurst wrote to A. S. Gaye, Solicitor to the Office of Woods, Forests, and Land Revenues, as follows:[19]

Somewhere in the archives of your department must be buried the papers which contain the history of the drafting of an Act of Parliament called The Cornish [sic] Submarine Mines Act, 21 & 22 Victoria, Chap. 109. It was an Act of Parliament which was passed to give statutory effect to an arbitration award, the arbitration having taken place for the purpose of settling a dispute between the Crown and the Duchy of Cornwall as to which party was entitled to the minerals won from workings underground beyond low-water mark. The arbitrator decided that the Crown was entitled to these minerals. When the Act was passed for the purpose of giving effect to this award, some words were introduced into the Bill which implied that the Crown was the proprietor of the bed of the sea below low-water mark. There is nothing in the arbitrator's award to justify this language, and I want, if I can, to find out how the words came to be introduced, whether it was mere inadventure or what.

. . . I am writing an article . . . on the question of whose is the bed of the sea, and what has led me to undertake it is the fact that Parliament has committed itself in this way to the above doctrine which seems to me to be open to question. The Duchy of Cornwall archives seem to contain no information on the subject of the preparation of this Bill; it must have been drafted by the Crown authorities and not by the Duchy authorities. [Parliamentary Counsel's] office had not in those days been established and, therefore, any records there are must be among your archives and I want you, if you would be so kind, to let me come across some day and ascertain what light the early papers throw on the subject.

I am afraid you will think me a great nuisance, but the subject is of great importance.

[18] Ibid., 43.
[19] The following account is from documents in CREST 37/252.

Gaye then arranged for relevant papers to be produced. On 13
December 1922 he wrote to Hurst, pointing out, *inter alia*, that
Coulson in his *Law of Waters* had stated that the realm of England
extended only to the low-water mark, all beyond being high seas,
but that later in the book Coulson had cited the cases of *Gammell*
and the *Whitstable Free Fishers* for the proposition that the Crown
had ownership of the soil as far as the 'three-mile limit'. The list of
documents produced for the inspection of Hurst when he visited
Gaye in March 1923 has survived; it reads:

1. Volume being Brief for the Crown containing (*inter alia*) various
   statements on behalf of the Crown and the Duchy of Cornwall
   respectively in regard to the title of minerals laid before Sir John
   Patteson.
2. Volume containing further documents in support of the Case of the
   Crown.
3. Print of Observations on behalf of the Crown 22nd May 1857.
4. Volume containing prints of Cornwall Submarine Mines Act 1858
   and of Agreement for reference to Sir J. T. Coleridge and of relative
   statements.
5. Print containing copies of Award or decision dated 10th June 1857 by
   Sir John Patteson.

It does not clearly appear from this list that Hurst saw all the
papers relating to both Cornwall arbitrations; in particular, it
seems doubtful whether all the voluminous papers relating to the
Coleridge arbitration were included in the general words 'relative
statements' in item 4 above.

The implications of Hurst's views on the bed and subsoil of
'territorial waters' were discussed within the Foreign Office in
December 1924.[20] Sir Thomas Barclay, who was *rapporteur* of the
Territorial Sea Committee of the *Institut de Droit International*, had
written to H. G. Maurice of the Ministry of Agriculture and
Fisheries, asking whether there had been any general order
respecting the utilization of the floor of territorial waters; he
asserted that modern development required recognition of the
right of the adjacent State to the 'absolute dominion' over the three-
mile belt, both under the sea and, subject to the right of innocent
passage, over it. The letter was referred to the Foreign Office for
advice. F. V. Adam considered that Maurice should send an
unofficial reply to Barclay calling his attention to Hurst's article
on the status of the bed of the sea. The second legal adviser, W.

---

[20] The following account is from documents in FO 372/2110, fos. 166–9.

Malkin, added:

The question put can, so far as I am aware, be answered simply in the negative, but there is no reason why a reference should not be given to Sir C. Hurst's article, provided that it is not suggested that it is official.

Sir Cecil Hurst continued to concern himself with the problem of the legal status of the maritime areas. In 1925, he delivered a statement in reply to various reports on the subject of the terri- torial sea made to the Conference of the *Institut de Droit International* held at the Hague in July and August of that year. After stating that, in his view, the high seas constituted a *res communis* rather than a *res nullius*, he went on:

A l'égard du sous-sol qui se trouve au-dessous du lit de la haute mer, on peut admettre que l'établissement d'un tunnel constitue un moyen par lequel ce sous-sol peut être effectivement occupé par l'Etat qui possède la souveraineté sur le territoire avoisinant et que nul autre Etat n'est en situation de l'empêcher. Dans cette mesure la condition juridique du sous-sol qui se trouve au dessous du lit de la haute mer se rapproche du status d'une *res nullius* en ce que le premier occupant peut s'assurer un titre qui sera bon contre tout le monde.

On peut admettre la même chose pour la surface du lit de la haute mer. L'occupation peut en être effectuée en posant des câbles ou en y établissant des parcs de pêche (huîtres, bêches de mer, perles, éponges, etc.) et le premier arrivant peut par cette occupation obtenir un titre valable.[21]

Shortly after this, Hurst was involved officially in an issue which raised the whole question of the status of the submarine areas, both within and without the territorial belt. The Imperial Conference of 1923 had requested the participating governments to submit a list of geographically defined waters which should be claimed as 'territorial inlets'. On 16 September 1926, the Indian Government submitted to the India Office a list[22] which included the Gulf of Manaar, an extensive area of water in the south of the sub-continent on the bed of which was an important pearl fishery. The status of the Gulf had been the subject of a decision in the High Court of Madras in 1904 which had held that it was an integral part of Her Majesty's dominions in the same way as the Bristol Channel and Conception Bay.[23] The Court dismissed *Keyn* very summarily:

The decision in the case of *The Queen* v. *Keyn* relied on by the respondents,

---

[21] *Annuaire de l'Institut de Droit International*, vol. 32, 1925, 159–60.
[22] FO 372/2285, fos. 456–8.
[23] *Annakumaru Pillai* v. *Muthupayal* (1904) I.L.R. 27 Madras 551.

referred to the jurisdiction of the Court of Admiralty over offences committed in the open sea, and has no application to such a state of facts as exists in the present case.[24]

Amongst the papers transmitted to the India Office in 1926 by the Government of India was an opinion of the Advocate-General of India given on 10 June 1917 on the subject of the Gulf of Manaar.[25] He had been asked to advise, *inter alia*, whether the Government could successfully prosecute any person, British subject or otherwise, who poached pearl oysters at a distance of more than three miles from the low-water mark. The Advocate-General replied that 'it is now fairly well established that the Crown is the owner of the sea and its bed within territorial limits'.[26]

He supported this conclusion by citing *Attorney-General of Southern Nigeria* v. *Holt (John) & Co. (Liverpool) Ltd.*, *Lord Fitzhardinge* v. *Purcell*, *Gammell* v. *Commissioners of Woods and Forests*, *Gann* v. *The Free Fishers of Whitstable*, *Lord Advocate* v. *Wemyss*, and *Secretary of State for India in Council* v. *Sri Raja Chelikani Rama Rao*, and continued:

The opinions to the contrary expressed in the *Franconia* case *R.* v. *Keyn* can no longer be regarded as law and have been set aside by the Territorial Waters Jurisdiction Act.[27]

According to the Advocate-General, the doubt expressed by Viscount Haldane in *Attorney-General for British Columbia* v. *Attorney-General for Canada* 'ignores the weight of authority which has already been referred to'. He concluded that a right of property existed in pearl fisheries situated within or without the three-mile belt as against subjects and foreigners alike.

On receipt of the above papers in London, the India Office referred them for information to other Departments. The Admiralty suggested an inter-departmental meeting to consider the status of the bed of the sea. In its view, the possibility that a foreign State might lawfully claim portions of the seabed under the high seas up to the outer limit of the territorial waters could have serious effects on questions of neutrality; for example, it would be impossible to lay a minefield even in areas outside the three-mile limit because the bed of the sea could be claimed as belonging to

[24] Ibid., 573.
[25] FO 372/2285, fos. 497–502.
[26] Ibid., fo. 497.
[27] Ibid., fo. 498.

some country; such a result, according to the Admiralty, followed from the conclusions in Sir Cecil Hurst's article on the subject of the bed of the sea outside territorial waters. Accordingly, an interdepartmental meeting was held on 1 February 1927, under the chairmanship of Sir Cecil Hurst.[28] After one of the Admiralty representatives had set out the problem, Hurst, disclaiming paternity for the theory discussed in his article, replied:

The difficulty started from the legislation in connection with the mines of Cornwall—'The Cornwall Submarine Mines Act, 1858'. Parliament there definitely committed itself to the view that the property and the sovereignty in the bed of the sea below low water mark was vested in the Crown.

Hurst was asked whether this meant as between the Crown and the subject or as between the Crown and the world. He replied:

In that case as between the Crown and the subject, but surely it is the same thing. Such rights as the Crown had in ancient days in the bed of the sea had now become limited to a range of three miles from the shore, but this was not inconsistent with the maintenance of sovereignty over specific areas of the bed of the sea, such as a pearl bank, where for all time effective control had been maintained. Occasions upon which such a claim would be made would, however, be extremely few.

Hurst was then asked whether the claim extended to private ownership of the soil as well as to ownership by the Sovereign. In reply, he stated:

Ownership is a matter of domestic law. The state must protect the ownership enjoyed by the individual. In Great Britain in the case of a sedentary fishery the private ownership would have to be traced back to a Crown grant. Where the Crown exercised both rights of sovereignty and property rights, there would have been nothing to prevent the Crown making a grant of the property rights while retaining the sovereignty. The real implications of the Cornish legislation are that the property and sovereignty must be vested in someone, because the possible opposite theory, upon which the Duchy of Cornwall relied, was that the bed of the sea was a *res nullius*. Parliament said 'No', the bed of the sea belongs to someone. The intention of the article in the Year Book was to show that as the rights of the Crown date back far beyond the origin of the doctrine of the three mile limit, but today may rightly be said not to extend in general in the bed of the sea off the coast beyond the three mile limit, there has been a tacit abandonment by the Sovereign of the rights beyond that limit. Here and there, however, there are areas where there has been effective control and use of the bed of the sea from time

[28] The minutes of this meeting are filed in FO 372/2410, fos. 283–93.

immemorial. In such cases it would be absurd to say that the Sovereign had tacitly abandoned its rights, when in fact it was maintaining them.

The question was then raised of the pearl banks in the Gulf of Manaar and in Palk's Strait between India and Ceylon. It is not clear from the ensuing discussion whether the departmental representatives were speaking about the seabed under territorial waters *stricto sensu* or about the solum under areas of sea beyond the territorial waters, or even, on the other hand, about the bed of internal waters. From a remark made by one of the Colonial Office representatives, Sir John Risley, it seems to have been the second of the above three possibilities. He was of opinion that the question turned on the distinction between sovereignty and jurisdiction:

You claim sovereignty over the bed of the sea, but only rights of juris-diction over the water in question in order to protect the bed of the sea. In the case of the Ceylon pearl fisheries, the Gulf of Manaar had never been claimed as territorial waters.

Hurst agreed with H. R. Cowell, the second Colonial Office representative, in thinking that a claim to rights in the bed of the sea must have been prior in date to the doctrine of territorial waters and that if such a claim had not so far been made it could not be made in future.

Towards the conclusion of the meeting, H. G. Maurice, of the Department of Agriculture and Fisheries, asked what attitude was to be accepted, if and when an international conference met to consider the subject of territorial waters, on the question of the bed of the sea. The minutes of the meeting then stated:

It was agreed that the best policy would be for His Majesty's Government not to raise the point at all. They did not want to admit any claims by other Powers and there was no need to call attention to their own claims.

In conclusion, the meeting agreed that the Gulf of Manaar and Palk's Strait should both be claimed as 'integral parts of His Majesty's Dominions'; this would meet the Admiralty objections 'as then no question of territorial waters in the technical sense would arise'.

D. The Gulf of Paria

Although this aspect of United Kingdom practice did not directly concern the solum adjacent to the coasts of the United Kingdom, it will be examined here since the views expressed were often of a general character, not confined necessarily to the case of colonies.

In a despatch to the Colonial Office dated 9 December 1935,[29] the Governor of Trinidad, Sir Claude Hollis, drew attention to the fact that oil boring activities had been successfuly carried out in the estuary of the Orinoco River in Venezuela but adjacent to the territorial waters of Trinidad; as a result of this success, there was renewed interest in an attempt to find oil under the Gulf of Paria in areas which were outside the territorial waters of the Colony, i.e. beyond three miles from the coast of Trinidad. The Governor went on to suggest that in respect of the submarine areas outside territorial waters a basis for negotiation might be found in the possible division of control of these areas between Venezuela and Trinidad.

In January 1936, the Colonial Office requested the advice of the Foreign Office on what, in the former's view, were the three possibilities: (a) a division of the whole area between Venezuela and Britain by means of drawing straight lines from headland to headland; (b) a claim to the sea floor 'even beyond territorial waters'; (c) the setting up a joint customs barrier with Venezuela at the exits from the Gulf, and also the imposition of a heavy duty on oil won subaqueously.[30]

Within the Foreign Office, the above request drew a succession of minutes from various officials both in the political and the legal branches. On 3 February 1936, J. M. Troutbeck wrote:

The first point that seems to arise is whether the ordinary rules about territorial waters govern the subsoil. Presumably they do, in which case it is difficult to see how we could claim any monopoly, even in conjunction with Venezuela, outside the 3 mile limit. It will be observed, however, that according to the attached map both entrances to the Gulf of Paria are covered within the territorial waters area, so possibly we could claim that the whole gulf belongs to Venezuela and ourselves. I doubt, though, whether this would be a just claim, as presumably we should not admit a similar use, e.g. in the Black Sea.[31]

G. G. Fitzmaurice, then third legal adviser, added a long minute dated 4 February 1936 which began:

There is a certain amount of authority for the view that it is possible to claim the subsoil beneath the open sea in the same way as one would

[29] CO 852/41.
[30] FO 371/19847, fo. 408.
[31] Ibid., fo. 378.

claim any piece of unoccupied territory. In other words, the idea is that the rule which prevents portions of the high seas being appropriated by individual countries does not apply to the subsoil beneath the sea.[32]

Fitzmaurice then turned to the status of the territorial subsoil:

In any case there is [little or] no doubt that the subsoil beneath actual territorial waters is automatically the property of the territorial State.[33]

He then added to the typewritten minute a handwritten note to the effect that authority for the last proposition could easily be found in Article 2 of the draft prepared at the 1930 Codification Conference. Fitzmaurice, however, did not consider that the whole of the Gulf of Paria could be dealt with on the assumption that it consisted of territorial waters. He remarked that an agreement could indeed be concluded between the two States by which the waters of the Gulf would be divided between Britain and Venezuela but added that such an agreement would bind only the two States concerned, although 'it might in time be possible to establish a valid claim internationally on grounds of prescription'. He continued:

There remains the possibility which I mentioned in the opening paragraph of this minute, namely to assert a claim to the subsoil beneath the open sea, i.e. outside territorial waters, in precisely the same way as one would assert a claim to any unoccupied territory on dry land. In this connexion I do not think I can do better than quote the passages from Oppenheim in which this possibility is discussed. I am not aware myself of any case in which a claim on this basis has been made. . . . I seem to have an idea, though, that in certain cases (the Cornish tin mines may be one of them) mining operations which have started on shore have gradually extended outwards under the bed of the sea and may in certain cases have extended even beyond the territorial water limit. This of course does not quite amount to asserting in terms a claim to the subsoil beyond the territorial limit. It merely is that such operations have been carried out from the shore, and could not have been carried out except from the shore, and the question of anyone else trying to challenge the 'occupation' by conducting such operations from the surface of the open sea in respect of the subsoil below it has never arisen.[34]

He attached a long extract from Volume 1 of the 5th edition of Oppenheim's *International Law* which sought to demonstrate that the bed of the open sea was a 'no man's land' and could be

[32] Ibid., fo. 379.
[33] Ibid. Fitzmaurice added to the typed minute the words in brackets.
[34] Ibid.

occupied by the littoral State starting from the subsoil beneath the bed of the territorial maritime belt.[35]

The above minute by Fitzmaurice was followed on 6 February 1936 by one by W. E. Beckett, then second legal adviser. He made no specific reference to the status of the soil under territorial waters, but on the general question raised by the Colonial Office he wrote:

The best view of the law is that the bed of the open sea and the subsoil beneath that bed is *res nullius* but that it is capable of acquisition by occupation in the same sort of manner as land which is above water and happens to belong to no-one. The best statement of the position with regard to this matter will be found in the article by Sir Cecil Hurst in the 1923 number of the British Year Book of International Law under the title 'Whose is the Bed of the Sea?'[36]

In answer to a request by Fitzmaurice for any evidence of claims to the subsoil of the sea beyond territorial waters, the Foreign Office Library produced the report of 10 May 1875 by the British members to the Joint Commission on the Channel tunnel project and also Foreign Office documents of 1929 on the same subject.[37]

The suggestion that the bed and subsoil of the high seas might be capable of being claimed by occupation caused concern at the Admiralty, which considered that such a theory might lead to claims to areas under the high seas anywhere, even adjacent to the territorial waters of another State.[38] Such a possibility was admitted by Fitzmaurice in a minute dated 28 April 1936 in which, however, he sought to allay the fears of the Admiralty that an occupation of the seabed by boring operations from above would lead to a claim to the superjacent waters as 'territorial', stating that for this conclusion 'there is certainly no warrant in international law'.[39]

Within the Colonial Office, certain doubts were being voiced over the Crown's title to the territorial seabed and subsoil, a question which would be of some importance if the exploitation of this area were to be assigned to the Trinidad authorities. On 5 May 1936, H. Duncan set out an extract from the advice of the Judicial Committee of the Privy Council delivered by Lord Haldane L.C. in *Attorney-General for British Columbia* v. *Attorney-*

[35] See now vol. 1, 8th ed., 1955, 629–30.
[36] FO 371/19847, fos. 382–3.
[37] Chapter VII above, and see FO 371/14075. fos. 185–201.
[38] FO 371/19847, fos. 412–20.
[39] Ibid., fo. 410.

General for Canada. In this case, wrote Duncan, the question whether the property in the soil of the sea under territorial waters vested in the Crown or not was raised but not decided.[40]

The Foreign Office, however, appeared to be heedless of such uncertainties and, in a despatch dated 28 July 1936 ad⌐.essed to the British Minister in Caracas asking him to beg... preliminary discussions with the Venezuelan Government, the legal position was stated to be as follows:

. . . in international law the bed of the sea beneath territorial waters and the subsoil beneath that bed are already considered as being in the possession of the territorial state. The bed of the sea and accompanying subsoil beneath the high seas on the other hand is *res nullius*, but is capable of acquisition by effective occupation in the same manner as any unoccupied territory above the level of the sea.[41]

On 18 September 1936, the Law Officers in Trinidad, J. L. Devaux A.G. and E. J. Davies S.G., wrote a minute to the Governor in which they suggested that an amending Ordinance be passed to the Crown Lands Ordinance of Trinidad declaring that the dominion of the land forming the bed of the sea within a distance of three miles from low-water mark belonged to and was vested in His Majesty with power to grant leases and licences in respect of it.[42] In view of the doubts which he had expressed in his minute of 5 May 1936, Duncan considered that the Imperial authorities, rather than the local legislature in Trinidad, should resolve the problem. As a result of his 'discovery' of the Judicial Committee's advice in *Chelikani*, Duncan asked C. C. Ross, the Attorney-General for Grenada, who was in London at this time, to prepare a minute. Accordingly, Ross set out extracts from *Chelikani* and from the later advice of the Judicial Committee in *Attorney-General for Canada* v. *Attorney-General for Quebec*, noting that there was no reference to the former in the latter. Duncan then drafted a letter which was sent to the Foreign Office and the Admiralty for their observations. This letter, sent on 15 January 1937 over the signature of G. L. M. Clauson, enclosed the minute of Devaux and Davies of 18 September 1936 and contained the following passage:

. . . the Secretary of State [for the Colonies] is advised that, in view (1) of the fact that the Colony's legislative powers are confined to its present

[40] CO 852/41.
[41] FO 371/19847, fo. 429.
[42] Sent to the Colonial Office with Governor's despatch of 10 October 1936; CO 852/41.

territorial limits and have no extra-territorial effect and (2) of the observations . . . of Lord Haldane L.C. in *Attorney-General for British Columbia* v. *Attorney-General for Canada* [1914] A.C. 153 at pages 174 and 175, and in *Attorney-General for Canada* v. *Attorney-General for Quebec* [1921] 1 A.C. 413 at page 431, on the question whether the property in the soil of the sea under territorial waters vests in the Crown (in this connection, however, cf. *Secretary of State for India in Council* v. *Sri Rajah Chili Pani Rama Rao and Others* [sic] reported in Law Journal Reports for 1916 volume 85 Part III (P.C.) at pages 222–228), it will be necessary to issue an Imperial Order in Council providing for the annexation to His Majesty's dominions of the portions of the bed of the sea . . . unless it is now definitely recognised in international law that the bed of the sea below low water mark to what is known as the three mile limit is the property of the State concerned.[43]

Within the Foreign Office, the views expressed above were discussed by Fitzmaurice in a minute dated 24 February 1937.[44] The relevant part of the minute was incorporated into a letter dated 2 March 1937, sent to the Colonial Office in reply to its above request for observations:

I am in conclusion to state that, in Mr Eden's view, the bed of the sea under *territorial waters* is, under international law as it now stands, automatically under the sovereignty of the territorial Power. He would therefore deprecate the issue of any Order-in-Council claiming or asserting sovereignty over such territory, since this would tend to throw doubt on what is believed to be the rule. Mr. Eden is advised that it would, however, be an advantage to enact legislation of a similar kind to that suggested above, either locally or by Imperial Order-in-Council, but preferably, if possible, by the former method, in respect of territory under territorial waters as well as in respect of territory under the high seas. Whereas, in the case of the territory under the high seas, the legislation would have been preceded by an act or document asserting sovereignty, the legislation in respect of territory under territorial waters would not be preceded by any such act or document but would be based on the assumption that sovereignty already existed in respect of this territory, but that no legislation had previously been enacted in respect of it.[45]

Although the Judicial Committee cases mentioned in the Colonial Office letter of 15 January 1937 were apparently not discussed within the Foreign Office at this time, they were still troubling the authorities in Trinidad. On 7 October 1937, the

---

[43] FO 371/20675, fos. 78–9.
[44] Ibid., fos. 76–7.
[45] Ibid., fos. 87–8. Mr Eden was Secretary of State for Foreign Affairs.

Governor of Trinidad sent a despatch to the Colonial Office in which he enclosed a memorandum dated 20 September 1937 written by E. J. Davies, now the acting Attorney-General of the Colony.[46] In this memorandum, Davies was much more outspoken than he had been in the earlier opinion written jointly with the Attorney-General of Trinidad. Davies noted that the Foreign Office considered the bed of the sea under territorial waters to be, according to contemporary international law, automatically under the sovereignty of the territorial power; it was not clear to Davies, however, whether the Foreign Office considered the enactment of local legislation to vest the solum in the Crown to be undesirable. In his view, there was some justification for the enactment of an amending clause in the Crown Lands Ordinance of Trinidad, since the question of ownership of such areas was not as clear as it might be. He then cited a passage from *Halsbury's Laws of England*,[47] an extensive extract from the judgment of Cockburn C.J. in *Keyn*,[48] and what he described as 'dicta to the contrary' in *Gammell* v. *Commissioners of Woods and Forests, Gann* v. *The Free Fishers of Whitstable, Lord Advocate* v. *Wemyss, Fitzhardinge (Lord)* v. *Purcell*, and *Denaby & Cadeby Main Collieries Ltd.* v. *Anson*. His conclusion read:

From the above it will be seen that the question of the Crown's rights to the bed of the sea and the sub-soil under territorial waters is not unattended by some doubt.

Davies noted that the Foreign Office considered that it would be of advantage to enact local legislation with respect to the soil under territorial waters on the same lines as that suggested with respect to that portion of the Gulf of Paria which might fall to the Colony under an agreement with Venezuela. He went on:

It appears to me that in view of the uncertainty of the law with regard to the title of, as distinguished from the sovereignty to, the bed of the sea under territorial waters, the suggestion of the Foreign Office needs careful consideration. . . .

The theory of the *prima facie* title of the Crown to the foreshore was a mere theory of abstract law; a theory of 'law taken for granted'. The law (if such be the law) relating to the title of the Crown to the bed of the sea under territorial waters is equally so, but in my view it has not been established with that wealth of authority which has supported, in Common Law, the claim of the Crown to the title of the foreshore. In these circumstances, there is in my view a stronger case for declaring the

---

[46] Ibid., fos. 123–38.
[47] Now 3rd ed., vol. 39, 556.
[48] (1876) 2 Ex.D. 63, 199–201.

title of such bed of the sea to be in the Crown than there was with regard to the title of the foreshore.[49]

The Colonial Office's view of the relevant legal position was summed up in a letter to the Foreign Office dated 21 December 1937 in which copies of the documents received from Trinidad were enclosed. The Colonial Office stated:

Mr Ormsby Gore proposes to reply that he is advised that the bed of the sea under territorial waters belongs to the Crown and that, notwithstanding the arguments put forward by the Acting Attorney General of Trinidad . . . there should be legislation to put the title to it in the Crown. . . .

Mr. Ormsby Gore proposes, subject to any observations which Mr Eden may have to offer, to inform the Governor that the management and control of the bed of the sea under territorial waters should be effected in the same way as the management and control of other Crown lands in Trinidad is effected, namely by non-statutory regulations approved by the Secretary of State.[50]

The reaction of the Foreign Office was simple. On 28 December 1937 an official wrote on the file that 'this matter really concerns the C[olonial] O[ffice] and, subject to Mr Fitzmaurice's views, I suggest that we may concur'.[51] The following day, Fitzmaurice, without comment, added his agreement.[52]

On 26 February 1942, a treaty was signed between Great Britain and Venezuela by which each party declared that it would not assert 'any claim to sovereignty or control' over certain parts of the submarine area of the Gulf of Paria and that it would 'recognise any rights of sovereignty or control which have been or may hereafter be lawfully acquired' by the other party over those parts. The term 'submarine areas' was described in the Treaty as denoting 'the sea-bed and subsoil outside of the territorial waters of the High Contracting Parties'. The Treaty came into force upon the exchange of ratifications on 22 September 1942.[53]

By an Order in Council, intituled the Submarine Areas of the Gulf of Paria (Annexation) Order 1942, promulgated on 6 August 1942,[54] certain submarine areas of the Gulf of Paria were 'annexed to and form part of His Majesty's dominions and shall be attached

[49] FO 371/20675, fos. 134–6.
[50] Ibid., fos. 121–2. Mr Ormsby Gore was Secretary of State for the Colonies.
[51] Ibid., fo. 120.
[52] Ibid.
[53] 144 *British and Foreign State Papers* 1065–8.
[54] Ibid., 970–1.

to the Colony of Trinidad and Tobago for administrative purposes'.

Finally, by the Submarine (Oil Mining) Regulations promulgated in Trinidad in 1945,[55] licences issued by the Sub-Intendant of Crown Lands were required for exploration and exploitation of crude oil or natural gas 'in a submarine area'. This area was described as 'land underlying the sea waters surrounding the coast of the Colony below high water mark at ordinary spring tides'.

E. Practice within International Organizations[56]

(i) THE LEAGUE OF NATIONS

As a result of a resolution of the Assembly of the League of Nations dated 22 September 1924, a Committee of Experts for the Progressive Codification of International Law was established. Among the topics which this Committee proposed to study was the law of the territorial sea. A sub-committee was appointed for this purpose, consisting of Schücking, Barbosa de Magalhaes, and Wickersham. On 29 January 1926, the sub-committee presented its report.[57] This took the form of a memorandum by Schücking followed by comments by the other two members, together with a proposed draft convention drawn up by Schücking and amended by him in the light of the above comments.

In his memorandum, Schücking put the seabed and subsoil of the territorial belt into the same category as the waters themselves. He wrote:

In virtue of its right of dominion over the whole area of its territorial waters, the riparian State possesses for itself and for its nationals the sole right of ownership over the riches of the sea. This right covers the fauna found in the waters, and also everything which may be found above or below the subsoil of the territorial sea (coral-reefs, oil-wells, tin mines).[58]

The first article of the proposed draft convention, as finally submitted by the sub-committee, ran as follows:

The character and extent of the rights of the riparian State
The State possesses sovereign rights over the zone which washes its

[55] Laws of Trinidad and Tobago, Revised Ordinances, 1950, vol. IX, 835–50.
[56] See also Marston, (1975–6) 48 *BYBIL* 322, 325–30.
[57] League of Nations Document C. 196. M.70. 1927. V.
[58] Ibid., p. 53. The original language was French but an unofficial translation was provided.

coast, in so far as, under general international law, the rights of common user of the international community or the special rights of any State do not interfere with such sovereign rights.

Such sovereign rights shall include rights over the air above the said sea and the soil and sub-soil beneath it.

Article 11 of the draft read in part:

Riches of the sea, the bottom and the subsoil
In virtue of its sovereign rights over the territorial sea, the riparian State shall exercise for itself and for its nationals the sole right of taking possession of the riches of the sea, the bottom and the subsoil.[59]

The report of the Schücking sub-committee was submitted to the League member States on 29 January 1926 for comment. The British Government confined itself to a statement that 'His Majesty's Government consider the amended draft convention . . . a useful basis for future discussion'.[60]

By a resolution of the Council of the League dated 28 September 1927, a Preparatory Committee for a future International Law Codification Conference was established.[61] This Committee asked member States to furnish information on the 'application of the rights of the coastal State to the air above and the sea bottom and the subsoil covered by its territorial waters'. The reply of the British Government to this simply stated:

The sovereign rights of the coastal State extend to the air space above, and to the sea bottom below, the belt of territorial waters and also to the subsoil below that sea bottom.[62]

After observing that 'unanimity exists on this point', the Committee drew up 'Basis of Discussion No. 2' which read:

The sovereignty of the coastal State extends to the air above its territorial waters, to the bed of the sea covered by those waters and to the subsoil.[63]

The Codification Conference opened at the Hague on 17 March 1930. Forty-eight States were represented. The Second Committee of the Conference undertook to study the 'Bases of Discussion' dealing with the territorial sea. At the fifth meeting of the Second Committee, Basis of Discussion No. 2 arose for consideration. The United States' delegate, D. H. Miller, put forward a revised

[59] Ibid., 72–3.
[60] Ibid., 145. Letter of 12 October 1926.
[61] The members were Basdevant, Castro-Ruiz, François, Hurst, and Pilotti.
[62] League of Nations Document C. 74. M. 39. 1929. V., p. 19.
[63] Ibid., 21.

formulation which read:

The territory of the coastal State includes the air above the territorial waters, the bed of the sea covered by those waters, and the subsoil.[64]

He considered that the air, water, and subsoil formed an undivided part of the territory of the State. In the debate following, the delegate of Great Britain, Sir Maurice Gwyer, the Treasury Solicitor, after 'fully accepting' the principle in the United States' amendment, stated:

The principle is that the belt of territorial water surrounding a State is to be regarded as an extension of its land territory, and, inasmuch as the sovereignty of a State over its land territory extends to the subsoil beneath and to the air above, that same principle must apply in the case of that portion of its territory which is covered by its territorial waters.[65]

The United States' amendment was carried by 24 votes to 7. The final draft, as annexed in Article 2 to the report adopted by the Second Committee on 10 April 1930, ran as follows:

The territory of a coastal State includes also the air space above the territorial sea, as well as the bed of the sea, and the subsoil.

Nothing in the present Convention prejudices any Conventions or other rules of international law relating to the exercise of sovereignty in these domains.[66]

In its written observations on the above draft article, the Committee noted that there were 'but few rules of international law' applying to the bed of the sea and the subsoil.

In the event, no instrument having treaty force emerged from the Conference.

(ii) THE UNITED NATIONS

The draft articles on the subject of the territorial sea which emerged from the Hague Codification Conference in 1930 formed the starting point for the International Law Commission's work of codifying the international law of the sea. The Commission's Special Rapporteur, J. P. A. François, who had been rapporteur to the Second Committee at the 1930 Conference, declared in his first report to the Commission presented on 4 April 1952:

Il s'ensuit de la souveraineté sur la mer territoriale, proclamée à l'article 2 [of François' draft], que le territoire de l'Etat riverain comprend, à

[64] League of Nations Document C. 351 (b). M. 145 (b). 1930. V., p. 48.
[65] Ibid., 50.
[66] Ibid., 213.

défaut de limitations expressément stipulées, le sol recouvert par la mer territoriale, ainsi que le sous-sol. Bien qu'il existe parmi les auteurs quelques opinions dissidentes, la pratique d'un certain nombre d'Etats accepte cette souveraineté. D'ailleurs la Commission du droit international dans les projets d'articles sur le plateau continental adoptés en 1951 . . . s'est déjà prononcée dans ce sens.[67]

He continued:

A toutes fins utiles le rapporteur se permet de rappeler que la Commission du droit international a décidé de séparer nettement le droit qui incombe aux Etats en ce qui concerne le plateau continental, d'une part, et les pouvoirs que les Etats peuvent exercer a l'égard du sol et du sous-sol de la mer territoriale, d'autre part.[68]

The relevant articles of François' draft ran as follows:

Article premier—Dénomination de la mer territoriale
    Le territoire de l'Etat comprend une zone de mer désignée sous le nom de mer territoriale.

Article 2—Caractère juridique de la mer territoriale
    La souveraineté sur cette zone s'exerce dans des conditions fixées par le droit international.

Article 3—Caractère juridique du sol et du sous-sol.
    1. Le territoire de l'Etat riverain comprend aussi le sol recouvert par la mer territoriale, ainsi que le sous-sol.
    2. Les dispositions du présent Règlement ne portent pas atteinte aux conventions et aux autres règles du droit international relatives à l'exercice de la souveraineté dans ces domaines.

The Commission at its eighth session in 1956 finally adopted the following draft articles:

Article 1
1. The sovereignty of a State extends to a belt of sea adjacent to its coast, described as the territorial sea.
2. This sovereignty is exercised subject to the conditions prescribed in these articles and by other rules of international law.
Article 2
The sovereignty of a coastal State extends also to the air space over the territorial sea as well as to its bed and subsoil.

[67] *Yearbook of the International Law Commission, 1952*, vol. II, 28.
[68] Ibid.

The Commission observed of draft article 2 that 'this article is taken, except for purely stylistic changes, from the regulations proposed by the 1930 Codification Conference.'[69]

In its written observations on the draft, the United Kingdom Government indicated its approval of the above two articles without comment.[70] In its written observations on the proposed régime for the contiguous zone, however, the United Kingdom Government incidentally expressed its views on the legal régime of the territorial sea:

The contiguous zone is not part of the territorial sea, but part of the high seas. It is not, like the territorial sea, under the sovereignty or jurisdiction of the coastal State. The laws of the coastal State are not, as such, applicable in the contiguous zone, as they are in the territorial sea.[71]

On 24 February 1958, the first United Nations' Conference on the Law of the Sea opened at Geneva. Eighty-six States were represented. The problems of the territorial sea and contiguous zone were entrusted to the First Committee under the chairmanship of K. H. Bailey of Australia.

During the Thirty-fifth Meeting of the First Committee, the United Kingdom proposed that draft article 1 be re-formulated to read as follows:

1. The sovereignty of a State extends, beyond its land territory and its internal waters, to a belt of sea adjacent to its coast, described as the territorial sea.
2. This sovereignty is exercised subject to the provisions of this convention and to other rules of international law.[72]

No reasons were given by the United Kingdom for the proposed reformulation which was carried at the Fifty-eighth Meeting by 61 votes to 1, with 8 abstentions.[73] Article 2 of the Commission's draft was adopted at the Fifty-ninth Meeting without objection.[74]

The full Conference, at its Nineteenth Plenary Meeting,

---

[69] *Yearbook of the International Law Commission, 1956*, vol. II, 265.
[70] Ibid., 83.
[71] Ibid., 82.
[72] United Nations Conference on the Law of the Sea, 1958, *Official Records*, vol. III, First Committee, 247.
[73] Ibid., 182.
[74] Ibid., 183.

adopted both draft articles as submitted by the First Committee, draft article 1 by 72 votes to none and draft article 2 by 75 votes to none.[75] They were then incorporated in substantially the above form into the Convention on the Territorial Sea and the Contiguous Zone which was opened for signature on 29 April 1958. The United Kingdom signed the Convention on 9 September 1958 and ratified it on 14 March 1960. It entered into force on 10 September 1964 for those States which had deposited instruments of ratification or accession.[76]

The Convention on the Continental Shelf, ratified by the United Kingdom on 11 May 1964, entered into force on 10 June 1964 for those States which had deposited instruments of ratifications or accession.[77] In Article 2(1) the Convention provides that 'the coastal State exercises over the continental shelf sovereign rights for the purpose of exploring it and exploiting its natural resources'; Article 2(3) provides that the rights of the coastal State 'do not depend on occupation, effective or notional, or on any express proclamation'; Article 2(4) states that the term 'natural resources' consists of 'the mineral and other non-living resources of the sea-bed and subsoil together with living organisms belonging to sedentary species'; Article 7 provides that the 'right' of the coastal State to exploit the subsoil by means of tunnelling irrespective of the depth of water above the subsoil is not prejudiced by the Convention, a provision which, on one view of this 'right', may permit a State to tunnel under the continental shelf appertaining to another State. As for the extent of the shelf for the purpose of the Convention, no breadth is specified. Article 1 provides that the shelf extends 'to a depth of 200 metres or, beyond that limit, to where the depth of the superjacent waters admits of the exploitation of the natural resources'; the shelf is stated in Article 1 to be 'adjacent to the coast but outside the area of the territorial sea'.

The domestic executive and legislative practice which followed the 1958 Conventions has been described to the extent that it concerns the subject matter of this study. Externally, the United Kingdom Government has concluded a number of bilateral treaties with States adjacent to the North Sea in which the shelf

---

[75] Ibid., vol. II, Plenary Meetings, 61–2.
[76] 516 *UNTS* 205.
[77] 499 *UNTS* 311.

'appertaining' to the respective Parties has been delimited.[78] The result of these instruments is that the seaward limit of shelf in the North Sea considered by the United Kingdom to 'appertain' to it is approximately the median line between the coast of the United Kingdom and those of the States opposite.

[78] The agreements are with Norway (Cmnd. 2757, 551 *UNTS* 213; in force 29 June 1965), Netherlands (Cmnd. 3254, 595 *UNTS* 113; in force 23 December 1966; as amended by Cmnd. 5173; in force 7 December 1972), Denmark (Cmnd. 5193; in force 7 December 1972) and the Federal Republic of Germany (Cmnd. 5192; in force 7 December 1972).

PART TWO

ANALYSIS

CHAPTER XI

The Delimitation of the Marginal Solum

A. The Shoreward Limit

The present work is not concerned with the solum of inland waters as such, i.e. waters that are within a county of one of the constituent parts of the United Kingdom. Nevertheless, in order to determine the shoreward limit of the solum under discussion it is necessary to discover the seaward limit of such inland waters. The two limits will coincide.

The leading case in English law is *Attorney-General* v. *Chambers* in 1854 which concerned the landward limit of the foreshore. There it was stated that 'the medium tides . . . of each quarter of the tidal period afford a criterion which we think best adopted . . . the average of these medium tides in each quarter of a lunar revolution during the year gives the limit, in the absence of all usage, to the rights of the Crown in the seashore'.[1]

This test has been applied in a rough and ready form in cases in which the issue has been the seaward extent of the county. Thus in *R.* v. *Musson*[2] in 1858, which concerned the rating of the Wellington Pier at Great Yarmouth, and in *Embleton* v. *Brown* in 1860, the seaward limit of the county was held to be the 'ordinary' low-water mark. *Coulson & Forbes* states:

The low water limit of the sea shore or foreshore has not been brought directly in issue as has been the case with the high water mark. In modern practice it has been considered to be the low water mark of the ordinary tides. If this is the correct view, and the seaward line of the foreshore is the limit of the kingdom on the coast, then the land left bare below the low water mark of ordinary tides is not part of the kingdom or within the jurisdiction of the county, and crimes committed there would be committed on the high sea.[4]

The Ordnance Survey accepts that *Chambers* is also relevant for

---

[1] (1854) 4 De G. M. & G. 206, 215.
[2] (1858) 22 J.P. 609.
[3] (1860) 30 L.J. M.C. 1.
[4] *Coulson & Forbes*, 6th ed., 24.

the seaward limits. In a leaflet—*High and Low Water Marks*—dated June 1965, it stated:

In 1854 the Lord Chancellor in giving judgment on the limits of foreshore boundaries around England and Wales defined these boundaries as following the High and Low Water Marks of a medium or average tide.

The leaflet goes on to explain that the present nomenclature is Mean Low Water (MLW). After explaining how tidal surveys are made, it concludes that low water presents greater difficulty than high water and 'its definition cannot be guaranteed to the same degree of accuracy'.

In Scotland, the position is different. In *Fisherrow Harbour Commissioners* v. *Musselburgh Real Estate Co. Ltd.*, the Court of Session had to consider the shoreward limit of the foreshore. Pressed to adopt the rule in *Chambers*, the Lord Ordinary, Lord Low, nevertheless held that the foreshore extended to the high-water mark of ordinary spring tides. On appeal, the judgment was affirmed by the Inner House. Lord Young remarked:

I regard the definition arrived at by our own law as the best, and I therefore consider that uniformity should be attained not by the Scottish authorities adopting the rule on this subject which has been determined in the law of England, but by the English authorities adopting the rule laid down in our own law.[5]

It has been assumed that the same principle applies to the seaward limit of the foreshore in Scotland. In its leaflet, the Ordnance Survey states inaccurately though authoritatively that in Scotland 'there has been no legal definition of foreshore boundaries but ancient custom has decreed that the extent of the foreshore shall be limited by mean spring tides'. This is known as Mean Low Water Springs (MLWS) in the Ordnance Survey.

It is not proposed in this work to enter into the technical complexities which are produced in practice by these judicial utterances. The Ordnance Survey, in the above leaflet, has explained how it constructs the relevant lines for use in its maps and plans. Nor is it proposed to discuss the seaward extent of the powers of various authorities for particular purposes, e.g., water management, planning, land drainage, and public health.[6] The

[5] (1903) 5 F. 387, 394.
[6] See, e.g., Gibson, [1977] *Journal of Planning and Environment Law* 762; Himsworth, ibid., 1.

importance of these matters is great and it would require a separate study to do justice to them.

The problem of accretions, natural and artificial, from the sea to the land has now been dealt with by s. 72 of the Local Government Act 1972, which provides:

(1) Subject to subsection (3) below, every accretion from the sea, whether natural or artificial, and any part of the sea-shore to the low water-mark, which does not immediately before the passing of this Act form part of a parish shall be annexed to and incorporated with—
   (a) in England, the parish or parishes which the accretion or part of the sea-shore adjoins, and
   (b) in Wales, the community or communities which the accretion or part of the sea-shore adjoins,
      in proportion to the extent of the common boundary.

(2) Every accretion from the sea or part of the sea-shore which is annexed to and incorporated with a parish or community under this section shall be annexed to and incorporated with the district and county in which that parish or community is situated.

(3) In England, in so far as the whole or part of any such accretion from the sea or part of the sea-shore as is mentioned in subsection (1) above does not adjoin a parish, it shall be annexed to and incorporated with the district which it adjoins or, if it adjoins more than one district, with those districts in proportion to the extent of the common boundary; and every such accretion or part of the sea-shore which is annexed to and incorporated with a district under this section shall be annexed to and incorporated with the county in which that district is situated.

The low-water mark, however, is not the uniform seaward limit of inland waters. Certain tidal waters, and their solum, are considered to be within the county by virtue of a common law doctrine. Furthermore, certain waters, and their solum, are considered to be under the unrestricted sovereignty of the Crown by virtue of the fact that they lie on the shoreward side of the baseline from which the United Kingdom territorial sea is measured. These situations will be examined separately.

(i) THE COMMON LAW DOCTRINE

This first arose in the context not of property but of 'jurisdiction'. The question was whether certain water areas fell within the ambit of adjudication of the common law courts, particularly in criminal matters. The strict territorial nature of English criminal law, evidenced by the fact that the jury had to be called from the 'pais' or county where the alleged crime was committed, made the delimitation of the county a matter of extreme importance; once certain water areas had been determined to be within the county, it was assumed without further question that not only was the subjacent soil equally within the county but that both were thereby part of the realm and, consequently, part of the Crown's territorial dominions. Jurisdictional rights, therefore, gave rise to property rights.

The earliest foundation in common law of a rule for these 'inland' tidal waters was a dictum by Stanton J. in about 1314, quoted in *Fitzherbert's Abridgement* as follows:

Que ceo nest pas saunce [or sauce] de mere ou home puit veier ce que est fait de l'un part de l'eive et de l'auter, come a veier de l'un terre tancque a l'auter, que le coroner viendra en ceo cas et fera son office; auxi come aventer avient en un brace del mere la ou home puit veier de l'un parte tancque a l'auter, de l'averter que en cel lieu avient puit pays avec conisans . . .[7]

The authority of this formulation was weakened in 1618 by Rolle's comment that it was denied by the judges to be the law.[8] Shortly afterwards, Hale reformulated the rule as follows:

The sea is either that which lies within the body of a county or without.

That arm or branch of the sea which lies within the *fauces terrae*, where a man may reasonably discerne between shore and shore, is or at least may be within the body of a county, and therefore within the jurisdiction of the sheriff or coroner. 8 E 2 Coron. 399.[9]

F. S. Reilly, in the opinion given in 1864 to the Office of Woods on the seaward extent of the county of Cornwall, stated that the dictum of Stanton J. ' . . . does not seem to rest on any principle, for the observation that a jury of the county will have cognizance of the facts would apply equally with respect to the open sea-shore; so that at that part a county should, be parity of reason, extend seawards far below low-water mark.'[10] He also criticized the ambiguity of Hale's reformulation. The Coleridge arbitral award of 1869 rejected the argument that the marginal solum around the Cornish coasts to a uniform distance was part of the county of Cornwall. There is no reason to consider that a different view would be taken elsewhere in the United Kingdom.

[7] *Fitzherbert's Abridgement, Coron.* 399.
[8] (1618) 2 Rolle 49.
[9] Hale, *De Jure Maris*, Ch. 4.
[10] FO 881/2290, p. 8.

The 'visibility' test of Hale was supplemented in *R.* v. *Cunningham* with a notion that waters (and presumably subjacent soil) were within the county if the local authorities had regarded them to be such by virtue of administrative acts. The case concerned the competence of a court in Glamorgan to try American seamen for alleged offences committed on board an American vessel while it was lying about a quarter of a mile from low-water mark in the Bristol Channel at a spot where the channel was not less than ten miles wide. The Court for Crown Cases Reserved, in a judgment delivered by Cockburn C.J., held that 'looking at the local situation of this sea' the ship was within the county of Glamorgan; the fact that certain islands between which and the shore the ship was lying had always been treated as part of the county was a 'a strong illustration of the principle on which we proceed, namely, that the whole of this inland sea between the counties of Somerset and Glamorgan is to be considered as within the counties by the shores of which its several parts are respectively bounded.'[11]

Thus the reasons for the decision remain obscure; the Court did not seem to act upon the fact that the *locus in quo* was within the port of Cardiff as defined by Treasury Warrant although this point had been relied on by the Crown; nor did the Court seem to apply the *intra fauces terrae* test, the vessel being in fact outside the headlands formed on the Glamorgan coast by Lavernock Point and Penarth Head. Sir Hardinge Giffard S.G., who had appeared as counsel for the defendants in *Cunningham*, claimed during the argument in *Keyn* that the earlier case had turned simply on a question of venue since he conceded that the Admiral would have had jurisdiction if this had been alleged by the Crown.[12]

According to the rival contentions in *The Fagernes*, the *locus in quo* was either 10½ or 12½ miles from the English coast and either 9½ or 7½ miles from the Welsh coast, at a point where the Bristol Channel was about 20 miles wide. At first instance, Hill J., 'on common law alone', held the *locus* to be 'within the jurisdiction'.[13] Although it was unnecessary for the Court of Appeal to consider the common law position in view of the opinion they formed of the effect of a statement by the Home Secretary on the extent of the Crown's 'territorial sovereignty', both Bankes and Lawrence L.JJ.

[11] (1859) Bell 72, 86.
[12] DPP 4/13: Transcript, 15 June 1876, p. 220.
[13] [1926] P. 185, 196–7.

stated that they did not agree with the reasoning of Hill J.[14]

The question remains whether there are in the United Kingdom any 'historic bays' or other tidal waters falling outside the *fauces terrae* test of visibility which are inland waters at common law. It might be argued that the 'King's Chambers' are such waters. These Chambers were areas of sea enclosed, by virtue of a decree of James I in 1604, within straight baselines drawn from headland to headland around the coasts of England and Wales (but not Scotland).[15] However, the very fact that the Chambers were proclaimed by James I as late as 1604 would, it is contended, thereby preclude them from being regarded by the common law as inland waters. Furthermore, they were originally proclaimed to delimit areas of neutral waters and no evidence exists to show that they were intended at the time to become part of the county.[16]

The application of specific legislation to adjacent tidal areas has sometimes been looked on as evidence of their incorporation within the county. Although there are local Acts, such as the Herne Bay and Ham oyster fisheries statutes,[17] no general legislation has been passed to constitute all areas of tidal enclosed water as inland waters. There are, nevertheless, statutes dealing with customs, pilotage, and fisheries which provide for the delimitation of particular areas. The most frequently relied on in the present context is the legislation enabling the delimitation of ports. In view of its pretended importance, this will be discussed in Chapter XII below. With regard to the compulsory pilotage areas delimited either by special Act or by Orders made under the Pilotage Act 1913, it is submitted that these are merely *ad hoc* administrative districts which provide no evidence for the incorporation of the water areas and subjacent soil as part of the county. As Hill J. remarked at first instance in *The Fagernes*:

. . . a provision that a ship entering a port must take a pilot at such and such a place does not, in my view, throw any light on the question

[14] [1927] P. 311, 323 (per Bankes L.J.), 329 (per Lawrence L.J.).
[15] A map, taken from Selden, which shows the Chambers is printed in Fulton, 121. See also Grant, (1915) 31 *LQR* 410.
[16] Atkin L.J. in *The Fagernes* [1927] P. 311, 326, indicated that he was not prepared to declare the King's Chambers dead. In the Anglo-Norwegian Fisheries Case before the International Court of Justice in 1950 and 1951, the United Kingdom Government claimed on several occasions that the King's Chambers had long snce been abandoned (*Pleadings, Oral Arguments, Documents*, vol. I, 90; vol. II, 451). It also pointed out that the locus in *Keyn* was within a Chamber (vol. I, 91–2).
[17] See Chapter II above.

whether that place is within the territory of the state which owns the port.[18]

Similarly, the creation of fishing zones cannot be construed as extending the ambit of inland waters, some of these zones, for example under the Fishery Limits Act 1976, extending beyond the limit currently claimed by the United Kingdom for its territorial sea.

As seen from such cases as *Lord Advocate* v. *Trustees of the Clyde Navigation*, the *intra fauces terrae* rule is applied in Scotland to constitute relatively narrow estuaries and lochs with their solum as part of the county. But the position of larger indentations is as uncertain as in England.[19] The problem was discussed to some extent in the cases of *Peters* v. *Olsen* in 1905[20] and *Mortensen* v. *Peters* in 1906,[21] although in both cases the court decided on grounds independent of property rights in the waters concerned. Both cases involved an appeal against the jurisdiction of the Dornoch Sheriff Court in prosecutions of the foreign masters of foreign trawlers who had used a certain type of trawl in a zone delimited by a regulation made under the Herring Fishery (Scotland) Act 1889 and subsequent Acts. The use of the particular trawl was stated to be forbidden. In the earlier case, the vessel was, or might have been, about 4½ miles from land in the Dornoch Firth, while in *Mortensen* v. *Peters* it was about 5 miles from land in the Moray Firth. In both cases, the High Court of Justiciary affirmed the jurisdiction of the Sheriff Court on finding that the vessels were using the forbidden type of trawl within the zone as delimited. In so doing, the judges all stated or implied that the cases turned on the construction of the legislation and bye-laws promulgated thereunder; the Lord Justice-General, Lord Dunedin, for example, remarked in *Mortensen* v. *Peters* that his decision in favour of the competence of the Scottish courts did not mean that the Moray Firth was for every purpose within the 'territorial sovereignty'.[22] In the same case, however, Lord Salvesen declared that the Act of 1889 was 'an assertion by the British Parliament . . . of their right . . . to treat [the area delimited] as within the

18 [1926] P. 185, 196–7.
19 So is that of the Solway Firth: *Annandale & Eskdale District Council* v. *North West Water Authority* [1978] S.C. 187.
20 (1905) 4 Adam's Justiciary Reports 608.
21 (1906) 8 F. 93.
22 Ibid., 102. He cited the view of the Scottish institutional writer, Bell, that 'the Sovereign . . . is proprietor of the narrow seas within cannon shot of the land, and the firths, gulfs, and bays around the Kingdom'.

territory over which the jurisdiction of the Scottish courts extends'.[23]

In conclusion, it appears that at common law the areas of tidal water below low-water mark classified as inland waters are strictly limited in extent. It is still an open question, for example, whether waters situated between an off-shore island and the mainland fall into the category of inland waters at all. This uncertainty in the common law position led the Minister for Local Government and Development to declare in the House of Commons on 13 April 1972:

> Generally, the local government areas extend to low water mark, but certain waters have been recognised as parts of counties by decisions of the courts. There have been specific decisions extended to Poole Harbour, Milford Haven, the Solent, Humber and the Bristol Channel, but the precise areas to which they extend are uncertain.[24]

Accordingly, s. 71 of the Local Government Act 1972 was framed to deal with the problem in England and Wales:

> (1) A Commission may at any time review so much of the boundary of any county as lies below the high-water mark of medium tides and does not form a common boundary with another county and may make proposals to the Secretary of State for making alterations to any part of the boundary so as to include in the county any area of the sea which at the date of the proposals is not, in whole or in part, comprised in any other county or to exclude from the county any area of the sea which at that date is comprised in the county.
>
> (2) The Secretary of State may direct a Commission to conduct a review under this section of a particular boundary or not to undertake during a specified period such a review of a particular boundary, and may give a Commission directions for their guidance in conducting a review and making proposals under this section. . . .
>
> (4) The Secretary of State may if he thinks fit by order give effect to any proposals made to him under this section, either as submitted to him or with modifications.
>
> (5) A statutory instrument containing an order under this section shall be subject to annulment in pursuance of a resolution of either House of Parliament.

---

[23] Ibid., 108.

[24] 834 *HC Debs.*, col. 1443. The Minister did not name the decisions but it is suggested that they are: *R.* v. *Forty-Nine Casks of Brandy* (1836) 3 Hagg. Adm. 257 (Poole Harbour); *R.* v. *Bruce* (1812) 2 Leach 1093 and *Mure* v. *Hore* (1877) 41 J.P. 471 (Milford Haven); *The Lord of the Isles* (1832) referred to in *The Public Opinion* (1832) 2 Hagg. Adm. 398 (Solent); *The Public Opinion* (Humber); *R.* v. *Cunningham* (1859) Bell 72 (Bristol Channel).

(ii) THE TERRITORIAL SEA BASELINE

The rules for the determination of the baseline of the territorial sea are in large part now embodied in the 1958 Convention on the Territorial Sea and the Contiguous Zone. Article 3 provides that, except where otherwise provided in the instrument, the 'normal baseline' is the low-water line along the coast; by Article 10, this rule applies also to islands which are above water at high tide. Article 7 provides for the position of bays, which are defined as well-marked indentations not being mere curvatures of the coast. Where such an indentation fulfils the technical requirements of the Article for being a 'bay' then a closing line, not exceeding 24 miles in length, may be drawn across 'its natural entrance points' or, if these are more than 24 miles apart, across the interior of the bay in such a manner as to enclose the maximum area of water that is possible with a line of that length. By virtue of Article 5(1), waters on the landward side of the baseline of the territorial sea form part of the 'internal waters' of the State.

The principal derogations from the 'normal baseline' and '24 mile' rules come firstly in Article 4, which provides that straight baselines may be drawn 'in localities where the coast line is deeply indented and cut into, or if there is a fringe of islands along the coast in its immediate vicinity'; the drawing of such baselines must not 'depart to any appreciable extent from the general direction of the coast'. The second derogation comes in Article 11 which provides that the low-water line on a low-tide elevation may be used as the baseline, provided the low-tide elevation is situated 'wholly or partly at a distance not exceeding the breadth of the territorial sea from the mainland or an island'.

Finally, the provisions of the Convention are stated in Article 7(6) not to apply to so-called 'historic' bays, nor, it would appear from a resolution adopted by the United Nations Conference on 27 April 1958, to other 'historic waters'.

The question is to what extent, if at all, have these rules replaced or supplemented the common law rules regarding inland waters. In particular, are the waters and their solum shoreward of the baseline now within the county?

The Convention's provisions on the determination of the baseline of the territorial sea were incorporated, in a redrafted form, into the Territorial Waters Order in Council effective on 30 September 1964 and now slightly amended by an Order effective on 18 June 1979. The 'general purport' of the 1964 instrument is set out in an explanatory note attached to but forming no part of it:

This Order establishes the baseline from which the breadth of the
territorial sea adjacent to the United Kingdom, the Channel Islands and
the Isle of Man is measured. This, generally, is low-water line round the
coast, including the coast of all islands, but between Cape Wrath and
the Mull of Kintyre a series of straight lines joining specified points lying
generally on the seaward side of the islands lying off the coast are used,
and where there are well defined bays elsewhere lines not exceeding 24
miles in length drawn across the bays are used.[25]

The Order does not make specific mention of the Convention
nor does it specify the legal status of the waters and subjacent soil
enclosed within the baselines. Although it provides for effect to be
given to low-tide elevations wholly or partly 'within the breadth of
sea which would be territorial sea if all low-tide elevations were
disregarded for the purpose of the measurement of the breadth
thereof',[26] it makes no special provision for the determination of
the baseline across the mouth of a river, whereas Article 13 of the
Convention provides for a mandatory straight line when a river
flows 'directly into the sea'.[27]

Is the outer line of delimitation of inland waters now concurrent
with the baseline of the territorial sea as determined by the provisions of the 1958 Convention and the 1964 and 1979 Orders in
Council? This is not an idle question; in *Post Office* v. *Estuary Radio
Ltd.*, Diplock L.J., on behalf of the Court of Appeal, said:

It is common ground that the area included in the internal waters of the
United Kingdom under the Convention, at any rate as respects 'bays', is
greater than that previously claimed by the Crown.[28]

From a chart showing the three-mile belt of the United
Kingdom as measured from the baselines in accordance with the
1958 Convention,[29] it appears that the Hydrographic Department
of the Admiralty considers that, for example, the spot in the Bristol
Channel which two Lords Justices in *The Fagernes* in 1927 thought

[25] Statutory Instruments, 1965, Part III, section 2, p. 6452A. The Order is not a
Statutory Instrument but is promulgated by Her Majesty 'by virtue and in exercise of all
the powers enabling Her in That Behalf'. The 1979 Order has not yet been printed in the
Statutory Instruments series.
[26] It was on the strength of this provision that the Kent Justices in *Lye* found that Red
Sands Tower was within territorial waters.
[27] In *Post Office* v. *Estuary Radio Ltd.* [1967] 1 W.L.R. 847, O'Connor J. at first instance
held that the Thames estuary was rather 'an indentation of the coast' and formed as to
some part of its extent a 'bay'.
[28] [1968] 2 Q.B. 740, 756.
[29] The chart is reproduced in (1964) 3 *International Legal Materials* 494–5.

was outside inland and even territorial waters is now within the above baselines; similarly, the spot in the Solent, held by Romilly M.R. in 1861 to be 'high seas',[30] is equally within the new baselines. As for Red Sands Tower, held by the Queen's Bench Division and the Court of Appeal in 1967 to be within internal waters on the basis of the 1964 Order,[31] this feature is probably outside the county on the common law test.

In the absence of authority, it is submitted that the Convention and the Orders in Council have not altered the area of tidal waters, and the solum thereof, which is within the county. Thus there is a basic difference between the tidal waters within the county (inland waters), and the tidal waters on the shoreward side of the baseline of the territorial sea (internal waters).[32] Nowhere would this be more obvious than in those areas where straight baselines have been constructed by the Orders, i.e., the west coast of Scotland. The waters and solum of the Minches, for example, though internal waters, would not necessarily thereby become inland waters, part of the nearby counties of Scotland.

Two arguments can be advanced to support this contention. Firstly, it would seem contrary to basic principle that as the legislature has specifically provided a complex mechanism for changing the seaward boundaries of the local government areas in s. 71 of the Local Government Act 1972, the Crown could still do this by a stroke of its prerogative pen. It seems a classic case of a statute abrogating any prerogative power there might previously have been to delimit the county.[33] Secondly, the low-water mark for the purposes of the baseline of the territorial sea is unlikely to be the Mean Low Water line (MLW) or the Mean Low Water Springs (MLWS) of common law and the Ordnance Survey, but rather the chart datum of the Admiralty which is the line of lowest astronomical tide (LAT), the lowest predictable tide under average meteorological conditions. Thus the baseline of the territorial sea will be seawards of the limit of inland waters except in places where the land ends in a vertical cliff.

[30] *The Eclipse and the Saxonia* (1862) 15 Moo. P.C. 262.
[31] *Post Office* v. *Estuary Radio Ltd.* [1967] 1 W.L.R. 847 (Q.B.D.), [1968] 2 Q.B. 740 (C.A.) The tower was some 4.9 miles from the nearest point on the low-water line on the coast though within 3 miles of a low-tide elevation which itself was within 3 miles of the low-water line on the coast.
[32] This distinction is crucial in the context of the federal/provincial dispute over Georgia Strait in Canada. See *Reference re Ownership of the Bed of the Strait of Georgia and related areas* (1976) 1 B.C.L.R. 97.
[33] *Attorney-General* v. *De Keyser's Royal Hotel Ltd.* [1920] A.C. 508.

B. The Seaward Limit

It will assist clarity here if the traditional claim of the Crown is discussed separately from the claim flowing from the public international law concept of territorial sea.

(i) THE TRADITIONAL CLAIM

The early authorities did not think that the extent seawards of the Crown's alleged rights in the soil of the marginal sea were other than co-extensive with its alleged rights in the waters of that sea. The location of the areas of sea in which the Crown claimed rights are vague. Often they were spoken of as the 'Four Seas' or *quatuor maria*. As late as 14 February 1878, Lord Cairns L.C., after mention of Bracton and Selden, declared in the House of Lords that the 'four seas' were the British Channel, the seas on the west and east coasts of Scotland and the German Ocean.[34] Another description of the sea areas in question was in terms of the 'narrow seas'. This term was used in particular to describe the claim to the English Channel. Thus on 29 May 1557, the Queen, Mary Tudor, wrote to Lord Admiral William Howard that the 'narrow seas' lay between the North Foreland and the Cape of Cornwall on the side of England and between Flushing and Guernsey on the side of France.[35] More widely used were the terms 'British Seas' or the 'seas of England'. Thus in the roll *De Superioritate Maris Angliae et Jure Officii Admirallatus in eodem*, written, according to Fulton, between 1304 and 1307, the following passage appeared:

That whereas the Kings of England by right of the said kingdom, from a time whereof there is no memorial to the contrary, had been in peaceable possession of the sovereign lordship of the sea of England and of the isles within the same . . .[36]

The extent of these seas was equally in doubt and conflicting views were given. In 1575, Plowden, appearing as counsel in the case of *Sir John Constable*, claimed that the 'bounds of England' extended to the middle of the adjoining sea, though the 'exclusive jurisdiction' of the Queen extended over the whole sea between England and both France and Ireland, 'but in other places, as towards Spain, she has only the moiety'.[37] According to Fulton, the first writer who appeared to attempt the definition of the

---

[34] 237 *P.Debs.*, 3rd series, col. 1606.
[35] SP 11/10, fo. 80.
[36] Fulton, 45–6.
[37] Moore, 227–8; see Chapter I above.

'English seas' was the scholar and mystic Dr John Dee. In a work published in 1577[38] Dee claimed that the surrounding seas half way to the shores of foreign princes were the Queen's 'peculiar seas' and that when both coasts of the sea were possessed by the Queen, 'her peculiar jurisdiction and sea royalty' extended over the whole breadth of the sea, even if the distance were one thousand miles or more. In a later treatise, addressed to Dyer and dated 1597,[39] Dee declared that the whole sea between the south coast of England and the north coast of France—Picardy, Normandy, and Brittany—was under the Queen's 'sea-jurisdiction and sovereignty absolute' inasmuch as she was a real monarch of France by direct inheritance and prior conquest. Dee also claimed sovereignty for the Queen in the sea to the west of England and Ireland, the sea around Scotland, 'at least to the mid-sea' between Scotland and the coasts of Norway and Denmark, and 'half seas over' between England and the coasts of Denmark, Friesland, and Holland.

Such wide claims, reminiscent of those by the Crowns of Spain and Portugal, and of various States in the Mediterranean, do not seem to have been espoused by the Crown itself at this period. In instructions sent to the English representatives at negotiations with Denmark at Bremen in 1602, the Queen declared that 'property of sea in some small distance from the coast may yield some oversight and jurisdiction' yet fishing and passage should not be forbidden by the prince holding the coast.[40]

With the ascent of the Stuart Kings, wide claims by the Crown became common and these were reflected by the writers. In Scotland, Welwood and Craig both claimed that the open sea appertained to the adjacent State as a general rule of international law. In England, John Selden ended his work *Mare Clausum*, first released in 1635, as follows:

It is certainly true, according to the mass of evidence set out above, that the very shores or ports of the neighbouring sovereigns on the other side of the sea are the bounds of the maritime dominion of Britain, to the southwards and eastwards; but in the vast ocean to the north and west they are to be placed at the farthest extent of the most spacious seas which are possessed by the English, Scots and Irish.[41]

[38] Dee, *The Brytish Monarchie*; Fulton, 99–103.
[39] Fulton, 103–4.
[40] *Rymer's Foedera*, vol. 16, 433.
[41] As quoted in Fulton, 374.

Hale, in his preliminary treatise written about 1636, referred to 'the sea, at lest so much thereof as adjoines nearer to our cost then to any other foren cost: as it is within the Kinges jurisdiction'.[42]

Various declarations of the extent of the 'British Seas' were made by the Admiralty Judges,[43] while in *R.* v. *Vaughan* in 1696 an alternative count in the indictment stated that the accused performed overt acts 'upon the high seas about fourteen leagues from Deal and within the dominion of the Crown of England and within the jurisdiction of the Admiralty of England'.[44] Furthermore, the term 'British Seas' continued to be inserted in treaties negotiated by Britain, although without any declaration of their extent.[45]

In a memorandum of 18 January 1815, concerning the sovereignty of the sea and the right of salute, John Wilson Croker, First Secretary to the Admiralty, stated:

What are the British Seas?

A majority of Authorities state them to be all the Seas contained to the eastward, by the meridian of Cape Finisterre and the latitude of the Cape of the land van Staten in Norway, but it is curious and *not much*, I think, to the *credit* of the then Court of Admiralty that on the conclusion of the Spanish Treaty 1719 when captures in the British Seas were to be restored after 14 days, the judge (Sir Nath. Lloyd) held (in the case of three Spanish Merchantmen taken within Cape Finisterre but beyond the chops of the Channel) that the Sovereignty extended to Cape Finisterre yet the British Seas intended by the Treaty were the Channel only and the ships were accordingly condemned as good prize.

It will have been observed that Sir William Temple and King William use the term 'narrow seas', now, it appears from the numerous patents of the Admirals and Vice Admirals of the Narrow Seas that the limits of these Seas are distinctly defined to be from the Thames to the Island of Scilly and in a proclamation of 1702 of Colours to be worn by Merchantmen, the British Seas seem by implication to be restricted to the Channel, and Sir Philip Meadows says of the old definition of *from Cape Finisterre to the Nase* that 'it is too wide for dominion and too narrow for respect'.[46]

Scepticism over the wide extent of the 'British Seas' increased

[42] Moore, 358.

[43] See Wynne, *Life of Sir Leoline Jenkins*, vol. II, 699–700; Marsden, *The Law and Custom of the Sea*, vol. II, 231–2, 256–7.

[44] (1696) 13 Howell's State Trials 485, 488.

[45] See Marston, (1980) 11 *Cambrian Law Review* 62.

[46] Printed in *The Naval Miscellany*, vol. III, 289–329, at 298, from ADM 7/667. In a footnote, Croker admitted that he meant Sir H. Penrice, not Sir Nath. Lloyd.

with the advance of the nineteenth century. With regard to the 'Hovering Acts', which rendered liable to forfeiture, in certain circumstances, foreign ships coming within a hundred leagues of the British coasts, the Law Officers, Robinson K.A., Copley A.G., and Wetherell S.G., advised the Foreign Office on 21 May 1825: 'Can it be supposed that England pretends to claim a property in the Sea to the distance of 100 leagues from her Shores? or to the distance of eight or four leagues?'[47]

The Crown clearly did not consider that such strictures applied to its solum claim. The extent of this was stated, for the first time divorced from considerations of the superjacent waters, in the Crown's *Preliminary Case* in the first Cornwall submarine mines arbitration in 1856; there it claimed, on the authority of Plowden's argument in *Sir John Constable's Case* and of *Comyn's Digest* that

[t]he jurisdiction and consequent ownership of the Crown, as Lord of the Sea, has been defined, with respect to the British Channel, to extend midway between England and France, and to the middle of the sea between England and Spain.[48]

Sir John Patteson's award itself made no mention of the seaward extent of the minerals below low-water mark awarded to the Crown.

The second Cornwall submarine mines arbitration could very easily have been the occasion for the extent of the Crown's particular claim to the solum to be defined. This was not to be so, however, since the Duchy of Cornwall, which delivered the first statement in the proceedings, claimed that the 'full limit on the open coast of the fundus below low water-mark, which the Sovereign might grant to an ordinary subject, as part of the maritime territories of the Realm' appeared to extend to three geographical miles off the shores of the Kingdom in general. This, in its first alternative submission, was the seaward extent of the county. In its *Reply*, the Duchy developed its argument on this point, citing numerous ancient authorities, some of which claimed vast distances, but concluding that

. . . the proprietary or territorial ownership of the Crown in the soil of the sea, adjoining the English coasts, (irrespective of the maritime jurisdiction or authority which would equally prevail within such limited area as beyond it) would be confined to the limit of a maritime league, or

---

[47] FO 83/2266; *Law Officers' Opinions to the Foreign Office 1793–1860*, vol. 30, 346.
[48] See Chapter IV above.

three miles from the shore, alluded to in the introduction to 'Angell on Tide Waters' as the limits of a nation's *territory*, and referred to by Chief Justice Erle, in the case of the 'Free Fishers of Whitstable v. Gann', as the extent to which the sovereign might grant the soil of the sea, even to an ordinary subject.

The Duchy then referred to the argument of the defendant in *Attorney-General* v. *Tomsett*[49] which, it maintained, erred in asserting that the Downs were not part of the Realm of England, though part of the Dominions of the King of England like the colonies. In the Duchy's view, the 'comparatively reasonable distance' of three miles was under the proprietary or territorial ownership of the Crown, while the dominion over the sea beyond 'might well be compared to that exercised over the Colonies, or any other part of the Crown dependencies, not forming an integral part of the Realm of England'.

In its *Rejoinder*, the Crown pointed out that the Duchy, by arguing that the proprietary right 'even of the Sovereign' was *confined* to a distance of three miles from the shore, and furthermore that this area was within the county, would leave nothing for the Cornwall Submarine Mines Act 1858 to operate upon, since that Act specifically assigned to the Crown 'all Mines and Minerals lying below Low-Water Mark under the open Sea adjacent to but not being Part of the County of Cornwall'. The Crown went on:

It is common ground to both the Duchy and the Crown that the jurisdiction and interest of the King [sic] extends to three miles at the least from the shore; and for the purposes of the present argument, the Crown may admit that a subject may hold by grant from itself not only lands between high and low water mark, but also lands below low-water mark.

The case of *R.* v. *Keyn* in 1876 provoked several remarks regarding the extent of the 'British Seas'. During the first hearing of the appeal, the Solicitor-General, Sir Hardinge Giffard, declared:

The extent to which other nations were agreed that this territorial limit extends to the distance of a cannon shot, is a matter settled I admit between nation and nation now. But if it is said that the existence of this territory of England is a matter of international law, I respectfully say that it is not so, that the claim of this country (which was a far wider claim than it is now) was to exercise a territorial dominion over it

[49] (1835) 2 C.M. & R. 170.

because it *was* part of this country; and was what this country claimed to be part of its own territorial dominion, and that other nations have conceded to the extent of the three miles. It is known historically that it was claimed to a much wider extent, and for this purpose it is enough for me to contend for what is the international limit.[50]

Later in the same argument, the Solicitor-General maintained that the three-mile belt was the 'modern version' of the 'Four Seas'.[51]

During his judgment, Cockburn C.J., who throughout the second hearing of the appeal had shown his contempt for the limits claimed by Selden and his followers, declared:

All these vain and extravagant pretensions have long since given way to the influence of reason and common sense. If, indeed, the sovereignty thus asserted had a real existence, and could now be maintained, it would of course, independently of any question as to the three-mile zone, be conclusive of the present case. But the claim to such sovereignty, at all times unfounded, has long since been abandoned.[52]

Two of the dissenting judges commented equally unfavourably on the extent of the traditional claim. Amphlett J.A. considered that 'these extravagant claims ... have been long since abandoned',[53] while Grove J., if not repudiating them categorically, implied that they belonged to the past rather than the present.[54] Lord Coleridge C.J., without making reference to the old claims, cautiously stated that the 'property of the State and Crown of England' extended 'at least so far beyond the line of low water' as to include the place where the collision took place.[55]

The Territorial Waters Jurisdiction Act 1878, though confined in its operation to 'any part of the open sea within one marine league of the coast measured from low-water mark', declares in its preamble that

. . . the rightful jurisdiction of Her Majesty, her heirs and successors, extends and has always extended over the open seas adjacent to the coasts of the United Kingdom and of all other parts of Her Majesty's dominions to such a distance as is necessary for the defence and security of such dominions.

[50] DPP 4/12: Transcript, 6 May 1876, p. 174.
[51] Ibid., Transcript, 19 May 1876, p. 172.
[52] (1876) 2 Ex.D. 63, 175.
[53] Ibid., 119.
[54] Ibid., 109.
[55] Ibid., 155.

In his speech in the House of Lords on 14 February 1878 introducing the Bill which became the above Act, Lord Cairns L.C. stated that 'as years went on and commerce extended, definitions as to distance were adopted; but the principle of the claim to a jurisdiction over the waters round the Kingdom was never given up'.[56]

In various other Parliamentary speeches, high Government spokesmen continued to declare that this 'jurisdiction' was not confined to a marine league. Thus on 6 May 1895 Lord Halsbury L.C., after pointing out that as Solicitor-General at the time he had been responsible for introducing the Territorial Waters Jurisdiction Bill in the Commons, declared that care had been taken in that measure to avoid measurements as to the territorial limit. 'The distance was left at such limit as was necessary for the defence of the Realm. Then the exact limit was given for the particular purpose in view'.[57] In the same debate, the Foreign Secretary, the Marquis of Salisbury, stated that 'great care had been taken [in preparing the Sea Fisheries Regulation (Scotland) Act 1895] not to name three miles as the territorial limit. The limit depended on the distance to which a cannon-shot could go'.[58]

All the above Parliamentary statements, however, were uttered in the context of the waters of the marginal belt and usually of 'jurisdiction' rather than property rights in it; they were not necessarily intended to refer to the subjacent soil. It will indeed have been noticed in the earlier part of this work that, in granting licences to lay cables on the bed of the sea, the Crown always stated that these were to extend 'so far as British territory extended', without any specific distance being indicated.[59] In the course of the discussions set out in Chapter VII above between the Commissioner of Woods, Charles Gore, and the Treasury in 1875 concerning the Channel tunnel scheme, the former declared that the exact seaward limit of the boundary of England was 'open to question'; he thought that 'for 3 miles at the least the Tunnel will be constructed through substrata belonging to the Crown of England'. Similarly, the British members of the Joint Commission on the tunnel scheme wrote a few months later that the Crown's right of property in the soil of the bed of the sea extended to a distance of three miles at least from the shore, and, on the basis of

[56] 237 *P.Debs.*, 3rd series, col. 1606.
[57] 33 *P.Debs.*, 4th series, col. 504.
[58] Ibid.
[59] See Chapter II above.

occupation and accretion, would extend further with the construction of the tunnel; they were of the opinion that the tunnel would
thus be 'situate in England'. In the Crown informations filed in the
subsequent abortive proceedings, no distance was specified as the
extent of the Crown's claim, although the President of the Board of
Trade declared in the Commons in 1884 that 'nobody disputed the
right of the Crown to the *solum* of the sea within the three-mile
limit'.[60] Brickdale, on the other hand, thought in 1893 that the bed
of the sea to an 'undefined distance' belonged to the Crown.[61] The
leases of submarine strata made by the Office of Woods frequently
used the distance of three miles as the seaward extent of the strata
leased, but in 1880 the Office first leased then sold the mineral
substances to a distance of ten miles from the coast of
Cumberland.[62]

As well as general statements disclaiming sovereignty over the
waters beyond the marginal belt,[63] there is evidence that the
Crown has abandoned its traditional claim to the solum beyond
the limit of the territorial sea. The Easington lease of 1938 was
based on occupation not existing property. Moreover, in a written
answer in the House of Commons on 21 December 1955, the Joint
Under-Secretary of State at the Foreign Office remarked that 'Her
Majesty's Government have not as yet put forward any claim to
the seabed and subsoil outside territorial waters in the English
Channel'.[64] This area was *par excellence* the location of the
traditional claim.

A more drastic argument might be advanced to support the
above view. By virtue of Article 2(1) of the 1958 Convention on the
Continental Shelf, the United Kingdom *qua* contracting Party has
'sovereign rights' not 'sovereignty' over the shelf appertaining to
it, rights which are confined 'for the purpose of exploring it and
exploiting its natural resources'. The Continental Shelf Act 1964,
enacted to implement the relevant provisions of the Convention,
applies 'outside territorial waters'. It makes no specific provision
for the saving of rights, if any, which may flow from the prerogative
of the Crown, and, indeed, during the passage of the Bill through
Parliament, the Crown indicated that it was putting its 'preroga-

[60] See Chapter VII above.
[61] See Chapter VIII above.
[62] Ibid. It is uncertain whether the area was considered to be within the Solway Firth
and thus under inland waters, or whether the whole of the channel between Cumberland
and the Isle of Man was still considered to be an 'inland sea'.
[63] E.g., 546 *HC Debs.*, Written Answers, col. *169* (28 November 1955).
[64] 547 *HC Debs.*, Written Answers, col. *328*.

tive and interest' so far as affected by the Bill at the disposal of Parliament.[65] There is thus the possibility of arguing that, since 'sovereign rights' are a lesser quantum than 'sovereignty' and *a fortiori* less than 'property', the Crown, by ratifying the Convention, has by implication abandoned in favour of the Convention régime whatever rights in municipal law it might previously have been able to claim in the submarine soil beyond the present limits of the territorial sea. Thus, if tomorrow the Crown were to claim a territorial sea of twelve international nautical miles in breadth, then the status in public law of the bed and subsoil of the nine extra miles so claimed would flow solely from the declaration of extension and not from any earlier title. In the absence of any judicial pronouncement on the effects of the Convention and the 1964 Act, it is difficult to assess the likely outcome of such an argument, although it is suggested that the courts are likely to construe strictly a provision which would derogate from the Crown's existing rights and powers.

(ii) THE CLAIM BASED ON THE TERRITORIAL SEA DOCTRINE

It is not proposed to discuss the evolution of the 'three-mile limit' doctrine in international law. It is sufficient to note that the United Kingdom has consistently since at least the eighteen-thirties confined its claim to 'sovereignty' to a belt of sea of a marine league (now three international nautical miles) when dealing with other States. Indeed, a glance at the open archives of the British Government shows that the policy followed, particularly under the pressure of the Admiralty, has been to confine the area of water under sovereignty to a minimum. There is little evidence, however, until the pioneering article of Sir Cecil Hurst in the early nineteen-twenties, that the extent of sovereignty over the marginal submarine soil was thoroughly considered.[66]

The problem today is that there does not seem to be any rule of customary international law regarding the maximum breadth of the territorial sea as this concept is defined in Articles 1 and 2 of the Convention on the Territorial Sea and the Contiguous Zone. This Convention provides nothing on the point and the 1960 United Nations Conference failed to reach agreement. Claims of up to 200 miles have been made by some States, which, when coupled with liberal application of the straight baseline system to

---

[65] 254 *HL Debs.*, col. 392 (19 December 1963).
[66] See Marston, (1975–6) 48 *BYBIL* 321.

archipelagic areas or deeply indented coasts have the potential to appropriate vast areas of the sea, including bed and subsoil, as 'territorial sea' subject to State sovereignty. It cannot now be invalid for the United Kingdom, by a stroke of the royal pen wielded by an anonymous functionary, to extend tomorrow to at least twelve miles the breadth of its territorial sea, and thus vest in the Crown Estate property rights in the solum thereof. The power in the Sea Fisheries (Shellfish) Act 1967 to confer a several fishery to a distance of six miles from the baseline of the territorial sea indicates that the legislature took the view that the Crown's property in the solum might already extend so far.[67]

The Downward Limit

There is little authority except the Roman law maxim *usque ad inferos* and the rule of land law that the fee simple owner is entitled to land down to the centre of the earth.[68] As the exploration and exploitation of the solum has not yet progressed to the depth that legal problems arise over it, it is proposed to curtail discussion on this last aspect of delimitation.

[67] See *A.G.* v. *Emerson* [1891] A.C. 649.
[68] *Egremont Burial Board* v. *Egremont Iron Ore Company* (1880) 14 Ch.D. 158.

Chapter XII

The Historical and Juridical Bases of the Crown's Claim to the Marginal Solum

A. The Historical Basis

It is clear from the practice described in Chapter VIII above that the Crown today claims to be the owner, *jure coronae*, of the marginal solum beyond the limits of inland waters. From this solum it receives a substantial income. Is the claim a continuation, unchanged in quality though possibly not in extent, of that advanced in the remote past (called for convenience the 'traditional claim'), or is it based on the relatively modern international law doctrine of the territorial sea?

There is a substantial body of opinion which considers that the traditional claim was abandoned, either on the demise of the Stuart dynasty, or later. Cockburn C.J. expressed this most forcefully when he remarked in *Keyn* that 'these assertions of sovereignty were manifestly based on the doctrine that the narrow seas are part of the realm of England. But that doctrine is now exploded . . . when the sovereignty and jurisdiction from which the property in the soil of the sea was inferred is gone, the territorial property which was suggested to be consequent upon it must necessarily go with it.'[1] A similar view was advanced by the Judicial Committee of the Privy Council in the British Columbia fisheries case of 1913 where it stated that the 'three-mile limit' owed its origin to 'comparatively modern authorities on public international law'.[2] Furthermore, the Cockburn view has been endorsed by the Supreme Courts of the United States,[3] and of Canada,[4] and by some members of the High Court of Australia.[5]

Some academic writers, too, have followed Sir Alexander Cockburn's interpretation of history. *Coulson & Forbes* continues to

[1] (1876) 2 Ex.D. 63, 196.

[2] [1914] A.C. 153, 174–5.

[3] *United States* v. *California* 332 U.S. 19 (1947), *United States* v. *Texas* 339 U.S. 707 (1950), *United States* v. *Maine & Others* 420 U.S. 515 (1975).

[4] *Reference re Offshore Mineral Rights of British Columbia* [1967] S.C.R. 792.

[5] *New South Wales & Others* v. *Commonwealth of Australia* (1975) 135 C.L.R. 337, 367 (Barwick C.J.), 461–2 (Mason J.). However both left the point undetermined.

declare that in the absence of legislation, the solum is not vested in the Crown 'as against other nations'.[6] Fulton asserted that the old claim to dominion of the British seas 'simply died out and vanished in the lapse of time, without apparently leaving a single juridical or international right behind it'.[7] O'Connell, writing in 1970, stated that 'by 1800 the Crown's traditional claims had been abandoned, and the new doctrine of territorial waters had been substituted for them'.[8]

The evidence of Crown practice set out in the earlier part of the present work, however, gives a different picture. Although there was a period of comparative desuetude during most of the eighteenth century, there is little evidence of outright abandonment of the traditional claim to the solum. In the first place, Crown practice has followed a remarkably consistent pattern. There is not a great deal of difference, for example, between the information against William Hammond in 1575 and that against the Channel tunnel companies in 1882. When the Crown resumed in earnest its foreshore and seabed activities in the early nineteenth century, the authorities invoked in support were Callis and Hale rather than Grotius and Bynkershoek, indicating that the claim was not based on the international law doctrine of territorial sea, a doctrine unknown in English law until a few years previously. Furthermore, there was, and perhaps still is, a reluctance to confine the claim to the 'international' distance of the marine league. Judges in English courts, both before and after *Keyn*, have not doubted the validity of the historical sources of the Crown's claim. In Commonwealth courts, there are still some judges who take a similar attitude.[9]

Some writers have not followed Cockburn's view. Thus Sir Cecil Hurst considered 'that the ownership of the bed of the sea within the three-mile limit is the survival of more extensive claims to the ownership of and sovereignty over the bed of the sea'.[10] O'Connell, moreover, changed his view from that set out above, for in an article published in 1973 he wrote that 'the common law tradition of the Crown's property in the sea descended into the caverns of lawyers' law, where it flowed as strongly as ever until it

---

[6] Coulson & Forbes, 6th ed., 1952, 9.

[7] Fulton, 538.

[8] O'Connell, *International Law*, vol. I, 470.

[9] *New South Wales & Others* v. *Commonwealth of Australia* (1975) 135 C.L.R. 337, 391–400 (Gibbs J.), 438 (Stephen J.), 487 (Jacobs J.). *Re Monashee Enterprises Ltd.* (1978) 90 D.L.R. (3d) 521, 530 (Supreme Court of British Columbia).

[10] Hurst, (1923–4) 4 *BYBIL* 34, 43.

reappeared on the surface in the nineteenth century in connection with the three-mile limit. This being so, the only possible way of regarding the matter is to suppose that the territorial sea, whatever dimensions it may have at any time possessed, was consistently part of the royal waste.'[11]

A further argument which makes it difficult to accept that the present claim is solely based on the international law concept of territorial sea is that only relatively recently did this latter concept extend to the bed and subsoil. Thus Gidel remarked of the draft rule formulated at the Hague Conference of 1930, which was in similar terms to the 1958 Convention text:

C'est, semble-t-il, la première fois qu'une disposition a jamais été formulée expressément dans un document international collectif d'ordre positif concernant le sol et le sous-sol de l'espace maritime en général et de la mer territoriale en particulier.[12]

As the Crown has consistently asserted ownership of the solum since the first half of the nineteenth century at the latest, this claim could not have been based during the entire period on sovereignty flowing from an international law source.

The Crown's claim to sovereignty, or at least jurisdiction, over large tracts of sea surrounding the British Isles was relevant in an international context, largely of the flag-salute and the enforcement of hovering legislation over foreign vessels. The Crown's claim to the solum only occasionally, as in the Channel tunnel negotiations, affected foreign States. It was a claim which sounded in municipal law rather than international law. Thus the tacit abandonment of the wide claim in respect of the surrounding waters[13] need not have involved the abandonment of the traditional claim to the solum and the evidence in the first part of this work indicates that it did not.

In conclusion, it is submitted that the traditional claim was not abandoned at any time prior to the reception of the doctrine of territorial sea, nor has it been abandoned since. There appear, therefore, to be at least two separate historical sources of the present-day claim to the solum, the traditional claim and the international law doctrine of territorial sea.

B. The Juridical Basis

[11] O'Connell, (1971) 45 *BYBIL* 303, 319.
[12] Gidel, vol. III, 326. See also Marston, (1975–6) 48 *BYBIL* 321.
[13] On this, see Marston, (1980) 11 *Cambrian Law Review* 62.

(i) STATUTE

The legislature has been reluctant to describe the Crown's interest in the solum outside inland waters. The statute Prerogativa Regis, enacted about 1324, made no mention of it. The reclamation statutes as well as the Great Yarmouth Wellington Pier Act 1855 and the Thames Conservancy Act 1857 contemplated that the Crown might have only a 'claim' to the solum. Even s. 7 of the Crown Lands Act 1866 did not specify what were the 'Parts and Rights and Interests' of the sovereign in the bed of the sea. The Crown Estate Act 1961 does not mention the solum.

Great importance has been placed on the Cornwall Submarine Mines Act 1858 as indicating that the solum is part of the Crown's territories. Thus Lord Coleridge C.J. considered that it was 'the express and definite authority of Parliament for the proposition that the realm does not end with low-water mark, but that the open sea and the bed of it are part of the realm and of the territory of the sovereign'.[14] The Act, however, dealt only with the mines and minerals adjacent to the County of Cornwall and thus cannot be the source of Crown ownership of solum elsewhere. Furthermore, the Act used the contradictory formula 'be it therefore enacted and declared' thus not indicating that the legislature necessarily approved of Sir John Patteson's ruling that the mines and minerals were already vested in the Crown. On the other hand, the provisions of the Act were of great persuasive authority as to the general legal status of the solum and were so applied by the executive to other areas of solum around the coasts.

The Territorial Waters Jurisdiction Act 1878 refers throughout to the 'open sea' and makes no reference to the solum. The preamble, which asserts the Crown's 'rightful jurisdiction' over the open seas adjacent to the coasts of its dominions, cannot, on general principles of statutory construction, have an enacting function. This point was emphasized by the United Kingdom Government in the course of its pleadings before the International Court of Justice in the Anglo-Norwegian Fisheries Case in 1950 where it stated that 'while this recital in the preamble is evidence of views entertained by some people in the United Kingdom at that time, the preamble has no operative force'.[15] The definition of 'territorial waters' in s. 7 of the Act as 'such part of the sea adjacent to the coast of the United Kingdom, or the coast of some other part

---

[14] (1876) 2 Ex. D. 63, 157–8.

[15] Anglo-Norwegian Fisheries Case, *Pleadings, Oral Arguments, Documents*, vol. II, 418. See also to the same effect Blain J. in *R.* v. *Kent Justices, ex parte Lye* [1967] 2 Q.B. 153, 186.

of Her Majesty's dominions, as is deemed by international law to be within the sovereignty of Her Majesty' has led some writers to consider that the Act provides a statutory mandate to assimilate territorial waters with land territory for the purposes of the delimitation of State territory. With respect, the provision cannot have such an effect. The fact that it appears in the definition section indicates that it does not have a wider effect than the enacting sections. These sections, however, provide only for the extension of the Admiral's criminal jurisdiction to foreign ships within a limited distance of the open coast. The Act nowhere constitutes the marginal sea to be British territory and, *a fortiori*, does not constitute it part of the United Kingdom or any part thereof. Furthermore, the expression 'deemed by international law' seems inconsistent with an intention thereby to declare British sovereignty over the marginal sea; it seems more consistent with an intention to leave such declaration to some other instrument. The executive certainly did not consider that the Act had extended the boundary of the United Kingdom. Thus on 20 July 1881, James A.G., Herschell S.G., and A. L. Smith advised the Board of Trade that since *Keyn* and the Act 'the United Kingdom must be held to terminate at low-water mark'.[16] The Territorial Waters Jurisdiction Act 1878 thus seems at the most neutral on the status of the solum of the 'territorial waters', or even on that of the 'three-mile belt' within those territorial waters.

Later statutes which contain references to the solum, such as the Coast Protection Act 1949, are equally incapable of being the source of the Crown's claim. It appears, therefore, that with the possible exception of the mines and minerals to an uncertain distance adjacent to the coasts of Cornwall, the Crown's claim to the solum cannot be based on statute.

(ii) THE ROYAL PREROGATIVE

There is much evidence that the Crown's traditional claim to ownership of the solum is founded on the royal prerogative, described by Dicey as 'the residue of discretionary or arbitrary authority which at any given time is legally left in the hands of the Crown.'[17] The earliest claims set out in Chapter I above, in 1575 against Hammond and in 1591 against Dulinge, were expressly based on the prerogative. The claim is frequently regarded as a

[16] CO 885/12; see Chapter VI above.
[17] Dicey, 10th ed., 424.

separate and valid head of the prerogative. Thus H. V. Evatt, in his unpublished dissertation on certain aspects of the royal prerogative, classified the ownership of 'the bed of the ocean within territorial limits' as one of the prerogatives in the nature of property.[18] *Halsbury* considers the matter settled: 'By prerogative right the Crown is prima facie the owner of all land covered by the narrow seas adjoining the coast'.[19]

If, however, it were ever authoritatively determined that the traditional claim lapsed with the demise of the Stuart Kings, or if the Crown were now to rely only on the territorial sea doctrine as the historical source, then it would be difficult to support a separate head of the prerogative. Are there any existing heads of the prerogative into which the Crown's claim to ownership of the solum could therefore fall? Two heads in the nature of powers come to mind: (1) the power of the Crown to extend its sovereignty to territory, including maritime territory, over which it has not previously claimed or exercised sovereignty (2) the power to create and delimit ports, and thereby the ownership of the solum therein, to the extent that this power has not been abridged by statute.

(1) *The power to extend sovereignty to territory hitherto outside it*

It is idle to deny that the Crown has such a power. In *Post Office* v. *Estuary Radio Ltd.*, Diplock L.J. for the Court of Appeal stated:

It still lies within the prerogative power of the Crown to extend its sovereignty and jurisdiction to areas of land or sea over which it has not previously claimed or exercised sovereignty or jurisdiction.[20]

But does the Crown thereby automatically acquire proprietary rights, amounting to ownership? The answer in English (and, outside Orkney and Shetland, Scottish) law is yes. Sir Kenneth Roberts-Wray, former legal adviser to the Colonial and Commonwealth Relations Offices, discusses the distinction between sovereignty and property by relying on the well-known dichotomy of *imperium* and *dominium*. He prefaces his discussion:

The distinction between these two conceptions has, however, become blurred by the doctrine that the acquisition of sovereignty over a Colony, whether by settlement, cession or conquest, or even of jurisdiction in

[18] Evatt, *Certain Aspects of the Royal Prerogative*, 40.
[19] *Halsbury's Laws of England*, 4th ed., vol. 8, paragraph 1418.
[20] [1968] 2 Q.B. 740, 753.

territory which remains outside the British dominions, imports Crown rights in, or in relation to, the land itself.[21]

There is a great deal of authority, most of it understandably in courts outside the United Kingdom, to support such a proposition.[22] It will suffice to give two illustrations from the High Court of Australia. In *Williams* v. *Attorney-General for New South Wales*, Isaacs J. (as he then was) stated:

It has always been a fixed principle of English law that the Crown is the proprietor of all land for which no subject can show a title. When Colonies were acquired this feudal principle extended to the lands oversea. The mere fact that men discovered and settled upon the new territory gave them no title to the soil. It belonged to the Crown until the Crown chose to grant it.[23]

In *Randwick Municipality* v. *Rutledge* in 1959, Windeyer J., with Dixon C.J., Fullagar, and Kitto JJ. concurring, asserted that 'on the first settlement of New South Wales (then comprising the whole of eastern Australia), all the land in the colony became in law vested in the Crown'.[24] Writing later extra-judicially in a general context, Sir Victor Windeyer stated that 'the concept of separate territorial sovereignties remained undisturbed. From it flowed proprietary rights of a state and its subjects. *Imperium* begat *dominium*.'[25]

A particularly illustrative case is the advice of the Judicial Committee of the Privy Council in *Amodu Tijani* v. *Secretary, Southern Nigeria*[26] which concerned the cession by treaty to the British Crown of 'the port and island of Lagos with all the rights, profits, territories and appurtenances thereto belonging'. The Judicial Committee remarked that '[n]o doubt there was a cession to the British Crown, along with the sovereignty, of the radical or ultimate title to the land, in the new colony' but it is clear from the advice that this title did not pass expressly by the treaty of cession, but arose out of the nature of the Crown's relationship to land in the common law feudal system.[27]

---

[21] Roberts-Wray, 625. See also O'Connell, *International Law*, vol. I, pp. 403–4.

[22] See, e.g., *Attorney-General* v. *Brown* (1847) 1 Legge 312, 316 (Supreme Court of New South Wales); *R. (McIntosh)* v. *Symonds* (1847) N.Z.P.C.C. 387, 388 (Supreme Court of New Zealand).

[23] (1913) 16 C.L.R. 404, 439.

[24] (1959) 102 C.L.R. 54, 71.

[25] Windeyer, (1974) 6 *Federal Law Review* 1, 9.

[26] [1921] 2 A.C. 399.

[27] Ibid., 407.

The question of how the Crown's sovereignty over territory leads necessarily to the Crown's ownership in a proprietary sense has not been the subject of much discussion in respect of territory within the United Kingdom itself. The Crown's acquisition of the islet of Rockall is the most recent instance in which the process would have occurred. The Crown would probably have acquired full proprietary rights amounting to the 'radical title' or ownership on its annexation on 18 September 1955 pursuant to a Royal commission addressed to the captain of a Royal Naval vessel.[28] The Island of Rockall Act 1972, which incorporated the rock into 'that part of the United Kingdom known as Scotland' would thus not have been the root of the Crown's proprietary rights. These rights were described in an entry made by the Crown in the General Register of Saisines in Edinburgh on 16 May 1975 as follows:

Be it known that the Queen's most excellent Majesty has right to All and Whole the Island of Rockall together with the small islands or rocks adjacent thereto known as Hazelwood Rock and Helen's Reef, all to low water mark together with the whole rights and pertinents thereof, including the fishings, and the mines, metals and minerals in and about same; . . . Which subjects are part of the Crown Estate vested in Her Majesty and Her Royal Predecessors in right of the Crown from time immemorial and from whom or in confirmation of which Her Majesty acquired right by the Island of Rockall Act 1972 . . . which incorporated the said Island of Rockall into that part of the United Kingdom known as Scotland. . . .[29]

Has the Crown expressly extended its sovereignty to the solum adjacent to the coasts of the United Kingdom? According to Anson, the Crown's pleasure may be expressed for administrative purposes in one of three ways:
1. By Order in Council.
2. By order, commission, or warrant under the sign manual.
3. By Proclamations, Writs, Letters Patent, or other documents under the Great Seal.[30]
No such instrument has ever been promulgated formally annexing or declaring the solum to be part of the territorial possessions of the Crown or to be British territory. Is such a formal expression of the Crown's will necessary?

[28] For the text of this commission, see Fisher, *Rockall*, 151.
[29] Gardner, [1976] Scots Law Times 257, 259. The Crown did not therefore claim specifically the ownership of the rock's marginal solum.
[30] *Anson's Law and Custom of the Constitution*, 4th ed., Vol. II, 62.

There is some authority for the view that land can become part of British territory under public law without a formal declaration to that effect by the Crown. Thus the Judicial Committee of the Privy Council in *Attorney-General for British Honduras* v. *Bristowe*[31] in 1880 considered that the Crown had assumed territorial domain in Honduras at the latest in 1817 on the evidence of land grants made by the Crown from that year. This was despite an Imperial Act of 1817, the Murders Abroad Act, which had described the area in question as 'not within the Territory and Dominions of His Majesty'.[32]

Similar situations exercised the minds of the Crown's Law Officers in the nineteenth century in the context of uninhabited guano islands in the Pacific, and it was in the midst of such problems that the key opinion of 16 March 1878 on the ownership of submarine minerals was given to the Office of Woods by Holker and Giffard. It will be recalled that in this opinion the Law Officers stated that

. . . the mere occupation of [the submarine areas], if they had not been part of Her Majesty's dominions and even without her previous authority that occupation had been by a subject such occupation would at Her Majesty's pleasure have vested the newly occupied territory in right of her Crown and by this we mean not only the right of dominion but the right of property.[33]

The 'guano island' opinions were conveniently collected by McNair in his *International Law Opinions*.[34] He analysed the problems to be: (i) whether the mere fact of the working of guano deposits by private individuals created in their State a title by occupation, (ii) whether a formal declaration of title by occupation should be made by a Government before issuing licences. During the late 1870s, conflicting opinions were given to the Foreign Office on these matters by Holker, Giffard and Deane. Their final opinion cited by McNair, given on 20 January 1880,[35] appeared to take the view that a formal declaration was unnecessary when the island was occupied by British subjects who

[31] (1880) 6 App. Cas. 143.
[32] 57 Geo. 3, c. 53. An opinion was given to the Colonial Office on 14 March 1851 by Dodson Q.A., Romilly A.G., and Cockburn S.G., stating that 'upon the whole' they considered the settlement was already part of Her Majesty's dominions by 1850 (CO 123/94). The settlement was not formally designated a Colony until 1862.
[33] CREST 40/94; See Chapter VI above.
[34] McNair, vol. I, 314–25.
[35] Ibid., 324. Different advice had been given by the same Law Officers on 11 November 1878 (ibid., 320–1) and on 21 March 1879 (ibid., 323).

notify their occupation by 'hoisting the British flag'. In this event, 'the island in question becomes part of Her Majesty's dominions, and will remain part of such dominions so long as Her Majesty shall find it expedient to retain the sovereignty thereto'.

Applying this conclusion to the submarine soil adjacent to the coasts of the United Kingdom, it would follow that mines to the extent of their construction would become British territory since they were apparently constructed by British subjects, and since the Crown, at least from the time of the Patteson award of 1857, issued leases of the strata through which the tunnels were drilled.[36] A similar result would presumably apply to seabed structures or to local occupation for the purpose of exploiting natural resources, e.g., sedentary fisheries. The soil would become British territory by virtue of the occupation, coupled with the will of the Crown to incorporate such soil within its territories. With respect to the structures themselves, separate from the bed on which they rest, Sir Charles Russell, arguing for the British Government in the Behring Sea Arbitration in 1893, considered that lighthouses built on submerged rocks or on piles driven into the bed of the sea would become 'part of the territory' of the State which constructed them.[37] A similar view was expressed by counsel for the Post Office in *R.* v. *Kent Justices, ex parte Lye* with regard to Red Sands Tower, a structure resting on piles affixed to the submarine soil, although he did not argue the point.[38]

The argument set out above is valid only for small areas of the submarine soil under discussion, i.e., those areas where physical occupation of one kind or another has taken place; it is not necessarily applicable to the whole solum as such, irrespective of such local occupation, yet the Crown's traditional claim clearly extends to the whole solum to one distance or another. Could it then be said that, outside the occupied areas, the Crown has a mere paper claim, the frequency of its repetition merely having the effect of adding zero to zero?

An answer to such an objection may be formulated as follows: the prerogative claim of the Crown to the submarine soil is based on the fact that such soil is more than adjacent to the Crown's

[36] See Chapter IV above. The Law Officers in the above opinions do not appear to have considered the motives of the first occupiers. Not all these acted initially in the name of the Crown, e.g., the Channel tunnel companies. Presumably an occupation by British subjects for whatever reason, coupled by a later assertion of title by the Crown, such as by issuing a writ for trespass, would have satisfied the requirements of the Law Officers.

[37] J. B. Moore, *International Arbitrations*, vol. I, 900.

[38] [1967] 2 Q.B. 153, 167.

realm, it is a continuation of the land, necessary to it for reasons of security and defence. Because the Crown may take measures for the defence of the realm, even against the ravages of the sea,[39] so it would seem to have power to hold land to serve as a bulwark of the realm; the submarine soil constitutes such land, held on the basis of 'constructive occupation', or in Hale's words 'a kind of possession', no other State being in a position to control or occupy it. Furthermore, the answer might run, this conclusion is supported by the preamble to the Territorial Waters Jurisdiction Act 1878 which declares that the 'rightful jurisdiction' of the Crown extends, not to a fixed distance, but to 'such a distance as is necessary for the defence and security of [the] dominions'. Whether such a view of the traditional claim to the soil of the marginal sea would be upheld by a United Kingdom court, however, remains to be tested.

But apart from the traditional claim, the Crown can also rely on a claim based on its 'sovereignty' over the solum by virtue either of Article 2 of the Convention on the Territorial Sea and the Contiguous Zone 1958 or of a rule of customary international law to the same effect. The Crown, it is clear, has 'sovereignty' over the solum of the territorial sea by virtue of the Convention or by virtue of a rule of customary international law in similar terms.[40] Has it therefore proprietary rights amounting to ownership in the said solum? According to the argument set out above, Crown ownership would flow automatically from Crown sovereignty. Furthermore, it could be argued that the instrument of ratification deposited by the Crown on 14 March 1960 with the Secretary-General of the United Nations in respect of the above Convention amounted in legal effect to a formal extension of sovereignty to the solum, in so far as sovereignty had not already been extended to it by other means. The principal difficulty in such a contention is that neither the Convention nor customary law lays down a specific breadth of the territorial sea; furthermore, the Convention leaves certain discretions to the coastal State in constructing the baseline from which the territorial sea is measured.[41] It might therefore be wrong to attribute legal effect to an instrument which makes such a vague claim. On the other hand, it might be asserted that thereby the Crown has made a claim to the solum to a breadth

---

[39] E.g., *Attorney-General* v. *Tomline* (1880) 14 Ch.D. 58, although it was doubted therein whether the power flowed from the prerogative.

[40] See Chapter X above.

[41] E.g., Article 4 (1).

as from time to time it will determine measured from a baseline as from time to time it will determine, and that such an 'ambulatory' claim is sufficiently certain at any one time. In any event, the uncertainty in respect of the baseline has now been resolved by the Territorial Waters Order in Council 1974,[42] in force on 30 September 1964, as amended by the Territorial Waters (Amendment) Order in Council 1979, in force on 18 June 1979.[43]

If the Crown's sovereignty is regarded as flowing from a rule of customary international law, Crown ownership in the solum ought to result by the operation of the same process as decribed above. Sovereignty is necessarily reflected in municipal law as Crown ownership. Here there is the possibility of reinforcing the conclusion by use of the general line of reasoning followed by Lord Denning M.R. and Shaw L.J. in *Trendtex Trading Co. Ltd.* v. *Central Bank of Nigeria*.[44] The customary rule of sovereignty is directly incorporated into municipal law where it can take the form only of proprietary rights amounting to ownership.

Finally, there is authority that notwithstanding the absence of an earlier clear expression of the Crown's will the courts cannot refuse to accept a declaration made before them by the Crown on the extent of its territorial possessions, including the maritime area it claims to be under its sovereignty.[45] Thus in *Post Office* v. *Estuary Radio Ltd.* Diplock L.J. for the Court of Appeal remarked: 'The Queen's courts, upon being informed by Order in Council or by the appropriate Minister or Law Officer of the Crown's claim to sovereignty or jurisdiction over any place, must give effect to it and are bound by it.'[46] In the same judgment, the learned judge considered that the courts would be 'constitutionally bound' to recognize a 'claim' to incorporate maritime areas within the United Kingdom, a statement which, as will be seen in the next chapter, goes even further.[47]

(2) *Ports and the soil thereof*

It has long been a rule of English municipal law that the soil of ports is vested in the Crown. This was expounded at great length by Matthew Hale in *De Portibus Maris*. It is also an uncontested

---

[42] Statutory Instruments, 1965 (Part III, section 2) p. 6452 A.

[43] Not yet published in the above series.

[44] [1977] Q.B. 529.

[45] See *The Fagernes* [1927] P. 311.

[46] [1968] 2 Q.B. 740, 754.

[47] For a discussion on the Crown's alleged prerogative to delimit the realm, see Edeson, (1973) 89 *LQR* 364.

rule that the Crown has the power to create ports. Thus it is not surprising that a view has arisen that the Crown can vest in itself the property in the soil of ports simply by setting up a port and delimiting its ambit.

One objection to this contention is that the first rule set out above does not apply simply by calling an area of water and subjacent soil a 'port'. Thus in its *Rejoinder* in the arbitration before Sir John Coleridge, the Crown argued against the Duchy that according to Hale only 'havens' and 'creeks' were capable of being held in property, and not 'ports' in the wider sense of that term.[48] The award of the arbitrator by implication negatived the Duchy's wider proposition, though he gave no reasons for his decision.

From the time at least of the statute 13 & 14 Car. 2, c. 11 in 1662, the power to delimit ports has been conferred on Commissioners of the Treasury for the purposes of customs regulation. Until well into the nineteenth century, the Commissioners usually delimited ports according to bearings, often based on the depth of water.[49] From the mid-eighteenth century, however, the ambit of some ports began to be expressed as a fixed distance from the shore, often three leagues, although as early as 17 August 1738 the port of Great Yarmouth was delimited as 'three miles into the sea to be measured from the low water mark of any point of the said shore'. From the eighteen-forties, most ports were delimited in terms of 'three miles from low-water mark out to sea', although some, e.g., Barnstaple and Bideford, were delimited as 'three miles from the headlands'. The result of these mid-nineteenth century delimitations was that all the sea within three miles of the low-water mark everywhere around the coast of the United Kingdom was within the ambit of a 'port'. But there was some reluctance on the part of the executive to press the matter further. In *Attorney-General* v. *Tomsett* in 1835, the Solicitor-General argued inconclusively that a spot two miles from the shore at Dover was within the United Kingdom because it was within the ambit of the port of Dover as delimited by warrant.[50] More than thirty years later in the course of the arbitration before Sir John Coleridge, however, the Crown stated:

The considerations of policy which extend the limits of fiscal ports to

---

[48] See Chapter IV above. See also *Willets* v. *Newport* (1615) 1 Rolle 250.

[49] Copies of the warrants, classified by ports, are kept in the Library of the Department of Customs and Excise, London. See also Masterson, *Jurisdiction in Marginal Seas*, Part I.

[50] (1835) 2 C.M. & R. 170, 173.

three miles seaward of low-water, do not apply so as to make it desirable to extend the limits of counties to the same distance.[51]

Although it is not clear whether the Crown in this arbitration thought that the delimitation of ports by warrant constituted the waters and subjacent soil *ipso facto* and *ipso jure* part of the United Kingdom though outside the counties, in *Keyn* seven years later it declined to argue the possibility that such delimitations gave power to the Central Criminal Court to adjudicate upon an indictment for manslaughter in respect of an act committed by a foreigner on board a foreign ship within three miles of the coast at Dover. During the first hearing of the appeal by way of case stated, the judges of the Court for Crown Cases Reserved showed their awareness of the system of Treasury warrants. During the opening address of Sir Hardinge Giffard S.G., the following discussion took place:

POLLOCK B. Take the constitution of the very port of Dover. The port of Dover you will find set out by a Commission in the time of Charles the Second.
SOLICITOR-GENERAL Yes, my Lord.
POLLOCK B. And that the port extends to the high seas.
LUSH J. There was a case in this Court some years ago in which the word port in the Act of Parliament was held to extend to the limits to which the authority of the commissioners extended.
SOLICITOR-GENERAL Yes, I believe there is an Act of Parliament which gives the limits I believe the jurisdiction used formerly to be exercised by the Admiral.[52]

During the second hearing, the Crown's position was clearly stated by the Solicitor-General:

If I were able to rely on the word 'port' as decisive of the question of jurisdiction, this particular accident happened in the port of Dover. I cannot say that that gives jurisdiction. I do not think it does, because a port is a thing which Her Majesty may fix within arbitrary limits, and for certain purposes it is binding on her subjects.[53]

In view of this disclaimer, it is hard to understand the remarks made by Lord Cairns L.C. in the House of Lords when intro-

---

[51] *Rejoinder on behalf of the Crown*, p. 39; see Chapter IV above.
[52] DPP 4/12: transcript 12 May 1876, pp. 99–100. Lush J. was probably referring to *Nicholson* v. *Williams* (1871) L.R. 6 Q.B. 632 in the Exchequer Chamber where it was held (Mellor, Lush and Hannen JJ.) that the word 'port' in 54 Geo. 3, c. 159, s. 14 meant the area within limits assigned by the Commissioners.
[53] DPP 4/13: transcript 17 June 1876, p. 136.

ducing the Territorial Waters Jurisdiction Bill on 14 February 1878. After citing the judgment of Lush J. in *Keyn*, the Lord Chancellor remarked:

As he [i.e., the Lord Chancellor] understood these words, if Sir Robert Lush had found that, in the particular place Parliament had stepped in and said that that portion of the sea was part of the United Kingdom, he would have been of opinion that the Crown had territorial jurisdiction over it, and that the conviction ought not to be quashed. It was fortunate for the prisoner in the *Franconia* case, though not fortunate for the vindication of the law, that Mr. Justice Lush was under the impression that that had not been done which really had been done.[54]

He then quoted a Treasury Warrant dated March 1848 which declared that the limits of the port of Dover extended to a distance of three miles from low-water mark. Thus he seems to have been of the view that the effect of the Warrant was to constitute the area enclosed as part of the United Kingdom.

Such a view lacks any foundation in the terms of the Customs legislation and, furthermore, the warrants, taken in their context, appear to lack the precision necessary for them to be construed as formal declarations of British territory, even less the extent of the United Kingdom. Three months after Lord Cairns's statement, the Law Officers, Holker A.G. and Giffard S.G., together with Parker Deane, significantly made no comment on a doubt expressed by the Foreign Office on whether the power to delimit ports was not vested in the Commissioners 'for customs purposes only'.[55] More significantly still, later Law Officers, Webster A.G. and Clarke S.G., together with R.S. Wright, in an opinion given to the Board of Trade on 7 June 1888, considered that a number of executive acts with regard to the Goodwin Sands, including the incorporation of the area within a port, were 'some, although far from conclusive, evidence of a dependency' within the meaning of

[54] 237 *P.Debs.*, 3rd series, col. 1604. Lord Cairns L.C. later declared that the judges were not responsible for the oversight. His own attention had been called to the existence of the warrant by a person 'connected with a Public Office' (238 *P.Debs.*, col. 141). The question of Treasury warrants had been discussed in the columns of *The Times* some months earlier in the context of a killing on board an American merchant vessel *New World* which was moored three-quarters of a mile from the nearest low-water mark near the Nore lightship. The 'local authorities' declined jurisdiction (*The Times*, 27 October 1877). This drew a letter from Sherston Baker who argued that the vessel was within the port of London at the relevant time (ibid.). On 29 October 1877 the newspaper carried a letter from one 'W', who drew attention to the Treasury Warrant of 1848 in respect of the port of Dover.
[55] FO 834/12; Foreign Office Confidential Print No. 4280, Opinion No. 58.

the expression 'dependent islands and banks' in the Sea Fisheries Act 1883.[56]

In conclusion, it is submitted that the power to delimit the ambit of ports, whether it be based on statute or on a delegation of the royal prerogative, cannot by itself constitute the waters, bed, and subsoil so enclosed as part of the United Kingdom or even as British territory.[57]

---

[56] McNair, vol. I, 370. For an extra-judicial opinion to the effect that a Warrant was irrelevant to criminal jurisdiction over a foreigner on board a foreign ship in the Roads off Deal, see Marston, (1972) 88 *LQR* 357, 374–5.

[57] The 'port' theory continued to attract dicta in its support. See, e.g., Lawrence L.J. in *The Fagernes* [1927] P. 311, 329 who considered that the locus in *R.* v. *Cunningham* (1859) Bell 72, was 'within the body of the county of Glamorgan' because it was within the area of the port of Cardiff.

Chapter XIII

The Legal Status of the Marginal Solum

A. On the Basis of the Traditional Claim

On the strength of the evidence set out in the first part of this work and on the argument in Chapter XII above, it seems likely that the courts in the United Kingdom today would uphold the Crown's claim to the ownership *jure coronae* of the marginal solum, either as the residue of the traditional claim or as the necessary consequence of the territorial sea doctrine. It is also likely that the courts would regard the claim as an Act of State, the validity of which they could not question. It is clear that the view of Cockburn C.J. in *Keyn* was made without a full appreciation of the historical background and, in any event, his view has become obsolete in its turn through the development of the international law concept of the territorial sea. This applies also to the doubts of the Judicial Committee of the Privy Council in the British Columbia and Quebec fisheries appeals.

Certain major questions remain unsolved. Of these, the most important is the status in United Kingdom constitutional law of the marginal solum outside inland waters. Three possibilities suggest themselves:

(1) the solum, though Crown property, is no part respectively of England and Wales, Scotland, or Northern Ireland, and is therefore no part of the United Kingdom;

(2) the solum is no part respectively of England and Wales, Scotland, or Northern Ireland, but is an integral part of the United Kingdom;

(3) the solum is part respectively of England and Wales, Scotland, and Northern Ireland, and is therefore an integral part of the United Kingdom.

Sir John Salmond, writing in 1918, was strongly of the opinion that (1) above was the correct answer. He concluded as follows:

Save in the case of enclosed waters the seaward boundary of every possession of the Crown is at common law low water-mark, and there is no belt of marginal waters forming part of the territory.[1]

[1] Salmond, (1918) 35 *LQR* 235, 249. See also Lord Herschell L.C. in 352 *P. Debs.*, 3rd series, col. 1459 (27 April 1891).

Salmond's main authority for this conclusion was, of course, the decision in *Keyn*, and it was seen in Chapter VI above that the executive took this same view in the years following the case. It was argued above, however, that *Keyn* did not decide that the marginal sea was outside the United Kingdom, at most this being a strong dictum. One must therefore look further than *Keyn* to see whether Salmond's view can be upheld on any ground of principle. For this exercise it is necessary to divide the United Kingdom into its component parts.

(i) ENGLAND AND WALES

It might be argued that basic principle dictates that the marginal solum is as a matter of public law an integral part of the land to which it is adjacent, as an extension under water of such land. There is respectable authority that the marginal sea, including the solum thereof, was regarded from early times as part of the realm of England. Hale's views were particularly clear. In *Pleas of the Crown* he wrote that 'the realm of England comprehends the narrow seas'.[2] In a treatise on the admiralty jurisdiction, unpublished and not cited in *Keyn*, Hale expanded his views:

And certainly for things done in the narrow seas that belong to and are part of the Dominions of the Crown of England, there seems very little reason to question it, for those offences that are done within the Dominion of the Crown of England are as much contra Pacem Domini Regis as those that are done within the bodies of the Counties and doubtless tryable and determinable by the Courts of the Common Law . . .[3]

[2] Hale, *History of the Pleas of the Crown*, vol. I, 154.

[3] BL, Hargrave MS 137, p. 32. The Hargrave MSS contain two copies of this work, Nos. 93 and 137. No. 137 is the earlier of the two, written probably in the 1730s. It is likely that this is the copy given to Hargrave by George Hardinge, Solicitor to the Queen of George III (*Dictionary of National Biography*, vol. xxiv, p. 22) as part of a gift which also included a copy of *De Jure Maris* (Hargrave MS 97). No. 93 was made for Hargrave with a view to publication. The author is indebted to Dr Stanley Boorman for palaeographic advice on these manuscripts.

The original manuscript of the treatise, like that of *De Jure Maris*, remains undiscovered. Pepys, writing in 1683–seven years after the death of Hale—remarked that the admiralty treatise was said to be in the hand(s?) of Hale's wife (*The Tangier Papers of Samuel Pepys*, 112). As far as is known, the treatise has not been referred to in any United Kingdom court. Its only known citation was by Gray C.J. in the Massachusetts case of *Commonwealth* v. *Macloon* in 1869 (101 Mass. 1; 100 Am. Decs. 89), from a copy made in London for Joseph Story in 1839 and now in Harvard Law School Library (LMS 1148). Gray C.J. cited it for the proposition that 'in the most ancient times of which we have any considerable records, the English courts of common law took jurisdiction of crimes committed at sea, both by English subjects and by foreigners'. Judah Benjamin QC, who throughout his argument in *Keyn* displayed a detailed knowledge of United States admiralty jurisprudence, made no reference to this case.

Later in the same manuscript, Hale wrote:

A few words are necessary touching Jurisdiction [of the] Admiral in the
narrow Seas, belonging to the Dominion of the Crown of England,
which hath this difference from the former [i.e. the high seas] because
those Seas though in a great part out of the Counties yet are parcel of the
Realm of England—deins le ligeance de coron d'Engleterre as the old
book stiles it.[4]

Coke and Callis had both taken the same view earlier. Coke, in
his *Commentary upon Littleton,* commented that 'if a man be upon the
sea of England, he is within the kingdom or realme of England,
and within the ligeance of the King of England, as of his crowne of
England'.[5] Callis in his lectures remarked that 'English seas being
within the realm, be within the bounds of my said Statute of
Sewers'.[6]

In the nineteenth-century reaffirmation of its claim, the Crown
did not specifically aver that the solum was within England or the
United Kingdom. The Cornwall submarine mines arbitration
before Sir John Coleridge, however, caused the issue to be raised,
and with it the two arguments which were to be advanced against
the view that the solum is within England or the United Kingdom,
namely (1) it lies outside any county (2) it is not subject to the
common law. These two arguments are closely linked. The
counties of England were in their inception areas of curial
competence, particularly for administering the common law of
crime. If an act or omission took place outside any county it could
not in the normal course be tried by the courts of oyer and terminer
appointed to hear and determine 'secundum legem et consuetudinem Angliae', since these courts were usually held under
commissions which limited them to trying offences presented by
the grand jury of a particular county or group of counties.[7] The
sea, outside a narrow concept of inland waters, was not and still is
not within any county. Consequently, the argument goes, the open
seas outside inland waters are outside the ambit of the common
law, and thus incapable of being within the realm of England. It
was no doubt because of this train of reasoning that the realm of
England was considered to be nothing more than the sum of the

[4] BL., Hargrave MS 137, p. 211.
[5] Coke, *Commentary upon Littleton*, s. 439.
[6] Callis, 42.
[7] See, for example, Lord Diplock's observations in *Treacy* v. *Director of Public Prosecutions*
[1971] A.C. 537, 559.

counties. In *R.* v. *Musson* in 1858 Wightman J. is reported to have remarked that 'all the realm of England is within some county',[8] while in 1884 Brett M.R. (ironically one of the strongest dissenters in *Keyn*) declared in a highways case that 'England is divided geographically into counties, at least to this extent, that there is no part of England which is not within a county'.[9]

The Crown, however, did not accept such a concept in its *Rejoinder* in the Coleridge arbitration in 1866.[10] It asserted therein, on the authority of Hale and Callis, that certain places were within the realm of England though outside any county. In particular, it attempted to overcome the argument that the common law did not run outside the county by emphasizing Hale's views in *Pleas of the Crown* that originally 'the King's Bench had usually cognizance of felonies and treasons done upon the narrow seas, though out of the bodies of counties; and it was presented and tried by men of the adjacent counties'.[11]

Moreover, the Crown relied on Hale for the existence of special commissions of oyer and terminer, not limited to particular places within counties.[12] In his admiralty manuscript, Hale went into more detail about special commissions. Writing of the early English jurisdiction over crimes at sea, he stated that 'it is most apparent that Piracies Depredations and Treasons committed upon the Seas were punishable in the King's Courts, 1. In his ordinary Court, the King's Bench. 2. By Special Commissions.'[13] Later in the same work Hale turned to discuss the narrow seas 'out of the confines of Counties':

As to the narrow Seas . . . and any Cause arising thereupon, I say as before touching Jurisdiction upon the great Sea
  1. As to Causes Civil that are transitory the Common Law and Admiralty have a concurrent Jurisdiction.
  2. As to Criminal Causes entirely arising upon the narrow Seas, though anciently the Court of King's Bench had Jurisdiction of it, as hath been said, yet at this day the Admiral hath an exclusive Jurisdiction of the Common Law.

But yet by Special Commission at this day it seems not unreasonable that it may be determined in the County next adjacent, without the aid of

---

[8] (1858) 4 Jurist N.S. 111, 112. Contrast the report of the same case in 8 E. & B. 336, where the remark is attributed to counsel.

[9] *Over Darwen (Mayor of)* v. *Lancashire Justices* (1884) 15 Q.B.D. 20.

[10] See Chapter IV above.

[11] Hale, *History of the Pleas of the Crown*, vol. II, 12.

[12] Ibid., 21.

[13] BL, Hargrave MS 137, p. 32.

the Statute of 28 Hen. 8 and the Trial, for ought I know to the contrary, might be by a Jury of the County adjacent, if the Commission be to proceed secundum legem et consuetudinem Regni Angliae. But this it seems will only extend to such as are felonies by the Common Law as murder, etc.[14]

In his memorandum of 10 May 1877 on a draft of a bill to amend the criminal jurisdiction of the Admiral,[15] Henry Thring relied on Hale for the opinion that 'for 300 years last past, there was a common law commission of oyer and terminer, and also a commission of peace and gaol delivery, for all offences against any penal laws on the sea'. He continued:

. . . Cockburn C.J., in the Franconia case, states that Hale was mistaken, but it may be doubted whether he has given sufficient weight to the ancient power of the Crown to issue, either in the character of admiral or otherwise, special commissions of oyer and terminer.

In *Keyn*, all concerned, including the Crown, agreed that the locality was not within the county of Kent and so the accused could not be tried before a general court of oyer and terminer for that county. There remains a possibility, however, that had *Keyn* been tried under a special commission of oyer and terminer, on an indictment that he had committed the offence within England, the Court for Crown Cases Reserved would have divided in favour of the Crown. Although Cockburn C.J. and his followers would not have changed their decision, since the locality would still in their view have been outside England, one can speculate that at least one judge, possibly Bramwell B., might have crossed the floor.

Against this speculation, one should put the opinion of Salmon L.J. in *R.* v. *Kent Justices, ex parte Lye* in 1967 that the meaning of the term 'United Kingdom' was 'fairly plain', namely the land down to the low-water mark.[16] Furthermore, the sale of submarine minerals to the Lonsdale trustees in 1880 is some evidence that the Crown considered the minerals demised to lie outside England, since by the Act of 1 Anne (St. 1), c. 7, 1702, it was prohibited from alienating Crown land 'within the Kingdom of England, Dominion of Wales or Town of Berwick upon Tweed', a restriction which was not removed until the enactment of s. 1(2) of the Crown Estate Act 1961. Other statutes relevant to this question will be treated later in this chapter.

---

[14] Ibid., pp. 211–12.
[15] Records of the Office of Parliamentary Counsel; see Chapter VI above.
[16] [1967] 2 Q.B. 153, 179.

It is sometimes asserted that the common law stops with the county at low-water mark because the open seas beyond are under the jurisdiction of the Admiral, and that the two jurisdictions are mutually exclusive. Leaving aside the possibility of a concurrent jurisdiction, for which there is authority in respect of some inland waters,[17] it appears unlikely that the Admiral's jurisdiction, which is confined *ratione materiae* to matters occurring on or in close connection with British ships, applies at all to the subsoil of the marginal sea.

In conclusion, the arguments for declaring the seaward limits of the counties of England to be the limit of the realm of England risk confusing the basic concepts of ambit of law and ambit of curial competence. The confusion stems from the dual meaning of 'common law' in the particular context of the marginal sea. The expression could mean either (1) the corpus of non-statutory law applicable within a certain area, namely that of England and Wales, or (2) the area in which the courts administering such corpus of law have competence. The two areas should, of course, ideally coincide, but it it not impossible that due to historical anomaly or oversight a particular place is within the ambit of the corpus of law but outside the competence of any court. The frequently uttered phrase—the common law stops at the low-water mark—is thus ambiguous. Appropriate in a rough and ready manner to the second meaning, it has come by error to be regarded as relevant also to the first.

(ii) SCOTLAND

In the view of O'Connell, 'the Scottish kings from time immemorial had property in the marginal sea, and differing streams of interpretation in Scotland and the rest of Great Britain are to be expected'.[18] However, O'Connell gave no authority for the first part of this assertion nor did he indicate whether the marginal sea was considered by the Scottish kings to be part of Scotland. Neither *Keyn* nor the two cases decided immediately after it, namely *Harris* v. *Owners of the Franconia* and the *Blackpool Pier Case*, were decisions on Scottish law; nor, furthermore, has the House of Lords on appeals from Scotland, e.g., *Wemyss* and *Parker*, shown itself willing to lay down a rule in the terms stated in the three English cases above.

[17] See, for example, *R.* v. *Bruce* (1812) 2 Leach 1093; *R.* v. *Mannion* (1846) 2 Cox Crim. Cas. 158.
[18] O'Connell, (1958) 34 *BYBIL* 199, 217, n. 2.

A Scottish writer commented:

It was a general principle of Scots law that a definite maritime territory lay within the realm as distinguished from the 'vast ocean' which was 'common to all mankind'. Within the maritime territory, therefore, the common law was valid and the common law jurisdiction might be exercised over ships even in the first instance provided that the concurrence of the Judge Admiral was obtained. In the maritime territory, therefore, the two jurisdictions were concurrent. In this respect Scots law differs materially from that of England, where the realm and the authority of the common law terminate alike at low-water mark, except in so far as the sea is within the body of a county, and no distinction is drawn between territorial waters and the high seas.[19]

(iii) NORTHERN IRELAND

The problem of the public law status of the marginal sea was raised in the case of *Director of Public Prosecutions for Northern Ireland* v. *McNeill*, decided by the Northern Ireland Court of Appeal in 1975.[20] The respondent, McNeill, was prosecuted on a charge of using a salmon net in the sea in a way prohibited by the Fisheries Act (Northern Ireland) 1966 of the Stormont Parliament. The location of the alleged offence was in the open sea within 150 feet of a vertical rock-face in County Antrim. The resident magistrate held for three reasons that he did not have competence to hear the charge:

(1) the Parliament of Northern Ireland, under the Government of Ireland Act 1920, had jurisdiction over six parliamentary counties and two parliamentary boroughs only, and these administrative areas did not include any part of the open sea;

(2) the 1921 Agreement between Great Britain and Ireland (later scheduled to the Irish Free State (Agreement) Act 1922) had the effect of vesting the territorial waters of the whole of Ireland, including those adjacent to Northern Ireland, in the Government of the Irish Free State;

(3) the 1966 Act could not derive its validity from the Fishery Limits Act 1964 of the United Kingdom Parliament since the latter no longer had rights of legislation in the waters concerned.

The Northern Ireland Court of Appeal reversed the magistrate's ruling on the short ground that a statute of the United Kingdom Parliament was incapable of challenge in any United Kingdom court. The Fishery Limits Act 1964 was thus effective

---

[19] McMillan, *Scottish Maritime Practice*, 1–2.
[20] [1975] N.I. 177.

and the 1966 Stormont Act valid. Lowry L.C.J. and Jones L.J. went on to discuss the wider issue. Lowry L.C.J. agreed that the counties and boroughs of Northern Ireland did not include the sea and its solum below low-water mark, but he considered that the Northern Ireland Parliament could validly legislate for the 'territorial waters' under its peace, order, and good government power. He denied that the 1921 Agreement had acknowledged that the territorial waters of the whole of Ireland were vested in the Dublin Government, pointing out that the Agreement gave Northern Ireland an election, which it later exercised, to exclude itself from the powers of the Free State Parliament. He concluded that 'once this election was made, it became inconceivable that waters adjacent to County Antrim could be regarded as the territorial waters of a State the powers of whose Parliament and Government no longer extended to County Antrim in particular and Northern Ireland as a whole'.

Jones L.J. first asked himself whether under the 1920 Act Northern Ireland consisted only of the land of the six counties, leaving Southern Ireland with the remainder of the land mass together with the territorial waters around the whole island. He concluded not, maintaining that 'Northern Ireland, as constituted by the 1920 Act, consisted not only of the land mass thereof but also of the former rights of the United Kingdom in the waters surrounding Northern Ireland'. He supported this conclusion by citing a reply given in the House of Commons on 27 November 1922 by the Attorney-General, Sir Douglas Hogg, which endorsed the theory that the territorial waters 'go with' the counties making up Northern Ireland.[21] Even if this were not the case, went on Jones L.J., the rights would have remained 'in the United Kingdom'. It may be significant that Jones L.J. considered that the term 'parliamentary counties' was one 'with internal implications only, generally with reference to electoral matters, and does not bear on the problem with which we are concerned'.

B. On the Basis of the Territorial Sea Doctrine

If the Crown's claim is based solely on the territorial sea doctrine, an additional set of problems arise. Can the Crown, by implied or even express annexation, extend the limit of the United Kingdom? There is high authority that it can. In 1968, Diplock L.J.,

[21] 159 *HC Debs.*, col. 451.

delivering the judgment of the Court of Appeal in *Post Office* v.
Estuary Radio Ltd., stated of the 1958 Territorial Sea Convention
and the 1964 Territorial Waters Order in Council:

. . . it is not disputed that, construing the Order in Council in the light of
the Convention and the law as it was before the Order in Council came
into operation, the Crown, in the exercise of its prerogative powers, was
thereby asserting a claim which the courts are constitutionally bound to
recognise, to incorporate within the United Kingdom that area of the sea
which lies upon the landward side of the baseline (that is, internal
waters) and within three nautical miles on the seaward side of the
baseline (that is, the territorial sea).[22]

The essential words here are 'within the United Kingdom'. As
the waters, beds, and subsoil are juridically inseparable under the
public international law concept of 'territorial sea', Diplock L.J.
would doubtless have come to the same conclusion if the Court
had been dealing with the solum instead of activities on a structure
resting on the bed but projecting above the surface of the water. If
the Crown does have this power, it will thereby have the power to
extend the applicability of the common law to areas once outside
its ambit and, furthermore, by the stroke of a pen to extend the
territorial scope of United Kingdom statutes. Indeed, the Court of
Appeal did not flinch from this result:

The area to which an Act of Parliament of the United Kingdom applies
may vary . . . as the Crown, in the exercise of its prerogative, extends its
claim to areas adjacent to the coast of the United Kingdom in which it
did not previously assert its sovereignty.[23]

Is there any support for the view that the Crown, quite independently of statute, can extend the area over which the common
law and statutes apply *proprio vigore*? When the realm of England
has been extended in the past, e.g., by the incorporation of
Berwick on Tweed and Wales, it was done by statute.[24] In *Keyn*,
some of the majority judges thought that legislation was impera-
tive. Thus Cockburn C.J. stated:

The law of England knows but of one territory—that which is within the
body of a county. All beyond it is the high sea, which is out of the
province of English law as applicable to the shore, and to which that law
cannot be extended except by legislation.[25]

---

[22] [1968] 2 Q.B. 740, 754.
[23] Ibid.
[24] 22 Ed. 4, c. 8; 2 Jac. 1, c. 28; 20 Geo. 3, c. 42 (Berwick): 27 Hen. 8, c. 26; 20 Geo. 2, c. 42
(Wales).
[25] (1876) 2 Ex.D. 63, 198.

Similarly, Lush J. declared:

> International law, which, upon this subject at least, has grown up since that period [i.e., the reign of Richard II] cannot enlarge the area of our municipal law, nor could treaties with all the nations of the world have that effect. That can only be done by Act of Parliament.[26]

Even the minority judges did not go so far as to say that the Crown could extend the realm by declaration, it being their view that the marginal sea and subjacent soil was and had always been part of the realm by virtue of the traditional claim. Yet during the argument in *R.* v. *Kent Justices, ex parte Lye*, counsel for the Post Office submitted that the Order in Council was 'legislation' within the scope of the above quotations, while Lord Parker C.J. took the view that the majority judges in *Keyn* had not directed their minds to the possibility of an Order in Council, their point being simply that something was needed to put the territorial waters within the ambit of the criminal law.[27] Moreover, in *Post Office* v. *Estuary Radio Ltd.*, the Court of Appeal considered that the courts would be 'constitutionally bound' to recognize a declaration by the Crown, in the exercise of its prerogative powers, to extend, not merely the area over which it claimed sovereignty, but the United Kingdom.[28]

There are great difficulties in conceding such a power to the Crown. It would mean that in a criminal case where the issue is whether the offence has been committed within the United Kingdom, the Crown could, by declaration, conclusively determine the point in its own favour. Would the Home Office, for example, have issued such a certificate in the *Lye* case if requested to do so by the Post Office? The Law Commission, in its report on the territorial and extra-territorial extent of the criminal law, stated that 'it would be inappropriate for Government Departments to supply evidence directly connected with an issue in a criminal case on which the court must make its own decision as a matter of law and as to which there may be a dispute. There is an understandable reluctance on the part of departments to be involved in the provision of certificates of this character.'[29] The problem has been well put by Edeson:

While it is not doubted that the Crown has a prerogative power to extend

---

[26] Ibid., 239.
[27] [1967] 2 Q.B. 153, 160.
[28] [1968] 2 Q.B. 740, 754.
[29] Law Commission Paper No. 91 (1978), 9.

or acquire territory, the view that it can also alter the scope of jurisdictions over offences conferred by statute is inconsistent with the
authorities. . . . The wide prerogative power approved by Diplock L.J.
seems, moreover, to cut across some of the traditional safeguards that
have been built into the common law to check the power of the executive,
such as the restrictions on the Act of State doctrine, and the requirements of parliamentary assent to treaties before their provisions can
have effect in English law.[30]

At best, it can be said that neither in *The Fagernes*[31] nor in the
Territorial Waters Orders in Council has the Crown expressly
purported to re-define the limits of the United Kingdom; it is only
some judicial statements which have so interpreted the Crown's
conduct.

C. The Application of Statutes

It has been seen in Chapter VIII above that some statutes, for
example the Mineral Workings (Offshore Installations) Act 1971,
apply expressly or by necessary construction to the marginal
solum outside inland waters. What of statutes in general? The
basic rule of statutory construction in this regard is set out in
Maxwell on the Interpretation of Statutes and approved by Cozens-
Hardy M.R. in *Tomalin* v. *S. Pearson & Son Ltd.*—'In the absence of
an intention clearly expressed or to be inferred either from its
language, or from the object or subject-matter or history of the
enactment, the presumption is that Parliament does not design its
statutes to operate on its subjects beyond the territorial limits of
the United Kingdom.'[32]

If statutes are in general construed to apply to the territorial sea,
it will indicate that the courts consider this area lies within the
limits of the United Kingdom. Unfortunately, there is little
practice on the matter other than the *Estuary Radio* case. In *Yorke* v.
British & Continental Steamship Co. Ltd. in 1945, which concerned
the application of Regulations made under the Factory and
Workshop Act 1901 to a ship in Gibraltar, Scott L.J. stated:

It is quite clear that the principle of law is that our territorial legislation

---

[30] Edeson, (1973) 89 *LQR* 364, 379. In *Nissan* v. *Attorney-General* [1970] A.C. 179, Lord
Reid (208) and Lord Pearce (225) assumed that the territorial waters or 'three-mile belt'
was within the 'realm' for the purposes of the doctrine of Act of State.
[31] It is not clear whether the 'territorial sovereignty' of the Home Office certificate was
intended to be co-extensive with the limits of the United Kingdom.
[32] [1909] 2 K.B. 61, 64. See *Maxwell on the Interpretation of Statutes*, 12th ed., 171.

does not extend out of the Realm, or at any rate outside territorial waters, unless Parliament has expressly said so.[33]

In *Fox* v. *Lawson*, a prosecution under the Transport Act 1968 for driving excessive hours, Lord Diplock, in giving the leading speech in the House of Lords, stated that it was conceded that nothing the driver did 'in France or on the ferry outside British territorial waters' was unlawful under the Act.[34] This remark has little persuasive value.

On the other hand, the legislature itself has on many occasions, described in Chapter VIII above, indicated that the territorial sea and its solum may not be within the United Kingdom. Thus the Sea Fisheries (Clam and Bait Beds) Act 1881, s. 2, the National Coal Board (Additional Powers) Act 1966, s. 1(1) (a), the Sea Fisheries (Shellfish) Act 1967, s. 12(2) (a), the Mineral Workings (Offshore Installations) Act 1971, s. 2(a), the Petroleum and Submarine Pipelines Act 1975, s. 20(2), the Petroleum (Production) Regulations 1976, reg. 3(1) (b), and the Ancient Monuments and Archaeological Areas Act 1979, s. 53(7), all envisage that the territorial sea is 'adjacent to' rather than 'in' the United Kingdom or Great Britain.[35]

Other authority is singularly lacking. *Craies on Statute Law* takes the view that the territorial sea is now within the 'realm', but on the contentious argument that the Territorial Waters Jurisdiction Act 1878 has 'reversed' *Keyn* on this point.[36] The Law Commission, on the other hand, has recently stated that 'at common law, the territory included the shore down to low water mark and internal, as distinct from territorial, waters'.[37] It seems that by 'internal waters' the Law Commission means what is

[33] (1945) 78 Lloyd's L.Rep. 181, 182.
[34] [1974] A.C. 803, 808.
[35] Even 'national waters' as well as the territorial sea have been regarded as being outside England and Scotland. S. 1 of the Sea Fisheries Regulation Act 1966 empowers the Minister to create sea fisheries districts comprising 'any part of the sea within the national or territorial waters of the United Kingdom adjacent to England or Wales'. A number of such districts were created by orders effective on 1 July 1980. Of these, the Cumbria Sea Fisheries District (Variation) Order 1980 defines the district so created as comprising 'so much of the sea within the national waters of the United Kingdom adjacent to England as is not included within the national waters of the United Kingdom adjacent to Scotland, and so much of the sea within three nautical miles from the baselines from which the breadth of the territorial sea of the United Kingdom adjacent to England is measured as is not included within three nautical miles from the baselines from which the breadth of the territorial sea of the United Kingdom adjacent to Scotland is measured . . .'. The author is indebted to Mr. Colin Warbrick for bringing these orders to his attention.
[36] *Craies on Statute Law*, 7th ed., 460. See also Wilkinson, (1950) 18 *Modern Law Review* 40.
[37] Law Commission Paper No. 91 (1978), 7.

called in this work 'inland waters' and it is not clear whether the Commission would include waters, other than inland waters, lying on the shoreward side of the baseline in the Territorial Waters Orders in Council. If the Commission does include these waters, and there is evidence in paragraph 17 of the Report that it does, then it is submitted respectfully that their inclusion is fraught with the difficulties pointed out in the previous section.

Finally, on 19 December 1963, the Minister of State for the Home Office, Lord Derwent, remarked in the course of a debate in the House of Lords that 'the Mines and Quarries Act will apply to a mine even if it extends from the land to a point beyond the territorial waters'.[38]

D. Conclusion

The status of the marginal solum in public law remains uncertain. Even the assumption that it is Crown land does not necessarily import the corpus of United Kingdom statute law in the absence of authority that it is within the United Kingdom. Furthermore, it is still doubtful whether the common law, either of England or Scotland, applies to it *proprio vigore*. If the area is, in Salmond's phrase, maritime territory in gross,[39] then doubtless the Crown has power to legislate for it by prerogative decree,[40] but the Crown has not yet done so. Like Mr. Bates on the Sealand Tower six miles from the Essex coast,[41] a person on or in the solum might be outside the ambit of United Kingdom law and the competence of its courts, provided that he does not operate from a British ship or seek to explore or exploit the natural resources of the continental shelf outside the United Kingdom territorial sea.

[38] Mines and Quarries Act 1954. The Act does not contain any express provision or indication that it applies to submarine workings. 254 *HL Debs.*, col. 394.

[39] Salmond, (1918) 35 *LQR* 235, 240.

[40] Roberts-Wray, 164.

[41] *R.* v. *Bates*, Essex Assizes, 1968; see Law Commission Paper No. 91, 17–18, and *The Times*, 22 October 1968.

Select Bibliography

A. Works of Reference

British and Foreign State Papers, London, 1841–.

Craies on Statute Law, 7th ed. by S. G. G. Edgar, London, 1971.

Halsbury's Laws of England, 3rd ed. by Viscount Simonds, 43 vols. London, 1952–62; 4th ed. by Viscount Hailsham, London, 1973–.

International Law Opinions, ed. by A. D. McNair, 3 vols., Cambridge, 1956.

International Legal Materials, Washington, 1962–.

Law Officers' Opinions to the Foreign Office 1793–1860, ed. by C. Parry, 95 vols., Farnborough, 1970.

The Law and Custom of the Sea, ed. by R. G. Marsden, 2 vols., Navy Records Society, London, 1925–6.

Maxwell on the Interpretation of Statutes, 9th ed. by P. Langan, London, 1969.

The Naval Miscellany, ed. by W. G. Perrin, vol. 3, Navy Records Society, London, 1928.

Select Pleas in the Court of Admiralty, ed. by R. G. Marsden, 2 vols., Selden Society, London, 1892–7.

United Nations Treaty Series, New York, 1946–.

B. Monographs

ANGELL, J. K., *A Treatise on the Right of Property in Tide Waters, and in the Soil and Shores thereof*, 2nd ed., Boston, Mass., 1847.

ANSON, SIR W., *Law and Custom of the Constitution*, 4th ed. by W. B. Keith, Oxford, 1935.

BLACKSTONE, SIR W., *Commentaries on the Laws of England*, 4 vols., London, 1765–69.

BOROUGHS, SIR J., *The Soveraignty of the British Seas, proved by Records, History, and the Municipal Laws of this Kingdom*, London, 1651.

CALLIS, R., *Reading upon the Statute of 23 H. 8, cap. 5 of Sewers*, London, 1647.

CHITTY, J., JR., *Law of the Prerogatives of the Crown*, London, 1820.

COKE, SIR E., *Commentary upon Littleton*, 11th ed., London, 1719.

COULSON and FORBES, *The Law of Waters and of Land Drainage*, 6th ed. by S. R. Hobday, London, 1952.

CRAIG, SIR T., *Ius Feudale*, Edinburgh, 1603.

DEE, J., *The Brytish Monarchie*, London, 1577.

DIGGES, T., *Arguments prooving the Queenes Maties. propertye in the Sea Landes, and salt shores thereof, and that no subiect cann lawfully hould eny parte thereof but by the Kinges especiall graunte*, London, 1569.

FISHER, J., *Rockall*, London, 1956.

FITZHERBERT, SIR A., *La Graunde Abridgement*, 3 vols., London, 1516.

FOX, A. W., *The Earl of Halsbury*, London, 1929.

FULTON, T. W., *The Sovereignty of the Sea*, Edinburgh and London, 1911.

GIDEL, G. C., *Le droit international public de la mer*, 3 vols., Paris, 1932–4.

HALE, SIR M., *De Jure Maris et Brachiorum ejusdem*, Hargrave's Law Tracts, London, 1787.

—— *De Portibus Maris*, ibid.

—— *A History of the Pleas of the Crown*, ed. by S. Emlyn, 2 vols., London, 1736.

HALL, R. G., *An Essay on the Rights of the Crown in the Sea-shore of the Realm*, London, 1830.

MCMILLAN, A. R. G., *Scottish Maritime Practice*, Edinburgh, 1926.

MASTERSON, W. E., *Jurisdiction in Marginal Seas with Special Reference to Smuggling*, New York, 1929.

MOORE., J. B., *History of the International Arbitrations to which the United States has been a Party*, 6 vols., Washington, 1898.

MOORE, S. A., *A History of the Foreshore and the Law Relating Thereto*, London, 1888 (cited in the present work as Moore).

O'CONNELL, D. P., *International Law*, 2nd ed., 2 vols., London, 1970.

OPPENHEIM, L., *International Law*, vol. I, 'Peace', 8th ed. by H. Lauterpacht, London, 1955.

PEPYS, S., *Naval Minutes*, ed. by J. R. Tanner, Navy Records Society, London, 1926.

—— *The Tangier Papers*, ed. by E. Chappell, Navy Records Society, London, 1935.

PYCROFT, J. W., *Arena Cornubiae*, 3rd ed., London, 1856.

ROBERTS-WRAY, SIR K., *Commonwealth and Colonial Law*, London, 1966.

SELDEN, J., *Mare Clausum: seu, de Dominio Maris libri duo*, London, 1635.

SMITH, H. A., *Great Britain and the Law of Nations*, 2 vols., London, 1935.

WYNNE, W., *The Life of Sir Leoline Jenkins*, 2 vols., London, 1724.

C. Periodical Literature

ANON., 'Title of the Crown to the Seashore' (1859) 6 *Law Magazine & Law Review* 99.

DOWRICK, F. E., 'Submarine Areas around Great Britain' [1977] *Public Law* 10.

EDESON, W. R., 'The Prerogative of the Crown to Delimit Britain's Maritime Boundary' (1973) 89 *LQR* 364.

FOSTER, D., 'The Case of the Franconia' (1877) 11 *American Law Review* 625.

GARDNER, D. L., 'Legal Storm Clouds over Rockall' [1976] *Scots Law Times* 257.

GIBSON, J., 'Foreshore: A Concept Built on Sand' [1977] *Journal of Planning and Environment Law* 762.

GRANT L., 'The King's Chambers' (1915) 31 *LQR* 410.

HIMSWORTH, C. M. G., 'The Limits of the Planning Realm' [1977] *Journal of Planning and Environment Law* 1.

HURST, SIR C., 'The Territoriality of Bays' (1922–3) 3 *BYBIL* 42.

—— 'Whose is the Bed of the Sea? Sedentary Fisheries Outside the Three-mile Limit' (1923–4) 4 *BYBIL* 34.

JOHNSON, D. H. N., 'Control of Exploitation of Natural Resources in the Sea off the United Kingdom' (1951) 4 *International Law Quarterly* 445.

MARSTON, G., 'Crimes on Board Foreign Merchant Ships at Sea: Some Aspects of English Practice' (1972) 88 *LQR* 357.

—— 'Some Legal Problems of the Channel Tunnel Scheme, 1874–1883' (1974–5) 47 *BYBIL* 290.

—— 'The Evolution of the Concept of Sovereignty over the Bed and Subsoil of the Territorial Sea' (1975–6) 48 *BYBIL* 321.

—— 'Colonial Enactments relating to the Legal Status of Offshore Submerged Lands' (1976) 50 *Australian Law Journal* 402.

—— 'The Centenary of the Franconia Case—The Prosecution of Ferdinand Keyn' (1976) 92 *LQR* 93.

—— 'The Abandonment of the "British Seas"' (1980) 11 *Cambrian Law Review* 62.

O'CONNELL, D. P., 'Problems of Australian Coastal Jurisdiction' (1958) 34 *BYBIL* 199.

—— 'The Juridical Nature of the Territorial Sea' (1971) 45 *BYBIL* 303.

SALMOND, SIR J., 'Territorial Waters' (1918) 34 *LQR* 235.

WADE, T. C., 'The Roll "De Superioritate Maris Angliae"' (1921–2) 2 *BYBIL* 99.

WILKINSON, G. S., 'The Application of Enactments within English Territorial Waters' (1950) 18 *Modern Law Review* 40.

WINDEYER, SIR V., 'The Seabed in Law' (1974) 6 *Federal Law Review* 1.

D. Unpublished Works

EVATT, H. V., 'Certain Aspects of the Royal Prerogative: A Study in Constitutional Law' LL.D. Dissertation, University of Sydney, 1924.

HALE, SIR M., 'A Disquisition touching the Jurisdiction of the Common Law and Courts of Admiralty in Relation to Things done upon or beyond the Seas and touching maritime and merchant contracts' British Library, Hargrave *MSS*, No. 137.

—— 'A Narrative Legall and Historicall Touching the Customes' British Library, Hargrave *MSS*, No. 98.

E. Other Publications

Annual Reports of the Crown Estate Commissioners.

'High and Low Water Marks as shown on Ordnance Survey Plans' Ordnance Survey, June 1965.

'Report on the Territorial and Extraterritorial Extent of the Criminal Law' Law Commission Paper No. 91, 1978.

Table of Statutes, Statutory Instruments, etc.

(In chronological order)

A. Public General Acts

1323–4	De Prerogativa Regis (17 Ed. 2, st. 1)	**p. 273**
1389	Admiralty Jurisdiction Act (13 Rich. 2, c. 5)	**pp. 132, 135**
1391	Admiralty Jurisdiction Act (13 Rich. 2, c. 3)	**pp. 132, 135**
1482	Berwick on Tweed Act (22 Ed. 4, c. 8)	**p. 294**
1531	Statute of Sewers (23 Hen. 8, c. 5)	**pp. 6–7**
1535	Laws in Wales Act (27 Hen. 8, c. 26)	**p. 294**
1536	Offences at Sea Act (28 Hen. 8, c. 15)	**p. 133**
1558	Customs Act (1 Eliz. 1, c. 11)	**p. 59**
1603	Berwick on Tweed Act (2 Jac. 1, c. 28)	**p. 294**
1662	Customs Act (13 & 14 Car. 2, c. 11)	**pp. 59, 101, 282**
1702	Crown Lands Act (1 Anne, st. 1, c. 7)	**pp. 15, 80, 183, 290**
1746	Wales and Berwick Act (20 Geo. 2, c. 42)	**pp. 183, 294**
1759	New Shoreham Harbour Act (33 Geo. 2, c. 35)	**p. 16 n.**
1769	Crown Suits Act (9 Geo. 3, c. 16)	**p. 51**
1786	Crown Land Revenues Act (26 Geo. 3, c. 87)	**p. 15**
1793	Free Fishers of Whitstable Act (33 Geo. 3, c. 42)	**p. 61**
1799	Offences at Sea Act (39 Geo. 3, c. 37)	**p. 133**
1814	Harbours Act (54 Geo. 3, c. 159)	**pp. 47, 283 n.**
1817	Murders Abroad Act (57 Geo. 3, c. 53)	**p. 278**
1825	Customs Act (6 Geo. 4, c. 108)	**p. 60**
1827	Malicious Injury to Property Act (7 & 8 Geo. 4, c. 30)	**p. 45**
1829	Crown Lands Act (10 Geo. 4, c. 50)	**pp. 22, 40, 183**
1833	Public Revenue Act (3 & 4 Will. 4, c. 13)	**p. 22 n.**
1836	Durham County Palatine Act (6 & 7 Will. 4, c. 19)	**p. 50**
1839	Fisheries Convention with France Act (2 & 3 Vict., c. 96)	**pp. 41, 109**
1843	Sea Fisheries Act (6 & 7 Vict., c. 79)	**pp. 41, 97, 102**
1845	Crown Lands Act (8 & 9 Vict., c. 99)	**p. 24**
1847	Harbours, Docks and Pier Clauses Act (10 & 11 Vict., c. 27)	**pp. 29–30**
1854	Merchant Shipping Act (17 & 18 Vict., c. 104)	**pp. 24, 60–1, 107, 150**
1858	Durham County Palatine Act (22 & 22 Vict., c. 45)	**pp. 50–1**
1858	Cornwall Submarine Mines Act (21 & 22 Vict., c. 109)	**pp. 39, 40, 50, 75, 91–4, 96–8, 103, 110, 112, 134, 147, 153, 154, 187, 193, 224, 226, 230, 264, 265–6, 273**
1860	Limitation of Actions, Duchy of Cornwall Act (23 & 24 Vict., c.53)	**p. 111**
1861	General Pier and Harbour Act (24 & 25 Vict., c. 45)	**p. 31, 34**
1861	Offences Against the Person Act (24 & 25 Vict., c. 100)	**p. 116 n.**
1862	General Pier and Harbour Act 1861 Amendment Act (25 & 26 Vict., c. 19)	**p. 31**
1862	Pier and Harbour Orders Confirmation Act (25 & 26 Vict., c. 51)	**p. 31**
1862	Harbours Transfer Act (25 & 26 Vict., c. 69)	**pp. 24, 49 n.**
1863	Pier and Harbour Orders Confirmation Act (26 & 27 Vict., c. 104)	**p. 33**
1864	—— (27 & 28 Vict., c. 93)	**p. 33**

1865   —— (28 & 29 Vict., c. 58)   **p. 33**
——   —— (—— c. 76)   **p. 33**
——   —— (—— c. 114)   **p. 33**
1866   —— (29 & 30 Vict., c. 56)   **p. 33**
——   —— (—— c. 58)   **pp. 33–4**
1866   Crown Lands Act (29 & 30 Vict., c. 62)   **pp. 24–7, 112, 165, 168, 185, 195, 273**
1866   Oyster and Mussel Fisheries Act (29 & 30 Vict., c. 85)   **p. 42**
1868   Sea Fisheries Act (31 & 32 Vict., c. 45)   **pp. 43–4, 153**
1868   Poor Law Amendment Act (31 & 32 Vict., c. 122)   **pp. 140, 196**
1878   Territorial Waters Jurisdiction Act (41 & 42 Vict., c. 73)   **pp. 144–9, 171, 184, 187, 193, 198, 223, 229, 265–6, 268, 273–4, 283–4, 297**
1878   Telegraph Act (41 & 42 Vict., c. 76)   **pp. 158–9**
1881   Sea Fisheries (Clam and Bait Beds) Act (44 & 45 Vict., c. 11)   **pp. 171, 297**
1883   Sea Fisheries Act (46 & 47 Vict., c. 22)   **p. 285**
1889   Herring Fishery (Scotland) Act (52 & 53 Vict., c. 23)   **p. 255**
1895   Sea Fisheries Regulation (Scotland) Act (58 & 59 Vict., c. 42)   **p. 266**
1901   Factory and Workshop Act (64 Vict. & 1 Edw. 7, c. 22)   **p. 296**
1913   Pilotage Act (2 & 3 Geo. 5, c. 31)   **p. 254**
1920   Government of Ireland Act (10 & 11 Geo. 5, c. 67)   **pp. 169, 292**
1922   Irish Free State (Agreement) Act (12 Geo. 5, c. 4)   **p. 292**
1932   Northern Ireland (Miscellaneous Provisions) Act (22 & 23 Geo. 5, c. 11) **pp. 169–70**
1934   Petroleum (Production) Act (24 & 25 Geo. 5, c. 36)   **pp. 176–7, 179**
1937   Coal (Registration of Ownership) Act (1 Edw. 8 & 1 Geo. 6, c. 56)   **pp. 175, 188, 189**
1938   Coal Act (1 & 2 Geo. 6, c. 52)   **pp. 175–6, 189–90**
1946   Coal Industry Nationalization Act (9 & 10 Geo. 6, c. 59)   **pp. 176, 179**
1949   Wireless Telegraphy Act (12, 13 & 14 Geo. 6, c. 54)   **pp. 201–2**
1949   Coast Protection Act (12, 13 & 14 Geo. 6, c. 74)   **pp. 170, 274**
1954   Mines and Quarries Act (2 & 3 Eliz. 2, c. 70)   **pp. 297–8**
1961   Crown Estate Act (9 & 10 Eliz. 2, c. 55)   **pp. 273, 290**
1964   Continental Shelf Act (c. 29)   **pp. vii, 171, 176–9, 267–8**
1964   Fishery Limits Act (c. 72)   **pp. 255, 292**
1966   Sea Fisheries Regulation Act (c. 38)   **p. 297**
1966   National Coal Board (Additional Powers) Act (c. 47)   **pp. 177, 178, 297**
1967   Sea Fisheries (Shellfish) Act (c. 83)   **pp. 171, 269, 297**
1968   Transport Act (c. 73)   **p. 297**
1971   Mineral Workings (Offshore Installations) Act (c. 61)   **pp. 178, 296, 297**
1972   Island of Rockall Act (c. 2)   **p. 277**
1972   Local Government Act (c. 70)   **pp. 251, 256, 259**
1973   Protection of Wrecks Act (c. 33)   **pp. 170–1**
1975   Offshore Petroleum Development (Scotland) Act (c. 8)   **p. 172**
1975   Petroleum and Submarine Pipelines Act (c. 74)   **pp. 171, 297**
1976   Fishery Limits Act (c. 86)   **p. 255**
1979   Ancient Monuments and Archaeological Areas Act (c. 46)   **pp. 171, 178, 297**

B. Local and Personal Acts

1844   Padstow Port Act (7 & 8 Vict., c. xxiv)   **pp. 102, 112**
1846   Norfolk Estuary Act (9 & 10 Vict., c. ccclxxxviii)   **pp. 28, 89, 225**
1851   Magnetic Telegraph Company Act (14 & 15 Vict., c. cxviii)   **p. 36**
1851   Lincolnshire Estuary Act (14 & 15 Vict., c. cxxxvi)   **pp. 28, 89, 225**

1852   South Essex Estuary Act (15 & 16 Vict., c. lxvi)   **p. 28**
1853   Great Yarmouth Wellington Pier Act (16 & 17 Vict., c. xv)   **pp. 30, 273**
1853   Castlemaine Estuary Act (16 & 17 Vict., c. cxci)   **p. 89**
1857   Atlantic Telegraph Act (20 & 21 Vict., c. cii)   **pp. 36, 39, 40**
1857   Thames Conservancy Act (20 & 21 Vict., c. cxlvii)   **pp. 45, 102, 273**
1859   British and Canadian Telegraph (Northern Line) Act (22 & 23 Vict., c. cvi)   **p. 36**
1864   Herne Bay Fishery Act (27 & 28 Vict., c. cclxxx)   **pp. 41, 185, 254**
1865   Ham Oyster Fishery Act (28 & 29 Vict., c. cxlviii)   **pp. 41, 185, 254**
1874   South Eastern Railway Company Act (37 & 38 Vict., c. ciii)   **p. 152**
1875   Channel Tunnel Company Act (38 & 39 Vict., c. cxc)   **p. 157**
1881   South Eastern Railway Company Act (44 & 45 Vict., c. cxcv)   **p.157**
1892   Colwyn Bay Pier Act (55 & 56 Vict., c. xxxiii)   **p. 194**
1948   Pier and Harbour Order (Redcar) Confirmation Act 1948 (11 & 12 Geo. 6, c. xxii)   **p. 172**
1966   Pier and Harbour Orders (Blackpool Pier and Great Yarmouth New Britannia Pier) Confirmation Act (c. xxxiv)   **p. 172 n.**
1966   Whitley Bay Pier Act (c. xxxv)   **p. 172**

C. Private Acts

1880   Lonsdale Settled Estates Act (44 & 45 Vict., c. 3)   **p. 180**

D. Statutory Instruments etc.

1964   Territorial Waters Order in Council (S.I. 1965, p. 6452A)   **pp. 202, 257–9, 281, 294–6, 297**
1976   Petroleum (Production) Regulations (S.I. 1976, No. 1129)   **pp. 177, 178**
1979   Territorial Waters (Amendment) Order in Council (Not yet included in S.I. volumes)   **pp. 257–9, 281, 297**
1980   Cumbria Sea Fisheries District (Variation) Order (S.I. 1980, No. 806) **p. 297 n.**

Table of Cases

Agnew v. *Lord Advocate* (1873) 11 M. 309. **p. 73**

Amodu Tijani v. *Secretary, Southern Nigeria* [1921] 2 A.C. 399. **p. 276**

Anna, The (1805) 5 C.Rob. 373; 165 E.R. 809. **p. 217**

Annakumaru Pillai v. *Muthupayal* (1904) I.L.R. 27 Madras 551. **p. 228**

Annandale and Eskdale District Council v. *North West Water Authority* [1978] S.C. 187. **p. 255**

Argyll & Bute District Council v. *Secretary of State for Scotland* [1977] S.L.T. Reps. 33. **p. 213**

Attorney-General v. *Burridge* (1822) 10 Price 350; 147 E.R. 335. **p. 222**

Attorney-General v. *Ceeley* (1662) Moore, 314. **pp. 11–12**

Attorney-General v. *Chambers* (1854) 4 De G.M. & G. 206; 43 E.R. 486. **pp. 58–60, 88, 102, 128, 189, 193, 225 n., 249–50**

Attorney-General v. *Constable, Sir Henry* (1601) 5 Co. Rep. 106a; 77 E.R. 218. **pp. 5, 6, 10, 86, 104**

Attorney-General v. *Constable, Sir John* (1575) 1 And. 86; 123 E.R. 367. **pp. 4–5, 85, 260, 263**

Attorney-General v. *De Keyser's Royal Hotel Ltd.* [1920] A.C. 508. **p. 259 n.**

Attorney-General v. *Emerson* [1891] A.C. 649. **p. 269**

Attorney-General v. *Farmen* (1676) 2 Lev. 171; 83 E.R. 503: *sub nom. A.G.* v. *Farmer, Sir Edward* Sir T. Raymond 241; 83 E.R. 125: *sub nom. A.G.* v. *Turner, Sir Edward* 2 Mod. 106; 86 E.R. 968. **pp. 15, 80**

Attorney-General v. *Hammond* (1575) 3 Dyer 326b; 73 E.R. 737. **p. 3**

Attorney-General v. *Hammond* (1580) Moore, 221–4. **p. 3**

Attorney-General v. *Hanmer* (1858) 6 W.R. 804. **p. 58**

Attorney-General v. *Johnson* (1819) 2 Wils. Ch. 87; 37 E.R. 240. **p. 222**

Attorney-General v. *South Eastern Railway Co. Ltd. and Submarine Continental Railway Co. Ltd. The Times,* 6 July 1882, 17 August 1882; *The Daily News,* 6 July 1882. **pp. 159–64**

Attorney-General v. *Manwaring and Jones* (1833) Moore, 464. **p. 80**

Attorney-General v. *Oldsworth; see Sutton Marsh Case.* ·

Attorney-General v. *Reeve* (1885) 1 T.L.R. 675. **p. 192**

Attorney-General v. *Richards* (1795) 2 Anst. 603; 145 E.R. 980. **p. 19**

Attorney-General v. *Tomline* (1880) 14 Ch. D. 58. **p. 280**

Attorney-General v. *Tomsett* (1835) 2 C.M. & R. 170; 150 E.R. 73. **pp. 59–60, 264, 282**

Attorney-General for British Columbia v. *Attorney-General for Canada* [1914] A.C. 153. **pp. 214, 229, 234, 236, 270, 286**

Attorney-General for British Honduras v. *Bristowe* (1880) 6 App. Cas. 143. **p. 278**

Attorney-General for Canada v. *Attorneys-General for Ontario, Quebec and Nova Scotia* [1898] A.C. 700. **pp. 197–8, 213–14**

Attorney-General for Canada v. *Attorney-General for Quebec* [1921] 1 A.C. 413. **pp. 217–18, 235–6, 286**

Attorney-General of New South Wales v. *Brown* (1847) 1 Legge 312. **p. 276**

Attorney-General of Southern Nigeria v. *Holt (John) & Co. (Liverpool) Ltd.* [1915] A.C. 599. **pp. 216, 229**

Banne, Case of the Royal Fishery of the (1610) Davis 55; 80 E.R. 540. **pp. 5, 6, 80**

Barwick v. *South Eastern and Chatham Railway Companies* (1920–1) 124 L.T. 71; (1920) 2 K.B. 387; [1921] 1 K.B. 187. **p. 196**

Beaufort (Duke) v. *Mayor of Swansea* (1849) 3 Exch. 413; 154 E.R. 905. **pp. 57–8, 89, 98–9**

Beckett (Alfred F.) Ltd. v. *Lyons* [1967] Ch. 449. **p. 199**

Benest v. *Pipon* (1829) 1 Knapp 60; 12 E.R. 243. **pp. 56–7**

Blackpool Pier Co. Ltd. & South Blackpool Jetty Co. Ltd. v. *Fylde Assessment Committee* (1877) 41 J.P. 344. **pp. 140, 196–7**

Blundell v. *Catterall* (1821) 5 B. & Ald. 268; 106 E.R. 1190. **pp. 20, 63, 89**

Brighton & Hove General Gas Co. v. *Hove Bungalows Ltd.* [1924] 1 Ch. 372. **pp. 197, 218**

Bristow v. *Cormican* (1878) 3 App. Cas. 641. **p. 192**

Calvin's Case (1608) 2 St. Tr. 559; 77 E.R. 377. **p. 7**

Chelikani's Case; see *Secretary of State for India in Council* v. *Sri Raja Chelikani Rama Rao.*

Commissioners of Woods v. *Gammell*; see *Gammell* v. *Commissioners of Woods.*

Commonwealth of Massachusetts v. *Macloon* (1869) 101 Mass. 1; 100 Am.Dec. 89. **p. 287 n.**

Corporation of Hastings v. *Ivall* (1875) L.R. 19 Eq. 558. **pp. 34, 68**

Crosse v. *Diggs* (1663) 1 Sid. 158; 82 E.R. 1030. **p. 85**

Crown Estate Commissioners v. *Fairlie Yacht Slip Ltd.* [1976] S.C. 161 **pp. 212–13**

Cuninghame v. *Assessor for Ayrshire* (1895) 22 R. 596. **p. 207**

Denaby & Cadeby Main Collieries Ltd. v. *Anson* [1911] 1 K.B. 171. **pp. 195, 237**

Direct United States Cable Co. Ltd. v. *Anglo-American Telegraph Co. Ltd.* (1877) 2 App. Cas. 394. **pp. 140, 213**

Director of Public Prosecutions for Northern Ireland v. *McNeill* [1975] N.I. 177. **pp. 292–3**

Eclipse, The; see *The Saxonia.*

Egremont Burial Board v. *Egremont Iron Ore Company* (1880) 14 Ch. D. 158. **p. 269**

Embleton v. *Brown* (1860) 30 L.J. M.C. 1. **pp. 95, 249**

Fagernes, The [1926] P. 185; [1927] P. 311. **pp. 197–9, 202, 253–5, 258, 285 n., 296**

Fisherrow Harbour Commissioners v. *Musselburgh Real Estate Co. Ltd.* (1903) 5 F. 387. **p. 250**

Fitzhardinge (Lord) v. *Purcell* [1908] 2 Ch. 139. **pp. 189, 193, 217, 225 n., 229**

Fox v. *Lawson* [1974] A.C. 803. **p. 297**

Franconia, The; see *R.* v. *Keyn.*

Free Fishers and Dredgers of Whitstable v. *Gann* (1861) 11 C.B. N.S. 387; 142 E.R. 847: (1863) 13 C.B. N.S. 853; 143 E.R. 337: *sub nom. Gann* v. *Free Fishers of Whitstable* (1865) 11 H.L.Cas. 192. **pp. 61–5, 66, 99, 102, 103, 126, 145, 204, 206, 214, 222, 225 n., 227, 229, 237, 264, 270**

Free Fishers of Whitstable v. *Foreman* (1867) L.R. 2 C.P. 688: (1868) L.R. 3 C.P. 578: *sub nom. Foreman* v. *Free Fishers and Dredgers of Whitstable* (1869) L.R. 4 H.L. 266. **pp. 65–6, 102**

Gammell v. *Commissioners of Woods, and the Lord Advocate* (1851) 13 D. 854: (1859) 3 Macqueen 419. **pp. 45 n., 69–72, 118, 125, 134, 206, 227, 229, 237**

Gann's Case; see *Free Fishers and Dredgers of Whitstable* v. *Gann.*

General Iron Screw Collier Co. v. *Schurmanns* (1860) 1 J. & H. 180; 70 E.R. 712. **p. 60**

Gifford v. *Yarborough*; see *R.* v. *Yarborough (Lord).*

Goodtitle d. Parker v. *Baldwin* (1809) 11 East 488; 103 E.R. 1902. **p. 80**

Harris v. *Owners of the Franconia* (1877) 2 C.P.D. 173. **pp. 139, 183, 198, 291**

Hull & Selby Railway Co., In re (1839) 5 M. & W. 327; 151 E.R. 139. **p. 57**

Ipswich Dock Commissioners v. *Overseers of St. Peter, Ipswich* (1866) 7 B. & S. 310. **p. 58**

Johannes, The (1860) Lush. 182; 167 E.R. 87. **p. 60**

Johnson v. *Barrett* (1646) Aleyn 10; 82 E.R. 887. **p. 11**

Jones v. *Bennett* (1890) 63 L.T. N.S. 705. **p. 193**

Kelsey v. *Baker* (1803) unreported. **p. 18**

Keyn's Case; see *R.* v. *Keyn.*

Lacey's Case (1582) 1 Leon. 270; 74 E.R. 246. **p. 6**

Leda, The (1856) Swabey Adm. 40; 166 E.R. 1007. **pp. 60, 151**

Le Strange v. *Rowe* (1866) 4 F. & F. 1048; 176 E.R. 903. **p. 65**

Liverpool & North Wales Steamship Co. Ltd. v. *Mersey Trading Co. Ltd.* [1908] 2 Ch. 460. **pp. 194–5**

Lonsdale (Earl) v. *Curwen* (1799) 3 Bligh 168; 4 E.R. 566. **p. 77**

Loose v. *Castleton* (1978) *The Times*, 21 June 1978; C.A. 366/78.   **pp. 43 n., 203–4**

Lord Advocate v. *Glengarnock Iron & Steel Co. Ltd.* (1908) 15 S.L.T. 769; [1909] 1 S.L.T. 15.   **pp. 211–12**

Lord Advocate v. *Trustees of the Clyde Navigation* (1891) 19 R. 174.   **pp. 166, 189, 204–6, 217, 225 n.**

Lord Advocate v. *Wemyss* [1900] A.C. 48.   **pp. 189, 207–10, 217, 225 n., 229, 237, 291**

Lord of the Isles, The (1832) unreported; mentioned in *The Public Opinion*.   **p. 256 n.**

Marwood v. *Lord Harewood* (1842) unreported.   **p. 57 n.**

Milford, The (1858) Swabey Adm. 362; 166 E.R. 1167.   **p. 60 n.**

Monashee Enterprises Ltd., In re (1978) 90 D.L.R. (3d) 521.   **p. 271**

Mortensen v. *Peters* (1906) 8 F. 93.   **pp. 255–6**

Mure v. *Hore* (1877) 41 J.P. 471.   **p. 256 n.**

Murphy v. *Ryan* (1868) I.R. 2 C.L. 143.   **p. 73**

Neill v. *Duke of Devonshire* (1882) 8 App. Cas. 135.   **p. 192**

New South Wales and others v. *Commonwealth of Australia* (1975) 135 C.L.R. 337.   **pp. 270–1**

Nicholson v. *Williams* (1871) L.R. 6 Q.B. 632.   **p. 283**

Nissan v. *Attorney-General* [1970] A.C. 179.   **p. 296 n.**

Officers of State for Scotland v. *Smith* (1846) 6 D. 711; appeal *sub nom. Smith* v. *Earl of Stair* (1849) 6 Bell 487.   **pp. 68, 206**

Over Darwen, Mayor of v. *Lancashire Justices* (1884) 15 Q.B.D. 20.   **p. 289**

Overseers of Woolwich v. *Robertson* (1881) 6 Q.B.D. 654.   **p. 192 n.**

Parker v. *Lord Advocate* [1904] A.C. 364.   **pp. 210, 291**

Parmeter v. *Gibbs, re Portsmouth Harbour* (1813) 10 Price 412; 147 E.R. 356.   **p. 19**

Pauline, The (1845) 2 Wm Rob. 358; 166 E.R. 790.   **p. 104**

Penang, Government of v. *Beng Hong Oon* [1970] 1 Malayan Law Journal 244: [1972] A.C. 425.   **p. 218**

Peters v. *Olsen* (1905) 4 Adam's Justiciary Rep. 608.   **p. 255**

Pianka and Hylton v. *The Queen* [1979] A.C. 107.   **p. 219**

Post Office v. *Estuary Radio Ltd.,* [1967] 1 W.L.R. 847: [1968] 2 Q.B. 740.   **pp. 200, 202–3, 258–9, 275, 281, 293–6**

Public Opinion, The (1832) 2 Hagg. Adm. 402; 58 E.R. 498.   **p. 256 n.**

Putbus, The [1969] P. 136.   **p. 203**

R. v. *Bates* (1968) unreported; see *The Times*, 22 October 1968.   **p. 298**

R. v. *Bruce* (1812) 2 Leach 1093; 168 E.R. 782.   **pp. 256 n., 291 n.**

R. v. *Coombes* (1786) 1 Leach 388; 168 E.R. 296.   **p. 104**

R. v. *Cunningham* (1859) Bell's C.C. 72; 169 E.R. 1171.   **pp. 95, 253, 256 n., 285 n.**

R. v. *Forty-Nine Casks of Brandy* (1836) 3 Hagg. Adm. 257; 166 E.R. 401.   **pp. 60, 104, 116, 256 n.**

R. v. *Hampden* (1636–8); see *Ship-money Case.*

R. v. *Kent Justices, ex parte Lye* [1967] 2 Q.B. 153.   **pp. 200–2, 273 n., 279, 290, 295**

R. v. *Keyn: The Franconia Case* (1876) L.R. 2 Ex. D. 63; 13 Cox Crim. Cas. 404.   **pp. 75 n., 114–37, 138–45, 149–5, 160, 161, 183, 189, 192, 194–5, 198, 201, 205–6, 207, 213, 215, 221, 223–4, 226, 228, 229, 237, 253, 264–5, 273, 274, 283–4, 286, 287, 289, 290, 291, 294–5**

R. v. *Mannion* (1846) 2 Cox Crim. Cas. 158.   **p. 291 n.**

R. v. *Musson* (1858) 8 E. & B. 900; (1858) 4 Jurist N.S. 111.   **pp. 58, 99, 103, 106, 249, 289**

R. v. *Nagle* (1868) unreported.   **pp. 105–6**

R. (McIntosh) v. *Symonds* (1847) N.Z. P.C.C. 387.   **p. 276**

R. v. *Vaughan* (1696) 13 How. St. Tr. 485.   **p. 262**

R. v. *Yarborough (Lord)* (1828) Bligh N.S. 147; 4 E.R. 1087.   **pp. 21, 87, 193**

Randwick Municipality v. *Rutledge* (1959) 102 C.L.R. 54.   **p. 275**

Reference re Offshore Mineral Rights of British Columbia [1967] S.C.R. 792.   **p. 270**

References re Ownership of the Bed of the Strait of Georgia and related areas (1976) 1 B.C.L.R. 97.   **p. 259 n.**

Saxonia, The Eclipse and The (1861) 1 Lush. 410; 167 E.R. 179.   **pp. 61, 107, 259**
Scratton v. *Brown* (1825) 4 B. & C. 485; 107 E.R. 1140.   **pp. 87, 101, 218**
Secretary of State for India in Council v. *Sri Raja Chelikani Rama Rao* (1916) L.R. 43 Ind.
   App.192.   **pp. 186, 198, 216–17, 225, 229, 235–6**
Ship-money Case (1636–8) 3 Cobbett's St. Tr. 825.   **pp. 10–11**
Smith v. *Earl of Stair*; see *Officers of State for Scotland* v. *Smith*.
Stephens v. *Snell* (No. 1) (1939) 55 T.L.R. 962.   **p. 199**
Stephens v. *Snell* (No. 2) (1954) *The Times*, 5 June 1954.   **p. 199**
Submarine Telegraph Company v. *Dixon* (1864) 10 L.T. N.S. 32; 33 L.J. C.P. 139; 10 Jurist 129;
   12 W.R. 384.   **pp. 66–7**
Sutherland (Duchess) v. *Watson* (1868) 6 M. 199.   **pp. 42, 72–3, 206, 210**
Sutton Marsh Case (1636–7) unreported; see Chapter I above.   **pp. 7–10, 14, 80**
Tanistry, Case of the (1608) Davis 28; 80 E.R. 516.   **p. 7**
Todd v. *River Clyde Trustees* (1841) 2 Rob. App. 333.   **p. 80**
Tomalin v. *S. Pearson & Son Ltd.* [1909] 2 K.B. 61.   **p. 296**
Treacy v. *Director of Public Prosecutions* [1971] A.C. 537.   **p. 288 n.**
Trendtex Trading Co. Ltd. v. *Central Bank of Nigeria* [1977] Q.B. 529.   **p. 281**
United States v. *California*, 332 U.S. 19 (1947).   **p. 270**
United States v. *Grush* (1829) 5 Mason 298.   **p. 109**
United States v. *Maine and others*, 420 U.S. 515 (1975).   **p. 270**
United States v. *Texas*, 339 U.S. 707 (1950).   **p. 270**
Willets v. *Newport* (1615) 1 Rolle 250; 81 E.R. 467.   **p. 282 n.**
Williams v. *Attorney-General of New South Wales* (1913) 16 C.L.R. 404.   **p. 276**
Yorke v. *British & Continental Steamship Co. Ltd.* (1945) 78 Lloyd's L.R. 181.   **pp. 296–7**

Index of Persons

Alderson B., 57–8, 59–60, 88, 89
Ali F. J., 218
Amphlett B., 120, 134–5, 265
Archibald J., 120, 130
Atherton, William, 45–7
Atkin L. J., 199, 254n.

Bailey, K. H., 243
Baker, Sherston, 284n
Bankes A. G., 8, 10–11
Bankes L. J., 199, 253–4
Barclay, Sir Thomas, 227–8
Barwick C.J., 270n.
Beckett, W. E., 234
Bell, G. J., 212, 255n.
Benjamin, Judah, 115–29, 139, 140, 160
Best C. J., 21
Bethell, Sir Richard, *see* Westbury, Lord
Blackburn, Lord, 58, 140, 152
Blain J., 201–2
Boroughs, Sir John, 7
Bovill C. J., 65–6
Brampston C. J., 11
Bramwell B., 66, 120–1, 128, 131, 137, 290
Brett, Sir Baliol:
    as S.G., 42, 44
    as judge, 120, 126, 128, 135, 289
Brickdale, M. I. F., 183–4, 187, 267
Bridge L. J., 204
Byles J., 62
Bynkershoek, Cornelius, 271

Caesar, Sir Julius, 107
Cairns, Earl (Sir Hugh Cairns):
    as S. G., 39, 92–3
    as L. C., 120, 138, 144, 260, 266, 283–4
Callis, Robert, 6–7, 64, 80, 85, 98, 99, 103, 197, 288, 289
Campbell, Lord, 58, 68
    as S. G., 112
Carmichael, Sir Ian, 40
Chamberlain, Joseph, 157–8
Chelmsford, Lord, 64–5, 71, 99
Chitty, Joseph jr., 157–8

Churchill, Winston S., 174
Clarke S. G., 112, 284
Cockburn, Sir Alexander:
    as A. G., 31, 79, 81, 82n
    as S. G., 278n
    as judge, 120–8, 130–3, 141, 142–4, 145, 151, 221, 237, 253, 264, 270–1, 286, 290, 294
Cockburn, Lord, 68
Coke, Sir Edward, 9, 71, 95, 101, 107–8, 123, 288
Coleridge, Sir John, 94–113, 136
Coleridge, Lord C. J., 114, 120–1, 123, 125, 126, 135–6, 139–40, 193, 196, 198, 206, 224, 265, 273
Copley A. G., 263
Coulson, H., 227
Cowell, H. G., 231
Cozens-Hardy M. R., 296
Craig, Sir Thomas, 18, 19, 70, 208
Cranworth, Lord, 40, 83, 93
Croker, J. W., 262
Cunliffe, R. E., 167–8

Darling J., 196–7
Davenport C. B., 9–11
Davey, Lord, 211
    as S. G., 221
Davies S. G. (Trinidad), 235, 237–8
Deane, Parker, 138, 156, 278, 284
Dee, Dr John, 261
Denman B., 9
Denman J., 120, 127, 134, 139
Derwent, Lord, 298
Devaux A. G. (Trinidad), 235
Digges, Thomas, 2–4
Dilhorne, Viscount, 220
Diplock, Lord, 203, 258, 275, 281, 288n., 293–4, 296, 297
Dodson Q. A., 278n
Dowrick, F. E., 191
Dulinge, 5
Duncan, H., 234–5
Dundas A. G., 78
Dunedin, Lord, 255

Dunpark, Lord, 212–13

Edeson, W. R., 295–6
Enever, F. A., 189–90
Erle C. J., 62, 64, 65, 67, 99, 102, 245, 264
Erskine, John, 69, 212
Evans, Morton, 186
Evatt, H. V., 275

Falmouth, Lord, 57, 76–82, 94, 104
Farrer, T. H., 25–7, 153, 159
Fenton, Sir Myles, 182
Field J., 115, 133
Finch L. C. J., 11
Finlay, Sir Robert, 215
    as S. G., 222
Fitzgerald J., 105–6, 109
Fitzmaurice, G. G., 232–4, 238
Follett S. G., 59, 76
François, J. P. A., 241–2
Fulton, T. W., 1–2, 260–1

Gaye, A. S., 226–7
Gibbs J., 270n
Giffard, Sir Hardinge (Earl of Halsbury),
    192n
    as S. G., 115–29, 138, 148–9, 156, 253,
        264–5, 278–9, 283, 284
    as L. C., 211, 266
Gill J., 218
Gordon L. A., 42
Gore, Charles A., 39–41, 50–1, 95–6,
    142–4, 146–7, 180–1, 266
Gorst, John, 141–2
Gorst, T. W., 143, 146–7, 184
Gray C. J., 287n
Grotius, 119, 271
Grove J., 120–1, 127–8, 134, 139–40, 196,
    265
Gwyer, Sir Maurice, 241

Haldane, Viscount, 215, 218, 229, 236
Hale, Sir Matthew, 11, 12–15, 19, 20, 23,
    46–7, 58, 59, 62–4, 80, 98–9, 101,
    103, 107, 110, 119, 123, 132, 192,
    225, 252–3, 262, 281–2, 287–8,
    289–90
Hall, Robert G., 22–3, 80
Halsbury, Earl of, *see* Giffard, Sir
    Hardinge
Hardie, Keir, 174–5
Heath J., 18
Heineccius, J. G., 70
Hellard, J., 184–5
Herschell, Lord, 197–8, 209, 286n
    as S. G., 150, 274

Hill J., 198, 253, 254–5
Hobart L. C. J., 107
Hobhouse, C. E., 175
Hogg A. G., 198, 293
Holker A. G., 114, 120, 138, 141–2,
    148–9, 156, 278–9, 284
Holroyd J., 20, 89, 101
Hope L. J.-C., 69–70
Horne A. G., 112
Horton, A. E., 187, 190
Hurst, Sir Cecil, 187, 223–31, 234, 268,
    271

Isaacs S. G., 174
Isaacs J., 276
Ivory, T., 42

Jacobs J., 271
James A. G., 150, 159–60, 274
James, W. M., 42
Jervis A. G., 78
Johnson, D. H. N., 169
Johnston, Lord, 212
Jones L. J. (Northern Ireland), 293

Karslake A. G., 42, 44
Kay J., 160–1
Keating S. G., 40
Kelly C. B., 115, 117, 124–5, 131, 145
    as S. G., 39
Kendall, Nicholas, 92
Ker, Bellenden, 112
Kincairney, Lord, 210
Kingscote, Sir Nigel, 185–6
Kinross, Lord, 211
Kyd, Stewart, 17
Kyllachy, Lord, 205–6

Lawrence J., 195
Lawrence L. J., 199, 253–4
Leigh, Pemberton, 83
Lindley J., 115, 133–4, 206
Littler, R., 161
Lonsdale, Earl of, 51–2, 179–82, 187
Low, Lord, 250
Lowry L. C. J. (Northern Ireland) 293
Lush J., 115, 119–22, 126, 133, 141, 283,
    284, 295
Lushington Dr, 60, 151

Macdonald L. J.-C., 206
Malcolm, W., 138
Malins V. C., 68
Malkin, W., 227–8
Mason J., 270n

Maule J., 58, 88
Maurice, H. G., 227, 231
Medwyn, Lord, 69
Mellor J., 63
Millar S. G. (Scotland), 42
Miller, D. H., 240–1
Moncrieff L. J.-C., 73
  as L. A., 45
Montague C. B., 15
Montague L. C. J., 107
Moore, Stuart, 1, 13
Morier, Robert, 149–50
Moulton, Fletcher L. J., 195–6
Murray, Lord, 69
Murton, W., 182

Neaves, Lord, 72–3, 210
Nedham, Marchamont, 1
Neville J., 195
Nicholl, Sir John, 60, 116
North J., 161

O'Connell, D. P., 271–2, 291
O'Connor J., 202, 258n
O'Hagan J., 73–4

Parker J., 194
Parker, Lord C. J., 201, 295
Parry, Serjeant, 115
Patteson, Sir John, 83–91, 136, 273
Paul, Dr G., 16–17
Pelham, T. H. W., 168
Phillimore, Sir Robert, 115, 117, 130–1, 145
Phillimore L. J., 203
Plowden, Edmund, 4–5, 260, 263
Poland, H., 115, 149 n.
Pollock A. G., 76
Pollock B., 115, 133, 283

Redgrave, J., 52, 55, 146–7
Reilly, F. S., 94–5, 101, 138–9, 252
Risley, Sir John, 231
Roberts-Wray, Sir Kenneth, 275–6
Robinson K. A., 263
Rolle, Henry, 101, 252
Romer J., 197
Romilly M. R., 259
  as A. G., 278n
Ross, C. C., 235
Runciman, Walter, 174
Russell A. G., 221–2, 279
Rutherford Clark, Lord, 207

Salisbury, Marquis of, 266
Salmon L. J., 201, 203, 209

Salmond, Sir John, 286–7
Salvesen, Lord, 255
Schücking, Walther, 239
Scott L. J., 296–7
Scrutton L. J., 197
Selden, John, 1, 6, 10, 13, 19, 23, 80, 85, 119, 123, 132, 145, 195, 260, 261, 265
Shand, Lord, 209–10
Smirke, E., 76
Smith, A. L., 150, 274
Smith, Augustus, 192
Smith, D. F., 188–90

Smyth, W. M., 51
Stanton J., 95n., 252
Stephen J., 270n
Stocks, A. D., 187–8
Story J., 109
Strabolgi, Lord, 179
Sullivan A. G. (Ireland), 44
Sutton, Henry, 113

Talbot, I., 76
Thring, Henry, 47–50, 144, 290
Trayner, Lord, 207
Trevor B., 9
Troutbeck, J. M., 232

Vaisey J., 199
Vane, Earl, 53

Watkin, Sir Edward, 152, 157–9
Watson B., 58
Watson, Lord, 209, 214
Watson, Horace, 50, 82, 154, 156
Webster A. G., 113, 222–3
Wellwood, Lord, 207
Wensleydale, Lord, 64, 71–2, 125
Westbury, Lord (Sir Richard Bethell), 64
  as S. G., 31, 40, 81, 82n
Weston B., 9
Wetherell S. G., 263
Wheatley L. J.-C., 213
Wightman J., 99, 103, 106, 289
Wilberforce, Lord, 219
Willes, James, 81
Windeyer, Sir Victor, 278
Winn L. J., 199–200
Wood V. C., 60
Wright, R. S., 284
Wynford, Lord, 58–9

Young, Lord, 206–7, 250

General Index

Abandonment of Crown's rights in sea and solum, 16, 123, 129, 132, 142, 145, 205, 215, 225–6, 230, 267, 270–2, 275

Accretion, 12, 13, 28–9, 87–8, 89, 100–1, 192–3, 196–7, 216, 218, 224–5, 251, 267

Act of State, 281, 286, 294–6

Admiral, jurisdiction of:
  extent of, 5, 6, 133, 217, 288
  whether applicable to solum, 13, 46–50, 86, 100, 104–5, 228–9, 291

Anchorage, public right of, 2, 8, 16–17, 63–4, 65–66, 100, 154–5, 194, 195

Arbitrations:
  Behring Sea (1893), 44, 220–1, 279
  Cornwall Submarine Mines:
    Coleridge (1866–9), 94–111, 227, 252, 282–3, 288–9; Patteson (1856–8), 83–91, 224, 226–7, 263, 273, 279

Baseline of territorial sea, 257–9, 280–1
Bed of marginal sea, 24–50, 144, 165–72
  See also Subsoil of marginal sea
British Seas, extent of, 4, 5, 8, 16–17, 19–20, 69, 85, 260–3, 264

Cables, submarine, 36–41, 66–7, 127, 144, 147, 153, 166, 169, 228, 266
Chambers, King's, 16, 254
Channel tunnel scheme, 121, 124, 151, 152–64, 182–3, 185, 234, 266
Coal, sea, 199–200
Coal, submarine mines and deposits of, 25, 51–5, 142–4, 153, 154, 173–91, 207–12, 267
Collisions:
  'City of Mecca'/'Insulano', 149–50
  'Fagernes'/'Cornish Coast', 197
  'Franconia'/'Strathclyde', 114
Common law:
  whether applicable to solum, 6–7, 39, 100, 123, 298
  whether common law courts have

jurisdiction over solum, 116, 151, 288–90
Continental shelf, 176–9, 242–3, 267, 298
Copper, submarine mines and deposits of, 75, 82, 94
Cornwall, *see* Subsoil of marginal sea: Cornwall
County, whether solum within, 43, 60, 85–111, 123, 288–91, 292–3
County Palatine:
  Durham, 50–1
  Lancaster, 169n

Derelict lands, 3, 7–10, 12, 13, 14–15, 20, 23, 57, 87–8, 197
Dominium, contrast with imperium, 275–6

England, seaward extent of, 80–1, 139, 140, 151, 154, 183–4, 187, 198–9, 201, 286–91

Feudal law, 17, 275–6
Fishery:
  limits, 171–2, 199, 255
  public right of, 70–1, 73, 80–1, 154–5, 167, 172, 194, 205, 212, 215
  salmon fishery in Scotland, 44, 69–72, 125
  See also Sedentary fisheries; Several fishery
Foreshore:
  defined, 2, 152, 168, 249–51
  Crown's property in, 13, 19, 22, 39, 40, 128, 158, 160, 161, 164, 168
  distinct from solum, 5, 19, 22, 39, 40, 128, 158, 160, 161, 164, 168
  in Bermuda, 222
  in Scotland, 42–3, 73, 210–11, 250–1
  in Straits Settlements, 223

Gravel, submarine deposits of, 25, 191

Harbours, Crown's property in solum of, 1, 2–3, 19, 29–36, 47, 101, 117, 150, 195

See also Havens; Piers; Ports
Havens:
  Contrast with ports, 107–8, 282
  Crown's property in solum of, 11, 16,
    19, 47, 63, 101

Imperium, contrast with dominium,
    275–6
Inland waters:
  contrast with internal waters, 259
  extent of, 257–9
International law:
  whether incorporated into municipal,
    129, 135, 281, 295
  whether source of Crown's rights in
    solum, 118, 132–3, 135, 215–16, 218,
    224, 264–5, 270, 272, 280–1
International Law Commission, 241–3
Ireland, including Northern Ireland, 5,
    73–4, 43–4, 105–6, 109, 166, 169–70,
    192, 292–3
  See also Northern Ireland
Islands arising in the sea, 2, 4–5, 7, 12,
    13–14, 20, 23, 153

Jurisdiction, contrast with property, 1,
    4–5, 6, 13, 14, 29, 70, 99, 117, 120,
    127, 132, 150, 197–8, 200, 206, 207,
    215, 224, 231, 266, 270, 275–6
  See also Sovereignty

League of Nations, 233, 239–41
Low-water mark, meaning of, 249–50,
    257–59

Magna Charta, 63, 194, 225
Mines and minerals, submarine, *see*
    Subsoil of marginal sea

Narrow seas, 11, 13, 14, 20, 59–60, 70, 71,
    119, 125, 192, 195, 205, 209, 215,
    225, 260, 262, 270, 287–8, 289–90
Navigation, public rights of, 24, 63, 65–7,
    70, 73, 154–5, 172, 195, 205, 212–13,
    222
Northern Ireland, 169–70, 192, 292–3

Occupation of solum as creative of rights
    in, 14, 21, 154, 189–90, 220–1,
    224–6, 228, 230–1, 232–6, 267,
    278–80

Paria, Gulf of, 231–9
Petroleum, submarine deposits of, 176–9,
    182, 232, 239

Piers, 11, 16, 25, 29–36, 58, 65, 68,
    112–13, 121, 139–40, 147, 165, 166,
    172, 194–5, 206, 222, 249
Pilotage areas, 254–5
Pipe-lines, submarine, 171, 297
Ports:
  creation for customs purposes, 47,
    59–60, 98, 107, 145, 253, 254, 275,
    282–5
  Crown's property in solum of, 2–3, 8,
    10, 11, 16, 19, 64, 66, 95, 150, 281–2
  extent of, 95, 97, 107–9, 111–12, 119
Prerogative, Crown, 2, 3, 5, 15, 18, 20, 30,
    47, 48, 68, 71, 81, 117, 161–3, 201,
    203, 211, 267–8, 274–85, 294–6

Reclamation of land from sea, 28–9
  See also Accretion; Derelict lands
Rockall, Island of, 277
Royalties, Crown, 30, 51–4, 94, 173–5,
    179, 181, 207

Sand, submarine deposits of, 191
Scilly, Isles of, 97, 111, 112
Scotland:
  baseline on coasts of, 250
  executive practice in respect of, 54–5,
    144, 166, 167
  inland waters of, 204–10, 212–13,
    255–6
  judicial decisions in, 68–73, 204–13,
    255–6
  marginal sea of, 68–73, 204–13, 291–2
Seaweed, 27, 56, 166
Sedentary fisheries, 17–18, 41–4, 72–3,
    121, 171, 203–4, 210–11, 224, 228,
    230–1, 279
Several fishery, 169, 171–2, 204, 225, 269
Solum, meaning of, vii
  See also Bed of marginal sea; Subsoil of
    marginal sea
Sovereignty, contrast with property, 270,
    275–7, 280–1
  See also Jurisdiction
Special Commissions, 104, 289–90
Subsoil of marginal sea:
  Cornwall, 50, 75–113, 123–4, 153, 154,
    173, 185, 233, 274
  Cumberland, 51–2, 147, 154, 173,
    179–82, 185
  Devon, 54
  Durham, 52–4, 142–3, 147, 153, 154,
    173, 185, 186, 191
  Kent, 174, 182–3, 185–6
  Northumberland, 54, 123, 147, 173,
    185

Scotland, 54–5, 185
Wales, 54, 144, 185
See also Bed of marginal sea

Territorial sea:
  breadth of, 268–9
  contrast with traditional claim, 65,
    116–18, 215–16, 218, 268–9, 293–6
  whether an existing concept, 65, 132–3,
    215–16, 218, 219, 220–1, 233, 235,
    236, 238, 239–44
  See also Baseline of territorial sea;
    Three-mile limit
Territory, British, extent of, 37–40, 41,
    45, 143–4, 219

Three-mile limit, 65, 70, 71, 72, 97, 101,
    103–6, 116, 119, 121, 129, 132–3,
    154, 158–9, 189–90, 193, 195–6, 198,
    206, 263–4, 268–9, 270
Tin, submarine mines and deposits of, 75,
    82, 94, 191, 233
Tunnel, channel, *see* Channel tunnel
    scheme

United Kingdom, seaward extent of,
    60–1, 150, 151, 201, 203, 274, 286,
    290, 294–6, 298
United Nations, 241–4, 257, 268

Wreck, 3, 4–5, 12, 60, 130–1, 170–1